A Field Guide to the Classroom Library E

Lucy Calkins

and

*The Teachers College
Reading and Writing
Project Community*

HEINEMANN
Portsmouth, NH

Heinemann
A division of Reed Elsevier Inc.
361 Hanover Street
Portsmouth, NH 03801–3912
www.heinemann.com

Offices and agents throughout the world

Library of Congress Cataloging-in-Publication Data
Calkins, Lucy McCormick.
A field guide to the classroom library / Lucy Calkins and the Teachers College Reading and Writing Project community.
v. cm.
Includes bibliographical references and index.
Contents: [v. 5] Library E : grades 3–4
ISBN 0-325-00499-4
1. Reading (Elementary)—Handbooks, manuals, etc. 2. Children—Books and reading—Handbooks, manuals, etc. 3. Children's literature—Study and teaching (Elementary)—Handbooks, manuals, etc. 4. Classroom libraries—Handbooks, manuals, etc. I. Teachers College Reading and Writing Project (Columbia University). II. Title.

LB1573 .C183 2002
372.4—dc21 2002038767

Editor: Kate Montgomery
Production: Abigail M. Heim
Interior design: Catherine Hawkes, Cat & Mouse
Cover design: Jenny Jensen Greenleaf Graphic Design & Illustration
Manufacturing: Louise Richardson

Printed in the United States of America on acid-free paper

06 05 04 03 VP 5

This field guide is dedicated to

Annemarie Powers

The Field Guides to the Classroom Library *project is a philanthropic effort. According to the wishes of the scores of contributors, all royalties from the sale of these field guides will be given back entirely to the project in the continued effort to put powerful, beautiful, and thoughtfully chosen literature into the hands of children.*

Contents

Acknowledgments

The entire Teachers College Reading and Writing Project community has joined together in the spirit of a barn-raising to contribute to this gigantic effort to put the best of children's literature into the hands of children.

There are hundreds of people to thank. In these pages, I will only be able to give special thanks to a few of the many who made this work possible.

First, we thank Alan and Gail Levenstein who sponsored this effort with a generous personal gift and who helped us remember and hold tight to our mission. We are grateful to Annemarie Powers who worked tirelessly, launching the entire effort in all its many dimensions. Annemarie's passionate love of good literature shines throughout this project.

Kate Montgomery, now an editor at Heinemann and a long-time friend and coauthor, joined me in writing and revising literally hundreds of the field guides. Kate's deep social consciousness, knowledge of reading, and her commitment to children are evident throughout the work. How lucky we were that she became a full-time editor at Heinemann just when this project reached there, and was, therefore, able to guide the project's final stages.

Tasha Kalista coordinated the effort, bringing grace, humor, and an attention to detail to the project. She's been our home base, helping us all stay on track. Tasha has made sure loose ends were tied up, leads pursued, inquiries conducted, and she's woven a graceful tapestry out of all the thousands of books, guides, and people.

Each library is dedicated to a brilliant, passionate educator who took that particular library and the entire effort under her wing. We are thankful to Lynn Holcomb whose deep understanding of early reading informed our work; to Mary Ann Colbert who gave generously of her wisdom of reading recovery and primary texts; to Kathleen Tolan who championed the little chapter books and made us see them with new eyes; to Gaby Layden for her expertise in the area of nonfiction reading; to Isoke Nia for passionate contributions to our upper grade libraries; and to Kathy Doyle who knows books better than anyone we know.

We thank Pam Allyn for her dedication to this effort, Laurie Pessah for working behind the scenes with me, and Beth Neville for keeping the Project on course when this undertaking threatened to swamp us.

Finally, we are grateful to Mayor Guiliani for putting these libraries into every New York City school. To Judith Rizzo, Deputy Chancellor of Instruction, Adele Schroeter, Director of Office of Research, Development and Dissemination, Peter Heaney, Executive Director of the Division of Instructional Support, and William P. Casey, Chief Executive for Instructional Innovation, we also offer our heartfelt thanks for contributing their wisdom, integrity, and precious time to making this miracle happen.

Contributors

Christina Adams
Lisa Ali Chetram
Pam Allyn
Francine Almash
Janet Angelillo
Liz Arfin
Anna Arrigo
Laura Ascenzi-Moreno
Maureen Bilewich
Melissa Biondi
Pat Bleichman
Christine Bluestein
Ellen Braunstein
Dina Bruno
Theresa Burns
Lucy Calkins
Adele Cammarata
Joanne Capozzoli
Laura Cappadona
Justin Charlebois
Linda Chen
Mary Chiarella
Danielle Cione
Erica Cohen
Mary Ann Colbert
Kerri Conlon
Denise Corichi
Danielle Corrao
Sue Dalba
Linda Darro
Mildred De Stefano
Marisa DeChiara
Erica Denman
Claudia Diamond
Renee Dinnerstein
Kathy Doyle
Lizz Errico
Rosemarie Fabbricante
Gabriel Feldberg
Holly Fisher
Sofia Forgione
Judy Friedman
Elizabeth Fuchs
Jerilyn Ganz
Allison Gentile
Linda Gerstman
Jessica Goff
Iris Goldstein-Jackman
Ivy Green
Cathy Grimes
David Hackenburg
Amanda Hartman
Grace Heske
Caren Hinckley
Lynn Holcomb
Michelle Hornof
Anne Illardi
Maria Interlandi
Erin Jackman
Debbie Jaffe
Helen Jurios
Kim Kaiser
Tasha Kalista
Beth Kanner
Michele Kaye
Laurie Kemme
Hue Kha
Tara Krebs
Joan Kuntz Verdino
Kathleen Kurtz
Lamson Lam
Gaby Layden
Karen Liebowitz
Adele Long
Cynthia Lopez
Natalie Louis
Eileen Lynch
Theresa Maldarelli
Lucille Malka
Corinne Maracina
Jennifer Marmo
Paula Marron
Marjorie Martinelli
Esther Martinez
Debbie Matz
Teresa Maura
Leah Mermelstein
Melissa Miller
Kate Montgomery
Jessica Moss
Janice Motloenya
Marie Naples
Marcia Nass
Beth Neville
Silvana Ng
Isoke Nia
Jennie Nolan Buonocore
Lynn Norton Manna
Beth Nuremberg
Sharon Nurse
Liz O'Connell
Jacqueline O'Connor
Joanne Onolfi
Suzann Pallai
Shefali Parekh
Karen Perepeluk
Laurie Pessah
Jayne Piccola
Laura Polos
Annemarie Powers
Bethany Pray
Carol Puglisi
Alice Ressner
Marcy Rhatigan
Khrishmati Ridgeway
Lisa Ripperger
Barbara Rosenblum
Jennifer Ruggiero
Liz Rusch
Jennifer Ryan
Karen Salzberg
Elizabeth Sandoval
Carmen Santiago
Karen Scher
Adele Schroeter
Shanna Schwartz
India Scott
Marci Seidman
Rosie Silberman
Jessica Silver
Miles Skorpen
Joann Smith
Chandra Smith
Helene Sokol
Gail Wesson Spivey
Barbara Stavetski
Barbara Stavridis
Jean Stehle
Kathleen Stevens
Emma Suarez Baez
Michelle Sufrin
Jane Sullivan
Evelyn Summer
Eileen Tabasko
Patricia Tanzosh
Lyon Terry
Kathleen Tolan
Christine Topf
Joseph Turzo
Cheryl Tyler
Emily Veronese
Anne Marie Vira
Marilyn Walker
Gillan White
Alison Wolensky
Michelle Wolf
Eileen Wolfring

Introduction: What Is This Field Guide?

Lucy Calkins

When I was pregnant with my first-born son, the Teachers College Reading and Writing Project community organized a giant baby shower for me. Each person came with a carefully chosen book, inscribed with a message for baby Miles. Since then, we have commemorated birthdays, engagements, graduations, and good-byes by searching the world for exactly the right poem or picture book, novel or essay, and writing a letter to accompany it. Inside the letter, it says "This is why I chose this piece of literature precisely for you." In this same way, the book lists and the written guides that accompany them in this field guide have become our gift to you, the teachers of our nation's children. We have chosen, from all the books we have ever read, exactly the ones we think could start best in your classroom, and with these books, we have written notes that explain exactly why and how we think these texts will be so powerful in your children's hands.

The book lists and guides in this field guide are the Teachers College Reading and Writing Project's literacy gift to New York City and to the nation. When, two years ago, patrons Alan and Gail Levenstein came to us asking if there was one thing, above all others, which could further our work with teachers and children, we knew our answer in a heartbeat. We couldn't imagine anything more important than giving children the opportunity to trade, collect, talk over, and live by books. We want children to carry poems in their backpacks, to cry with Jess when he finds out that his friend Leslie has drowned, to explore tropical seas from the deck of a ship, to wonder at the life teeming in a drop of water. We want our children's heroes to include the wise and loving spider Charlotte, spinning her web to save the life of Wilbur, and the brave Atticus Finch.

We told the Levensteins that for teachers, as well as for children, there could be no finer gift than the gift of books for their students. We want teachers to be able to read magnificent stories aloud as the prelude to each school day, and to know the joy of putting exactly the right book in the hands of a child and adding, with a wink, "When you finish this book, there are more like it." We want teachers to create libraries with categories of books that peak their students' interests and match their children's passions, with one shelf for Light Sports Books and another shelf for Cousins of the Harry Potter books, one for Books That Make You Cry and another for You'll-Never-Believe-This Books. With this kind of a library, how much easier it becomes to teach children to read, to teach them what they need to become powerful, knowledgeable, literate people!

Even as we embarked on the effort to design magnificent classroom libraries, we knew that the best classroom library would always be the one assembled by a knowledgeable classroom teacher with his or her own students in mind. But, in so many cities, twenty new teachers may arrive in a school in a single year, having had no opportunity to learn about children's books at all. Even though some teachers have studied children's books, they may not be the ones given the opportunity to purchase books. Or, too often, there is no time to make book selections carefully—funds are discovered ten minutes before they must be spent or be taken from the budget. For these situations, we knew it would be enormously helpful to have lists and arrangements of recommended books for classroom libraries. Even without these worries, we all know the value of receiving book recommendations from friends. And so, our commitment to the project grew.

Our plan became this: We'd rally the entire Project community around a gigantic, two-year-long effort to design state-of-the-art classroom libraries and guides, exactly tailored to the classrooms we know so well. Simultaneously, we'd begin working with political, educational, and philanthropic leaders in hopes that individuals or corporations might adopt a school (or a corridor of classrooms) and create in these schools and classrooms the libraries of our dreams. Sharing our enthusiasm, colleagues at the New York City Board of Education proposed that idea to the mayor. Two years later, that dream has come true—In his January 2001 state of the city address, Mayor Giuliani promised $31.5 million of support to put a lending library in every New York City classroom, kindergarten through eighth grade.

Hearing this pronouncement, educational leaders from around the city joined with us in our philanthropic effort. People from the New York City Board of Education reviewed the lists and added suggestions and revisions. The Robin Hood Foundation, which had already been involved in a parallel effort to develop *school* libraries, contributed their knowledge. Readers from the Teachers Union and from the Office of Multicultural Education and of Early Childhood Education and of Literacy Education all joined in, coordinated by Peter Heaney, Executive Director of the Division of Instructional Support, and Adele Schroeter, Director of the Office of Research, Development and Dissemination. The book selections for the classroom libraries became even more carefully honed, and the written guides became richer still.

Over the past few months, boxes upon boxes of books have arrived across New York City, and in every classroom, children are pulling close to watch, big-eyed, as one exquisite, carefully chosen book after another is brought from the box and set on the shelf. Each teacher will receive between three and four hundred books. With most of these books, there will be a carefully crafted guide which says, "We chose this book because . . ." and "On page . . ." and "You'll notice that . . ." and "If you like this book, these are some others like it. . . . " I cannot promise that in every town and city across the nation the effort to put literature in the hands of students and guidance in the hands of their teachers will proceed so smoothly. But I'm hoping these book lists and these ready-made libraries bearing a stamp of approval will catch the eye of funders, of generous patrons, and of foresighted school leaders. And, every penny that comes to the authors from the sale of these field guides will go directly back into this project, directly back into our efforts to get more books into children's hands.

In the meantime, we needn't be idle. We'll comb through the book sales at libraries, and we'll write requests to publishers and companies. In a letter home to our children's parents, we might say, "Instead of sending in cupcakes to honor your child's birthday, I'm hoping you'll send a book. Enclosed is a list of suggestions." We can and will get books into our children's hands, by hook or by crook. And we can and will get the professional support we need for our reading instruction—our vitality and effectiveness as educators depend on it.

About the Books

When hundreds of teachers pool their knowledge of children's books as we have here, the resulting libraries are far richer than anything any one of us could have imagined on our own. We're proud as peacocks of these selections and of the accompanying literary insights and teaching ideas, and can't wait to share them both with teachers and children across the country. Here is a window into some of the crafting that has gone into the book selections:

- We suggest author studies in which the texts that students will study approximately match those they'll write and will inform their own work as authors.
- In upper-grade libraries, we include books that are relatively easy to read, but we have tried to ensure that they contain issues of concern to older children as well.
- We include books that might inform other books in the same library. For example, one library contains three books about dust storms, another contains a variety of books on spiders.
- We know that comprehension and interpretive thinking must be a part of reading from the very beginning, so we include easy to read books that can support thoughtful responses.
- We try to match character ages with student ages, approximately. For example, we have put the book in which Ramona is five in the library we anticipate will be for kindergartners, and put fourth-grade Ramona in the library we anticipate will be for fourth graders.
- We include complementary stories together when possible. For example, Ringgold's *Tar Beach* and Dorros' *Abuela* appear in the same library, anticipating that readers will recognize these as parallel stories in which the narrator has an imagined trip.
- We have never assumed that books in a series are all of the same level. For example, we have determined that some of the *Frog and Toad* books are more challenging, and this is indicated in our libraries.
- We understand that books in a series cannot always be easily read out of sequence. Because we know the *Magic Treehouse* series is best read in a particular sequence, for example, we have been careful with regard to the books we select out of that series.
- We selected our libraries to reflect multicultural values and bring forth characters of many different backgrounds and lives.

- We try to steer clear of books that will not meet with general public approval. We do not believe in censorship, but we do believe that books purchased en masse should not bring storms of criticism upon the unsuspecting teacher.

At the same time that we are proud of the work we've done, we also know that there are countless magnificent books we have omitted and countless helpful and obvious teaching moves we have missed. We are certain that there are authors' names we have inadvertently misspelled, opinions expressed with which we don't all agree, levels assigned that perhaps should be different, and so on. We consider this work to be a letter to a friend and a work in progress, and we are rushing it to you, eager for a response. We are hoping that when you come across areas that need more attention, when you get a bright idea about a guide or booklist, that you will write back to us. We have tried to make this as easy as possible for you to do—just go to our website and contact us!

Choosing the Library for Your Class

We have created seven libraries for kindergarten through sixth grade classrooms. The libraries are each assigned a letter name (A–G) rather than a grade-level in recognition of the fact that the teacher of one class of fourth graders might find that Library D is suited to her students, and another fourth grade teacher might opt for Library E or Library F.

In order to determine which classroom library is most appropriate for a particular class in a particular school, teachers need to determine the approximate reading levels of their students in November, after the teachers have had some time to assess their students as readers. Teachers can compare the book the middle-of-the-class reader tends to be reading with the books we note for each level, and choose the library that corresponds to that average text level. More detail follows this general description. In shorthand, however, the following equivalencies apply:

Library Ⓐ is usually Kindergarten
Library Ⓑ is usually K or 1st grade
Library Ⓒ is usually 1st or 2nd grade
Library Ⓓ is usually 2nd or 3rd grade
Library Ⓔ is usually 3rd or 4th grade
Library Ⓕ is usually 4th or 5th grade
Library Ⓖ is usually 5th or 6th grade

The system of saying, "If in November, your children are reading books like these," usually doesn't work for kindergarten children. Instead, we say Library A is suitable if, in November, the average student cannot yet do a rich, story-like, emergent (or pretend) reading of a familiar storybook, nor can this child write using enough initial and final consonants that an adult can "read" the child's writing.

It is important to note that all of the books in any given library are not at the same level of difficulty. Instead, we have created a mix of levels that tend to represent the mixed levels of ability of readers in the classes we have studied. The composition of the libraries, by level, is described on pages xlv–liv.

Once you have chosen the library that best corresponds to the average level of your students as readers, you will need to decide which components of the library best suit your curriculum. Each library is divided into components—a core and some modules. The core is the group of books in the library we regard as essential. Each library also contains six modules, each representing a category of books. For example, in each library there is a module of nonfiction books, and in the upper-grade libraries there are modules containing five copies each of ten books we recommend for book clubs. Each module contains approximately fifty titles. The exact quantity from module to module varies slightly because we have tried to keep the cost of each module approximately equal. This means, for example, that the nonfiction module that contains more hardcover books has fewer books overall.

There are a variety of ways to assemble a library. Some teachers will want to purchase the entire library—the core plus the six modules. Sometimes, teachers on the same grade level in a school each purchase the same core but different modules, so a greater variety of books will be available across the hall for their students. In New York City, teachers automatically received the core of their library of choice, 150 books, and then could choose three of the six possible modules.

The Contents of Each Library

Researchers generally agree that a classroom should contain at least twenty books per child. Obviously, the number of books needs to be far greater than this in kindergarten and first grade classrooms, because books for beginning readers often contain fewer than 100 words and can generally only sustain a child's reading for a short while. We would have liked to recommend libraries of 750 titles but decided to select a smaller number of books, trusting that each teacher will have other books of his or her choice to supplement our recommendations.

Because we predict that every teacher will receive or buy the core of a library and only some teachers will receive any particular module, we tried to fill the core of the libraries with great books we couldn't imagine teaching, or living, without. Because we know children will borrow and swap books between classrooms, it is rare for books to be in the core of more than one library, even though some great books could easily belong there.

Usually, these classroom libraries include enough books from a particularly wonderful series to turn that series into a class rage, but the libraries frequently do not contain all the books in a series. Often, more books in the series are included in Modules One and Two, which always contain more books for independent reading, divided into the same levels as those in the core. Our expectation is that once readers have become engrossed in a series, teachers or parents can help them track down sequels in the school or public library.

Within the core of a library, we include about a dozen books of various genres that could be perfect for the teacher to read aloud to the class. These are all tried-and-true read aloud books; each title on the read-aloud list is one that countless teachers have found will create rapt listeners and generate rich conversation.

In every library we have included nonfiction books. They were not chosen to support particular social studies or science units; that would be a different and admirable goal. Instead, our team members have searched for nonfiction texts that captivate readers, and we imagine them being read within the reading workshop. The nonfiction books were chosen either because their topics are generally high-interest ones for children (animals, yo-yo tricks, faraway lands, disgusting animals), or because they represent the best of their genre.

Each library contains about fifteen books that could be splendid mentor te xts for young writers. That is, they contain writing that students could emulate and learn from easily since it is somewhat like the writing they are generally able to create themselves.

In each core library, an assortment of other categories is included. These differ somewhat from one library to another. Libraries D and E, for example, contain many early chapter books, but since it is also crucial for children at this level to read the richest picture books imaginable, the core contains a score of carefully chosen picture books. Some cores also contain a set of books perfect for an author study. The categories are indicated on the book lists themselves, and under "Teaching Uses" in the guides.

The vast majority of books in each library are single copies, chosen in hopes that they will be passed eagerly from one reader to another. The challenge was not to find the number of books representing a particular level, but instead to select irresistible books. The chosen books have been field tested in dozens of New York City classrooms, and they've emerged as favorites for teachers and children alike.

The few books that have been selected in duplicate are ones we regard as particularly worthwhile to talk over with a partner. We would have loved to suggest duplicate copies be available for half the books in each library—if libraries had more duplicates, this would allow two readers to move simultaneously through a book, meeting in partnerships to talk and think about the chapters they've read. The duplicate copies would allow readers to have deeper and more text-specific book talks, while growing and researching theories as they read with each other. Duplicates also help books gain social clout in a classroom—allowing the enthusiasm of several readers to urge even more readers to pick the book up. If teachers are looking for ways to supplement these libraries, buying some duplicate copies would be a perfect way to start.

Many of the libraries contain a very small number of multiple (four or five) copies of books intended for use in guided reading and strategy lessons. Once children are reading chapter books, we find teachers are wise to help children into a new series by pulling together a group of four readers, introducing the text, and guiding their early reading. Teachers may also want to offer extra support to children as they read the second book in a series, and so we suggest having a duplicate of this next book as well, so that each child can read it with a partner, meeting to retell and discuss it.

The Levels Within the Libraries

We've leveled many, but purposely not all, of the books in every classroom library. The fact that we have leveled these books doesn't mean that teachers should necessarily convey all of these levels to children. We expect teachers will often make these levels visible on less than half of their books (through the use of colored tabs), giving readers the responsibility of choosing appropriate books for themselves by judging unmarked books against the template of leveled books. "This book looks a lot like the green dot books that have been just-right for me, so I'll give it a try and see if I have a smooth read," a reader might say. It is important that kids learn to navigate different levels of difficulty within a classroom library on their own or with only minimal support from a teacher.

We do not imagine a classroom lending library that is divided into levels as discrete as the levels established by Reading Recovery© or by Gay Su Pinnell and Irene Fountas' book, *Guided Reading: Good First Teaching for All Children* (Heinemann, 1996). These levels were designed for either one-to-one tutorials or intensive, small group guided reading sessions, and in both of these situations a vigilant teacher is present to constantly shepherd children along toward more challenging books. If a classroom lending library is divided into micro-levels and each child's entire independent reading life is slotted into a micro-level, some children might languish at a particular level, and many youngsters might not receive the opportunities to read across a healthy range of somewhat-easier and somewhat-harder books. Most worrisome of all, because we imagine children working often with reading partners who "like to read the same kinds of books as you do," classroom libraries that contain ten micro-levels (instead of say, five more general levels) could inadvertently convey the message that many *children* as well as many *books* were off-limits as partners to particular readers.

There are benefits to micro-levels, however, and therefore within a difficulty level (or a color-dot), some teachers might ascribe a plus sign to certain books, signifying that this book is one of the harder ones at this level. Teachers can then tell a child who is new to a level to steer clear of the books with plus signs, or to be sure that he or she receives a book introduction before tackling a book with this marker.

When assigning books to levels, we have tried to research the difficulty levels that others have given to each text and we have included these levels in our guides. Fairly frequently, however, our close study of a particular text has led us to differ somewhat from the assessments others have made. Of course leveling books is and always will be a subjective and flawed process; and therefore teachers everywhere *should* deviate from assigned levels, ours and others, when confident of their rationale, or when particularly knowledgeable about a reader. You can turn to the tables at the back of this section, on pages xxv–lviii, to learn more about our leveling system.

Building the Libraries

When we started this project two years ago, we initiated some intensive study groups, each designed to investigate a different terrain in children's literature. Soon, a group led by Lynn Holcomb, one of the first Reading Recovery teachers in Connecticut, was working to select books for a K–1 library. Members of this group also learned from Barbara Peterson, author of *Literary Pathways: Selecting Books to Support New Readers* (Heinemann, 2001), who conducted groundbreaking research at Ohio State University, examining how readers actually experience levels of text complexity. The group also learned from Gay Su Pinnell, well-known scholar of literacy education and coauthor with Irene Fountas of many books including *Guided Reading*. Of course, the group learned especially from intensive work with children in classrooms. The group searched for books that:

- Represent a diverse range of shapes, sizes, authors, and language patterns as possible. The committee went to lengths to be sure that when taken as a whole, primary-level libraries looked more like libraries full of real books than like kits full of "teaching materials."
- Use unstilted language. A book that reads, "Come, Spot. Come, Spot, come," generally would not be selected.
- Contain many high frequency words. If one book contained just one word on a page ("Scissors/paste/paper/etc.") and another book contained the reoccurring refrain of "I see the scissors./ I see the paste." we selected the second option.
- Carry meaning and were written to communicate content with a reader. If the book would probably generate a conversation or spark an insight, it was more apt to be included than one that generally left a reader feeling flat and finished with the book.
- Represent the diversity of people in our world and convey valuable messages about the human spirit.

A second group, under the leadership of Kathleen Tolan, an experienced teacher and staff developer, spent thousands of hours studying early chapter books and the children who read them. This group pored over series, asking questions: Is each book in the series equally difficult? Which series act as good precursors for other series? Do the books in the series make up one continuous story, or can each book stand alone? What are the special demands placed on readers of this series?

Yet another group, led by Gaby Layden, staff developer at the Project, studied nonfiction books to determine which might be included in a balanced, independent reading library. The group studied levels of difficulty in nonfiction books, and found authors and texts that deserved special attention. Carefully, they chose books for teachers to demonstrate and for children to practice working through the special challenges of nonfiction reading.

Meanwhile, renowned teacher-educator Isoke Nia, teacher extraordinaire Kathy Doyle, and their team of educators dove into the search for the very best chapter books available for upper-grade readers. Isoke especially helped us select touchstone texts for writing workshops—books to help us teach children to craft their writing with style, care, and power.

Teacher, staff developer, and researcher Annemarie Powers worked full-time to ensure that our effort was informed by the related work of other groups across the city and nation. We pored over bibliographies and met with librarians and literature professors. We searched for particular kinds of books: books featuring Latino children, anthologies of short stories, Level A and B books which looked and sounded like literature. We researched the classrooms in our region that are especially famous for their classroom libraries, and took note of the most treasured books we found there. All of this information fed our work.

Reading Instruction and the Classroom Library: An Introduction to Workshop Structures

These classroom libraries have been developed with the expectation that they will be the centerpiece of reading instruction. When I ask teachers what they are really after in the teaching of reading, many answer, as I do, "I want children to be lifelong readers. I cannot imagine anything more important than helping children grow up able to read and loving to read. I want students to initiate reading in their own lives, for their own purposes."

There is, of course, no one best way to teach reading so that children become lifelong readers. One of the most straightforward ways to do this is to embrace the age-old, widely shared belief that children benefit from daily opportunities to read books they choose for their own purposes and pleasures (Krashen 1993, Atwell 1987, Cambourne 1993, Smith 1985, Meek 1988).

More and more, however, we've come to realize that students benefit not only from opportunities to read, read, read, but also from instruction that responds to what students do when they are given opportunities to read. I have described the reading workshop in my latest publication, *The Art of Teaching Reading* (Calkins 2001). The reading workshop is an instructional format in which children are given long chunks of time in which to read appropriate texts, and also given explicit and direct instruction. Teachers who come from a writing workshop background may find it helpful to structure the reading workshop in ways that parallel the writing workshop so that children learn simultaneously to work productively inside each of the two congruent structures. Whatever a teacher decides, it is important that the structures of a reading workshop are clear and predictable so that children know how to carry on with some independence, and so that teachers are able to assess and coach individuals as well as partnerships and small groups.

Many teachers begin a reading workshop by pulling students together for a minilesson lasting about eight minutes (unless the read aloud is, for that day, incorporated into the minilesson, which then adds at least twenty minutes). Children then bring their reading bins, holding the books they are currently reading, to their assigned "reading nooks." As children read independently, a teacher moves among them, conferring individually with a child or bringing a small group of readers together for a ten- to fifteen-minute guided reading or strategy lesson. After children have read independently for about half an hour, teachers ask them to meet with their partners to talk about their books and their reading. After the partners meet, teachers often call all the readers in a class together for a brief "share session" (Calkins 2001). The following table shows some general guidelines for the length of both independent reading and the partnership talks based on the approximate level of the texts students are reading in the class.

How Long Might a Class Have Independent Reading and Partnership Talk?

Class Reading Level	*Independent Reading Duration*	*Partnership Talk Duration*
Library A	10 minutes	20 minutes
Library B	15 minutes	20 minutes
Library C	20 minutes	20 minutes
Library D	30 minutes	10 minutes
Library E	40 minutes	10 minutes
Library F	40 minutes	10 minutes
Library G	40 minutes	10 minutes

Periodically, the structure of the minilesson, independent reading, partnership, and then share time is replaced by a structure built around book clubs or "junior" book clubs, our own, reading-intensive version of reading centers.

Minilessons

During a minilesson, the class gathers on the carpet to learn a strategy all readers can use not only during the independent reading workshop but also throughout their reading lives. The content of a minilesson comes, in part, from a teacher deciding that for a period of time, usually a month, he needs to focus his teaching on a particular aspect of reading. For example, many teachers begin the year by devoting a month to reading with stamina and understanding (Calkins 2001). During this unit, teachers might give several minilessons designed to help children choose books they can understand, and they might give others designed to help readers sustain their reading over time. Another minilesson might be designed to help readers make more time for reading in their lives or to help them keep a stack of books-in-waiting to minimize the interval between finishing one book and starting another.

The minilesson, then, often directs the work readers do during independent reading. If the minilessons show students how to make sure their ideas are grounded in the details of the text, teachers may establish an interval between independent reading time and partnership conversations when children can prepare for a talk about their text by marking relevant sections that support their ideas.

Sometimes minilessons are self-standing, separate from the interactive read aloud. Other minilessons include and provide a frame for the day's read aloud. For example, the teacher may read aloud a book and direct that day's talk in a way that demonstrates the importance of thinking about a character's motivations. Then children may be asked to think in similar ways about their independent reading books. Perhaps, when they meet with a partner at the end of reading, the teacher will say, "Please talk about the motivations that drive your central characters and show evidence in the text to support your theories."

Conferences

While children read, a teacher confers. Usually this means that the teacher starts by sitting close to a child as he or she continues reading, watching for external behaviors that can help assess the child. After a moment or two, the teacher usually says, "Can I interrupt?" and conducts a few-minute-long conversation while continuing the assessment. A teacher will often ask, "Can you read to me a bit?" and this, too, informs any hunches about a child and his or her strengths and needs as a reader. Finally, teachers intervene to lift the level of what the child is doing. The following table offers some examples of this.

General Examples of the Conferring That Can Help Readers Grow

If, in reading, the child is . . .	*Teachers might teach by . . .*
able to demonstrate a basic understanding of the text	nudging the child to grow deeper insights, perhaps by asking: ■ Do any pages (parts) go together in a surprising way? ■ Why do you think the author wrote this book? What is he (she) trying to say? ■ If you were to divide the book into different sections, what would they be? ■ How are you changing as a reader? How are you reading this book differently than you've read others? ■ What's the work you are doing as you read this?
talking mostly about the smallest, most recent details read	generalizing what kind of book it is, giving the child a larger sense of the genre. If it is a story, we can ask questions that will work for any story: ■ How is the main character changing? ■ How much time has gone by? ■ What is the setting for the story? If the text is a non-narrative, we could ask: ■ What are the main chunks (or sections) in the text? ■ How would you divide this up? ■ How do the parts of this text go together? ■ What do you think the author is trying to teach you?
clearly enthralled by the story	asking questions to help the reader tap into the best of this experience to use again later. ■ What do you think it is about this story that draws you in? ■ You seem really engaged, so I'm wondering what can you learn about this reading experience that might inform you as you read other books. ■ When I love a book, as you love this one, I sometimes find myself reading faster and faster, as if I'm trying to gulp it down. But a reading teacher once told me this quote. "Some people think a good book is one you can't put down, but me, I think a good book is one you must put down—to muse over, to question, to think about." Could you set some bookmarks throughout this book and use them to pause in those places to really think and even to write about this book? Make one of those places right now, would you?

Partnerships

When many of us imagine reading, we envision a solitary person curled up with a book. The truth is that reading is always social, always embedded in talk with others. If I think about the texts I am reading now in my life and ask myself, "Is there something *social* about my reading of those texts?" I quickly realize that I read texts because people have recommended them. I read anticipating conversations I will soon have with others, and I read noticing things in this one text that I have discussed with others. My reading, as is true for many readers, is multilayered and sharper because of the talk that surrounds it.

There are a lot of reasons to organize reading time so that children have opportunities to talk with a reading partner. Partner conversations can highlight the social elements of reading, making children enjoy reading more. Talking about books also helps children have more internal conversations (thoughts) as they read. Putting thoughts about texts out into the world by speaking them allows other readers to engage in conversation, in interpretations and ideas, and can push children to ground their ideas in the text, to revise their ideas, to lengthen and deepen their ideas.

For young children, talking with a partner usually doubles the actual unit of time a child spends working with books. In many primary classrooms, the whole class reads and then the teacher asks every child to meet with a partner who can read a similar level of book. Each child brings his bin of books, thus doubling the number of appropriate books available to any one child. The child who has already read a book talks about it with the other child, giving one partner a valuable and authentic reason to retell a book and another child an introduction to the book. Then the two readers discuss how they will read together. After the children read aloud together, the one book held between them as they sit hip to hip, there is always time for the partners to discuss the text. Sometimes, teachers offer students guidance in this conversation.

More proficient readers need a different sort of partnership because once a child can read short chapter books, there are few advantages to the child reading aloud often. Then too, by this time children can sustain reading longer. Typically in third grade, for example, individuals read independently for thirty minutes and then meet with partners for ten minutes to talk over the book. Again, the teacher often guides that conversation, sometimes by modeling—by entertaining with the whole-class read-aloud text—the sort of conversations she expects readers will have in their partnerships.

Book Clubs

Teaching children to read well has a great deal to do with teaching children to talk well about books, because the conversations children have in the air between one another become the conversations they have in their own minds as they read. Children who have talked in small groups about the role of the suitcase in Christopher Paul Curtis's book, *Bud, Not Buddy* will be far more apt to pause as they read another book, asking, "Might *this* object play a significant role in this book, like the suitcase did in *Bud, Not Buddy*?"

When we move children from partnership conversations toward small-group book clubs, we need to provide some scaffolding for them to lean on at first. This is because partnerships are generally easier for children to manage than small group conversations. It is also generally easier for students to read for thirty-minute reading sessions with ten-minute book talks than it is to read for a few days in a row and then sustain extended book talks, as they are expected to do in book clubs.

Children need some support as they begin clubs. One way to do this is to begin with small book club conversations about the read aloud book—the one book we know everyone will be prepared to talk about. Another way to get started with book clubs is for the teacher to suggest that children work in small groups to read multiple copies of, say, a mystery book. The teacher will plan to read a mystery book aloud to the class during the weeks they work in their clubs. Meanwhile, each group of approximately four readers will be reading one mystery that is at an appropriate level for them. The whole class works on and talks about the read-aloud mystery, and this work then guides the small group work. On one day, for example, after reading aloud the whole-class mystery, the teacher could immerse the class in talk about what it's like to read "suspiciously," suspecting everything and everyone. For a few days, the class can try that sort of reading as they listen to the read aloud. Meanwhile, when children disperse to their small groups to read their own mysteries, they can read these books "suspiciously."

Eventually the book clubs can become more independent. One small group of children might be reading several books by an author and talking about what they can learn from the vantage point of having read so many. Another group might read books that deal with a particular theme or subject. Either way, in the classrooms I know best, each book club lasts at least a few weeks. Teachers observe, and coach and teach into these talks, equipping kids with ways to write, talk, and think about texts. However, teachers neither dominate the clubs nor steer readers toward a particular preordained interpretation of a text. Instead, teachers steer readers toward ways of learning and thinking that can help them again and again, in reading after reading, throughout their lives.

Library E Contents Description

Library E consists of

I.	Independent Reading & Partner Reading Chapter Books (Levels 7–11)			
		Level 7	37 Titles	39 Texts
		Level 8	46 Titles	53 Texts
		Level 9	95 Titles	111 Texts
		Level 10	44 Titles	50 Texts
		Level 11	17 Titles	20 Texts
	Nonfiction		57 Titles	57 Texts
	Picture Books		24 Titles	24 Texts
	Poetry		12 Titles	12 Texts
	Short Stories		7 Titles	7 Texts
II.	Guided Reading		12 Titles	48 Texts
III.	Book Club/Literature Circle		26 Titles	132 Texts
IV.	Author Study		10 Titles	20 Texts
V.	Read Alouds		12 Titles	12 Texts
VI.	Books to Support the Writing Process		9 Titles	9 Texts
Total Number of Texts in Library E			**408 Titles**	**594 Texts**

(Because of substitutions made in the ordering process, this number may not be precise.)

Library E Book List

Group Description	Level	#	Author	Title	ISBN	Publisher	Quantity	Heinemann Write-Up
CORE								
Independent Reading		1	Cooney, Barbara	*Island Boy*	140507566	Penguin Putnam	1	Y
		2	Oppenheim, Shulamith	*Fireflies for Nathan*	140557822	Penguin Puffin	1	Y
		3	Woodson, Jacqueline	*We Had a Picnic This Sunday Past*	786802421	Hyperion Books	1	Y
	7	1	Bonsall, Crosby	*Case of the Cat's Meow, The*	64440176	Harper Collins	1	
		2	Coerr, Eleanor	*Big Balloon Race, The*	64440532	Harper Collins	1	
		3	Cristaldi, Kathryn	*Baseball Ballerina*	679817344	Random House	1	
		4	Komaiko, Leah	*Annie Bananie Moves to Barry Avenue*	440410355	Bantam Doubleday Dell	1	
		5	Marshall, Edward	*Fox Series/Fox in Love*	140368434	Penguin Puffin	1	Y
		6	Marshall, Edward	*Fox Series/Fox on Stage*	140380329	Penguin Puffin	1	
		7	Paterson, Katherine	*Smallest Cow in the World, The*	64441644	Harper Collins	1	
		8	Ross, Pat	*M&M Series/Santa Secrets*	141300949	Penguin Puffin	1	Y
		9	Rylant, Cynthia	*Poppleton and Friends*	590847880	Scholastic Inc.	1	Y
		10	Rylant, Cynthia	*Poppleton in Spring*	590848224	Scholastic Inc.	1	Y
		11	Sharmat, Marjorie Weinman	*Nate the Great*	44046126X	Bantam Doubleday Dell	1	
		12	Sharmat, Marjorie Weinman	*Nate the Great and the Snowy Trail*	440462762	Bantam Doubleday Dell	1	Y
		13	Sharmat, Marjorie Weinman	*Nate the Great/The Case of the Fleeing Fang*	440413818	Bantam Doubleday Dell	1	
	8	1	Adler, David	*Cam Jansen Series/Mystery of the Dinosaur Bones*	590461230	Scholastic Inc.	1	Y
		2	Adler, David	*Cam Jansen Series/Mystery of the Stolen Corn Popper*	141304618	Penguin Publishing	1	
		3	Blume, Judy	*One in the Middle is a Green Kangaroo, The*	440467314	Bantam Doubleday Dell	1	Y

BLUE DOT

DOUBLE YELLOW

Group Description	Level	#	Author	Title	ISBN	Publisher	Quantity	Heinemann Write-Up
		4	Bos, Burny	*Molesons/Meet the Molesons*	1558584099	North South Books	1	
		5	Brown, Marc	*Arthur Adventure Series/Arthur's Eyes*	316110698	Little Brown & Co	1	
		6	Brown, Marc	*Arthur Adventure Series/Meets the President*	316112917	Little Brown & Co	1	Y
		7	Byars, Betsy	*Beans on the Roof*	440403146	Dell Publishing	1	Y
		8	Byars, Betsy	*Seven Treasure Hunts, The*	60208856	Harper Trophy	1	Y
		9	Conford, Ellen	*Jenny Archer Series/A Case for Jenny Archer*	316153524	Little Brown & Co	1	
		10	Conford, Ellen	*Jenny Archer Series/Nibble, Nibble, Jenny Archer*	316152064	Little Brown & Co	1	
		11	Cosby, Bill	*Little Bill Series/Best Way to Play*	59052190X	Scholastic Inc.	1	
		12	Cosby, Bill	*Little Bill Series/Worst Day of My Life*	59052190X	Scholastic Inc.	1	
		13	Dadey, Debbie	*Triplet Trouble and the Class Trip*	590907301	Scholastic Inc.	1	
		14	Delton, Judy	*Pee Wee Scouts/Lights, Action, Land-Ho! (#18)*	44040732X	Dell Publishing	1	Y
		15	Delton, Judy	*Pee Wee Scouts/Stage Frightened*	440413273	Bantam Doubleday Dell	1	
		16	Giff, Patricia Reilly	*Kids of Polk Street Series/ December Secrets*	440417953	Dell Publishing	1	Y
		17	Giff, Patricia Reilly	*Kids of Polk Street Series/In the Dinosaurs Paw*	440441501	Dell Publishing	1	Y
		18	Howe, James	*Pinky & Rex Series/Double Dad Weekend*	689808356	Aladdin	1	Y
		19	Howe, James	*Pinky & Rex Series/Go to Camp*	689825889	Simon & Schuster	1	Y
		20	Hurwitz, Johanna	*Russell Sprouts*	140329420	Penguin Puffin	1	Y
		21	Kline, Suzy	*Horrible Harry Series/the Green Slime*	140389709	Penguin Publishing	1	Y
		22	Kline, Suzy	*Song Lee and the Leech Man*	140372555	Viking Penguin	1	

Group Description	Level	#	Author	Title	ISBN	Publisher	Quantity	Heinemann Write-Up
		23	Levy, Elizabeth	*Invisible Inc Series/The Karate Class*	59060323X	Scholastic Inc.	1	
		24	Levy, Elizabeth	*Invisible Inc Series/The Mystery of the Missing Dog*	590474847	Scholastic Inc.	1	
		25	Osborne, Mary Pope	*Magic Tree House Series/Day of the Dragon King*	679890513	Random House	1	Y
		26	Osborne, Mary Pope	*Magic Tree House Series/Vacation on a Volcano*	679890505	Random House	1	
		27	Pilkey, Dav	*Adventures of Captian Underpants, The*	590846280	Scholastic Inc.	1	Y
		28	Rosenbloom, Joseph	*Deputy Dan and the Bank Robbers*	39487045X	Random House	1	
		29	Rosenbloom, Joseph	*Deputy Dan Gets His Man*	394872509	Random House	1	
		30	Rylant, Cynthia	*Cobble Street Cousins/Special Gifts*	689817150	Simon & Schuster	1	
		31	Sachar, Louis	*Marvin Redpost: Alone in his Teacher's House*	679819495	Random House	1	Y
		32	Sachar, Louis	*Marvin Redpost: Kidnapped at Birth?*	679819460	Random House	1	Y
		33	Sachar, Louis	*Marvin Redpost: Why Pick on Me?*	679819479	Random House	1	Y
		34	Yolen, Jane	*Commander Toad Series/in Space*	698113551	Penguin Putnam	1	
		35	Yolen, Jane	*Commander Toad Series/the Voyage Home*	69811602X	Putnam & Grosset	1	
	9	1	Bulla, Clyde Robert	*Lion to Guard Us, A*	64403335	Harper Collins	1	Y
		2	Bulla, Clyde Robert	*Shoeshine Girl*	64402282	Harper Trophy	1	Y
		3	Cameron, Ann	*Julian, Dream Doctor*	395732379	Houghton Mifflin	1	
		4	Cameron, Ann	*Julian, Secret Agent*	394819497	Random House	1	
		5	Cameron, Ann	*Stories That Julian Tells, The*	394828925	Alfred A Knopf	1	Y
		6	Christopher, Matt	*Soccer Cat's Series/Captain Contest*	316141690	Little Brown & Co	1	
		7	Cleary, Beverly	*Dear Mr. Henshaw*	380709589	Avon Books	1	

Group Description	Level	#	Author	Title	ISBN	Publisher	Quantity	Heinemann Write-Up
		8	Cleary, Beverly	*Ramona and Her Father*	688221149	William Morrow & Co	1	Y
		9	Cleary, Beverly	*Runaway Ralph*	380709538	William Morrow & Co	1	
Freckle Juice?		10	Dahl, Roald	*George's Marvelous Medicine*	140346414	Penguin Publishing	1	Y
		11	Danziger, Paula	*Amber Brown Series/ is Feeling Blue*	439071682	Scholastic Inc.	1	Y
		12	Danziger, Paula	*Amber Brown Series/ is not a Crayon*	59045899X	Scholastic Inc.	1	Y
		13	Danziger, Paula	*Amber Brown Series/ Sees Red*	590947281	Scholastic Inc.	1	Y
		14	DeGross, Monalisa	*Donovan's Word Jar*	64420892	Harper Trophy	1	
		15	Duffey, Betsy	*Hey New Kid!*	140384391	Penguin Puffin	1	
		16	Estes, Eleanor	*Hundred Dresses, The*	156423502	Harcourt Brace	1	Y
		17	Gerstein, Mordicai	*Behind the Couch*	786811390	Hyperion Books	1	
DOUBLE ORANGE		18	Giff, Patricia Reilly	*Ballet Slippers Series/Rosie's Big City Ballet*	141301678	Penguin Puffin	1	Y
		19	Giff, Patricia Reilly	*Polk Street Kids on Tour/Let's Go, Philadelphia!*	440413680	Bantam Doubleday Dell	1	
		20	Giff, Patricia Reilly	*Polk Street Kids on Tour/Next Stop, New York City!*	440413621	Bantam Doubleday Dell	1	
		21	Giff, Patricia Reilly	*Polk Street Special/Look Out, Washington DC*	440409349	Bantam Doubleday Dell	1	
		22	Giff, Patricia Reilly	*Polk Street Special/Postcard Pest, The*	44040973X	Bantam Doubleday Dell	1	
		23	Holmes, Barbara Ware	*My Sister the Sausage Roll*	786822600	Hyperion Books	1	
		* 24	Hurwitz, Johanna	*Aldo Applesauce*	140340831	Penguin Putnam	1	Y
		25	Hurwitz, Johanna	*Busybody Nora*	64421430	Harper Collins	1	
		26	Hurwitz, Johanna	*Class Clown*	590418211	Scholastic Inc.	1	Y
		27	Hurwitz, Johanna	*New Neighbors for Nora*	140345949	Penguin Putnam	1	
		28	Hurwitz, Johanna	*One Small Dog*	688173829	Harper Collins	1	

Group Description	Level	#	Author	Title	ISBN	Publisher	Quantity	Heinemann Write-Up
		29	Hurwitz, Johanna	*Spring Break*	688166725	Beech Tree	1	Y
		30	Kingman, Lee	*Best Christmas, The*	688118380	William Morrow & Co	1	Y
DOUBLE ORANGE		31	King-Smith, Dick	*Jenius The Amazing Guinea Pig*	786811358	Hyperion Books	1	
		* 32	King-Smith, Dick	*School Mouse, The*	786811560	Hyperion Books	1	
		33	Leverich, Kathleen	*Flower Girl Series/Rose*	64420205	Harper Trophy	1	Y
		34	Moss, Marissa	*Amelia Writes Again*	1562477862	Pleasant Company	1	
		35	Patrick, Denise Lewis	*Adventures of Midnight Son, The*	80504714X	Henry Holt & Co	1	
		36	Roy, Ron	*A to Z Mysteries/Absent Author (#1)*	679881689	Random House	1	Y
		37	Sachar, Louis	*Marvin Redpost: A Magic Crystal?*	679890025	Random House	1	
		38	Soto, Gary	*Too Many Tamales*	698114124	Penguin Putnam	1	
		39	Spinelli, Eileen	*Lizzie Logan Wears Purple Sunglasses*	689818483	Aladdin	1	
		40	Warner, Sally	*Lily Series/Private Lily*	375800565	Alfred A. Knopf	1	
		41	Warner, Sally	*Lily Series/Sweet & Sour Lily*	375800557	Alfred A. Knopf	2	Y
	10	1	Adler, David	*Andy and Tamika*	152019014	Harcourt Brace	1	Y
		2	Adler, David	*Many Troubles of Andy Russell*	152019006	Harcourt Brace	1	
		3	Beverly Clearly	*Ramona Forever* ✓	3800709600	Avon Books	1	Y
		4	Blume, Judy	*SuperFudge* ✓	440484332	Bantam Doubleday Dell	1	Y
DOUBLE GREEN		5	Blume, Judy	*Tales of a Fourth Grade Nothing* ✓	44048474X	Bantam Doubleday Dell	1	
		6	Cameron, Ann	*Most Beautiful Place in World, The*	394804244	Alfred A. Knopf	1	
		7	Cleary, Beverly	*Ramona Quimby, Age 8* ✓	440473500	Bantam Doubleday Dell	1	Y
		8	Dahl, Roald	*Fantastic Mr. Fox* ✓	140328726	Penguin Publishing	1	
		9	Dahl, Roald	*James & the Giant Peach* ✓	140374248	Penguin Publishing	1	
		10	Forward, Toby	*Pie Magic*	688158560	Beech Tree	1	
		11	Hiller, B.B.	*Got a Job to Do? Rent a Third Grader*	590409662	Scholastic Inc.	1	

Group Description	Level	#	Author	Title	ISBN	Publisher	Quantity	Heinemann Write-Up
		12	Koller, Jackie French	*Dragon Trouble*	671013998	Pocket Books	1	
		13	Koller, Jackie French	*Dragonling, The*	671867903	Pocket Books	1	
		14	Koller, Jackie French	*Dragons of Krad*	671001949	Pocket Books	1	
DOUBLE GREEN		15	Murphy, Jill	*Worst Witch at Sea, The*	76361257X	Candlewick Press	1	
		16	Murphy, Jill	*Worst Witch, The*	763612545	Candlewick Press	1	
		17	Park, Barbara	*Almost Starring Skinnybones*	394825918	Random House	1	
		18	Sachar, Louis	*There's a Boy in the Girls' Bathroom*	394805720	Random House	1	
		19	Smith, Robert Kimmel	*Chocolate Fever*	440413699	Bantam Doubleday Dell	1	Y
		20	Spinelli, Jerry	*Fourth Grade Rats*	590442449	Scholastic Inc.	1	Y
		21	Spyri, Johanna	*Heidi*	789453908	DK Publishing	1	Y
		22	Wagner, Jane	*J.T.*	440442753	Bantam Doubleday Dell	1	Y
	11	1	Coerr, Eleanor	*Sadako and The Thousand Paper Cranes*	440474655	Bantam Doubleday Dell	1	
		2	Hermes, Patricia	*Mama, Let's Dance*	316358614	Berkeley	1	
DOUBLE RED		3	Lowry, Lois	*Taking Care of Terrific*	440484944	Bantam Doubleday Dell	1	
		4	MacLachlan, Patricia	*Skylark*	64406229	Harper Collins	1	
		5	Naidoo, Beverley	*Journey to Jo'burg*	64402371	Harper Collins	1	Y
		6	Scieszka, Jon	*Time Warp Trio Series/The Good the Bad and the Goofy*	59098165X	Scholastic Inc.	1	
		7	Simont, Marc	*In the Year of the Boar and Jackie Robinson*	64401758	Harper Trophy	1	
		8	Taylor, Mildred	*Friendship and the Gold Cadillac*	440413079	Bantam Doubleday Dell	1	
	12	1	Atwater, Richard	*Mr. Popper's Penguins*	590477331	Little Brown & Co	1	Y
		2	Avi	*Poppy*	380727692	William Morrow & Co	1	
		3	Fleischman, Sid	*Whipping Boy, The*	816710384	William Morrow & Co	1	Y
DOUBLE BLACK		4	Fletcher, Ralph	*Spider Boy*	440414830	Bantam Doubleday Dell	1	

Group Description	Level	#	Author	Title	ISBN	Publisher	Quantity	Heinemann Write-Up
		5	Hermes, Patricia	*Our Strange New Land: Elizabeth's Diary, Jamestown, Virginia, 1609*	439112087	Scholastic Inc.	1	Y
		6	Lewis, C.S.	*Chronicles of Narnia/Lion, the Witch and the Wardrobe*	64409422	Harper Trophy	1	Y
		7	Lowry, Lois	*Anastasia Krupnik*	440408520	Bantam Doubleday Dell	1	Y
		8	Myers, Walter Dean	*Me, Mop & the Moondance Kid*	440403960	Delacorte Press	1	
		9	Paterson, Katherine	*Great Gilly Hopkins, The*	64402010	Harper Trophy	1	Y
	13	1	Avi	*Ragweed*	380801671	Harper Trophy	1	Y
		2	MacLachlan, Patricia	*Unclaimed Treasures*	64401898	Harper Collins	1	
	14	1	Paulsen, Gary	*Hatchet*	689808828	Simon & Schuster	1	Y
Anthologies of Short Stories		1	Scieszka, Jon	*Stinky Cheese Man and Other Fairly Stupid Tales*	67084487X	Viking Penguin	1	
Author Studies		1	Greenfield, Eloise	*For the Love of the Game*	64435555	Harper Trophy	1	Y
		2	Greenfield, Eloise	*Grandpa's Face*	698113810	Penguin Putnam	1	Y
		3	Greenfield, Eloise	*Nathaniel Talking*	863162010	Writers & Readers Publishing	1	Y
		4	Greenfield, Eloise	*Rosa Parks*	64420256	Harper Collins	1	
		5	Greenfield, Eloise	*Sister*	64401995	Harper Trophy	1	
		6	Greenfield, Eloise	*Talk About a Family*	64404447	Harper Collins	1	
Teaching Writing		1	Baylor, Byrd	*Table Where Rich People Sit, The*	689820089	Simon & Schuster	1	Y
		2	Jarrell, Randall	*Bat-Poet, The*	6205905X	Harper Collins	1	
		3	Merriam, Eve	*Wise Woman and Her Secret, The*	689823819	Simon & Schuster	1	Y
		4	Schotter, Roni	*Nothing Ever Happens on 90th St.*	531071367	Orchard Books	1	
		5	Winter, Jonah	*Once Upon a Time in Chicago*	786804629	Hyperion Books	1	
		6	Yolen, Jane	*Nocturne*	152014586	Harcourt Brace	1	

Group Description	Level	#	Author	Title	ISBN	Publisher	Quantity	Heinemann Write-Up
Memoir		1	MacLachlan, Patricia	*What You Know First*	64434923	Harper Trophy	1	Y
		2	Myers, Walter Dean	*Angel to Angel*	64462420	Harper Trophy	1	Y
		3	Wyeth, Sharon Dennis	*Always My Dad*	679889345	Alfred A. Knopf	1	Y
Nonfiction		1	Ammon, Richard	*Conestoga Wagons*	823414752	Holiday House	1	Y
		2	Bruchac, Joseph	*Crazy Horse's Vision*	1880000946 (hc)	Lee & Low Books	1	
		3	Lauber, Patricia	*Fur, Feathers, Flippers*	590450719	Scholastic Inc.	1	Y
		4	Montgomery, Sy	*Snake Scientist, The*	395871697	Houghton Mifflin	1	Y
		5	Oneal, Zibby	*Long Way to Go, A /Once Upon America*	140329501	Penguin Publishing	1	
Poetry		1	Giovanni, Nikki	*Spin a Soft Black Song*	440845025	Scholastic Inc.	1	
		2	Hopkins, Lee Bennett	*Good Books, Good Times*	64462226	Harper Collins	1	
		3	Stepanek, Mattie	*Journey Through Heartsongs*	786869429	Hyperion	1	
ReadAloud Texts		1	Bridges, Ruby	*Through My Eyes*	590189239	Scholastic Inc.	1	Y
		2	Burleigh, Robert	*Flight*	698114256	Penguin Putnam	1	Y
		3	DiCamillo, Kate	*Because of Winn Dixie*	763607762	Candlewick Press	1	
		4	DiCamillo, Kate	*Tiger Rising*	763609110	Candlewick Press	1	
		5	Fletcher, Ralph	*Fig Pudding*	44041203X	Bantam Doubleday Dell	1	Y
		6	Hesse, Karen	*Music of Dolphins, The*	590897985	Scholastic Inc.	1	Y
		7	Leverich, Kathleen	*Flower Girl Series/Violet*	64420183	Harper Collins	1	
		8	Marshall, James	*Rats on the Roof and Other Stories*	140386467	Penguin Publishing	1	Y
		9	Philbrick, Rodman	*Freak the Mighty*	590474138	Scholastic Inc.	1	
		10	Rawls, Wilson	*Where The Red Fern Grows*	553274295	Bantam Doubleday Dell	1	
		11	Settel, Joanne	*Exploding Ants*	689817398	Simon & Schuster	1	Y
		12	Spinelli, Jerry	*Crash*	679885501	Alfred A. Knopf	1	Y

Group Description	Level	#	Author	Title	ISBN	Publisher	Quantity	Heinemann Write-Up
MODULE 1: More Independent Reading: Filling in the Lower Portion of the Library								
	7	1	Bonsall, Crosby	*Case of the Dumb Bells, The*	64440303	Harper Collins	1	
		2	Komaiko, Leah	*Annie Bananie and the People's Court*	440410371	Random House	1	
		3	Komaiko, Leah	*Annie Bananie Best Friends to the End*	440410363	Bantam Doubleday Dell	1	
		4	Krensky, Stephen	*Lionel and Louise*	140386173	Penguin Publishing	1	
		5	Krensky, Stephen	*Louise, Soccer Star?*	803724950	Penguin Publishing	1	
		6	Marzollo, Jean	*Soccer Cousins*	59074254X	Scholastic Inc.	1	
		7	Mills, Claudia	*Gus and Grandpa and the Christmas Cookies*	374428158	Farrar Strauss & Giroux	1	
		8	Mozelle, Shirley	*Zack's Alligator Goes to School*	64442489	Harper Collins	1	
		9	Mozelle, Shirley	*Zack's Alligator*	64441865	Harper Collins	1	
		10	Ross, Pat	*M&M Series/The Mummy Mess*	141306548	Penguin Puffin	1	
		11	Rylant, Cynthia	*Poppleton Forever*	590848445	Scholastic Inc.	1	
		12	Sharmat, Marjorie Weinman	*Nate the Great/Stalks Stupid Weed*	44040150X	Bantam Doubleday Dell	1	
	8	1	Adler, David	*Cam Jansen Series/Mystery of the Stolen Diamonds*	590461214	Scholastic Inc.	1	
		2	Avi	*Keep Your Eye on Amanda!*	380803372	Avon Books	1	Y
		3	Cazet, Denys	*Minnie & Moo and the Mask of Zorro*	789426536	DK Publishing	1	
DOUBLE YELLOW		4	Cohen, Barbara	*Molly's Pilgrim*	688162800	William Morrow & Co	1	
		5	Conford, Ellen	*Jenny Archer Series/Can Do, Jenny Archer*	316153729	Little Brown & Co	1	
		6	Conford, Ellen	*Jenny Archer Series/What's Cooking, Jenny Archer?*	316153575	Little Brown & Co	1	
		7	Cosby, Bill	*Little Bill Series/Day I Was Rich*	59052173X	Scholastic Inc.	1	

Group Description	Level	#	Author	Title	ISBN	Publisher	Quantity	Heinemann Write-Up
		8	Dadey, Debbie	*Triplet Trouble and the Cookie Contest*	59090728X	Scholastic Inc.	1	
		9	Dale, Jenny	*Kitten Friends Series/Felix the Fluffy Kitten*	689841086	Simon & Schuster	1	
		10	Howe, James	*Pinky & Rex Series/Spelling Bee*	689828802	Aladdin	1	Y
		11	Kline, Suzy	*Horrible Harry Series/the Ant Invastion*	141300825	Penguin Publishing	1	Y
		12	Kline, Suzy	*Horrible Harry Series/the Purple People*	590682695	Scholastic Inc.	1	
		13	Marzollo, Jean	*Soccer Sam*	39488406X	Random House	1	Y
		14	Stanley, George	*Third Grade Detective Series/Puzzle of the Pretty Pink Handkerchief*	689822324	Simon & Schuster	1	
		15	Wyeth, Sharon Dennis	*Ginger Brown Series/The Nobody Boy*	679856455	Random House	1	
	9	1	Cleary, Beverly	*Ralph S. Mouse*	380709570	Harper Trophy	1	
		2	Fleischman, Sid	*Here Comes McBroom*	688163645	William Morrow & Co	1	Y
		3	Gannett, Ruth S.	*My Father's Dragon*	394890485	Random House	1	Y
		4	Kline, Suzy	*Herbie Jones*	140320717	Penguin Publishing	1	
		5	Kline, Suzy	*Herbie Jones and Hamburger Head*	140345833	Penguin Puffin	1	
		6	Lasky, Kathryn	*Grace the Pirate*	786811471	Hyperion Books	1	
		7	Leverich, Kathleen	*Flower Girl Series/Daisy*	64420191	Harper Collins	1	
		8	Leverich, Kathleen	*Flower Girl Series/Heather*	64420213	Harper Collins	1	
		9	Levy, Elizabeth	*Frankenstein Moved In On the Fourth Floor*	64401227	Harper Collins	1	
		10	Myers, Walter Dean	*Ace Crime Detective/The Case of the Missing Ruby and Other Stories*	590676660	Scholastic Inc.	1	
		11	Roy, Ron	*A to Z Mysteries/Bald Bandit (#2)*	679884491	Random House	1	
		12	Roy, Ron	*A to Z Mysteries/Falcon's Feathers (#6)*	679890556	Random House	1	

Group Description	Level	#	Author	Title	ISBN	Publisher	Quantity	Heinemann Write-Up
		13	Sachar, Louis	*Wayside School Gets a Little Stranger*	68813694X	William Morrow & Co	1	
		14	Sachar, Louis	*Wayside School is Falling Down*	380754843	Avon Books	1	
		15	Shreve, Susan Richards	*Flunking of Joshua T. Bates*	679841873	Alfred A. Knopf	1	
		16	Stolz, Mary	*Coco Grimes*	64405125	Harper Collins	1	
		17	Warner, Gertrude	*Boxcar Children Series/Mystery at the Ballpark*	59048415X	Scholastic Inc.	1	
		18	Warner, Gertrude	*Boxcar Children Series/Mystery in Washington DC*	590475347	Scholastic Inc.	1	
		19	Warner, Sally	*Lily Series/Accidental Lily*	375801820	Alfred A. Knopf	1	
		20	Wells, Rosemary	*Lassie Come-Home*	805064230	Henry Holt & Co	1	
MODULE 2: More Independent Reading: Filling in the Upper Portion of the Library								
		1	Kinsey-Warnock, Natalie	*Canada Geese Quilt*	440407192	Bantam Doubleday Dell	1	
	10	1	Cleary, Beverly	*Ellen Tebbits*	380709139	William Morrow & Co	1	
		2	Dahl, Roald	*Giraffe and the Pelly and Me, The*	141302283	Penguin Publishing	1	
		3	Dengler, Marianna	*Worry Stone, The*	873586425	Rising Moon	1	
		4	Donnelly, Judy	*Tut's Mummy: Lost . . . and Found*	394891899	Random House	1	
		5	Greenfield, Eloise	*Koya Delaney and the Good Girl Blues*	590432990	Scholastic Inc.	1	
		6	Hurwitz, Johanna	*Faraway Summer*	380732564	Harper Trophy	1	
		7	King-Smith, Dick	*Cukoo Child, The*	786813512	Hyperion Books	1	Y
		8	Leverich, Kathleen	*Best Enemies Again*	688161979	William Morrow & Co	1	
		9	Leverich, Kathleen	*Best Enemies Forever*	688158544	William Morrow & Co	1	
		10	Rylant, Cynthia	*Birthday Presents*	531070263	Orchard Books	1	Y
		11	Schultz, Irene	*Missing Will, The*	322019567	Wright Group	1	

Group Description	Level	#	Author	Title	ISBN	Publisher	Quantity	Heinemann Write-Up
		12	Smith, Robert Kimmel	*War with Grandpa, The*	440492769	Bantam Doubleday Dell	1	Y
		13	Sobol, Donald	*Encyclopedia Brown Series/E B and the Case of Pablo's Nose*	55348513X	Skylark Books	1	
		14	Sobol, Donald	*Encyclopedia Brown Series/E B Solves Them All*	553480804	Bantam Doubleday Dell	1	
	11	1	Belton, Sandra	*Ernestine and Amanda Series/ Mysteries on Monroe Street*	689816626	Simon & Schuster	1	
		2	Chocolate, Deborah Newton	*Elizabeth's Wish, Vol. 2*	940975459	Just Us Books	1	
		3	Christopher, Matt	*Reluctant Pitcher, The (Vol. 54)*	316141275	Little Brown & Co	1	
		4	Dahl, Roald	*Matilda*	141301066	Penguin Publishing	1	
		5	Eager, Edward	*Magic by the Lake*	152020764	Harcourt Brace	1	
		6	Fletcher, Ralph	*Flying Solo*	395873231	Clarion Books	1	
DOUBE RED		7	George, Jean Craighead	*There's a Tarantula in My Purse*			1	
		8	Hahn, Mary D.	*Doll in the Garden, The*	380708655	William Morrow & Co	1	
		9	Henry, Marguerite	*Misty of Chincoteague*	689714920	Simon & Schuster	1	
		10	Park, Barbara	*My Mother Got Married: And Other Disasters*	394850599	Alfred A Knopf	1	
		11	Paulsen, Gary	*Project: A Perfect World*	606088512	Demco Media	1	
		12	Paulsen, Gary	*Puppies, Dogs & Blue Northers*	152928812	Harcourt Brace	1	
		13	Pinkney, Andrea Davis	*Silent Thunder*	786804394	Hyperion Books	1	
		14	Schotter, Roni	*F is for Freedom*	789426412	DK Publishing	2	
	12	1	Hahn, Mary D.	*Stepping on the Cracks*	380719002	William Morrow & Co	1	
		2	King-Smith, Dick	*Pigs Might Fly*	14034537X	Penguin Putnam	1	Y
DOUBLE RED		3	Lisle, Jane & Taylor	*Afternoon of the Elves*	698118065	Penguin Putnam	1	Y

Group Description	Level	#	Author	Title	ISBN	Publisher	Quantity	Heinemann Write-Up
		4	Lowry, Lois	*Attaboy, Sam!*	440408164	Bantam Doubleday Dell	1	
		5	Lowry, Lois	*See You Around, Sam!*	440414008	Bantam Doubleday Dell	1	
		6	Mohr, Nicholasa	*Magic Shell, The*	590471104	Scholastic Inc.	1	Y
		7	Mowat, Farley	*Owls in the Family*	440413613	Bantam Doubleday Dell	1	
		8	Myers, A.	*Red-Dirt Jesse*	14038734X	Penguin Putnam	1	
		9	Paulsen, Gary	*Boy Who Owned the School, The*	440405246	Bantam Doubleday Dell	1	
		10	Paulson, Gary	*River, The*	440407532	Bantam Doubleday Dell	1	
		11	Pinkwater, Jill	*Tails of the Bronx*	689716710	Simon & Schuster	1	
MODULE 3: Multiple Copies for Small Group Work								
	6	1	Lobel, Arnold	*Frog and Toad Series/Frog and Toad Are Friends*	64440206	Harper Trophy	5	Y
	7	1	Rylant, Cynthia	*Poppleton*	59084783X	Scholastic Inc.	4	Y
	8	1	Blume, Judy	*Freckle Juice*	440428130	Bantam Doubleday Dell	5	Y
		2	Cazet, Denys	*Minnie & Moo Go Dancing*	78942536X	DK Publishing	5	
		3	Hurwitz, Johanna	*Rip-Roaring Russell*	140329390	Penguin Puffin	5	Y
	9	1	Cameron, Ann	*More Stories Julian Tells*	394824547	Alfred A. Knopf	5	
		2	Danziger, Paula	*Amber Brown Series/ Goes Fourth*	590934252	Scholastic Inc.	5	
		3	Warner, Sally	*Lily Series/Leftover Lily*	375803475	Alfred A. Knopf	5	
	10	1	Hinton, S.E.	*Puppy Sister, the*	440413842	Bantam Doubleday Dell	4	Y
		2	Koller, Jackie French	*Dragon in the Family, A*	671897861	Pocket Books	5	
	11	1	Eager, Edward	*Time Garden, The*	152020705	Harcourt Brace	5	
MODULE 4: Enrichment								
Author Studies		1	Bunting, Eve	*Day's Work, A*	395845181	Clarion Books	1	Y

Group Description	Level	#	Author	Title	ISBN	Publisher	Quantity	Heinemann Write-Up
		2	Bunting, Eve	*Night of the Gargoyles*	395968879	Clarion Books	1	Y
		3	Bunting, Eve	*Smoky Night*	152018840	Harcourt Brace	1	Y
		4	Bunting, Eve	*Someday A Tree*	395764785	Clarion Books	1	
		5	Bunting, Eve	*Wednesday Surprise, The*	395547768	Clarion Books	1	
		6	Fox, Mem	*Feathers and Fools*	152023658	Harcourt Brace	1	
		7	Fox, Mem	*Koala Lou*	152005021	Harcourt Brace	1	Y
		8	Fox, Mem	*Possum Magic*	440843820	Harcourt Brace	1	Y
		9	Fox, Mem	*Tough Boris*	152018913	Harcourt Brace	1	
		10	Fox, Mem	*Wilfrid Gordon McDonald Partridge*	91629126X	Kane/Miller Book Publishers	1	Y
Memoir		1	Cisneros, Sandra	*House on Mango Street, The*	679734775	Random House	1	Y
		2	Gray, Libba Moore	*My Mama Had a Dancing Heart*	531071421	Orchard Books	1	Y
		3	Greenfield, Eloise	*Childtimes: A Three-Generation Memoir*	64461343	Harper Collins	1	Y
		4	Little, Jean	*Little by Little*	140323252	Penguin Putnam	1	
		5	MacLachlan, Patricia	*All the Places to Love*	60210982	Harper Collins	1	Y
		6	Myers, Walter Dean	*Glorious Angels*	64467260	Harper Collins	1	
		7	Polacco, Patricia	*Chicken Sunday*	698116151	Putnam Publishing	1	Y
		8	Rylant, Cynthia	*When I Was Young in the Mountains*	140548750	Penguin Publishing	1	
New York Studies		1	Cobblestone	*Cobblestone's New York City Reader*	382409612	Cobblestone Publishing	1	
		2	Harness, Cheryl	*Amazing Impossible Erie Canal, The*	689825846	Simon & Schuster	1	Y
		3	Jacobs, William Jay	*Ellis Island: New Hope in a New Land*	684191717	Simon & Schuster	1	
		4	Marx, David F.	*New York City/Rookie Read-About Geography*	51626558X	Children's Press	1	
		5	Whitecraft, Melissa	*Hudson River*	531117391	Franklin Watts, Grolier	1	

Group Description	Level	#	Author	Title	ISBN	Publisher	Quantity	Heinemann Write-Up
Nonfiction		1	Davis, Meredith	*Up & Away Taking a Flight*	157255214X	Mondo Publishing	1	
		2	Krull, Kathleen	*Wilma Unlimited*	152020985	Harcourt Brace	1	
		3	Locker, Thomas	*Water Dance*	152012842	Harcourt Brace	1	
		4	Pinkney, Andrea Davis	*Duke Ellington*	786801786	Hyperion Books	1	
		5	Snow, Alan	*How Do Dogs Really Work?*	316801348	Little Brown & Co	1	Y
Picture Books		1	Hesse, Karen	*Lester's Dog*	517583577	Random House	1	Y
		2	Howe, James	*I Wish I Were a Butterfly*	15200470X	Harcourt Brace	1	Y
		3	Joyce, William	*Leaf Men and the Brave Good Bugs, The*	60272376	Harper Collins	1	Y
		4	Lionni, Leo	*Alexander & the Wind Up Mouse*	590430122	Scholastic Inc.	1	Y
		5	Polacco, Patricia	*My Rotten Red Headed Older Brother*	44083449X	Bantam Doubleday Dell	1	Y
		6	Shannon, David	*Bad Case Of Stripes, A*	590929976 (hc)	Scholastic Inc.	1	Y
		7	Thaler, Mike	*Teacher from the Black Lagoon*	590419625	Scholastic Inc.	1	
		8	Waber, Bernard	*Ira Says Goodbye*	395584132	Houghton Mifflin	1	Y
		9	Yolen, Jane	*Dove Isabeau*	152015051	Harcourt Brace	1	Y
		10	Yolen, Jane	*Owl Moon*	590420445	Scholastic Inc.	1	Y
		11	Zolotow, Charlotte	*Mr. Rabbit & the Lovely Present*	64430200	Harper Trophy	1	Y
Poetry		1	Graves, Donald	*Baseball, Snakes and Summer Squash*	156397570X	Boyds Mills Press	1	
		2	Greenfield, Eloise	*Honey, I Love*	64430979	Harper Collins	1	Y
		3	Hopkins, Lee Bennett	*Been to Yesterdays: Poems of a Life*	1563978083	Boyds Mills Press	1	
		4	Worth, Valerie	*All the Small Poems & Fourteen More*	374403457	Farrar Strauss & Giroux	1	
Qualities of Good Writing		1	Rosen, Michael, ed.	*Home*	60217898	Harper Collins	1	

Group Description	Level	#	Author	Title	ISBN	Publisher	Quantity	Heinemann Write-Up
		2	Woodson, Jacqueline	*Sweet, Sweet Memory*	786821914	Hyperion Books	1	
Short Fiction		1	Avi	*What Do Fish Have To Do With Anything?*	763604127	Candlewick Press	1	
		2	Hurwitz, Johanna	*Birthday Surprises*	688131948	William Morrow & Co	1	Y
		3	Mazer, Anne	*America Street*	892551917	Persea Books Inc.	1	
		4	Rylant, Cynthia	*Every Living Thing*	689712634	Simon & Schuster	1	
		5	Smith, Janice Lee	*Adam Joshua Capers Series/ Kid Next Door and Other Headaches, The*	60257938	Harper Collins	1	
MODULE 5: Multiple Copies for Book Clubs								
	6	1	Marzollo, Claudio	*Kenny and the Little Kickers*	59045417X	Scholastic Inc.	5	
	8	1	Clifton, Lucille	*Lucky Stone, The*	440451108	Bantam Doubleday Dell	5	Y
		2	Howe, James	*Pinky & Rex Series/the School Play*	689817045	Simon & Schuster	5	Y
	9	1	Bulla, Clyde Robert	*Chalk Box Kid, The*	590485237	Scholastic Inc.	4	Y
		2	Flor Ada, Alma	*My Name is Maria Isabel*	68980217X	Simon & Schuster	5	Y
		3	Lowry, Lois	*All About Sam*	440402212	Bantam Doubleday Dell	4	
		4	Mead, Alice	*Junebug*	440412455	Bantam Doubleday Dell	5	Y
	11	1	MacLachlan, Patricia	*Sarah Plain & Tall*	64402053	Harper Collins	5	
		2	Naylor, Phyllis Reynolds	*Shiloh*	440407524	Bantam Doubleday Dell	5	Y
		3	Rylant, Cynthia	*Van Gogh Café, The*	590907174	Scholastic Inc.	4	Y
MODULE 6: Nonfiction								
		1	Ardley, Neil	*How Things Work: 100 Ways Parents and Kids Can Share the Secrets of Technology*	895776944	Reader's Digest	1	
		2	de Paola, Tomie	*Cloud Book, The*	59008531X	Scholastic Inc.	1	Y
		3	Dean-Myers, Walter	*Young Martin's Promise*	81148050X	Steck-Vaughn	1	
		4	Donnelly, Judy	*True-Life Treasure Hunts*	679839801	Random House	1	

Group Description	Level	#	Author	Title	ISBN	Publisher	Quantity	Heinemann Write-Up
		5	Eaton, Deborah & Susan Halter	*No One told the Aardvark*	881068713	Charlesbridge Publishing	1	
		6	Forman, Michael H.	*From Wax to Crayon*	516203606	Children's Press	1	
		7	George, Jean Craighead	*Look to the North: A Wolf Puppy Story*	64435105	Harper Trophy	1	Y
		8	Hodge, Deborah	*Whales*	1550744186	Kids Can Press	1	
		9	Jean-Hopping, Lorraine	*Sports Hall of Fame*	1572557761	Mondo Publishing	1	
		10	Kalman, Bobbie	*What Is a Primate?*	865059225	Crabtree Publishing	1	
		11	Kalman, Bobbie	*What Is a Rodent?*	865059233	Crabtree Publishing	1	
		12	Knight, Bertram T.	*From Cow to Ice Cream*	516260669	Children's Press	1	
		13	Lasky, Kathryn	*Monarchs*	152552979	Harcourt Brace	1	Y
		14	Nayer, Judy	*Next Stop Mars*	765213745	Modern Curriculum	1	
		15	Relf, Patricia	*What's Happening? A Book of Explanations*	1572558415	Mondo Publishing	1	
	7	1	Baker, Jeannie	*Story of Rosy Dock, The*	68811938 (hc)	Greenwillow Books	1	Y
	7; 8; 9	1	Most, Bernard	*Catbirds & Dogfish*	152007792	Harcourt Brace	1	
	8	1	Brenner, Barbara	*Wagon Wheels*	64440524	Harper Trophy	1	Y
	9	1	Barrett, Judi	*Polar Animals*	531152073	Franklin Watts, Grolier	1	
		2	Esiason, Boomer	*Boy Named Boomer, A*	590528351	Scholastic Inc.	1	
		3	Fritz, Jean	*George Washington's Mother*	448403846	Grosset & Dunlap	1	
	9; 10	1	Adoff, Arnold	*Malcolm X*	6442118X	Harper Trophy	1	Y
		2	Biddulph, Fred & Jeanne	*What Is Soil?*	780227212	Wright Group	1	
		3	Dubowski, Mark	*Ice Mummy*	679856471	Random House	1	
		4	Little, Emily	*Trojan Horse, The*	394896742	Random House	1	Y
	9; 10; 11	1	Ballard, Robert	*Finding the Titanic*	590472305	Scholastic Inc.	1	

Group Description	Level	#	Author	Title	ISBN	Publisher	Quantity	Heinemann Write-Up
		2	Berger, Melvin	*Whale is Not a Fish and Other Animal Mix-Ups, A*	590474774	Scholastic Inc.	1	
		3	Dobson, Philip	*How Faucets Work*	780226879	Wright Group	1	
		4	Gibbons, Gail	*Planet Earth Inside Out*	688158498	William Morrow & Co	1	
		5	Hurwitz, Johanna	*Dream Come True, A*	1572741937 (hc)	Richard C. Owen Publishers	1	
		6	Jackson, Ellen	*Winter Solstice, The*	761302972	Millbrook Press	1	Y
		7	Lopez, Orlando	*Whoops! It Works!*	765211653	Modern Curriculum	1	
		8	Mochizuki, Ken	*Passage to Freedom: The Sugihara Story*	1880000490	Lee & Low Books	1	
		9	Mondo Publishing-Explorers	*Every Body Tells A Story*	769904971	Mondo Publishing	1	
		10	Pinkney, Andrea Davis	*Alvin Ailey*	786810777	Hyperion Books	1	
		11	Short, Joan & Bettina Bird	*Whales*	1572551909	Mondo Publishing	1	Y
		12	Simon, Seymour	*Crocodiles & Alligators*	60274735	Harper Collins	1	
	10	1	Cole, Joanna	*Magic School Bus Series/Electric Field Trip*	590446835	Scholastic Inc.	1	Y
		2	Miller, William	*Richard Wright & the Library Card*	1880000881	Lee & Low Books	1	Y
	10; 11	1	Hudson, Wade	*Five Notable Inventors*	590480332	Scholastic Inc.	1	
	10; 11; 12	1	Aliki	*William Shakespeare and the Globe*	64437221	Harper Collins	1	Y
		2	Armstrong, Kristin	*Lance Armstrong: The Race of His Life*	44842407X	Grosset & Dunlap	1	
		3	Facklam, Margery	*Creepy, Crawly Caterpillars*	316273422	Little Brown & Co	1	
		4	Guiberson, Brenda	*Into the Sea*	805064818	Henry Holt & Co	1	Y
		5	Jackson, Ellen	*Book of Slime, The*	761300945	Millbrook Press	1	
		6	Kaner, Etta	*Animal Defenses: How Animals Protect Themselves*	1550744216	Kids Can Press	1	

Group Description	Level	#	Author	Title	ISBN	Publisher	Quantity	Heinemann Write-Up
		7	Kelso, Richard	*Walking for Freedom*	811480585	Steck-Vaughn	1	Y
	11	1	Fritz, Jean	*Where Do You Think You're Going Christopher Columbus?*	698115805	Putnam & Grosset	1	
	11; 12	1	Maynard, Christopher	*Days of the Knights*	789442531	DK Publishing	1	
	11; 12; 13	1	Wade, Mary Dodson	*Amelia Earhart: Flying for Adventure*	156294763X	Millbrook Press	1	

Benchmark Books for Each Text Level

TC Level	Benchmarks: Books that Represent Each Level
1	*A Birthday Cake* (Cowley) *I Can Write* (Williams) *The Cat on the Mat* (Wildsmith)
2	*Rain* (Kaplan) *Fox on the Box* (Gregorich)
3	*It Looked Like Spilt Milk* (Shaw) *I Like Books* (Browne) *Mrs. Wishy-Washy* (Cowley)
4	*Rosie's Walk* (Hutchins) *The Carrot Seed* (Krauss) *Cookie's Week* (Ward)
5	*George Shrinks* (Joyce) *Goodnight Moon* (Brown) *Hattie and the Fox* (Fox)
6	*Danny and the Dinosaur* (Hoff) *Henry and Mudge* (Rylant)
7	*Nate the Great* (Sharmat) *Meet M&M* (Ross)
8	*Horrible Harry* (Kline) *Pinky and Rex* (Howe) Arthur Series (Marc Brown)
9	*Amber Brown* (Danziger) *Ramona Quimby, Age 8* (Cleary)
10	*James and the Giant Peach* (Dahl) *Fudge-A-Mania* (Blume)
11	*Shiloh* (Naylor) *The Great Gilly Hopkins* (Paterson)
12	*Bridge to Terabithia* (Paterson) *Baby* (MacLachlan)
13	*Missing May* (Rylant) *Where the Red Fern Grows* (Rawls)
14	*A Day No Pigs Would Die* (Peck) *Scorpions* (Myers)
15	*The Golden Compass* (Pullman) *The Dark Is Rising* (Cooper) *A Wizard of Earthsea* (Le Guin)

Descriptions of Text Levels One Through Seven

TEXT LEVEL ONE

This level roughly corresponds to the following levels in other systems:

Reading Recovery© (RR) Levels 1–2
Developmental Reading Assessment (DRA) Levels A–2

Text Characteristics for TC Level One

- The font is large, clear, and is usually printed in black on a white background.
- There is exaggerated spacing between words and letters. (In some books, publishers have enlarged the print but have not adjusted the spacing which can create difficulties for readers.)
- There is usually a single word, phrase, or simple sentence on a page, and the text is patterned and predictable. For example, in the book *I Can Read*, once a child knows the title (which is ideally read to a Level One reader) it is not hard for the child to read "I can read the newspaper," "I can read the cereal box." These readers are regarded as "preconventional" because they rely on the illustrations (that support the meaning) and the sounds of language (or syntax) and not on graphophonics or word/letter cues to read a sentence such as, "I can read the newspaper."
- Usually each page contains two or three sight words. A Level One book *may* contain one illustrated word on a page (such as "Mom," "Dad," "sister," "cat") but it's just as easy for a child to read "I see my mom. I see my Dad. I see my sister. I see my cat." because the sight words give the child a way into the text.
- The words are highly supported by illustrations. No one would expect a Level One reader to solve the word "newspaper." We would, however, expect a child at this level to look at the picture and at the text and to read the word "newspaper."
- Words are consistently placed in the same area of each page, preferably top left or bottom left.

Characteristics of the Reader

Readers in this group will demonstrate most of these behaviors.

- Remember the pattern in a predictable text
- Use picture cues

- Use left to right directionality to read one or two lines of print
- Work on matching spoken words with printed words and self-correcting when these don't "come out even"
- Rely on the spaces between words to signify the end of one word and the beginning of another. These readers read the spaces as well as the words, as the words are at first black blobs on white paper
- Locate one or two known words on a page

Benchmarks

The following titles are representative of the kinds of books found in this grouping.

A Birthday Cake, Joy Cowley
Cat on the Mat, Brian Wildsmith
The Farm, Literacy 2000/Stage 1
Growing Colors, Bruce McMillan
I Can Write, Rozanne Williams
Time for Dinner, PM Starters

Assessment

The following titles can be used to determine if a reader is ready to move on to the next grouping of books. This type of assessment is most effective if the text is unfamiliar to the reader. If these titles will be used as assessment texts, they should *not* be part of the classroom library.

My Home, Story Box
The Tree Stump, Little Celebrations
DRA Assessments A–2

We move children from Level One to Level Two books when they are consistently able to match one spoken word with one word written on the page. This means that they can point under words in a Level One book as they read and know when they haven't matched a spoken word to a written word by noticing that, at the end of the line, they still have words left on the page or they've run out of words. When children read multisyllabic words and compound words and point to multiple, instead of one, word on the page, we consider this a successful one-to-one match.

TEXT LEVEL TWO

This level roughly corresponds to the following levels in other systems:

Reading Recovery© (RR) Levels 3–4
Developmental Reading Assessment (DRA) Levels 3–4

Text Characteristics of TC Level Two

- There are usually two lines of print on at least some of the pages in these books, and sometimes there are three. This means readers will become accustomed to making the return sweep to the beginning of a new line.
- The texts are still patterned and predictable, but now the patterns tend to switch at intervals. Almost always, the pattern changes at the end of the book. The repeating unit may be as long as two sentences in length.
- The font continues to be large and clear. The letters might not, however, be black against white although this is generally the case.
- Children still rely on the picture but the pictures tend to give readers more to deal with; children need to search more in the picture to find help in reading the words.
- High frequency words are still helpful and important. The sentences in Level One books tend to begin with 2 to 3 high frequency words, for example, "I like to run. I like to jump." At this level, the pages are more apt to begin with a single high frequency word and then include words that require picture support and attention to first letters, for example, "A mouse has a long tail. A bear has a short tail."
- Sentences are more varied, resulting in texts that include a full range of punctuation.

Characteristics of the Reader

Readers in this group will demonstrate most of these behaviors.

- Get the mouth ready for the initial sound of a word
- Use left to right directionality as well as a return sweep to another line of print
- Locate one or two known words on a page
- Monitor for meaning: check to make sure it makes sense

Benchmarks

The following titles are representative of the kinds of books found in this grouping.

All Fall Down, Brian Wildsmith
I Went Walking, Sue Williams
Rain, Robert Kalan
Shoo, Sunshine

Assessment

The following titles can be used to determine if a reader is ready to move on to the next grouping. This type of assessment is most effective if the text is unfamiliar to a reader. If these titles will be used as assessment texts, they should *not* be part of the classroom library.

The Bus Ride, Little Celebrations, DRA 3
Fox on the Box, School Zone, DRA 4

We generally move children from Level Two to Level Three texts when they know how to use the pictures and the syntax to generate possibilities for the next word, when they attend to the first letters of unknown words. These readers will also read and rely on high frequency words such as *I*, *the*, *a*, *to*, *me*, *mom*, *the child's name*, *like*, *love*, *go*, and *and*.

TEXT LEVEL THREE

This level roughly corresponds to the following levels in other systems:

Reading Recovery© (RR) Levels 5–8
Developmental Reading Assessment (DRA) Levels 6–8

Text Characteristics of TC Level Three

It is important to note that this grouping includes a wide range of levels. This was done deliberately because at this level, readers should be able to select "just right" books for themselves and be able to monitor their own reading.

- Sentences are longer and readers will need to put their words together in order to take in more of the sentence at a time. When they are stuck, it's often helpful to nudge them to reread and try again.
- The pictures are not as supportive as they've been. It's still helpful for children to do picture walks prior to reading an unfamiliar text, but now the goal is less about surmising what words the page contains and more about seeing an overview of the narrative.
- Readers must rely on graphophonics across the whole word. If readers hit a wall at this level, it's often because they're accustomed to predicting words based on a dominant pattern and using the initial letters (only) to confirm their predictions. It takes readers a while to begin checking the print closely enough to adjust their expectations.
- Children will need to use sight words to help with unknown words, using parts of these familiar words as analogies, helping them unlock the unfamiliar words.
- The font size and spacing are less important now.
- Words in the text begin to include contractions. We can help children read these by urging them to look all the way across a word.

Characteristics of the Reader

Readers in this group will demonstrate most of these behaviors.

- Reread and self-correct
- Read with some fluency

- Cross check one cue against another
- Monitor for meaning: check to make sure what has been read makes sense and sounds right
- Recognize common chunks of words

Benchmarks

The following titles are representative of the kinds of books found in this grouping.

Bears in the Night Stan and Jan, Berenstain
The Chick and the Duckling, Ginsburg
It Looked Like Spilt Milk, Charles G. Shaw
Mrs. Wishy-Washy, Joy Cowley

Assessment

The following titles can be used to determine if a reader is ready to move on to the next grouping. This type of assessment is most effective if the text is unfamiliar to a reader. If these titles will be used as assessment texts, they should *not* be part of the classroom library.

Bread, Story Box, DRA 6
Get Lost Becka, School Zone, DRA 8

We move a child to Level Four books if that child can pick up an unfamiliar book like *Bread* or *It Looked Like Spilt Milk* and read it with a little difficulty, but with a lot of independence and with strategies. This reader should know to reread when she is stuck, to use the initial sounds in a word, to chunk word families within a word, and so on.

TEXT LEVEL FOUR

This level roughly corresponds to the following levels in other systems:

Reading Recovery© (RR) Levels 9–12
Developmental Reading Assessment (DRA) Levels 10–12

Text Characteristics of TC Level Four

- In general, the child who is reading Level Four books is able to do more of the same reading work he could do with texts at the previous level. This child reads texts that contain more words, lines, pages, and more challenging vocabulary.
- These texts contain even less picture support than earlier levels.
- Fluency and phrasing are very important for the Level Four reader. If children don't begin to read quickly enough, they won't be able to carry the syntax of the sentence along well enough to comprehend what they are reading.

- These books use brief bits of literary language. That is, in these books the mother may turn to her child and say, "We shall be rich."
- These books are more apt to have a plot (with characters, setting, problem, solution) and they tend to be less patterned than they were at the previous level.

Characteristics of the Reader

Readers in this group will demonstrate most of these behaviors.

- Reread and self-correct
- Read with fluency
- Integrate cues from meaning, structure, and visual sources
- Monitor for meaning: check to make sure what has been read makes sense, sounds right, and looks right
- Make some analogies from known words to figure out unknown words
- Read increasingly difficult chunks within words

Benchmarks

The following titles are representative of the kinds of books found in this grouping.

The Carrot Seed, Ruth Krauss
Cookie's Week, Cindy Ward
Rosie's Walk, Pat Hutchins
Titch, Pat Hutchins

Assessment

The following titles can be used to determine if a reader is ready to move on to the next grouping. This type of assessment is most effective if the text is unfamiliar to a reader. If these titles will be used as assessment texts, they should *not* be part of the classroom library.

Are You There Bear?, Ron Maris, DRA 10
The House in the Tree, Rigby PM Story Books
Nicky Upstairs and Downstairs, Harriet Ziefert
William's Skateboard, Sunshine, DRA 12

We move a child to Level Five books if that reader can independently use a variety of strategies to work through difficult words or parts of a text. The reader must be reading fluently enough to reread quickly, when necessary, so as to keep the flow of the story going. If a reader is reading very slowly, taking too much time to work through the hard parts, then this reader may not be ready to move on to the longer, more challenging texts in Level Five.

TEXT LEVEL FIVE

This level roughly corresponds to the following levels in other systems:

Reading Recovery© (RR) Levels 13–15
Developmental Reading Assessment (DRA) Level 14

Text Characteristics

- Sentences in Level Five books tend to be longer, more varied, and more complex than they were in previous levels.
- Many of the stories are retold folktales or fantasy-like stories that use literary or story language, such as: "Once upon a time, there once lived, a long, long time ago. . . . "
- Many books may be in a cumulative form in which text is added to each page, requiring the reader to read more and more text as the story unfolds, adding a new line with every page turn.
- The illustrations tend to be a representation of just a slice of what is happening in the text. For example, the text may tell of a long journey that a character has taken over time, but the picture may represent just the character reaching his destination.
- There will be more unfamiliar and sometimes complex vocabulary.

Characteristics of the Reader

Readers in this group will demonstrate most of these behaviors.

- Reread and self-correct regularly
- Read with fluency
- Integrate a balance of cues
- Monitor for meaning: check to make sure what has been read makes sense, sounds right, and looks right
- Demonstrate fluent phrasing of longer passages
- Use a repertoire of graphophonic strategies to problem solve through text

Benchmarks

The following titles are representative of the kinds of books found in this grouping.

George Shrinks, William Joyce
Goodnight Moon, Margaret Wise Brown
Hattie and the Fox, Mem Fox
Little Red Hen, Parkes

Assessment

The following titles can be used to determine if a reader is ready to move on to the next grouping. This type of assessment is most effective if the text is unfamiliar to a reader. If these titles will be used as assessment texts, they should *not* be part of the classroom library.

The Old Man's Mitten, Bookshop, Mondo
Who Took the Farmer's Hat?, Joan Nodset, DRA 14

We move children from Level Five to Level Six texts when they are consistently able to use a multitude of strategies to work through challenges quickly and efficiently. These challenges may be brought on by unfamiliar settings, unfamiliar language structures, unfamiliar words, and increased text length. The amount of text on a page and the length of a book should not be a hindrance to the reader who is moving on to Level Six. The reader who is ready to move on is also adept at consistently choosing appropriate books that will make her a stronger reader.

TEXT LEVEL SIX

This level roughly corresponds to the following levels in other systems:

Reading Recovery© (RR) Levels 16–18
Developmental Reading Assessment (DRA) Level 16

Text Characteristics of TC Level Six

- The focus of the book is evident at its start
- Descriptive language is used more frequently than before
- Dialogue often tells a large part of the story
- Texts may include traditional retellings of fairy tales and folktales
- Stories are frequently humorous
- Considerable amount of text is found on each page. A book in this grouping may be a picture book, or a simple chapter book. These books offer extended stretches of text.
- Texts are often simple chapter books, and often have episodic chapters in which each chapter stands as a story on its own
- Texts often center around just two or three main characters who tend to be markedly different from each other (a boy and a girl, a child and a parent)
- There is limited support from the pictures
- Texts includes challenging vocabulary

Characteristics of the Reader

Readers in this group will demonstrate most of these behaviors.

- Reread and self-correct regularly
- Read with fluency
- Integrate a balance of cues
- Demonstrate fluent phrasing of longer passages
- Use a repertoire of graphophonic strategies to problem solve through text

Benchmarks

The following titles are representative of the kinds of books found in this grouping.

Danny and the Dinosaur, Syd Hoff
The Doorbell Rang, Pat Hutchins
Henry and Mudge, Cynthia Rylant
The Very Hungry Caterpillar, Eric Carle

Assessment

The following titles can be used to determine if a reader is ready to move on to the next grouping. This type of assessment is most effective if the text is unfamiliar to a reader. If these titles will be used as assessment texts, they should *not* be part of the classroom library.

Bear Shadow, Frank Asch, DRA 16
Jimmy Lee Did It, Pat Cummings, DRA 18

TEXT LEVEL SEVEN

This level roughly corresponds to the following levels in other systems:

Reading Recovery© (RR) Levels 19–20
Developmental Reading Assessment (DRA) Level 20

Text Characteristics of TC Level Seven

- Dialogue is used frequently to move the story along
- Texts often have 2 to 3 characters. (They tend to have distinctive personalities and usually don't change across a book or series.)
- Texts may include extended description. (The language may set a mood, and may be quite poetic or colorful.)
- Some books have episodic chapters. (In other books, each chapter contributes to the understanding of the entire book and the reader must carry the story line along.)
- There is limited picture support
- Plots are usually linear without large time-gaps
- Texts tend to have larger print and double spacing between lines of print

Characteristics of the Reader

Readers in this group will demonstrate most of these behaviors.

- Reread and self-correct regularly
- Read with fluency, intonation, and phrasing
- Demonstrate the existence of a self-extending (self-improving) system for reading
- Use an increasingly more challenging repertoire of graphophonic strategies to problem solve through text
- Solve unknown words with relative ease

Benchmarks

The following titles are representative of the kinds of books found in this grouping.

A Baby Sister for Frances, Russell Hoban
Meet M&M, Pat Ross
Nate the Great, Marjorie Sharmat
Poppleton, Cynthia Rylant

Asessment

The following titles can be used to determine if a reader is ready to move on to the next grouping. This type of assessment is most effective if the text is unfamiliar to a reader. If these titles will be used as assessment texts, they should *not* be part of the classroom library.

Peter's Pockets, Eve Rice, DRA 20
Uncle Elephant, Arnold Lobel

More Information to Help You Choose the Library That is Best for Your Readers

Library A

Library A is appropriate if your children enter kindergarten in October as very emergent readers with limited experiences hearing books read aloud. Use the following chart to help determine if Library A is about right for your class.

Approximate Distribution of Reading Levels of a Class Matched to Library A

Benchmark Book	*Reading Level*	*Percentage of the Class Reading at about This Level*
The Cat on the Mat, by Wildsmith	TC Level 1	45%
Fox on the Box, by Gregorich	TC Level 2	30%
Mrs. Wishy-Washy, by Cowley	TC Level 3	25%

Library B

Library B is appropriate for a class of children if, in October, they are reading books like *I Went Walking*. Use the following chart to help determine if Library B is about right for your class. (Note to New York City teachers: Many of your students would score a 3 on the ECLAS correlated with titles such as, *Things I Like to Do* and *My Shadow*.)

Approximate Distribution of Reading Levels of a Class Matched to Library B

Benchmark Book	*Reading Level*	*Percentage of the Class Reading at about This Level*
The Cat on the Mat, by Wildsmith	TC Level 1	10%
Fox on the Box, by Gregorich	TC Level 2	10%
Mrs. Wishy-Washy, by Cowley	TC Level 3	30%
The Carrot Seed, by Krauss	TC Level 4	25%
Goodnight Moon, by Brown	TC Level 5	15%
Henry and Mudge, by Rylant	TC Level 6	5%
Nate the Great, by Sharmat	TC Level 7	5%

Library C

Library C is appropriate for a class of children if, in October, many of your students are approaching reading books like *Mrs. Wishy-Washy* and *Bears in the Night.* (Note to New York City teachers: Many of your students would be approaching a 4 on the ECLAS that would be correlated with *Baby Bear's Present* and *No Where and Nothing.*)

Approximate Distribution of Reading Levels of a Class Matched to Library C

Benchmark Book	*Reading Level*	*Percentage of the Class Reading at about This Level*
Fox on the Box, by Gregorich	TC Level 2	8%
Mrs. Wishy-Washy, by Cowley	TC Level 3	8%
The Carrot Seed, by Krauss	TC Level 4	20%
Goodnight Moon, by Brown	TC Level 5	20%
Henry and Mudge, by Carle	TC Level 6	20%
Nate the Great, by Sharmat	TC Level 7	15%
Pinky and Rex, by Howe	TC Level 8	5%
Ramona Quimby, by Cleary	TC Level 9	2%
James and the Giant Peach, by Dahl	TC Level 10	2%

Library D

Use the following chart to help determine if Library D is right for your class.

Approximate Distribution of Reading Levels of a Class Matched to Library D

Benchmark Book	*Reading Level*	*Percentage of the Class Reading at about This Level*
Good Night Moon, by Brown	Level 5	8%
Henry and Mudge, by Rylant	Level 6	20%
Nate the Great, by Sharmat	Level 7	25%
Pinky and Rex, by Howe	Level 8	30%
Ramona Quimby, by Cleary	Level 9	10%
James and the Giant Peach, by Dahl	Level 10	2%

Library E

Library E is appropriate for a class of children if, in October, a readers list tends to look approximately like the following chart.

Approximate Distribution of Reading Levels of a Class Matched to Library E

Benchmark Book	*Reading Level*	*Percentage of the Class Reading at about This Level*
Nate the Great, by Sharmat	Level 7	10%
Pinky and Rex, by Howe	Level 8	25%
Ramona Quimby, by Cleary	Level 9	30%
James and the Giant Peach, by Dahl	Level 10	22%
Shiloh, by Naylor	Level 11	5%
Baby, by MacLachlan	Level 12	5%
Missing May, by Rylant	Level 13	2%
Scorpions, by Myers	Level 14	1%

Library F

Library F is appropriate for a class of children if, in October, a readers list tends to look approximately like the following chart.

Approximate Distribution of Reading Levels of a Class Matched to Library F

Benchmark Book	*Reading Level*	*Percentage of the Class Reading at about This Level*
Pinky and Rex, by Howe	Level 8	2%
Ramona Quimby, by Cleary	Level 9	20%
James and the Giant Peach, by Dahl	Level 10	25%
Shiloh, by Naylor	Level 11	30%
Baby, by MacLachlan	Level 12	20%
Missing May, by Rylant	Level 13	2%
Scorpions, by Myers	Level 14	1%

Library G

Library G is appropriate for a class of children if, in October, a readers list tends to look approximately like the following chart.

Approximate Distribution of Reading Levels of a Class Matched to Library G

Benchmark Book	*Reading Level*	*Percentage of the Class Reading at about This Level*
James and the Giant Peach, by Dahl	Level 10	10%
Shiloh, by Naylor	Level 11	10%
Baby, by MacLachlan	Level 12	30%
Missing May, by Rylant	Level 13	30%
Scorpions, by Myer	Level 14	20%

About the Guides

Soon we'd begun not only accumulating titles and honing arrangements for dream libraries, but also writing teaching advice to go with the chosen books. Our advice to the contributors was, "Write a letter from you to others who'll use this book with children. Tell folks what you notice in the book, and advise them on teaching opportunities you see. Think about advice you would give a teacher just coming to know the book." The insights, experience, and folk wisdom poured in and onto the pages of the guides.

A written guide accompanies many of the books in the libraries. These guides are not meant to be prescriptions for how a teacher or child should use a book. Instead they are intended to be resources, and we hope thoughtful teachers will tap into particular sections of a guide when it seems fit to do so. For example, a teaching guide might suggest six possible minilessons a teacher could do with a book. Of course, a teacher would never try to do all six of these! Instead we expect one of these minilessons will seem helpful to the teacher, and another minilesson to another teacher. The teaching guides illustrate the following few principles that are important to us.

Teaching One Text Intensely in Order to Learn About Many Texts

When you take a walk in the woods, it can happen that all the trees look the same, that they are just a monotony of foliage and trunks. It is only when you stop to learn about a particular tree, about its special leaf structure and the odd thickness of its bark, about the creatures that inhabit it and the seeds it lets fall, that you begin to see that particular kind of tree among the thickets. It is when you enter a forest knowing something about kinds of trees that you begin to truly see the multiplicity of trees in a forest and the particular attributes and mysteries of each one. Learning about the particulars of one tree leads you to thinking about all of the trees, each in its individuality, each with its unique deep structure, each with its own offerings.

The same is true of texts. The study of one can reveal not just the hidden intricacies of that story, but also the ways in which truths and puzzles can be structured in other writings as well. When one book holds a message in the way a chapter ends, it gives the reader the idea that any book may hold a message in the structure of its chapter's conclusions. When one book is revealed to make a sense that is unintended by the author, we look for unintended sense in other books we read. Within these guides, then, we hope that readers like you will find truths about the particular books they are written about, but more, we hope that you find pathways into all the books you read. By showing some lengthy thinking and meditations on one book, we hope to offer you paths toward thinking about each and every book that crosses your desk and crosses your mind.

Suggesting Classroom Library Arrangements

Many the attributes of a book, detailed in a guide, can become a category in a classroom library. If a group of students in a class seems particularly energized by the Harry Potter books, for example, the guide can be used to help determine which books could be in a bin in the library marked, "If You Like *Harry Potter*—Try These." The similarity between the *Harry Potter* books and the other books in this group may be not only in difficulty gradient, but also in content, story structure, popularity, or genre. That is, a class of children that like *Harry Potter* might benefit from a bin of books on fantasy, or from a collection of best-selling children's books, or from a bin of "Long-Books-You-Can't-Put-Down," or from stories set in imagined places. As you browse through the guides that accompany the books you have chosen, the connections will pop out at you.

Sometimes, the guides will help you determine a new or more interesting placement for a book. Perhaps you have regarded a book as historical fiction, but now you realize it could alternatively be shelved in a collection of books that offer children examples of "Great Leads to Imitate in Your Own Writing." Or, perhaps the guides will suggest entirely new categories that will appeal to your class in ways you and your students haven't yet imagined. Perhaps the guides will help you imagine a "Books That Make You Want to Change the World" category. Or maybe you'll decide to create a shelf in your library titled, "Books with Odd Techniques That Make You Wonder What the Author Is Trying To Do."

Aiding in Conferring

Teachers' knowledge of what to ask and what to teach a reader who says, "this book is boring" comes not only from their knowledge of particular students but also from their knowledge of the text they are talking about. Does "boring" mean that the book is too easy for the reader? Perhaps it means instead that the beginning few chapters of the book are hard to read—confusing because of a series of flashbacks. A guide might explain that the book under discussion has mostly internal, emotional action, and, if the reader is accustomed to avalanche-and-rattlesnake action in books, she may need some time to warm up to this unfamiliar kind of "quiet" action. The guide can point out the kinds of reactions, or troubles, other readers have had with particular books. With the guides at our fingertips, we can more easily determine which questions to ask students, or which pages to turn to, in order to get to the heart of the conference.

Providing a Resource for Curriculum Planning

One Friday, say, we leave the classroom knowing that our students' writing shows that they are thirsting for deeper, more complicated characters to study and imitate. As we plan lessons, we can page through the guides that correspond with some of the books in our library, finding, or remembering, books that students can study that depict fascinating characters.

On the other hand, perhaps we need a book to read aloud to the class, or perhaps we need to recommend a book to a particular struggling reader.

Maybe a reader has finished a book he loves and has turned to you to help him plan his reading for the next weeks. When designing an author study or an inquiry into punctuation and its effects on meaning, it also helps to have the guides with you to point out books that may be helpful in those areas. In each of these cases, and many more, the guides can be a planning aid for you.

Reminding Us, or Teaching Us, About Particular Book Basics

No teacher can read, let alone recall in detail, every book that every child will pick up in the classroom. Of course, we read many of them and learn about many more from our colleagues, but there are far too many books in the world for us to be knowledgeable about them all. Sometimes, the guides will be a reminder of what you have read many years ago. Sometimes, they will provide a framework for you to question or direct your students more effectively than you could if you knew nothing at all about the book. "Probably, you will have to take some time to understand the setting before you can really get a handle on this book, why don't you turn to the picture atlas?" you might say after consulting the guide, or "Sharlene is reading another book that is similar to this one in so many ways! Why don't you go pair up with her to talk." You might learn to ask, "What do you think of Freddy?" in order to learn if the student is catching on to the tone of the narrator, or you might learn you could hint, "Did you get to chapter three yet? Because I bet you won't be bored any more when you get there. . . ." The guides provide a bit of what time constraints deny us: thoughtful insights about the content or unusual features of a given book.

Showcasing Literary Intricacies in Order to Suggest a Reader's Thinking

Sometimes, when we read a book, our idea of the author's message is in our minds before we even finish the story. Because we are experienced readers, much of our inferring and interpreting, our understanding of symbols and contexts, can come to us effortlessly. In the guides, we have tried to slow down some of that thinking so that we can all see it more easily. We have tried to lay out some of the steps young readers may have to go through in order to come to a cohesive idea of what the story is about, or a clear understanding of why a character behaved the way she did. As experienced readers, we may not even realize that our readers are confused by the unorthodox use of italics to show us who is speaking, for example. We may not remember the days when we were confused by changing narrators, the days when it took us a few chapters to figure out a character wasn't to be believed. In these guides, we have tried to go back to those days when we were more naïve readers, and have tried to fill in those thoughts and processes we are now able to skip over so easily.

By bringing forth the noteworthy features of the text, features experienced readers may not even notice, we are reminded of the thinking that our students need to go through in order to make sense of their reading. It gives us an idea of where to offer pointers, of where readers may have gone off in an unhelpful direction, or of where their thinking may need to go instead of where it has gone. By highlighting literary intricacies, we may remember that every bit about the construction of texts is a navigation point for students, and every bit is something we may be able to help students in learning.

Providing a Community of Readers and Teachers

The guides are also intended to help teachers learn from the community of other teachers and readers who have used particular texts already. They make available some of the stories and experiences other teachers have had, in order that we might stand on their shoulders and take our teaching even higher than they could reach. These guides are intended to give you some thinking to go with the books in your classroom library, thinking you can mix with your own ideas.

In the end, we don't all have a community of other teachers with whom we can talk about children's literature. The guides are meant not to stand in for that community, but instead to provide a taste, an appetizer, of the world of supportive professional communities. We hope that by reading these guides and feeling the companionship, guidance and insight they offer, teachers will be nudged to recreate that experience for the other books that have no guides, and that they will ask their colleagues, librarians, and the parents of their students to talk with them about children's literature and young readers. Then, when teachers are creating these guides for themselves, on paper or in their minds' eyes, we will know this project has done the work for which it was created.

Bibliography

Atwell, Nancie. 1987. *In the Middle: Writing, Reading, and Learning with Adolescents.* Portsmouth, NH: Boynton/Cook.

Calkins, Lucy. 2001. *The Art of Teaching Reading.* New York: Addison-Wesley Educational Publishers, Inc.

Cambourne, Brian. 1993. *The Whole Story: Natural Learning and the Acquisition of Literacy in the Classroom.* Auckland, NZ: Ashton Scholastic.

Krashen, Stephen. 1993. *The Power of Reading: Insights from the Research.* Englewood, CO: Libraries Unlimited.

Meek, Margaret. 1988. *How Texts Teach What Readers Learn.* Thimble Press.

Smith, Frank. 1985. *Reading Without Nonsense.* 2nd ed. New York: TC Press.

A Bad Case of Stripes

David Shannon

FIELD GUIDE

E

Illustrator
David Shannon

Publisher
Scholastic (Blue Sky Press), 1998

ISBN
0590929976

TC Level
8

Book Summary

Camilla Cream loves lima beans, but she won't admit it because no one else likes them. Suddenly, her skin becomes rainbow-striped. At first, her mother has her stay home from school, but when nothing else seems wrong with her, she goes. Once there, the other students make fun of her mercilessly, and Camilla turns the colors and patterns of whatever they suggest to her, despite herself. Specialists, doctors and herbalists all try to help her, but each makes the situation worse by suggesting cures that Camilla then has to turn into. Finally, a friendly old woman offers Camilla lima beans. At first she won't take them because she doesn't want to seem weird. Then she does, and POOF-her real self reappears. In the end, Camilla admits to the world that she likes lima beans, takes the teasing she gets for it-and she's happier for it.

Basic Book Information

This large size picture book has substantial amounts of print on each page, and the illustration pictures only one of the several episodes described per page.

Noteworthy Features

This picture book's otherwise realistic illustrations overlay fantastical colors and patterns on Camilla, making it enticing and popular in the classroom. The pictures alone create a crowd around it every time.

The vocabulary is a bit harder than some others at this reading level, but it shouldn't pose too much of a problem. Words like "fretted," "uncontrollable twitching," "allegiance," and "contagious" appear with a frequency of one per page.

Teaching Ideas

Most readers come away from the book with the understanding that Camilla's condition came about because she wouldn't eat lima beans. However, this understanding usually comes after a little thinking and sometimes even after a little rereading and discussion. The question "Why did Camilla get stripes?" is the one that groups may choose to start their discussion.

After students find a correlation between Camilla's sickness and lima beans, the talks get deeper. Some groups ask themselves, was her sickness because she was telling people things that weren't true about her? Sometimes children will start off with "Eat your lima beans" as the theme of the book. But when others come up with "Be true to yourself," the first group usually sees it their way easily enough, with explanations.

What is most difficult for kids to see in the interpretation of the book is that in her self-denial, Camilla is forced to follow the whims of those around her. Kids tend to see the disease, not the way she gets the disease or its nature. Partly, this is due to the compelling pictures that center the reader's attention on the disease itself. This might be something teachers point out to children after they have finished their study.

One way children might get deeper into the book is to do a character study of Camilla. There are more than enough hints about her willingness to ignore her true feelings in order to fit in and impress others. Studying other characters may prove to be fruitless, as they are not as fully developed in the story.

Book Connections

David Shannon has written and illustrated many picture books, including the recent and popular *No, David!* series. Comparing the illustrations in these books and their styles might be a productive activity.

The Story of Imelda Who Was Small by Morris Lurie is an interesting book to consider alongside this one, as it, too, is the story of an oddly sick little girl and the strange ways people try to help her before a wise old person offers a straightforward cure.

Of course, it might also be productive to read this book together with other ones that offer similar messages about being true to oneself, even in the face of peer pressure.

Genre
Picture Book

Teaching Uses
Independent Reading; Interpretation; Character Study; Read Aloud

A Lion to Guard Us

Clyde Robert Bulla

FIELD GUIDE

E

POST-IT MOMENT

Book Summary

Amanda Freebold lives in London, England in 1609, in the home of a wealthy woman, Mistress Trippett. She works as a servant because her mother is very sick and unable to provide for the family. Amanda's little brother and sister live in the house as well, but they are not allowed to move around or play. They sleep on a pallet on the floor. Amanda soon learns that their father is in Jamestown, a new colony across the ocean in the New World. After their mother dies, Amanda is determined to go to Jamestown to escape the terrible conditions in London and be with their father. Luckily, a kind doctor offers to take the children with him on a voyage across the ocean on a large sailing ship. Amanda encounters many adventures and dangers. This story is fiction, but it is based on a real sea voyage.

Illustrator
Michele Chessare

Publisher
Harper Trophy, 1981

ISBN
0064403335

TC Level
9

Basic Book Information

A Lion to Guard Us is a 115-page historical fiction book. Pictures appear in some chapters, supplementing the text. The chapter titles focus on the main events of each chapter. There is alternating dialogue, sometimes without references. The plot is chronological, except for brief explanations of the past, which aid in understanding the setting.

Noteworthy Features

Historical fiction, even simply written, may present special challenges to readers. They may not understand the context in which the story is set, and that it is different from their own lives. This story is based on a true event-the voyage of the Sea Venture from England in 1609 to save the Jamestown colony. The book is loaded with action and the location changes several times. The action requires the reader to follow all the changes. Also, the story moves swiftly: "...one day, in the dark of the morning, they were on their way." It may be difficult for students to sort out the large cast of characters in the beginning because the relationships are unclear and the structure of the household and its hierarchy of mistress and servants is not clearly explained. The reader learns early on from Amanda, through a story she is telling her siblings, that their mother once worked for Mistress Trippett, and that they moved into Mistress Trippett's house when their father left for the Jamestown colony. There is some inferring to do; however these inferences are not crucial to understanding.

Although the story is set in a distant place and time, the language is not archaic. The speech is different from modern speech, but not incomprehensible: "I'll take my leave."

Teaching Ideas

Many teachers introduce this story by providing historical context to the students, at times even having them research the period and events before reading. The book can be enjoyed as an adventure without background information, but it is much richer when the context is understood. Most teachers recommend careful reading of the first several chapters. Some teachers find that guided study through the beginning helps students grasp the inferences and better understand the context. Along with the main problem-will the children make it safely to Virginia and will their father still be alive? -other problems also drive the action. For example, the lion's head doorknocker their father gave them as a good luck charm, first explained early on, becomes important when people threaten to steal it, and then carry out that threat. One teacher suggested that students make story maps or lists of the problems and the characters to help keep them straight.

There is alternating dialogue here that is not always referenced. A mini-lesson using an overhead projection of this dialogue from the text can help students identify who is speaking.

Book Connections

Similar books include the *Dragon* series by Jackie French Koller and *The Hundred Dresses* by Eleanor Estes. *The American Girls* series is slightly harder and would make a good next step for readers. Many of Clyde Robert Bulla's other books are written for new chapter book readers. *A Lion to Guard Us* is clearly much more challenging than many of his other books, though.

Genre
Historical Fiction; Chapter Book

Teaching Uses
Independent Reading; Language Conventions; Reading and Writing Nonfiction

Afternoon of the Elves

Janet Taylor Lisle

FIELD GUIDE

E G

Publisher
Scholastic Inc., 1989

ISBN
0590439448

TC Level
12

Book Summary

This book tells the story of the friendship that develops between Hillary, who is middle class, and Sara-Kate, who is poor. The story centers around the miniature villages Sara-Kate builds and the community of elves she imagines lives there. The two girls' growing friendship is tested by peers who discourage the mixing of different social classes.

As the girls' friendship grows stronger, Hillary learns that her friend is doing everything in her home from buying all the food to paying the bills. As it turns out, Sara-Kate's mother is sick and the young girl does not want to be taken away from her. Ultimately, Hillary is unable to protect her friend from being taken away, and is left to stand guard over elf village herself.

Basic Book Information

This book has 122 pages, and is divided into 15 chapters. It is realistic fiction. Another book by this author is *Forest*, a fantasy tale about the world of squirrels.

Noteworthy Features

One aspect that could challenge readers is that Sara-Kate speaks of the elf village she builds as if it were real. Readers might mistakenly think that the elves are, in fact, real and miss the more important details about Sara-Kate and Hillary's friendship.

Teaching Ideas

This is a captivating story that moves along quickly. It is the kind of book that helps reluctant readers want to read. Student might use post-its or charts to help them gather evidence about what is real and what is make-believe in the story. Rereading, monitoring for sense, and coming to a part of the text with a question in mind are all strategies teachers can help readers use to get more out of this text.

As this is an early read, conferences might include helping students remember and retell the story well. A teacher might make sure readers use the basic story elements of character, events, setting, movement of time, and change in these retellings.

Readers could challenge each other with questions that push their thinking and force them to support their ideas with evidence from the text. Since this is a book that tends to generate questions in readers easily, various questioning strategies work especially well here. This might also be a time to help children learn to integrate and revise their ideas with their partner's ideas in order to understand more completely what is going on in the book.

Teachers could use the book to teach strategies for conversation. For example, it is not enough to come up with a prediction; the reader should find the clues in the chapter that support that prediction, that way, readers can talk and decide which predictions are most accurate. Without such evidence, the conversation tends to just go around in a circle without any overlap, without any weighing of evidence or measuring of opinions.

To assign a set of readers a single chapter a night is one way to focus the conversation on a particular aspect or small chunk of the book. Different focusing possibilities include, but are not limited to: the perspective of each major character; Sara-Kate's relationship to each of the other characters; specific examples of both time and setting in each chapter and how changes in both become apparent through the text; and the developing trust between the two friends.

Book Connections

Books with similar themes include *Crazy Lady* by Connolly, *The Great Gilly Hopkins* by Katherine Paterson, Lois Lowry's *Atta Boy Sam,* Robert Kimmel Smith's *The War with Grandpa* and some of the Jerry Spinelli books, including *Picklemania.* Another book by this author is *Forest*, a fantasy tale about the world of squirrels.

Genre

Fantasy; Chapter Book

Teaching Uses

Independent Reading; Partnerships

Alexander and the Wind-Up Mouse

Leo Lionni

FIELD GUIDE

E

Illustrator
Leo Lionni

Publisher
Dragon Fly Books, 1987

ISBN
0590430122

TC Level
8

Book Summary

Alexander is a real mouse with one wish. After seeing all the attention paid to Willy, the wind-up mouse, Alexander wants to become one himself. Alexander is not particularly liked or understood by his family and friends; he thinks becoming a wind-up mouse will solve his problems. In the end, however, when Willy is thrown away, Alexander realizes that his magic wish could be best used to help his friend become real.

Basic Book Information

Leo Lionni won the Caldecott Honor with his collage illustrations of this classic. It has about 26 pages with anywhere from one line to a full paragraph on each double-page spread.

Noteworthy Features

There are a few aspects of the book that kids seem to find tricky: The story begins in the middle of the action, with no gradual introduction to the characters, what the setting is, or what is happening. There is a fair amount of idiomatic languagee.g., "as fast as his little legs could carry him;" and "heavy heart." This may be especially tricky for children learning English as a second language. When kids read "wind-up mouse" they sometimes end up pronouncing "wind" to rhyme with "pinned" instead of "find," and then have trouble understanding that Willy is a toy. Children these days do not have as many wind-up toys as kids used to have. Even if they pronounce the word "wind" correctly, they may not have experience with the kind of toy that requires someone to turn a key. In the middle of the story, Alexander tells Willy of his adventures with "brooms, flying saucers and mousetraps." Willy talks about "the penguin, the wooly bear and Annie." This leads some children to feel they have missed something. They don't remember any stories about flying saucers or penguins, and who is Annie? This however, is just the author's way of saying that the two characters talked with each other about many things.

Teaching Ideas

In the case of *Alexander and the Wind-Up Mouse*, and lots of other picture books in which an animal or toy is the main character, there are a few simple, easily internalized, sequential questions that can help students get started in assembling an interpretation of the text. Teachers may want to phrase the questions using words your children have used before to talk about the texts. Of course, these questions are only a few out of hundreds that might work, but they can serve as a start:

What kind of a person would the animal or toy in the story be in real life?

What kind of action does the character take? Would that choice or action be the same in the real world?

What are the consequences of that action? What would the consequences be for the action in the real world?

This book is wonderful for the kind of reading aloud during which kids are given a break to discuss the book with a partner. If two children are partnering to read this book, they could set markers at two or three intervals in the text. When they come to these markers, they can stop to talk. Alternatively, readers may read through the entire book once and then return to the book for a reread, expecting to find more as they look more closely at the text and prepare to talk or jot down their thoughts. This sort of revisiting of a rich, layered book is worthwhile to teach readers that great books deserve to be revisited, and that readers can approach a second read-through expecting to notice more and to grow important ideas.

In any case, thoughtful readers may notice that in this text a great deal is left unsaid. For example, Lionni never explains directly who is chasing after Alexander and who loves Willy, or why either circumstance is happening. Lionni also leaves it to the reader to interpret Alexander's motivation at the end of the book when he chooses to help his friend rather than turn himself into a wind-up mouse. Since all this is left to reading "between the lines," stopping to talk is especially helpful and relevant with this book.

Alexander is also the perfect book to use in a writing workshop when children are considering ways to write strong leads to their texts. The first sentences of the text read, "'Help! Help! A Mouse!' There was a scream. Then a crash. Cups, saucers and spoons were flying in all directions. Alexander ran for his hole as fast as his little legs would carry him." Lionni draws his readers into the story by starting with an action, and by writing about that action in a colorful way, using dialogue, sound effects, and short fragments to recreate the scurry of the moment. Children who tend to begin their narratives in a long-winded fashion may benefit from seeing that Lionni begins in the middle of the action, with no lengthy introduction to the characters, setting or plot.

Some communities of readers and writers collect language they love in the books they read. They try to describe and borrow the literary technique the authors use. Alexander has a nice sprinkling of idiomatic language that isn't heavy-handed. Lionni uses "as fast as his little legs could carry him," "cups, saucers and spoons were flying in all directions," "heavy heart" and several other turns of phrase that some children relish.

This book can be used for a reading mini-lesson to help children figure out new vocabulary words from context. The text is constructed of fairly common words, so it is a good basis from which to deduce the meaning of the few new words. Words like "pebble," "envy," "saucers," "vain," "baseboard," "quivering" and "alas" are examples of words that might challenge readers to do some productive work.

Book Connections

Lionni has written many other books that readers can turn to next.

Genre
Picture Book

Teaching Uses
Independent Reading; Interpretation; Read Aloud

All the Places to Love

Patricia MacLachlan

FIELD GUIDE

E

Illustrator
Mike Wimmer

Publisher
Harper Collins, 1994

ISBN
0060210982

TC Level
9

Book Summary

Eli lives in the countryside on his grandparents' farm. Each of his family members has shared with him a beautiful favorite place that they love. Now he is ready to share all these places, as well as his own special wonder at the beauty of the natural world, with his new baby sister.

Basic Book Information

Patricia MacLachlan is the author of many well-loved novels and picture books, including *Sarah, Plain and Tall*, winner of the Newbery Medal, and its sequel, *Skylark*, as well as *What You Know First*, also illustrated by Mike Wimmer.

Noteworthy Features

The cover of this beautiful picture book makes many adults sigh, feeling nostalgia for childhood and country living. But it seems less enticing to some children, perhaps because the children pictured on it are turning away. Despite this, the interior paintings are captivating, and the author is so beloved in many classrooms that children, like adults, find themselves drawn to the book.

The story has a fairly straightforward structure, starting with Eli telling of his birth and then of the beautiful places each of his family members has shown him as he has grown. The story then moves away from memories, and Eli describes his own favorite place that he will show his new baby sister one day, and the reverence for nature that he will impart to her. Some readers may not realize that Eli is reminiscing during the early part of the book and that, in the story, Eli's sister has already been born.

When characters "speak" in this book, Eli is actually remembering what they said much earlier in time. These words are written in italics. The "I love you, Eli" message that Grandmother sailed to Eli on the river is also written in italics. Readers may find this slightly confusing, and they may find it fascinating.

The penultimate page of the book is a double-page spread of a country landscape with no words, the same picture as appears on the book's cover. Some children take this and the closing-like words of the previous page to mean the book is over and they never turn to the very last page. It is not an earth-changing last page, perhaps, but it will add to an understanding of the book, especially if children are going to discuss the story.

Teaching Ideas

This picture book has won over the hearts of thousands of teachers who, in turn, help children to feel its magic. It's the sort of book that deserves to be simply savored and enjoyed first, then studied in multiple ways. One teacher holds some books back from her class, bringing them out as celebrations for special days-the first day of spring, an author's birthday, the first day after vacation. This book is worthy of such a celebration.

Later, the class will probably return to this book to study it with care. This is a very sophisticated memoir and it can be studied in upper grades (perhaps four and above) as an example of the kind of memoir children aim to write. But it can also be appreciated in the younger grades as a book that helps children get the sound of grand texts into their heads and hearts.

When looking more closely at this book, readers may want to pay attention to the setting. The book is largely about setting, an overlooked element in many children's stories. Children often read stories and focus on what happens and to whom. A teacher might want to design mini-lessons for a reading workshop that highlight the importance of setting. How does an author make a place come alive? What would a really good "read" of a book that is rich in setting entail? What's happening in your mind as you read these words? These prompts could, of course, lead a teacher to demonstrate the way he or she envisions place in the midst of reading a book. "Today, while reading your independent reading books, please pay special attention to the setting of the story. I'll stop your reading after fifteen minutes and ask you to talk with partners about the setting you're envisioning."

Of course, there are stories in which the setting is not very developed and readers may claim this to be true in their books. Sometimes it's not true that the setting is absent; it's just not explicitly described. Other times it will be true that an author has decided not to develop all the elements in a story. *All the Places to Love* can be revisited with readers asking, "Does MacLachlan develop all the story elements here?" This may lead to the discovery that some elements in this text have fallen into the background. As a follow up, readers can ponder why the author might choose to do this.

Readers will probably want to set this book alongside others. One way to do this is to look at other MacLachlan books, and examine their settings. MacLachlan's *Baby* is an obvious choice because images of nature are woven throughout that novella, too, and MacLachlan's *What You Know First* is very similar to this book, though it has a more developed character. This book could also profit from being read alongside some of Barbara Cooney's books, including *Island Boy*, *Miss Rumphius* or *Basket Moon*. All of these books revel in the beauty and goodness of living close to the land, but some of them also show the difficult aspects of such a life. Reading them together may highlight the messages and feelings in each of these books more than reading each one in isolation.

The messages here about the beauty of the farm and of nature are easy to accept without a second thought. But if teachers want children to begin to engage that second thought, this book may be an easy place to start. The second-to-last sentence of the book reads, "All the places to love are right here, no matter where you may live." Merely asking kids, especially those who know and love the city or suburbs best, if they agree or disagree with that statement may get a hearty discussion going. Talking about ways in which the sound of a cow chewing or the sight of an old turtle crossing the road "makes all the difference in the world" can also be interesting, since some children will undoubtedly agree and others will not, and they can help each other understand the two points of view.

We might also use this book to help students write using their own detailed descriptions of places and actions so that instead of writing, "The dog, oh the brown happy dog," they write, "The dogs ran ahead, looking back with sly smiles." A child might read this book looking for places where the writer works hard to help the reader see the places to love. Or a child might make a chart of how the writer makes the reader see. What is the writer doing on the pages that allow the reader to see the pictures without pictures in the text (which aren't as detailed as the words are)? We'd want upper grade students to know that words sometimes paint a clearer picture than illustrations.

This memoir begins in an unusual way with the birth of the person: "On the day I was born..." It's perfect for showing students that even when the writer uses this kind of beginning, she does not tell her entire life story, but chooses the moments she shares carefully. The events subtly follow the growth of the child, bringing the reader from one important person in her life to another, first showing the places she loves, and then showing those places with the important people in them.

This story spans many years, but there is no true way of seeing how many years it spans. Time isn't important; it's the places that are important.

This book is an example of a well-written text that is structured as a list. Readers may notice that in this list, dialogue has been woven throughout. The author says at least three things about each element on her list, moving between what is present now and what used to be.

Children have also gotten into grand conversations after noticing that Eli's grandfather cried when he saw Eli as a newborn and again when he sees Eli's newborn sister. This has led to conversations about an emotional quality in the text and in the pictures.

Book Connections

Other picture books written by MacLachlan include *Three Names* and *What You Know First*. Barbara Cooney has written books with similar themes, including *Island Boy*, *Miss Rumphius* and *Basket Moon.*

Genre
Picture Book; Memoir

Teaching Uses
Independent Reading; Read Aloud; Teaching Writing; Critique

Always My Dad

Sharon Dennis Wyeth

FIELD GUIDE

E

Illustrator
Ral Colón

Publisher
Alfred A Knopf, 1997

ISBN
0679889345

TC Level
8

Book Summary

A young girl remembers a summer spent on her grandparents' farm, when her father comes for a visit. She and her brothers play games with him and he gives them treats. Then, all too soon, he has to leave. The children don't know when they will see or hear from him again. But they are reassured to hear him say that he loves them and that wherever he is, he is always their dad.

This is a gentle story of a young girl's love for her absent father. Readers learn in the beginning that the young narrator sees her father only "once in a while." The sole explanation is "he moves around a lot." But Wyeth puts a positive spin on the relationship, focusing not on the father's absence, but on the time he is present. The four children spend a summer with their paternal grandparents on a farm. One evening Dad shows up and what follows is a description of the children playing together with their father. Later, the little girl uses these memories to remind herself, when Dad is away, that he is "Always my Dad." Colón's soft pastel illustrations reflect this very positive attitude of dealing with a parent who is not always there.

Basic Book Information

This is a 30-page picture book. The length and placement of text varies from page to page. On the first page, for example, two lines of text appear above the illustration. On the next page a six-line paragraph is on the left, with a collage-type illustration, depicting the details in the paragraph on the right-hand page. Wyeth states specifically what the characters are doing-and the illustrator, using the textured technique that is his trademark, captures these details well. Thus, the text and pictures complement each other. The limited amount of text on each page-ranging from two lines (or approximately 20 words) to eleven lines-also makes reading easier.

Noteworthy Features

If children read this book during independent reading and need to talk it over with a partner, they inevitably end up discussing whether the father is a good father or not. Kids are easily able to find textual evidence for their arguments-for some reason the details seem to stick in their minds more easily in this book than in other stories.

A small difficulty readers sometimes have in making sense of the book is in the section where the dad teaches his four children a game involving pies, a door and a devil. Some children get confused as to what is going on in the game, but with persistence, they can usually figure it out well enough without outside explanation to go on reading.

The story is told in the first person, from the point of view of the oldest child in the family. Although the author only implies that the dad does not live with the children, readers can infer that the two parents are separated when the dad admits, "I've been having trouble getting my life together." At the end of the story, back home in the city with her mother, the young narrator says that she dreams of her father often.

The text contains dialogue and complex sentences, which raise the level of difficulty somewhat. Although the sentences sometimes extend to two lines, they follow a logical sequence that would not be difficult for second or third graders to comprehend, particularly with the aid of the illustrations. Within paragraphs, Wyeth alternates between verb forms like "we played" and "we would play," alternating between telling about the children's lives in general and on one single day. Such inconsistency in verb form makes it a bit difficult to follow the time line of the action. That is a minor challenge, however.

Teaching Ideas

Discussions about the father often bring out personal response from the readers. Some children report that they would be angry with the dad if they were the girl in the story because the dad isn't dependable. Some children say that they would be angry if they were the mom or the grandparents in the story because they are the ones who do all the hard work of raising and caring for the children. The girl is always dreaming about her wonderful daddy, but he is never around to help. Some kids though, will say the best thing is to just be happy for what you can get in a dad, like the girl is, because some children don't have any dad at all. The discussions can be moving and deeply thoughtful since children are familiar with the topic.

Once reading partners have had their first responses to this story, a teacher might ask them whether the author (not they, but the author) seems to approve of this sort of fatherhood or not. Is the author supporting being the kind of father we see in the story, or is the author presenting this as an example of a not-so-good dad? Taking this a step farther, a teacher could nudge readers to ask some classic critical questions: Whose story is this? Who benefits from it being told this way? How else could it have been told? Even if children decide the man is not a good father, they can still revel in all the fun moments he has with his children. And of course, they can still love the story, and even the character himself.

If a teacher wanted to briefly set a child up to successfully read this book, the teacher could tell children that in this book, the oldest child in a family tells about her dad who is separated from her mom and from the kids. "You'll have to think hard," the teacher might say, "about what the title *Always My Dad* could mean in this book."

A teacher might want to say a little more to support readers with the inconsistency of verb tense. "Some pages tell about what the kids always would do," the teacher could say and perhaps point to such a page. "Some pages-like this one-tell about what happened one time."

This book also serves well if the class conversation is revolving around the characters in books. If a reader, or a small group of readers, studied the father in this story, they could discuss many things about the dad that aren't explicitly talked about in the book, but could be inferred. That is, a close look at the father would involve (at least with nudging from the teacher) not only developing theories about the father with specific references to the text, but also developing theories that emerge out of what readers already know about fathers from their own lives. Then, too, in a conference with a reader or a partnership of readers, a teacher might use this opportunity to stress that when they are reading, it is important to notice not only what is said, but also what is not said, which can be just as revealing. For some children, the study can be a very difficult one, because gathering information and making judgments about the man in the book can be very much like gathering information and making judgments about their own loved ones. In some cases, this subject is too painful for children to probe deeply on their own.

We can also use this book as an example of a memoir for children to study when they write their own memoirs. The structure the author uses is one that some children could adopt. Instead of telling about her entire wonderful summer, the narrator writes about the important parts of it-the parts that were related to her father. She includes details of the summer that weren't directly related to her father to create a setting and to build a mood, but only the events related to her father are told in detail here. The craft and figurative language of the writing also provide worthy examples for children as they write their own memoir.

Book Connections

Especially if this book is used as part of a study of memoir, readers might compare and contrast it to other memoirs including *The Relatives Came* and *When I Was Young in the Mountains* , both by Cynthia Rylant; *The Two of Us* by Aliki, *When I Was Nine* by James Stevenson, and *My Mama Had a Dancing Heart* by Libba Moore Gray.

Genre
Picture Book; Memoir

Teaching Uses
Independent Reading; Critique; Teaching Writing

Amber Brown Is Feeling Blue

Paula Danziger

FIELD GUIDE

E

Series
Amber Brown books

Illustrator
Tony Ross

Publisher
Scholastic (Little Apple), 1999

ISBN
0439071682

TC Level
9

Book Summary

In this book, Amber must decide between spending Thanksgiving with her mother and her mother's new boyfriend or with her father. A second plot line involves the arrival of Kelly, a new student in her class. After first feeling jealous of the new arrival, Amber and Kelly become friends. By the end of the book Amber has decided to spend Thanksgiving with her father. She has realized that her life will always be "colorful" and not as easy as she wishes it would be.

Basic Book Information

Besides the Amber Brown series, which was inspired by her niece Carrie, Paula Danziger is also the author of many other award-winning children's books, including *The Cat Ate My Gymsuit*, *Can You Sue Your Parents for Malpractice?* and *The Pistachio Prescription.*

Over the course of the *Amber Brown* series, Amber grows up from third to fourth grade, and her internal thinking becomes more sophisticated and reflective. The later books are more difficult than the earlier ones. For this reason it makes sense to read the series in order, but it's not completely necessary. Reading the earlier books will help readers understand this particular book better-by now, Amber's personality and her life are familiar. Because of the reflective and sophisticated thinking, the book is more appropriate for older readers than for young advanced readers.

Noteworthy Features

Amber Brown is the first-person narrator of this book. Some of her thinking is expressed in incomplete sentences. Some, but not all, dialogue is referenced. Pictures appear every several pages, and they match the text. There are no chapter titles.

Amber's strong personality and internal thinking tie all the events in the book together. Amber is a very consistent character with a distinct voice. She is a precocious fourth grader. While upper-grade readers are likely to understand her speech and thoughts, younger students may find her to be unique and even puzzling.

The settings are familiar: school and home. Readers will easily identify with many of Amber's family problems and her reflections on life. Since Amber usually says just what she is feeling, the reader is not expected to infer a great deal.

There are several characters in the book besides the main ones, but they should be familiar from past books, and they are distinctive enough so as not to be confusing. It is not a struggle to keep characters straight, as might be with one-dimensional "cardboard" characters. Paula Danziger makes the characters come alive in the reader's mind in a way that helps students hold onto them across the series.

There is some advanced vocabulary, colloquialisms, and humor here, but readers will probably be able to cope with words such as "cologne," "eau de pizza," "beheading Barbie dolls," "gullible," "detention," "intentionally," "nervous breakdown," and "yuckoid." There is also word play, as in "Feat-feet" and "friend-fiend." Some children may need help with the idiomatic expressions and word play in some titles: ...Sees Red, ...Feeling Blue, and ...Goes Fourth.

The text structure may merit attention as well. Although the thread of Amber's decision to be with her father is woven through the book, there are discrete episodes and subplots that have nothing to do withthis thread. The book also deals with Amber's relationship with Brenda the babysitter, Halloween, the Kelly Green story and school life. There is a warm, "real" feeling to this writing, as if you are living right along with Amber.

Teaching Ideas

In talking to a student reading this book, it's important to learn right away whether the reader is making his or her way through the series, or just pulled this book from the shelves. In general, it's probably advisable for children to stay within a series for a bit before switching to another series, because reading books in a series supports a lot of good reading behaviors. If a child is going to read within the *Amber Brown* series, this probably isn't the best one to start with. Amber is older here than in earlier books, and the story is more internal and sophisticated than the more plot-based previous books.

An obvious line of discussion to pursue with this book, as with so many series books, will be to ask how this book compares to earlier books in the series. Children may enjoy researching whether Amber is growing older and studying to see if they notice other changes across the different texts. They may also want to study Amber's friendships through the series. Brandi appears as a friend, but never has a major role. Kelly is her first real friend since she lost Justin in the first book. Amber's relationship to Max changes over the series, too. If readers have read most of the series, the most important commonality across the books will be Amber. Amber is a distinctive personality, yet she changes subtly through the series, from acting out her feelings to being more internal and reflective.

If a child has read several books across the series, it'll be interesting to launch that child into a cross-book inquiry. For example, the word play in this book's title is a feature one sees across the books, and even the reference to color in *Amber Brown Is Feeling Blue* is part of a pattern. There is, for example, another book entitled, *Amber Brown Sees Red.*

Book Connections

Amber Brown Is Feeling Blue is similar in difficulty to *Aldo applesauce* and *Russell Rides Again*, both by Johanna Hurwitz. It is more difficult than *The Bailey School Kids(*Debbie Dadey), *Junie B. Jones* (Barbara Park) and *Marvin Redpost* (Louis Sachar) series. If students can successfully read the *Amber Brown* books and other books of comparable difficulty, then they may find themselves well prepared to read the *Ramona* (Beverly Cleary) and *Flower Girls* (Kathleen Leverich) series.

Genre
Chapter Book

Teaching Uses
Independent Reading; Book Clubs; Character Study

Amber Brown Sees Red

Paula Danziger

FIELD GUIDE

D E

Book Summary

Amber has noticed that she is going through a growth spurt, which bothers her. Amber is ambivalent about her mother's fiancé, Max; Amber still loves her dad and feels torn and unsure about how this will affect her. When Dad announces he wants joint custody, Amber suffers from being in the middle. When Dad arrives home from Paris, Amber suddenly decides everything will be okay.

Series
Amber Brown books

Illustrator
Tony Ross

Publisher
Scholastic, 1998

ISBN
0590947281

TC Level
9

Basic Book Information

Amber Brown Sees Red is a 116-page chapter book. There are no chapter titles. Illustrations occur every several pages and support the text. Paula Danziger is the award-winning author of many books, including *The Cat Ate My Gymsuit*, *The Pistachio Prescription,* and *Can You Sue Your Parents for Malpractice?* The character of Amber was inspired by Danziger's niece, Carrie.

There are currently six books in the *Amber Brown* series. The books get longer and more complex as Amber ages, and the later books sometimes allude to events in earlier books. The author reintroduces characters and past events in each new book so that it is not necessary for readers to read them in sequence.

Noteworthy Features

Amber Brown Sees Red uses a straightforward plot with a linear time structure. There is a subplot, about school, but this comes in and out in an easily recognized setting change. Amber narrates the story in the first person. As a narrator, Amber likes to use colloquialisms. This can be thought of as kid language or puns, like "skunkorama" and "scrunchies." This book uses several idioms, most notably "Sees Red." Often students do not know that seeing red means being angry.

Difficult issues such as divorce are treated and explained honestly in the text. This book helps students reflect on the inevitable emotional impact that divorce has on children.

There is a lot of dialogue in this book that is not always easy to follow. Quite often, the author does not reference who is speaking, relying instead on paragraph changes to indicate new speakers. Occasional big words such as "apprehend" may need some support. Sentences are of varied length and complexity. Sentence fragments are present in Amber's internal monologues.

Teaching Ideas

Amber Brown Sees Red works well as a read aloud or book club book because of the conversation it engenders about divorce. This book also makes a good choice for partnership reading and reading centers dedicated to character development. Readers should pay special attention to inferring the causes of Amber's anger.

Amber thinks a lot during her narration, which makes this book a good one for introducing the concept of internal monologue. Issues such as how much the reader trusts the narrator should be addressed. Students can take their learning about narrators to their other books and other writing projects.

Book Connections

Amber Brown Sees Red is the sixth book in the Amber Brown series. Amber ages as the books progress, which may make them best read in sequence. If readers are interested in series books at this level, they might try *The Bailey School Kids*. *Junie B. Jones* and the *Marvin Redpost* series are a bit easier, and offer similar opportunities for studying character. The *Flower Girls* series would make a good follow-up series.

Genre

Short Chapter Book

Teaching Uses

Book Clubs; Independent Reading; Read Aloud

Anastasia Krupnik

Lois Lowry

FIELD GUIDE

E G

Series
Anastasia

Publisher
Houghton Mifflin, 1979

ISBN
055315253X

TC Level
12

Book Summary

Anastasia Krupnik, age 10, has a mother who paints, a professor/poet father, and a teacher she dislikes. She also has a green notebook where she keeps lists of favorite words and important private information. Most significant to the story are the lists of things Anastasia loves and hates, which trace the themes that make up the plot of the book. The story is not action-oriented -- the strongest element of suspense lies in learning what name Anastasia will choose for her new baby brother.

During the nine months before the baby arrives, Anastasia has a crush on a boy, tries to write poetry, considers becoming a Catholic, learns the importance of memories, changes her feelings about her very elderly grandmother, and comes to terms with her mother having a second child. By the end of the book, her grandmother has died, Anastasia's baby brother has arrived, and Anastasia has taken her teacher off her list of "things I hate" after the teacher calls Anastasia to express sympathy over the death of Anastasia's grandmother. Despite the lack of an action-driven plot, the incidents that make up the story are highly engaging, and Anastasia's decisions about a name for her baby brother resolves the book in a satisfying way.

Basic Book Information

This book received strong reviews at publication (The Bulletin of the Center for Children's Books named *Anastasia Krupnik* "A Book of Special Distinction"), and *Anastasia Krupnik* was so popular with readers that it engendered a series and has stayed in print for over twenty years. Lowry has written many books for young readers from lower middle grades, as well as young adult books. She has received the Newbery Medal for *Number The Stars* and *The Giver.*

This middle-grade novel contains eleven chapters, which are each six to eight pages long. Though quietly plotted, the book is written in a lively, humorous style that may appeal to a wide range of readers. Because the book was first published in 1979, some minor details are dated (e.g., Mrs. Westvessel wears stockings with seams up the back), but Anastasia's experiences are so interesting these details don't undercut the story's authenticity.

Noteworthy Features

The story uses third-person point of view with Anastasia as the central character. The plot unfolds chronologically, covering nine months of

Anastasia's fourth grade year in school. Lowry's writing style is engaging and accessible. She includes vivid details that create memorable characters. Anastasia has hair the color of Hubbard squash and a pink wart in the middle of her left thumb. Her father has a beard the same color, but not much hair on his head. Her mother paints and smells sometimes of turpentine, sometimes of vanilla and brown sugar, sometimes of Je Reviens perfume. Mrs. Westvessel, Anastasia's teacher, has brown spots on her hands, large, lop-sided bosoms, and a faint moustache. Children may take note of Lowry's style and try it in their own writing.

Each chapter ends with a reproduction of Anastasia's latest list of things she loves and things she hates. The alterations to the lists-items added, deleted, or moved from one column to the other-provide insight into the developing themes of the book and reflect growth and change in Anastasia. Students may well note this in a character study.

Teaching Ideas

Lowry's depiction of the only African American character in the book needs special attention from the teacher. Washburn Cummings, a sixth grader, wears an enormous Afro, wiggles his hips as he bounces an imaginary basketball, listens to music on his transistor radio, and shows up for school in a tee shirt with an obscenity on the front. Anastasia develops a brief crush on him, but no other details are added to move the character beyond the stereotype. Readers will need to critique this stereotypical depiction, with or without help from a teacher.

Anastasia's attitude toward several people changes significantly, especially her grandmother, her teacher, and the owner of the drugstore, Mr. Belden. To understand why and how Anastasia's feelings change, students might make a list of the things Anastasia dislikes about each person and a list of the things that eventually make her feel differently. This list could be compiled as readers move through the book, in order to help them understand the changes as they happen in the story.

Book Connections

Lois Lowry is a prolific writer for children. Her *Anastasia* series includes *Anastasia Krupnik, Anastasia Again!, Ask Your Analyst, Anastasia on Her Own, Anastasia at Your Service, Anastasia Has the Answers, Anastasia's Chosen Career, and Anastasia at This Address*. She's also written the richly layered book *Autumn Street*, which would be an appropriate precursor book to this series.

This is one of many books in which the main character writes. Readers could make a collection of these writing books to see what they can discover. See other Anastasia books, Kimmel Smith's *War With Grandpa*, Moss's *Amelia's Notebook*, MacLaughlan's *Arthur for the Very First Time*, or *Cassie Binegar*.

Genre

Chapter Book

Teaching Uses
Independent Reading; Teaching Writing; Character Study

Andy and Tamika

David A. Adler

FIELD GUIDE

E

Series
Andy Russell books

Illustrator
Will Hillenbrand

Publisher
Gulliver Books, 1999

ISBN
0152019014

TC Level
10

Book Summary

Andy is a fourth grader who is into everything. He has a pet snake, many gerbils, a newly adopted goldfish, a best friend who is moving in with his family, a pet kitten at school and a new sibling on the way! Andy and his friends Tamika and Bruce help each other deal with life's ups and downs.

Basic Book Information

This is the second book in the *Andy Russell* series by David Adler. Adler is also the beloved author of the *Cam Jansen* series. This series is more difficult than the *Cam Jansen* series because not only are the books longer, but the characters are more fleshed out and complex. This 129-page book has 10 chapters, which are titled and lend support to the goings on of the chapter.

While it is not necessary to start with the first book in this series, *The Many Troubles of Andy Russell*, it will make understanding the characters a lot easier. In that book, Tamika's parents are in an accident and so she goes to live with Andy's next-door neighbors, the Perlmans. Tamika deals with issues of abandonment and loss, which can help the reader to understand why she is reluctant to leave the Perlmans when they go on sabbatical to South America in the later book, *Andy and Tamika*.

Noteworthy Features

Andy is in fourth grade, and school is described in more detail than in many early chapter books. The life of Andy and his friends in school is regulated by the "RRRR!" of the period bells, as classes change from science to reading to lunch and to math and so on. There is enough shifting around of subjects to be a bit confusing, especially to readers who haven't been exposed to this kind of timekeeping.

There is often a subversive tone to Andy in his attitudes toward his teacher and school. Andy does well in math, for instance, without paying attention in class. For these reasons, the story is more reminiscent of middle school in its setting and humor.

One supportive element of this book is its dialogue referencing. The author makes it easier to understand who is saying what by always including, "he said" or "she said" next to the words spoken.

The story is told in the third person, but from Andy's point of view, making it easy for the reader to identify with him. However, there are so many characters in the book that it can make for difficulty at times. Andy's world is made up of many people, including those at school (Tamika, Bruce, Stacy Ann Jackson, and Mrs. Roman the teacher) and at home (Mom, Dad, Andy's older sister Rachel, the new baby, and the Perlmans next door). Adler keeps the characters close to their settings and Tamika is the only character besides Andy who crosses over from one setting to the other.

Teaching Ideas

The content of this book makes it a bit more suitable for fourth and fifth graders than for third graders. The author assumes readers understand quite a lot about pregnancy, global warming and division and addition of fractions.

Andy and Tamika shows a supportive friendship between a white child and an African-American child, and for this alone it is valuable. The world of Andy and Tamika is integrated and accepting. The Perlmans living next door have a menorah at one point and Andy asks what it is. It is assumed that the reader knows what Hanukkah is. Although this kind of interest in and acceptance of varied ethnicity can't be assumed in today's world, Adler's portrayal gives the reader an image of what could be.

Book Connections

There are several other popular books in which fourth grade figures prominently. They include *Fourth Grade Rats* (Jerry Spinelli), *Amber Brown Goes Fourth* (Paula Danziger) and Judy Blume's *Tales of a Fourth Grade Nothing*. It would be interesting to compare and contrast any of these books and their treatment of fourth grade.

Genre
Chapter Book

Teaching Uses
Independent Reading; Partnerships

Beans on the Roof

Betsy Byars

FIELD GUIDE

E

Book Summary

This is a charming portrait of life in a loving family of modest means. They cheer on each other's efforts to write poems and then support Anna through her crisis when her poem is not chosen for the school poetry book. Teachers may not be thrilled to see that poetry is depicted only as rhyming jingles, but this does not detract from the warm family story.

Publisher
Dell Yearling, 1988

ISBN
0440403146

TC Level
8

Basic Book Information

Betsy Byars has written many books for older readers. This book, along with easy readers *My Brother Ant*, and *The Seven Treasure Hunts* (which is more difficult) is among her few for young readers.

Beans on the Roof is 63 pages long, with 9 chapters of 6 to 9 pages each, with intriguing titles such as "The Number of Beans of the roof keeps increasing." The pictures are realistic and attractive, usually placed on the opposite page or overleaf following the action in the text. Towards the end of the story, Anna is shown crying in her bedroom. This picture gives the reader a glimpse behind the closed door, hidden from the rest of the family, who are all in the kitchen trying to figure out why Anna went to her room.

Noteworthy Features

This story is told chronologically, with all the action taking place in the same afternoon. The only exception is one place where time jumps ahead to the next day. There are two plot lines in the book. Readers will follow the story of Anna's poem and what happens when it is not accepted for the school poetry book. They'll also read about her brother "String," who is frustrated until he is able to write his own poem.

Except for some unreferenced alternating dialogue, this book, like *The Chalk Box Kid* by Clyde Robert Bulla, is a truly easy chapter book for newly fluent readers. Although the sentences are short and simple, and most of the story is explicitly told rather than left for readers to infer, the book has a literary quality, with good writing and a story readers can care about.

There is one section that may confuse some readers. At one point, students have to link Anna's statement, "We hand them [the poems] in tomorrow," with her crying the next day after school in her room, and then link this to the "mystery" of why Anna is upset when her poem was not chosen for the book.

Teaching Ideas

Children who are new to chapter books may still find it challenging to read and follow alternating dialogue. Although passages written in dialogue will eventually provide support for readers, there will be some children who read this book and find that the dialogue in it poses some problems. In a small group strategy lesson, a teacher could help several readers to read aloud the dialogue on a page or two of this book and to do so almost as if they were characters speaking their roles in a play. This may help readers to eventually read dialogue silently, making an internal play as they do so. Alternatively, a teacher could do a whole-class mini-lesson on reading dialogue and could create an overhead of a page or two from this book. Then a teacher could point out not only the alternating pattern of characters speaking, but also the way in which readers are expected to discern which character would be likely to say a line based on the logic of the conversation and the personality of the character.

In a guided reading introduction or in a conference with a reader who is just embarking on this book, a teacher could call attention to the time gap in the plot. "You'll notice that at one point in the story, time jumps ahead." Later, the reader(s) could reflect on ways an author signals that time in a story is going to jump forward or backward.

The readers of this book will be apt to wonder why Anna was crying. They might attach Post-its to "clues," discussing in conferences or partnership conversations how they figured out why Anna was crying.

Students could infer character traits, list the traits and cite evidence for these traits in a two-column chart. For example, although "String" is ecstatic about finally creating his own poem, he is willing to put his own happiness aside when his mother tells him his sister is probably upset because her poem was not chosen, and that no one should mention poems around her. This shows that he really loves his sister and can put aside his own needs to respect hers.

Book Connections

Readers who enjoy this book may also like *The Chalk Box Kid* by Clyde Robert Bulla, *The Dog That Pitched a No-Hitter* by Matt Christopher, and the *Cam Jansen* series by David Adler. Before long, these students will be reading *Tooter Pepperday* and *Blue Ribbon Blues* by Jerry Spinelli and the *Jigsaw Jones* series by James Preller.

Genre
Short Chapter Book; Poetry

Teaching Uses
Independent Reading; Teaching Writing; Character Study

Birthday Presents

Cynthia Rylant

FIELD GUIDE

A E

Book Summary

The narrators of this story are the parents of a child. They remind her of her real birthday, the day she was born and the things she did on that historic day. They also tell her about each of her subsequent birthdays and the things that they did to show her how special she was. Before her sixth birthday, the parents tell the girl how she herself will give the family gifts, make cards and help them to have special days. Then, when her sixth birthday arrives, they tell how the girl talks to them about things in the world, even things they hadn't known, and how they spend time together. The book ends with the words: "Birthday presents."

Illustrator
Sucie Stevenson

Publisher
Orchard Books, 1987

ISBN
0531070263

TC Level
10

Basic Book Information

Rylant is a prolific writer of many award-winning children's books. She received the Newbery Honor Award for *A Fine White Dust*, the Caldecott Honor Award for the titles *When I Was Young in the Mountains* and *The Relatives Came*. *Birthday Presents* and *A Blue-Eyed Daisy* were named Children's Choice books by a joint committee of the International Reading Association and the Children's Book Council.

Noteworthy Features

This is a fairly simple, straightforward book with cute, cartoon-type pictures. Usually, without a teacher's recommending it, boys don't tend to pick it up to read off the shelves, probably because of the girl protagonist pictured on the cover.

The predictable structure of the text in this book lends great support to readers who are not yet confident. Every few pages describes one year's birthday. The descriptions all begin, "On your first [or second or third, etc.] one," and all end "Happy birthday." In the middle, there is always a description of the cake, and of what the little girl and the parents did. Only near the very end of the book does the pattern vary. Instead of a sixth birthday, there is a part beginning "Before your sixth birthday" and containing a description of all the things the little girl did to make other people's birthdays, and lives, special.

Some children find this book hysterically funny. They laugh at the baby's screaming and spitting up, the young child's refusal to share and the chocolate-covered faces of the older child and her friends. These readers seem to enjoy imagining all the shapes a birthday cake can take and the presents and festivities of the party. Because the book is fairly simple, and very enjoyable, it may be one to keep in mind for the indifferent reader who usually puts everything aside. Of course, a book is always more fun with two readers, so a partnership might also be in order here.

Teaching Ideas

The book lends itself easily to making personal connections. Kids often find themselves comparing what their guardians have told them about their own babyhoods to the little girl's story. Despite this it may not be the easiest book for teachers to use as a starting point to help children make deeper personal connections. There aren't many behaviors in the book that lend themselves to questions about motivations or emotional conflicts that would be fleshed out by personal response. Perhaps this book is best used to get personal response started in an unthreatening way for children who are having trouble vocalizing or writing their reactions.

This story has an unusual narrative voice in that it is told from a second person plural, or "We," point of view. When children are making decisions about which point of view to employ in their own writing, it may be handy to have this book around as a model of this perspective.

The first page may be the hardest of the book. For one thing, the pattern hasn't been established yet, and the reader doesn't know which way the text will go. Next, the writer uses, "little piggies on your hands and feet" to mean fingers and toes. To the literal-minded child or the child not versed in nursery rhymes, this may pose a problem. An early reader might not think that it is normal for a baby to cry, and that reader might startle at the thought that the baby "screamed" upon hearing that her parents loved her. The page ends with the words, "We promised you more...," which can leave the reader wondering, "More what? love? screaming? birthdays?" Of course the answer is birthdays, but the thought process needed to get there might not be a smooth one for the reader. If this book is in the hands of a struggling reader, the teacher or the partner might be better off reading (and perhaps talking through) the first page and then letting the reader get started on the next pages.

Book Connections

Other memoirs structured in this year-by-year fashion are: *When I Was Little* by Jamie Lee Curtis, and *Another Important Book* by Margaret Wise Brown. These books, too, recall one small thing at a time from early childhood, and can all serve as examples for children trying to write memoir.

Of course, Cynthia Rylant has written many, many memoirs and other books for children (see Basic Book Information), a few of which could be paired with this one for an author study.

Genre

Memoir; Picture Book

Teaching Uses

Independent Reading; Read Aloud; Teaching Writing

Birthday Surprises

Various, Edited by Johanna Hurwitz

FIELD GUIDE

E G

Book Summary

This is a collection of short stories, written by noted children's authors and centering on the theme of receiving an empty box as a present. Each author has taken the idea of the empty box and fashioned a unique story. Writers include Jane Yolen, Richard Peck, James Howe, Karla Kuskin, Ann M. Martin, and David Adler.

Publisher
Morrow Junior Books, 1995

ISBN
0688131948

TC Level
12

Basic Book Information

This is a collection of short stories, ranging in length from ten to fifteen pages. The stories explore the nature of family relationships, friendships, hope, and humor.

All proceeds of this book are generously donated to the Teachers College Reading and Writing Project at Columbia University and to the National Writing Project of the University of California, Berkeley.

Noteworthy Features

At the end of the book there is a selected bibliography of the authors and their works. This information encourages readers to pursue other writing of authors they like. There is also a letter to the reader from Johanna Hurwitz, who has contributed to, as well as edited,this collection. It is interesting to know that these stories were contracted, and not just collected over time. This was a project that Hurwitz conceived of, prompting writers with a theme and seeing what would happen. This is an example of how prompts can work in writing, especially for authors who are experienced at finding their own topic out of their lives. Giving a prompt like this to students may be less advisable.

Teaching Ideas

Birthday Surprises can be used for a study of interpretation. In each story, all of the story elements (plot, character, setting) combine with an empty box to create the story. All of these stories have a major piece that is the same, and yet there are many other pieces that are different.

There is one story, "What the Princess Discarded," by Barbara Ann Porte that has a fairy tale structure. However, the story ends abruptly, with a change in tone of the narrator. Until this part, the narrator had kept a distance from the story, telling it as the third person omniscient (all-knowing) narrator, with an impartial stance. At the very end, the story reads, "And that's a true story." This brings the narrator front and center to the reader as well as unveiling the fairy tale as really a true story. This shift can create some difficulty. Yet none of this was done accidentally, and readers will want to muse over how this form supports the author's meaning. How does the last line in the story change everything that has gone before it? Readers should be encouraged to re-read this story (and others) to see if the subsequent read is different than the first. And if so, how?

Birthday Surprises can also serve as an introduction to some children's authors that are unfamiliar to readers as well as the genre of story collections. The stories are short, and yet provide a rich introduction to the author and his or her style. Some teachers have even used these stories as advertisements for these authors, reading them one at a time between other Read Alouds, to whet the appetite of curious readers.

Short texts such as those in this book are also treasures when we want to teach children to talk, think, and write well about a text. Short stories like these are also perfect to use when the teacher wants to model use of a particular writing tool (like a highlighter) or strategy (like marking the most interesting parts for a discussion).

With permission, teachers can duplicate one of these stories and ask children to read it in preparation for a book talk. Perhaps the talk begins with, "So what are some of the ideas you developed while reading this story?" but after laying out an array of possibilities, the class will probably agree upon a focus for their discussion. The great thing about a short story is that students can re-read it, marking it up, so as to be prepared for a talk which deepens a shared, agreed upon focus.

This book is a treasure chest of short texts, each of which can be used in some depth to demonstrate strategies good readers use when they read. Short stories are precious teaching tools because they allow teachers and children to hold themselves accountable to more of the text. When a child has read a novel, that child can usually say quite a few things about the story and there is *always* so much that by definition *must* be left unsaid that it's hard for a teacher to really see what children delete from their accounts. But when children read a short story that teachers know well, it's much easier to get an accurate glimpse of what any particular reader sees and overlooks in a text. If, for example, a child misses the motivation for the central action, and has no sense of how much time passed over the course of a story, this tends to show up when a teacher and child discuss the story together.

Book Connections

Johanna Hurwitz, the overall editor of this book, is famous for her *Russell* series, as well as many other older books for upper grade readers. Ann M. Martin has written the *Babysitter's Club* as well as the *California Diaries* series that many adolescent readers love. Pam Conrad has written *My Daniel* and *Holding Me Here*. Richard Peck has written many books, most notably the *Soup* series and a follow-up book, *Blossom Culp and the Sleep of Death*. David Adler is the author of the *Cam Jansen* series and the *Andy Russell* books. James Howe may be best known for his *Bunnicula* series. Karla Kuskin is mostly known as a poet and a picture book writer.

Genre

Short Story Anthology

Teaching Uses

Whole Group Instruction; Interpretation; Small Group Strategy Instruction

Cam Jansen and the Mystery of the Dinosaur Bones

FIELD GUIDE

E

David Adler

Series
Cam Jansen

Illustrator
Susanna Natti

Publisher
The Viking Press, 1981

ISBN
0590461230

TC Level
8

Book Summary

Cam Jansen and the Mystery of the Dinosaur Bones is about a fifth-grade detective with a photographic memory. (Cam is short for "the camera," a nickname she got because of this skill.) On a field trip to a natural history museum, Cam discovers that there are three missing bones from the skeleton model of the Coelophysis dinosaur. She tries to alert various adults, all of whom appear strangely unconcerned. She returns with her friend, Eric, to the museum, and the two get suspicious when they see a truck delivering milk to the museum in the middle of the day. Cam also notices that the name of the milk truck is different than the brand she was served at the museum that day. Cam and Eric follow the "milkman" and find him-along with the museum guide from their trip-with a garage full of stolen dinosaur bones. After being trapped with the thieves in the garage, they quickly think of a scheme involving dog whistles and Cam's photographic memory to escape their captors and alert the museum director.

Basic Book Information

Cam Jansen and the Mystery of the Dinosaur Bones is 57 pages long with 9 chapters. The chapters are untitled. There are one or two black-and-white illustrations per chapter. The illustrations are not always on the same page as the corresponding text, and often match only a small detail of the content. The text has from four to six short paragraphs per page. There is quite a bit of dialogue throughout the book. The dialogue is usually referenced, but the references are often embedded in the sentence, or at the beginning or end of a long string of several sentences. This book is part of a series that generally includes the same characters each time. The text, the mystery and the way in which Cam and her friends go about solving the case are also consistent from book to book.

Noteworthy Features

There are two features of this book (as well as other *Cam Jansen* books) that are essential to the plot: Cam's photographic memory and the mystery genre itself. These two features demand that certain parts of the story be filled with details. For example, on pages 30-31, the text reads:

"A sign painted on the side of the truck said 'Beth's Milk Tastes Best.'

'That's strange,' Cam said. 'Milk is usually delivered early in the morning, not late in the afternoon.'

A man in a white uniform got out of the truck. He was carrying an empty milk box.

'Maybe some of the milk went bad,' Eric said, 'and he's picking it up.'

The milkman knocked on the garage door. The door opened and he went inside. He came out a few minutes later, carrying a large brown bag in the box. He put it in the truck.

'There's probably containers of sour milk in that bag,' Eric said.

Cam and Eric heard the door on the other side of the truck open and someone get inside, but they couldn't see who it was. Then the truck backed up. As the truck passed them, Cam read the sign again... 'The museum doesn't use Beth's milk. It uses Edna's,' Cam said."

The details are included by the author for Cam to memorize, so that she can later use her photographic memory to recall them and to help her solve the mystery. The inclusion of many details is also an integral part of all mystery stories. Readers need to be aware of all the details so that they may begin to solve the mystery on their own. It is up to the reader to figure out which details are significant and which are not. And, of course, the multitude of details lend themselves to the fun of being "stumped" as the mystery unfolds. Although these details are essential to the mystery, they can also be difficult for many readers-especially those who are unfamiliar with the mystery/detective genre-to hold onto as they read.

There are several quick setting changes throughout the story. The mystery begins in a cafeteria of a natural history museum and continues to lead Cam and Eric through the museum lobby, the Air Travel room, a weather station and a dinosaur exhibit. These and other settings are well defined in the text. But they come very quickly and are likely to create challenges for readers at this level.

There are a few minor, but important characters in the story. The museum director, the "milkman" and the museum guide, Janet, are all crucial characters in the story. They do not play big roles, but their roles are important to recognize and understand in order to follow the mystery and have full comprehension of the story.

The text in *Cam Jansen and the Mystery of the Dinosaur Bones* is not written with difficult vocabulary or concepts. Yet it can appear easier than it is. Because it is a mystery, there are several elements that are crucial for readers to notice, such as plot twists, people wearing disguises, people lying and small but significant details.

There are many dinosaur names, which are often spelled out phonetically by the teacher (such as, Coelophysis, spelled out as "Seel-o-fy-sis") and many museum-related terms (such as plaster of Paris) that may be difficult for readers to decode or may be unfamiliar to many readers.

Teaching Ideas

Cam Jansen and the Mystery of the Dinosaur Bones, like all of the books in the *Cam Jansen* series, is a good book for readers as a class, in partnerships or independently, who are beginning a study of, or who already enjoy, the genre of mystery/detective books. Teachers may use this book as a read aloud to model good reading behaviors that are specific to the genre. In introducing the book a teacher may say: "*Cam Jansen and the Mystery of the Dinosaur Bones* is about a girl named Cam who is trying to solve a mystery with her friend Eric. On a trip to a dinosaur museum, Cam notices that one of the skeletons is missing some bones. She tries to tell the museum guide and the museum director but no one believes her. Later, she notices a milkman making a strange delivery. She gets very curious and starts to try to figure out the answers to all the questions she is beginning to have. While I am reading today, try to notice all the things that 'just don't seem to make sense' to you. Remember those things, because that's how a detective begins to solve a case."

This is also a good book for partner and independent reading for the reader who is beginning to read longer, more detailed and more complexly structured books. This book can be used to teach readers how to: look for clues in the text, gather lists of "evidence," notice how the author tries to throw the reader off track, ask and answer questions about the case, and figure out what is important to the story. Readers may use Post-its to mark examples of these things. They can jot down little notes to themselves on Post-its as to what they're thinking, noticing and wondering about the case. They can discuss their observations with other readers, make predictions, reread to find places where they may have missed a clue, and write lists of clues and predictions to share with other readers.

As readers become more familiar with the mystery/detective genre, they may like to do a comparison "across series" and explore ways in which the *Cam Jansen* series is like other mystery books they've read or heard. They can look for, discuss and write about the things that seem universal in all mystery/detective stories, how the detective stories are alike in their methods, what literary devices the authors use consistently and how they differ.

Book Connections

There are many other titles in the *Cam Jansen* series. Some of these titles include: *Cam Jansen and the Chocolate Fudge Mystery*, *Cam Jansen and the Mystery of Flight 54*, *Cam Jansen and the Mystery of the Stolen Diamonds* and *Cam Jansen and the Mystery of the Babe Ruth Baseball.* Other mystery series that are slightly more difficult include: *A to Z Mysteries*, the *Magic Tree House* series, and the *Polka Dot Private Eye* series. Mystery series at a slightly easier level include: the *Young Cam Jansen* series and the *Nate the Great* series.

Genre

Mystery; Short Chapter Book

Teaching Uses

Independent Reading; Partnerships

Chicken Sunday

Read Aloud

Patricia Polacco

FIELD GUIDE

E

Illustrator
Patricia Polacco

Publisher
Philomel Books, 1992

ISBN
0698116151

Book Summary

Three youngsters in a Southern community want to buy an elegant hat for Miss Eula Mae Walker. Two of the children are Miss Eula's grandsons. The third child, a little girl, also loves Miss Eula. This child, who is white, is the one telling the story. Looking for a way to earn money, the children go to Mr. Kodinski's hat shop, hoping to sweep his floor. Instead, Mr. Kodinski mistakes them for the vandals who have just thrown eggs at his back door. When Miss Eula finds out, she tells the children they need to prove to Mr. Kodinski that they are good people. That's when the narrator of the story suggests that they color eggs pysanky style, the way her "bubbie" taught her. Touched by their kindness, Mr. Kodinski suggests that the children make more decorated eggs to sell in his shop. The children earn enough money to buy the hat. To their surprise, he gives it to them-a gift for Miss Eula.

Basic Book Information

This 32-page picture book is illustrated by the author. Each two-page spread contains a large, full-color illustration and a block of text. The story is recounted in the first person by an adult remembering an incident from her childhood. A few words in the text may be unfamiliar to most children-"babushka," "pysanky," "chutzpah." The personal quality of the narrative voice also makes the book a marvelous read aloud. The brightly colored illustrations feature animated characters in detailed, realistic settings. The author notes that a local Baptist church provided her with paper fans, hymnals, and choir robes as models for the scenes that take place at church. In Miss Eula's house, family photos-real photographs, not drawings-occupy every available space. The walls of the narrator's house hold Russian icons, and a tea samovar is visible.

Noteworthy Features

The illustrations bear Patricia Polacco's unique style. Her characters are gently humorous, yet given great dignity. The title *Chicken Sunday* refers to the delicious chicken dinners Miss Eula prepared every Sunday, which the children, grown up by the end of the book, commemorate every year by visiting her burial place and symbolically pouring chicken soup over her gravestone.

Because Patricia Polacco is both writer and illustrator she has more control of the images that readers see and take away from her books. Her books are each designed to put the reader into the setting of the story and to create a mood that will accompany the text. The pictures in this book are drawn, but on many pages the illustrations include actual photographs from her life placed in appropriate places (such as the photos on the china cabinet in Miss Eula's dining room She also tells some parts of this story only through pictures. For example, it is never said in the text what Mr. Kodinski's troubles are, but a careful study of both pictures and words in this book leads a reader to identify tiny numbers printed on his arm. These numbers can explain his past.

Teaching Ideas

Patricia Polacco is at her best in this classic memoir. From word one to the end, *Chicken Sunday* is a rich example of her classic storyteller style.

This book contains all of the traditional story elements-characters, setting, plot, change, movement through time, setting-as do all of Patricia Polacco's books. She prides herself at being a storyteller, not a craftsperson. In fact, some teachers use this book to teach the elements of story. All stories must move through time. They must give the reader that "What happens next?" feeling. Many young writers find it challenging to grasp the techniques for making stories move though time, and this is a hallmark of all of Polacco's books. She uses dialogue, time words and a clear accounting of an event to help readers move through the story. Many teachers have used this text when they are trying to get students to tell their stories orally in a clear fashion before beginning to write those stories. This is also an excellent book for helping students learn to retell another person's story well. It can also be used to teach writers the power of shrinking and stretching time, of writing so that some moments are summarized in passing and others unroll in great detail. Not every event in this book is given equal attention.

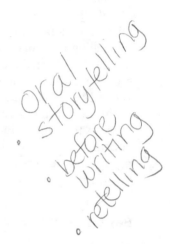

Many teachers use *Chicken Sunday* to demonstrate the different ways a story can begin. Some teachers and children name the type of beginning in this text as an "always/one day" beginning. In a mini-lesson, a teacher could show an overhead of just pages one and two, and ask students to read along as the text is read aloud. The teacher could comment on the list-like nature of the beginning and help students see that here Polacco is talking about what she, Winston and Stewart do all the time. This early part of the text is not set in a particular time, but is instead about always. It fills up the reader with valuable information about the characters.

Paragraph six begins, "One Sunday..." This marks the end of the "always" part and puts the reader into the story that the author is going to tell in this text. Some teachers name this the "one day" part. Children benefit from seeing that Polacco could have chosen any story of her adventures with Winston and Stewart, but has chosen this one as significant. Many teachers rewrite this part of the story including names of the characters to show that Polacco could have started her story right here. Everything in the book from this point on is about this event.

After demonstrating how to write a beginning like Polacco, teachers could ask students to look in their writing notebooks for entries that are either "one day" entries or "always" entries. The teacher could ask students to then get additional pages of paper, and to staple a new paper onto an "always" entry, trying to juxtapose this with a "one day" entry (and vice versa). Students might be encouraged to internalize this strategy and to use it often in future drafts.

Looking at just the first page of this book, the "always" part, teachers might nudge students to pay attention to the details of Polacco's list. Every word seems carefully chosen and does a job. Many students write list books and write other texts that are structured as lists, but they use generalities. The specificity (or smallness) of the items on Polacco's list make the writing powerful. In five paragraphs, she reveals her entire relationship with two friends and their grandmother. She makes their grandmother into a character quickly by including the details taken from one moment in their lives and placing it as an example in the always list ("Even though we been churchin' up like decent folks ought to..."). Readers remember and fall in love with Miss Eula because of the significant details given in this little bit of text, and because of the words used to describe her. "She had a voice like slow thunder and sweet rain" is a line that is remembered by all who read the book. The phrase only appears in the text on three pages, and many students comment that Polacco could have used this more often, as a repeating refrain, had she chosen to write in such a structure. As it is, repetition of the phrase pulls the text together. Teachers could ask students to go back to the "always parts" of their own writing and add significant details that will help readers learn about their characters. They may add tiny little observations that shape the characters they are writing about.

Teachers might also use this book to teach significant qualities of memoir. In many memoirs, there is a connection between the beginning and the ending of the text. In fact, in most well written memoirs, readers can read the beginning and the ending together and it should feel complete (even when the entire middle of the story has been left out). In this text, everything before the "One Sunday" can be regarded as the beginning; the ending probably begins on the very last page ("Winston, Stewart, and I are grown up now. Our old...."). These two sections of the text fit together like one complete text. Some teachers include this beginning and ending on a sheet of beginnings and endings. After reading and demonstrating how to connect the beginning and the ending of this memoir, some teachers have asked students to write the beginning of their own memoirs at the top of one sheet of draft paper and on another sheet, to write the ending. They can do this even before writing the middle of their memoirs.

Good stories have dialogue. This story is filled with dialogue that does a job. It helps the reader learn more about the characters and it moves the action of the story; teachers can use this book to teach both skills. There are also several places where Polacco has chosen to use various dialects so readers hear the true voices of the characters. This adds dimension and particularity to them.

Polacco uses words in unusual ways that help the reader see more clearly what she is seeing as she writes. It's challenging and fun for students to try some of the things she has done here, such as writing metaphorically, with phrases like "chicken-fried air."

Genre

Picture Book; Memoir

Teaching Uses

Teaching Writing; Read Aloud; Independent Reading; Partnerships

Childtimes, A Three-Generation Memoir

Eloise Greenfield; Lessie Jones Little

FIELD GUIDE

E F

Book Summary

This three-generation memoir, beginning in the 1880s and ending around 1950, revolves around the childhood memories of three Black women: Pattie Frances Ridley Jones, Lessie Blanche Jones Little and Eloise Glynn Little Greenfield. A preface for the book entitled "Landscape" tells how people are a part of their time, shaped by big and small things that happen in their worlds, such as a war, an invention like radio or television, a birthday party or a kiss. Subsequent chapters also begin with a "landscape" section, which gives an overview of the world each woman was living in at the time. Readers then follow the family through three generations, with each woman recounting the memories that most strongly affected her.

Pattie's section, for example, notes that the 1880s were a time of westward movement for the United States. But they were also a time of disappointment for many Black people in the post-slavery South. Wages for Black workers were low; jobs were hard to come by; Black schools and homes were burned; and people were dragged from their homes and murdered by the Ku Klux Klan. Pattie's family plants sweet potatoes and butter beans. They sweep their dirt yard every day, and Pattie and her sister, Mary, do all the cooking and ironing. Memories include picking mulberries, candy-pulling parties, reading and memorizing poems, and playing Sunday School with her little sisters. Pattie's story tells of a hard life of strenuous work, but one filled with good times, too.

Pattie's daughter, Lessie, lives in happier times. Her "landscape" section describes the bright beginning of the twentieth century, which brought the advent of the airplane, telephones and the automobile. Black people, looking for ways to end racism, had begun to demand rights, such as education for their children. Lessie describes herself as always singing at the top of her voice, jumping rope or running so fast she thinks her feet wouldn't touch the ground. Her days are filled with playing dolls and paper dolls, school, hide-and-go-seek and jacks. However, her father has trouble finding work, and even when he does, the pay is scarcely enough to buy what the family needs. Often Lessie is so hungry it is hard to play because of the pulling feeling inside her stomach. She has strong, fond memories of her parents. Her mama, a waitress at the local café, teaches the children how to draw and make rag dolls. She sits the children in chairs around her to tell them stories, read to them or recite poems. Papa is a quiet man who likes to read and study his Bible. He calls his children his "little duckies" and is the first one up on frigid winter mornings to build a roaring fire in the two stoves. One of Lessie's fondest memories is of school. They are proud of their school with its radiators and wide desks, and when Lessie graduates from high school, she receives a pin for having the best grades.

Publisher
HarperCollins Publishers
(Harper Trophy), 1979

ISBN
0064461343

TC Level
12

The third section of the book involves Lessie's daughter, the famous writer Eloise. She, too, was born in Parmele, North Carolina, right before the Great Depression, but her family soon moved to Washington, D.C., so her father could find work. But they often returned to Parmele, where their granny would make apple jelly and green tomato pickles, and their grandfather would entertain them with ghost stories. Eloise's fondest memories of her childhood are from Langston Terrace, the low-rent housing project where her family lives. With the playground in front of her house and a library within walking distance, Eloise is happy. She and her friends play hide-and-seek, paddle tennis, shuffleboard, dodge ball and jacks. They jump rope, have parties and take bus trips to the beach. For Eloise, Langston Terrace is a good growing-up place. Her happy memories include vendors coming through selling apples, fish and fruit-flavored snowballs. The organ grinder comes, too, his monkey on his shoulder, and the photographer, taking pictures of children sitting on his pony. And yet, behind the good times, linger traces of segregation. Eloise and her Black friends can't sit down at the drugstore soda fountains. The schools are segregated. The ads for the best jobs say, "White Only." But people still work together for Black freedom. "There was always, in my Washington, a sense of people trying to make things better."

Basic Book Information

Each part of this 176-page story is broken into vignettes with self-explanatory titles, such as, "Chores," "School," "Getting Baptized," "Spanish Flu," "Candy" and "Horses and Cows." The vocabulary and sentence structure are fairly simple as the stories are told in a conversational manner. A black-and-white photograph of each of the three women is included at the beginning of her section. There are also six pages of black-and-white photographs of other family members. At the beginning of each section is a sketch of where the person lived. Also, at the beginning of the book is a family tree. Although the book pretty much proceeds in chronological fashion, within each section the author may jump around a little in her memories.

Eloise Greenfield has received a citation from the Council on Interracial Books for Children in recognition of her "outstanding and exemplary contribution to children's literature." Lessie Jones Little's first book, *I Can Do It By Myself*, also a collaboration with Eloise Greenfield, was named a Notable Children's Trade Book in Social Studies by the National Council for the Social Studies/Children's Book Council Joint Committee.

Noteworthy Features

Each section of this lyrical memoir is told in the first person. Indeed, each voice is so strong that the readers feel as if they are sitting around a fire, while the author spins out her tale. In spite of hard times, these women are humorous. They use the dialect of Black people of their time, and place, which adds to the flavor of the stories and is never hard to understand.

Teaching Ideas

This book is a staple in classrooms in which children are invited to draft, revise and publish the stories of their lives. To do this well, children need models, and the short vignettes in *Childtimes* make this one of a small handful of texts that is regarded by many teachers as absolutely essential in a writing workshop. Teachers have found countless ways to use particular excerpts of *Childtimes*. "The Play," for example, has been used by many teachers as part of a lesson on the elements of story. "All stories have plot, character, setting, movement through time, and a change that is central to the plot and the characters," teachers have told children, and then they've asked children to listen to a reading of "The Play" and to later retell it, weaving together all the story elements. In "The Play," the passage of time needs to be inferred, and teachers remind children to draw on all they know about school plays in order to speculate how much time passed between the first rehearsal and the performance. Later, teachers have told children that when they read stories, it can help to keep an eye out for these elements of story. "You should be able to retell the stories you read, weaving together a mention of these elements."

The excerpt, "Mama Sewing" is another favorite. Children have spent many days noticing the features of this text and inferring the features of a memoir from it.

Every teacher who owns this book will go to it often, as one might go to an attic treasure chest, confident that each time it's opened, new treasures will be found.

Book Connections

Students may enjoy reading more books by Eloise Greenfield, such as *Africa Dream*, *Me and Neesie*, *Talk About a Family*, *Under the Sunday Tree*, or *I Can Do It By Myself* by Eloise Greenfield and Lessie Jones Little.

This book is a memoir, and its structure resembles a favorite memoir-like novel, Sandra Cisneros' *The House on Mango Street*, which is another favorite teacher resource for writing workshops.

Genre
Memoir; Chapter Book

Teaching Uses
Author Study; Teaching Writing; Read Aloud; Partnerships

Chocolate Fever

Robert Kimmel Smith

FIELD GUIDE

E

Illustrator
Gioia Fiammenghi

Publisher
Dell Publishing, Inc., 1972

ISBN
0440413699

TC Level
10

Book Summary

This delightful book is about Henry Green, a boy who eats chocolate morning, noon and night. Henry is the chocoholic of all chocoholics. A usual breakfast for Henry is chocolate cake, a bowl of chocolate cereal and milk (with chocolate syrup in the milk to make it more chocolatey), washed down by a big glass of chocolate milk and five or six chocolate cookies. While Henry never gets fat or develops a cavity, he soon learns that there can be "too much of a good thing": he develops a very rare case of Chocolate Fever.

Soon, Henry is the focus of a team of physicians who want to see this rare disease firsthand. Their unwelcome attention drives Henry to run away from the hospital with a team of doctors trailing behind him. On the streets, Henry learns just how cruel people can be when you have chocolate spots all over you.

After running away from a group of boys who torment him, he hitchhikes with Mac, a Black truck driver who is no stranger to discrimination. Mac is the first person who looks past his chocolate spots and sees Henry for himself. The camaraderie they develop helps them escape from a group of crooks who try to hijack the candy-filled truck, thinking it is filled with furs. When they escape, Mac introduces Henry to his kind boss, the first person ever to be diagnosed with Chocolate Fever. He gives Henry the antidote to Chocolate Fever-vanilla, of course. Soon, Henry is reunited with his family. The cured Henry declines chocolate for the first time in his life, wondering, "Could you ever have too much cinnamon?"

Basic Book Information

Chocolate Fever is 93 pages long. The book contains 12 chapters, each with an interesting title that clues the reader into what it will be about such as "Meet Henry Green" and "Hijacked." These chapters are outlined in the Table of Contents at the start of the book. Fiammenghi's black-and-white illustrations appear every four or five pages of text.

Noteworthy Features

The chapters are not episodic, stand-alone chapters, so readers must retain the developing plot for the duration of the book. This may be difficult for new readers of chapter books. Fiammenghi's illustrations, however, provide good picture support to the story. The detailed illustrations are well matched to the text that appears on the same or opposite pages. In addition, the chapter titles help the reader to stay focused on the developing story by supporting the section's plot.

The book follows Henry's bout with Chocolate Fever over the course of a weekend. The story moves in chronological order and all jumps in time are noted, (e.g., "It was almost two hours later now"). The book contains a lot of unreferenced dialogue that may be somewhat confusing. Though the narration is done in the third person, the narrator does explore Henry's thoughts.

The cover, which is characteristic of 70s artwork and a little dated, may discourage some readers, but once children get past the cover, they will find the book entertaining. Kimmel Smith incorporates a certain "grossness" in his book that appeals to many children. For instance, Henry is finally rescued from the hijackers when a group of dogs smell his chocolate spots: "Henry, of course, was the star attraction for the animal army. They were licking him as if he were some sort of new dog yummy."

Teaching Ideas

The New York Times called this book, "A pleasantly unpreachy cautionary tale." The book treads the serious issues of excess, racism, illness and the stigma of disease, in a lighthearted way. Teachers may find the book a good introduction to whole-group discussions on these serious issues. Or students may simply focus on the line, "Although life is grand and pleasure is everywhere, we can't have everything we want every time we want it."

This book can be read independently or in book partnerships. Children may want to explore the motives behind the meanness of the children in the schoolyard. Did they fear that they would get the disease? Were they mean to him because he was different than them? Were they just plain mean?

It also may be interesting to compare and contrast how the group of boys treats Henry as opposed to how Mac treats Henry. Children can look for evidence in the text and attach Post-its to pages that support their ideas.

To support readers, teachers may want to discuss how the dialogue and inner thoughts of the characters are represented. All of Henry's inner thoughts are in italics and everything he says is in quotations. When the character exclaims, both quotations marks and italics are used ("*Candy bars*").

It may be interesting for readers to mark with Post-its the times when Henry has inner thoughts, and discuss with a partner why he talks to himself at these specific times. They may conclude that when Henry is hungry, afraid or needs to make sense of something, his inner thoughts emerge. For instance, when Mac picks him up from the side of the road after no one else will, Henry's inner dialogue takes over as he struggles to figure out why Mac isn't afraid of him.

Retelling may be helpful so that children can keep track of the plot, which develops at breakneck speed and includes an exciting chase scene, a hijacking scene and an escape scene.

Book Connections

Robert Kimmel Smith has written many widely read children's books, including *The War with Grandpa.*

A Field Guide to the Classroom Library, Lucy Calkins and the Teachers College Reading and Writing Project, Heinemann, ©2002 Teachers College, Columbia University; http://www.heinemann.com/fieldguides

Genre
Chapter Book

Teaching Uses
Independent Reading; Partnerships; Book Clubs

Class Clown*

Johanna Hurwitz

FIELD GUIDE

E

Publisher
Scholastic Little Apple, 1987

ISBN
0590418211

TC Level
9

Book Summary

Lucas just can't seem to do what he's supposed to do. The kids raise their hands, but he calls out. It's silent reading time, but he makes noises with his Velcro sneakers. His teacher, Mrs. Hockaday, thinks he's "obstreperous." Even when Lucas tries to do things right, he gets in trouble. But little by little, Lucas starts to realize it's more enjoyable to change his behavior than to keep annoying people.

Basic Book Information

Class Clown has 98 pages and eight chapters ranging in length from eight to 18 pages. Chapter titles focus readers' attention on the main event of the chapter: "Eyeglasses," and "Turning Over a New Leaf." There are 26 lines to a page. Sentences are mostly simple and compound. Pictures appear once in each chapter and sometimes illustrate events described in the text that may be difficult to visualize. The plot is chronological and spans a school year, except for one flashback.

Noteworthy Features

The setting is a suburban or small-town home and school. Although the school situations described may not match every reader's experience, children will probably have no trouble understanding it. The narrative moves in linear time, with one flashback on pp. 47-48. The third-person narration includes Lucas thoughts.

This is not a book for beginning chapter book readers. There is a lot of challenging vocabulary, and most difficult words do not have context clues to help. If readers are following Lucas' changes, they have to read carefully. Readers may have to infer or pick up on a meaningful situation or change that is mentioned only briefly or indirectly. Most readers will still enjoy the book even if they don't catch everything, but less sophisticated readers may miss out and not understand some situations or changes.

Teaching Ideas

In guided reading groups, it may be useful to point out some of the more difficult vocabulary words and to demonstrate various strategies for figuring out their meaning.

In partnerships or reading clubs, students may come up with a question like, "Are Lucas antics funny?" This might be an interesting question for readers to debate. Students do not always agree. Younger readers might want to mark funny parts with a Post-it and discuss why they feel these sections are funny.

If more sophisticated students are following the character's changes and digging for motivation, they may notice that a gradual metamorphosis occurs over the whole school year, with one important event in each chapter. Chapters 1 and 2 have Lucas distracting the class and wasting the nurse's time, without seeming to care. In Chapter 3 he tries to behave to please his mother, but impulsively overdoes it (brings a whole bag instead of a few leaves) and makes a mess. In Chapter 4 he begins to get small emotional rewards for not disrupting, and discovers that he is actually interested in the work he formerly avoided. He is moved by the teacher's expression of caring about him when she thinks he is sick. In the barbershop (Chapter 5), he is complimented when he helps the barber and feels good about himself. Chapter 6 has Lucas in trouble again, but this time he unintentionally gets his head stuck in a chair. When his former rival Cricket sticks up for him and asks the teacher not to punish him, Lucas realizes she is on his side. In Chapter 7, Lucas is upset to be assigned the clown role in the class circus show; by now he doesn't want to be identified as a clown. But when the ringmaster gets sick, Lucas is able to get the part he wanted, and he performs it well. The last chapter, at the end of the school year, shows Lucas firmly in the mainstream and winning the award for most improved conduct. Students can try to decide what the "big event" is in each chapter as they read. This can help them build a clearer picture of Lucas transformation.

The turning point for Lucas is not abrupt but begins in a small way in Chapter 3. Students might notice this shift when he really starts to care and try. They should be aware of the long time frame (10 months). They could use a T-chart to list changes and the change agents in each chapter.

The relationship between Lucas and Cricket changes as well. Students could track these changes and try to figure out why. There is a similar rivalry between a boy and girl character in *Tooter Pepperday* by Jerry Spinelli, and probably many other books. In *Tooter Pepperday*, the girl (Tooter) has been mistrustful and tries to take revenge on Jack, who has been kind and helpful. Their relationship changes at the end. Comparing these books could be a good way for older students to think about relationships between characters.

Book Connections

Books similar in difficulty, although longer, are the *Ramona* series by Beverly Cleary and the *Babysitters Club* series by Ann Martin. Similar books by Johanna Hurwitz, such as *Teacher's Pet*, *School's Out* and *Spring Break* feature the same characters. The *Aldo* series by this author is also similar. This book is more difficult than the Russell series, also by Hurwitz, as well as the *Littles* series by Peterson and *Zack Files* by Greenburg. Readers could follow up with the *Bunnicula* series by James Howe and the *Time Warp Trio* series by Jon Scieszka. Note: Although one of the reviews quoted on the back cover reads: "... a fine choice for children just beginning chapter books," this book is by no means appropriate for beginners.

Genre

Chapter Book

Teaching Uses
Independent Reading; Character Study; Small Group Strategy Instruction

Conestoga Wagons

Richard Ammon

FIELD GUIDE

E G

Book Summary

Conestoga wagons were the tractor-trailers of colonial America. Built in Lancaster County, Pennsylvania, they were named after the Conestoga Valley, which lies in the heart of Pennsylvania Dutch country. These sturdy wagons transported goods from state to state between 1750 and 1850.

Basic Book Information

Bill Farnsworth depicts these massive wagons and the historical period they thrived in through beautiful paintings that both support and enhance the text (e.g., An enlarged painting of a wheel lies on the page opposite the one where the wheels are described). A map of Pennsylvania and its surrounding states is found at the beginning of the book. This helps children to see the routes the wagons traveled.

Noteworthy Features

The author helps the reader understand the colonial period by making comparisons to the familiar. He points out that these rugged wagons could haul up to 5 tons of supplies or as the author points out-"the weight of about 160 fourth graders." Horses, the author says, weigh 1800 pounds-or the same as 29 fourth graders. Richard Ammon states that Conestoga wagons were not built in factories as today's cars are, but were made by hand. The author does this throughout the book, which makes things more concrete for children and gives them a frame of reference.

The author describes how the teamsters would stop at taverns to rest. Whenever these men ordered beer, the innkeeper would keep a tab on a slate: P = pint; Q = quart. If the tab started to mount, the innkeeper would remind the wagoneers "to mind his P's and Q's." Ammon goes on to tell the reader that today this expression is a reminder to mind our manners. This example illustrates how the author, whenever possible, connects the past with the present to help the reader.

Conestoga Wagons is full of information about the massive wagons. A specific topic is addressed on each page or double pages. Some of the topics covered include: Conestoga wheels, Conestoga brakes, Conestoga features of horses, and teamsters. Surprisingly, there are no headings to tell the reader what he or she will be reading about. In addition, there is no index for easy reference for the reader who is interested in finding out specifically about any of the topics covered in the text. As mentioned, this is an informative text. It is not a book that takes the reader on a journey and does not necessarily have to be read from beginning to end. If the book had headings and/or and index, the reader would have the freedom to choose to read what interested him or her.

Illustrator
Bill Farnsworth

Publisher
Holiday House, 2000

ISBN
0823414752

TC Level
9; 10; 11

Teaching Ideas

This informative text describes the Conestoga wagons and the vital role they played in American history. Obviously, it can be used for researching transportation during the colonial period. Additionally, the text generates questions that can lead to an inquiry into colonial ports, colonial craftsmen, American locomotives, or the Pennsylvania Dutch country.

If students have been reading other Nonfiction books which have sub-headings that tell them how the text can be divided into sections and what the key concept in each section is, it would be interesting for them to notice that this book lacks sub-headings and to see if they could read, using captioned post-it notes to create their own sub-headings. This, of course would take students one step toward learning to take notes. If a teacher wanted to go a few steps farther with teaching students to take notes, he or she could suggest that students record their sub-headings on paper, and then jot down some of the main things the author wants them to know that fit under these sub-headings. Then, in order for students to understand the purpose for note-taking, it would be important to ask students to use their notes as a scaffold while they retell what they've read to a partner.

Of course, the system just described for taking notes assumes that students are trying to use their notes to outline and eventually reconstruct the main gist of what they have read. This sort of outlining should not be an every day practice for readers of Nonfiction, but when a text seems especially interesting as this one is, this sort of outlining will help readers "hold onto a text" and will meanwhile teach them to pay attention to the structure of a Nonfiction text and to the author's main ideas.

Book Connections

Other books that relate to Westward Expansion include: The Coyote Bead *(Hausman) and* Adaline Falling Star *(Osbourne).*

Genre

Nonfiction

Teaching Uses

Reading and Writing Nonfiction; Content Area Study

Crash

Jerry Spinelli

FIELD GUIDE

E G

Publisher
Alfred A. Knopf, Inc., 1996

ISBN
0679879579

Book Summary

This book is about a seventh grader named John Patrick Coogan, nicknamed "Crash." The story is of how Crash lives up to his nickname and then how he undergoes change. Crash lives in Pennsylvania with his mother, father, and younger sister, Abby. The story begins with Crash looking back seven years when he first encountered a new neighbor named Penn Webb. Crash learns that Penn's family is Quaker, vegetarians, and live in a small garage-like house. This gives Crash reason to tease Penn unmercifully. Despite Crash's teasing, Penn remains friendly and good-natured. But, Crash continuously rejects Penn's attempt at friendship. At the beginning of sixth grade, Crash meets a new boy named Mike Deluca. They find that they have a lot in common. Crash and Mike play many pranks on Penn.

Crash experiences disappointment when his parents don't attend his football games or do many things as a family. Then, Crash's much-loved grandfather, Scooter, comes to live with the Coogans. Now that Scooter has moved in, he attends Crash's games and is there when Crash breaks the school's touchdown record. Right before Christmas, Scooter suffers a stroke. This dramatic change in his family begins to cause change in Crash and his relationships. Crash also experiences a shift in his family dynamic as his mother cuts back her work to spend more time with the family. Crash then moves toward undoing two of Mike's nasty pranks on Penn. As time goes on, the name Crash doesn't seem to fit him anymore; he has changed.

The final change in Crash comes when he gives the ultimate gift-letting Penn win a race-off to qualify for the Penn Relays. The story ends with significant changes in the way Crash's life works. His final statement is "Penn Webb is my best friend."

Basic Book Information

The story is told in the first person narrative, from Crash's point of view.

Jerry Spinelli has written numerous young adult novels. In 1991, Spinelli won the Newbery Award for *Maniac Magee,* and in 1998, *Wringer* was named a Newbery Honor book. Whenever students ask him where he gets his ideas, he replies, "From you. You're the funny ones."

Noteworthy Features

The illustration on the cover of the book provides for a good talk. There are no other illustrations, but students tend to think hard about the cover illustration and how it could be different.

This book provides a good character study. It gives strong evidence for Crash's metamorphosis. The reader can track how Crash undergoes change as he moves through the story. One way is to follow his involvement with Penn from when they first meet to the book's closing that announces that they are best friends. Different situations that involve Penn have an impact on Crash. They allow the reader to see one of the ways that Crash's strange-bad feelings change to strange-good feelings, as they did when Crash sacrifices winning the race as a gift to Penn and his great-grandfather. Crash's behavior also changes as a result of Scooter's stroke, when he faces Scooter's survival and recovery.

Students should re-read any passages that contribute to the significant changes that Crash undergoes. They can talk and write about these passages and carry them over into texts where character study is also possible.

Teaching Ideas

Students can learn about Crash from the other characters in this story. The beginning of the book sees Crash living up to his nickname by not allowing anyone to stand in his way. Students can see how the different characters react to Crash. Readers can learn about Crash from his family members. Crash has strong feelings about his parents' commitment to their work and leaving little time for him. Seeing Crash and his relationship with his sister Abby and becoming part of her world is significant. Also seeing how Crash connects with Scooter is a noteworthy study. Students can relate this family dynamic with their own.

Crash can also be viewed by his relationship with his friend Mike and how he breaks away from things that had bonded them. Readers also get a glimpse of Crash and his interest in the new girl, Jane Forbes. An investigation into how Jane sees Crash as a person and then how things turn around with an invitation to her Fourth of July party is noteworthy.

Reading and writing about Penn's effect on Crash gives students a good grasp on what's going on inside of Crash. It becomes evident that Crash begins to see the things in his life that are most important. As the story unfolds around Crash, his shell begins to crack allowing him to see things in a different light.

The different ways in which the author tells the reader about Crash make this book an excellent choice for a character study.

Book Connections

Jerry Spinelli has written numerous books for young readers on various topics and of various levels. Most of them have young boys as the protagonists.

Genre
Chapter Book

Teaching Uses
Character Study

Day of the Dragon King

Mary Pope Osborne

FIELD GUIDE

E

Book Summary

In *Day of the Dragon King*, one book in the *Magic Tree House* series, Annie and Jack are called away to ancient China to save a lost story that the Dragon King is trying to burn. They learn that he is the first emperor and then are introduced to different clothing and people of this time. They learn about things that ancient China is well known for: silk, the Great Wall, books made out of bamboo, and an ancient tomb with hundreds of sculptures of soldiers.

All of the books in this series follow this same basic plot structure. The beginning of this book is very predictable and establishes the setting and plot line of the story. Jack and Annie (who are brother and sister) go to a magic tree house in their backyard, knowing it will take them to another time and place. They want a new assignment from Morgan le Fey, the owner of the magic tree house. Then they go on their adventure, learn new things about the particular time and place, and return home enlightened. In each adventure, they achieve their goal and return with notes and newfound knowledge from their journey.

Series
Magic Tree House

Illustrator
Sal Murdocca

Publisher
Random House, 1998

ISBN
0679890513

TC Level
8

Basic Book Information

Day of the Dragon King is 68 pages long. Most sentences are short and simple, and there is dialogue throughout. There are pictures on every third or fourth page that depict the setting and characters. There are 10 chapters that represent changes in scene and have descriptive titles that support the reader's comprehension.

This series should be read in order, perhaps in groups of four, due to the continuing plot lines. In books 1 through 4, Jack and Annie discover Morgan le Fey, the mysterious owner of the magic tree house. In books 5 through 8, Jack and Annie are linked together by their mission to help free Morgan le Fey from a spell. In 9 through 12, Jack and Annie solve four ancient riddles to become Master Librarians. In books 13 through 16, they are Master Librarians. And books 17 through 20 are linked together by Jack and Annie being given four gifts to help free a dog from a spell. *Day of the Dragon King* is number 14 in the series.

Noteworthy Features

The book is ideal for readers who have just recently become accustomed to longer chapter books. *Magic Tree House* books present an exciting adventure every time, which creates high interest. The book pushes the student to read on without stopping, so it stretches the reader's stamina. In addition, the settings are interesting and usually hold the reader's attention.

The dialogue used in this book is very simple and mostly comes from

Annie, Jack and another central figure who guides them through the new land. The speaker is always identified clearly so students are not confused.

Sources of difficulty lie in isolated vocabulary words (like "scholar" and "silk weaver") and references to the people and culture of ancient China, which will probably be unfamiliar to most kids.

Teaching Ideas

Because these characters remain the same throughout the series, students often become quite attached to them. They can be the subject of character studies-the kind of studies in which students swap information they have collected over the course of many books. However, the characters are mainly there to carry out the plot and are not the sources of deep psychological understandings.

Students may want to use this series to launch them into nonfiction studies of the times or places in the books. Sometimes groups like to read or reread a certain book in the series before they begin a social studies project on a linked topic.

Some teachers like to use these books as a bridge for readers reluctant to start nonfiction reading.

Book Connections

Day of the Dragon King is similar in difficulty to the *Ginger Brown* series by Sharon Dennis Wyeth and the *Marvin Redpost* series by Louis Sachar. *Pee Wee Scouts* (Judy Delton) and *Junie B. Jones* (Barbara Park) are good precursors to this series. *The Hit- Away Kid* by Matt Christopher and *The Bailey School Kids* series would be good follow-up books.

Mary Pope Osborne has written historic fiction for a wide range of levels. This means that she could become the subject of an author study, with readers of every level in the class reading one of her books.

Genre
Chapter Book

Teaching Uses
Independent Reading; Character Study; Book Clubs

December Secrets

Patricia Reilly Giff

FIELD GUIDE

E

Book Summary

December Secrets is #4 in the series known as *The Kids of the Polk Street School.* The main characters in the series are the 13 kids in Ms. Rooney's class: Alex, Timothy, Noah, Matthew, Derrick, Jill, Wayne, Linda, Sherri, Richard, Jason, Dawn and Emily. Each numbered book in the series takes place in a different month of the year; this story happens in December. Ms. Rooney tells the class that they will each choose a special "secret" person. They will spend the month of December doing special things for that person including: drawing pictures, doing favors and making gifts. At the end of the month they will each reveal who their secret person is. By the time Emily decides who she wants as her secret person, only "fat" Jill Simon (the "crybaby") is left. Emily decides that Jill will be happier if she is thinner and decides to give her gifts that will inspire Jill to go on a diet. At the same time, Emily is receiving gifts from Dawn Bosco-or so she believes-who she has recently argued with. This sets up an internal conflict for Emily. As the month progresses, Emily has several good experiences with Jill and learns to like her as she is. As the final gift, Emily gives Jill a gift she treasures, which feels really good to Emily. The final twist occurs when Emily discovers that the nice gifts she's been receiving have been from Jill Simon all along!

Series
The Kids of the Polk Street School

Illustrator
Blanche Sims

Publisher
Bantam Doubleday Dell, 1984

ISBN
0440417953

TC Level
8

Basic Book Information

December Secrets is 75 pages long with 9 chapters. The chapters are numbered and do not have titles. Each chapter averages 6 to 7 pages in length. There is one full-page illustration in each chapter that represents a small part of the action taking place on either the facing page, or the pages after the illustration. The story takes place over several days in December and is generally set in and around Miss Rooney's classroom at the Polk Street School. The author, Patricia Reilly Giff, has written many popular books for children and this series in particular is an old favorite of early chapter book readers.

Noteworthy Features

The vocabulary in the text tends to be simple, but some of the writing can be tricky and confusing for less sophisticated readers. Throughout the story, Emily's thoughts are written into the text, so the reader has to be able to decipher when this is happening. For example, on page 22, the text states: "It was hard to think of something to do for Jill. Emily walked around a telephone pole. Too bad Jill was such a fat crybaby."

Although most of the dialogue is written simply, and always referenced, some passages have dialogue that tends to jump around a bit. There are also times when characters interrupt each other or their sentences drift off, to show them thinking. For example, on pages 34-35 the text reads: "Emily shook her head. 'Not Yet.' 'I thought I saw someone put-' Beast began. Then he closed his mouth. 'In my desk?' Emily asked. Beast pressed his lips together. 'Who was it?' Emily asked. Beast covered his mouth with his hand. He shook his head. 'Don't ask me,' he said. 'All right, class' Miss Rooney said."

Teaching Ideas

Readers at this level can use *December Secrets* to begin making deeper character studies. Readers can learn the names of characters, the traits (both good and bad) and the relationship between characters (e.g., Emily doesn't like Jill because Jill is fat and a crybaby. Beast is always fooling around in class. He is also a good friend of Emily's). Because this is one book in a series, readers can compare specific characters to ones in other titles from the series. Readers can write a list of characteristics. They can also compare the characters in this story to themselves, other people they know, or characters in other books they've read and heard. These are all great opportunities for the student to reread, write, and have relevant discussions with reading partners or members of a reading. .

Often in this series, the main character goes through some kind of change. For example, in *December Secrets*, the main character, Emily, feels pretty consistently negative about Jill throughout most of the book. As Emily has more of an opportunity to get to know Jill, she begins to become more reflective and more open to changing her opinion. Teachers may discuss with readers how to use Post-its and notebooks to chart when, how and why the character has changed. These chartings are also great opportunities for discussion with reading partners and members of a class.

Another opportunity for teaching readers at this level is to discuss with children how to predict what is going to happen within the character, or in the story. Teachers may set readers up with a brief introduction, such as: "In this story, Miss Rooney's class is learning how nice it is to give presents to other people-even if they don't know who they are getting gifts from. The class is keeping the names of the givers secret until the end of December! When Emily learns that Jill Simon, who Emily thinks she dislikes, is her 'secret' person to give to, she is not happy. But as she gives and gets more and more gifts, her feelings about Jill begin to change. While you're reading today, try to find the places in the story where Emily's feelings begin to shift. When you find those places, see if you can guess what happens next." The teacher may suggest and model questions or comments that readers can ask themselves, or each other, at these points, such as: "I'm getting a funny (or exciting, or bad) feeling here that something is going to happen." Or, "I wonder if Emily will ever really tell Jill that she thinks Jill should go on a diet?" or, "I think Emily is starting to like Jill because they were laughing together in the hallway. I bet they will be friends in the end." These are also great opportunities for the teacher to model how readers actually think as they read. Teachers can demonstrate for readers "out loud" some of the questions, predictions and feelings readers have as they continue the story-the "internal dialogue" the reader has with a book.

Because *December Secrets* is longer than the very early chapter books that children may have just moved on from, teachers may want to work with readers on the ending or resolution of the story, and discuss where that actually occurs. The resolution of the story does not always happen in or on the last page. Teachers can work with children on noticing places in their reading where the character has fully changed, or the main events of the story have come together, or the "problem" has been resolved. It is important for the teacher to lead readers to discover where these things happen in the story, and how they are revealed in the text.

Book Connections

There are many titles in *The Kids of the Polk Street School* series, including *The Beast in Miss Rooney's Room*, *Snaggle Doodles*, *Purple Climbing Days* and *Fish Face*. Other chapter book series that are similar to these are: *The Pee Wee Scouts*, *The Adventures of The Bailey School Kids* series and *The New Kids of the Polk Street School*, which is about Emily Arrow's little sister and her friends. (This series, though, is easier than the regular *Kids of the Polk Street School* series.)

Genre
Short Chapter Book

Teaching Uses
Independent Reading; Partnerships; Character Study

Dove Isabeau

Jane Yolen

FIELD GUIDE

E

Book Summary

A beautiful and fiery young woman, Dove Isabeau is turned into a vicious dragon by her jealous stepmother. The young men who came to court her now come to kill the dragon and end up being killed themselves. Only the king's son, Kemp Owain, who has studied good magic, remains to save her. When he arrives, a white cat speaks with Dove Isabeau's true mother's voice, and tells the prince her secret. He kisses the dragon three times, frees Dove and turns himself to stone. Dove kills her stepmother and returns to the side of her prince. With the help of the white cat, she brings the prince back to life and they live happily ever after, despite the changes within them.

Illustrator
Dennis Nolan

Publisher
Voyager Books, Harcourt Brace & Co., 1997

ISBN
0152015051

TC Level
10

Basic Book Information

This book is about 30 pages long, with about four paragraphs on every two-page spread. Each spread has one full-page picture or two half-page pictures. The book is written in the English particular to fairy tales and stories of kings and dragons, with a touch of the elegant and the ancient in the vocabulary.

Noteworthy Features

The realistic, stark and captivating pictures usually attract readers to the book immediately. Others are drawn to the book because its award-winning author is so well loved.

Many teachers choose this fairy tale for the classroom because it's a bit different from other fairy tales. Though a beautiful maiden is saved by a brave prince, the prince is also saved by the maiden. Also, though the maiden is good and kind, she is also vengeful and murderous.

Though she is fair, her husband calls her a mighty warrior. The brave prince's horse is not pure white but gray.

The morality here is more complicated than in a traditional fairy tale, and the heroine is not a passive woman. Students will undoubtedly notice this if they begin comparing this fairy tale with other ones that involve evil stepmothers and brave princes rescuing damsels in distress. Character studies of the women in fairy tales would also bring this point to light.

Teaching Ideas

For readers who find the decoding of this book smooth, the story itself will probably unfold smoothly as well. To help it unfold, teachers may guide students to think more deeply about concepts they may have understood already. In order to go deeper into a story, readers can answer some questions, such as: 1) Do I know what each of the pictures mean? 2) Do I have any questions about what is happening or why characters do what they do? 3) Do I hear any echoes, either within the story or between this story and others?

In *Dove Isabeau,* many of the pictures are stark, and have meaning beyond decoration. Some titles, such as this one, will only reveal their meaning after the entire book has been read. On the cover, under the title *Dove Isabeau,* there are pictures of both a young woman and a dragon. Only after the book has been read will readers be able to see that both of those images represent Dove Isabeau. On the title page, there is a picture of a cat drinking a spilled potion. Only after reading the story can the reader put together that that cat gained its magical powers with the help of that potion. There are other small pictures and details like this that bear fruit upon second examination.

When working with the second question, "Do I have any questions about what is happening or why characters do what they do?" many readers need to reread the book. Many may end up with the same questions even after a second reading. For example, after Dove Isabeau's stepmother is thrown from the window and Dove throws the sword out after her, why doesn't Dove hear her sword hit the stone? Why does she smile a dragon smile when she hears that there is no sound?

Experienced readers will probably agree that the reason the sword makes no sound is that it has plunged into the body of the evil stepmother. Young readers do not always come to that conclusion, however. Some decide that the sword has fallen into the sea, never to be seen again, and Dove Isabeau smiles because that is the end of the violence. But in that case, why a dragon's smile and not a maiden's prayer, since both are within her, as the earlier line reads? Teachers will have to decide whether to confront readers with evidence to support the more violent interpretation, or the more peaceful one. Readers may also come across other questions and pursue them instead of this one.

The third question, involving looking for echoes in stories, is a bit harder to explain to readers who haven't done it before. The best way to explain may be to give readers examples, either from this book or others. In *Dove Isabeau,* there are "echoes" of dragons in the scales that form on Isabeau's mother before she dies, or in the red of the wyrm's skin, the stepmother's red star pentagram, and Isabeau's wedding dress. There are "echoes" of the stepmother's fate as she throws the lizard out the window just as she herself is thrown out the window. The cold hard stones of the setting "echo" the cold hard stones of the stepmother's heart and the cold hard stone from which Isabeau releases the prince. Readers can find meaning in the echoes by seeing how the images relate to each other. Readers might also sees echoes of other fairy tales, and the places that stand out from the standard pattern may be worth closer examination.

Book Connections

Readers may want to turn to fairy tales from the Brothers Grimm next.

Genre

Picture Book; Fairy and Folk Tale

Teaching Uses
Independent Reading; Interpretation

Exploding Ants: Amazing Facts about How Animals Adapt

Joanne Settel

FIELD GUIDE

E G

Publisher
Simon & Schuster

ISBN
0689817398

TC Level
11; 12; 13

Book Summary

This book is full of short vignettes that convey interesting and disgusting information about what animals do to adapt in order to survive. For example, readers will learn that swallowtail butterfly larva mimic the appearance of bird droppings and in this way, avoid being eaten by predators. Soldier Ants are designed to explode in order to defend their colony from invaders. When they explode, they spray a glue that holds their opponents in place.

At a glance, this resembles a picture book but it's actually closer to a Nonfiction chapter book. But, rather than reading vast expanses of text, readers can quickly glean the author's content. The sections are several pages long and each contains several smaller vignettes. In this way, the text is structured a bit like the memoir *Childtimes* by Eloise Greenfield or *The House on Mango Street* by Sandra Cisneros.

Basic Book Information

The book is well written. The author sometimes uses technical vocabulary such as "regurgitate" but she quickly follows this word with the more accessible term, "throw-up." The author is a biology professor and writes with that voice. For example, she begins one vignette by saying, "When a male deep-sea angler fish finds a female, he gets really attached." The book contains a glossary and an index and has a scattering of small color photographs.

Noteworthy Features

Kathy Doyle, a teacher renowned for her work with Nonfiction reading and writing, says, "If I could choose one book to give kids a feeling for how interesting and compelling Nonfiction can be; this would be the book. Just reading aloud the introduction, 'Why Animals Do Gross Things,' will captivate children who have not yet learned to love Nonfiction."

Teaching Ideas

This book deserves to be read aloud. If it was to simply be shelved in a Nonfiction shelf, children may be apt to overlook it. But, once a section of the book has been read aloud, children will be clamoring to read it themselves.

After oohing and ahhing and sharing the required "yuck" responses, a teacher might decide to use this book as a way to teach children that when you are the kind of person who knows things about the world, it's fun to drop these facts into conversations and see what happens. "At lunch today," a teacher might say, "Try turning to someone from a different classroom and saying, 'Did you know that . . .' Bring their reactions back to our class and let's talk about them."

Teachers can also encourage kids to fact-drop at home. "When parents ask, 'What did you learn today?' try telling them that male fireflies that flash in search of friendly females risk being eaten if they flash at the wrong species." Over time, students can become more sophisticated at fact-dropping. They can learn how to listen to what's being said so as to insert information when it fits. They can learn, also that the point of all of this is not merely to show-off or to raise eyebrows but that, in fact, it's thrilling and fascinating to live the life of a person intoxicated by ideas and information. One bizarre fact can lead to big, thoughtful conversations.

This book also serves well within the writing workshop. Because the vignettes are short, full of both voice and interesting information, children benefit from using sections of this book as models for their own Nonfiction writing.

Genre
Picture Book; Nonfiction; Chapter Book

Teaching Uses
Reading and Writing Nonfiction; Content Area Study; Read Aloud; Partnerships; Book Clubs

Fig Pudding

Ralph Fletcher

FIELD GUIDE

E

Book Summary

Fletcher's book spends a year with the Abernathy family: Mom, Dad, five boys and one girl. The oldest, 12-year-old Cliff, narrates the story. On the surface, the Abernathys seem like an ordinary family. There is "wild" Teddy, whose antics confine him to "time-outs" under the kitchen table; almost-talking Josh, whose Christmas gift wish, a "yidda yadda," is a puzzle to all the family members; Cyn, who struggles to find herself among her five male siblings; Brad, whose naiveté makes him a marvelous target for Nate's mischief; and Cliff, who, because he's the oldest, gets blamed for everything. Readers also meet Grandma Annie, a colorful figure with a flair for baking. Underlying the hustle and bustle of the household is the message that a family like this one survives sickness, teasing, sibling rivalry, and even tragedy, through love and humor.

Publisher
Clarion Books, 1995

ISBN
044041203X

TC Level
12

Basic Book Information

This book is 136 pages long and has 9 chapters. This book was written by Ralph Fletcher, a former member of the Teachers College Reading and Writing Project staff. Ralph is also the author of many books on teaching writing, including *What a Writer Needs*, *Craft Lessons* and *The Writing Life*. People who know the author well know this book is grounded in his own experiences as the oldest in a family of nine children. Fletcher's brother died at a young age, and that tragedy is very much a part of this book.

Noteworthy Features

The story, told in the first person by Cliff, runs chronologically from Christmas to Christmas. The passage of time is noted at the beginning of each chapter with such reference points as New Year's Day, April fifth (Cliff's birthday), and late that summer. Each chapter centers on a vignette about one or more of the members of the family. "Under the Kitchen Table," for example, describes Mom's attempt to discipline Teddy for the "wild" things he does, while "The Headless Chicks" tells how Brad is finally able to pay back Nate for his teasing. Fletcher tells the stories with humor and compassion. Readers will easily make connections to their own families, where both sibling rivalry and emotional support are commonplace.

The dialogue is cleverly written with realistic exchanges, such as the one that took place about the naming of Cyn's kitten: "Lemme guess, you're going to name the kitten Salt? Marshmallow? Sugar? Snow. Just Snow? How about Snowflake or Snow White? Snowball? Snowball fight? Snow. How 'bout Snowball? How 'bout Snowstorm? Snow. Snowdrop, Snowshoe? Snowshoe? Well, her feet are white. How about Snowy? Her name is Snow, period."

There are references to the Christmas holiday-most of which center around food-that may not be familiar to all children, such as "fig pudding," "stollen," and "she-crab bisque". Fletcher takes care to explain those items that are critical to comprehension. This is especially true for the fig pudding, which brings the story to an end on a note of humor.

Teaching Ideas

This is a touching memoir-like novel that portrays a loving family that must change its dynamic to deal with the death of a child. In time, the family members realize that though they'll never forget the tragedy, life goes on and can still be embraced.

A character study would work well with this book. A reader may want to jot down the siblings in the order of their ages, and note what the student learns about each. It is possible to connect these human beings to the ones a reader knows from his or her own life. Are any of the traits of the siblings similar to the traits of their own family members? What can the reader learn about his own family from studying the one in the book, and what can she learn about the one in the book from studying her own?

This book is worthy of in-depth interpretation: What is the message that the reader is left with? What is the book really about?

Students sometimes focus on the steaming bowl of sadness that Uncle Billy tells Cliff about -"When someone you love dies, you get a big bowl of sadness put down in front of you, steaming hot. You can start eating now, or you can let it cool and eat it bit by bit later on. Either way, you end up eating the whole thing. There's really no way around it."

As children may have already learned about literature, it is always important to determine a title's significance. This is especially true in this case. Before Brad dies, the father locked himself in the kitchen every year to make his special fig pudding. After Brad's death, he invites the kids to help him. It is the fig pudding in the end that unites the family-and laughter brings them through their pain. The fig pudding becomes the big "family secret" that brings them closer to healing, as children will no doubt discover in their discussions.

Another way to examine the text would be to study the genre of memoir. This is not technically a memoir, but excerpts of it work as touchstone texts in a memoir unit of study. A teacher may wish to bring in a few memoirs, or memoir-like texts, and have the class come up with a list of options an author has available to him when he puts a life onto the page. Then students could choose from among these options to write their own pieces. Many more things probably happened to the Abernathy family in that year. Students could discuss why they think Cliff chose the episodes he did, and not others, to tell his story. How did these scenes contribute to the final message of the story? (Of course, Cliff is not the author of this story, but the narrator, which is why it is not strictly a memoir.)

Genre

Chapter Book; Memoir

Teaching Uses

Read Aloud; Independent Reading; Book Clubs; Partnerships

Fireflies for Nathan

Shulamith Levey Oppenheim

FIELD GUIDE

E

Illustrator
John Ward

Publisher
Penguin Puffin, 1996

ISBN
0140557822

Book Summary

Six-year-old Nathan is dropped off to stay with his grandparents. The three of them spend an enchanted evening by the pond catching fireflies in a jar, just the way Nathan's dad used to when he was six. As the grandparents tuck him in, Nathan asks them to let the fireflies out of the jar when he is asleep-just the way his dad did when he was a boy.

Basic Book Information

This short, small picture book has realistic-looking illustrations that often draw readers into the book.

Noteworthy Features

Although the language and structures of this story are fairly simple, the type size is very small and the words are close together. Adding to the difficulty, the quoted dialogue is not always referenced, that is, followed by a "he said" or a "Nathan said." This can make following the conversation very confusing to inexperienced readers. Reading the story to a young student before she tries to read it on her own may help the dialogue make more sense to her. Of course, teachers can also explain how the reader can tell who is talking: by the new line each speaker gets on the page.

At the beginning of the story, Nathan says that he is six years old. Some children will be older than six by the time they are reading this story on their own. Finding that the main character is six may make some students feel that the book is babyish. Teachers can remind children that there are often things to relate to in characters, even if they at first seem very different. Or, teachers can help children to think of the six-year-olds they know in order to decide if they would like to have this book read to them. Sometimes, this book works best as a read aloud choice for children who are about six years old, like Nathan.

Teaching Ideas

The first page of this wholesome little book is wordless, and many readers pass right over it as they look for the first words in the story. Examining the illustration might help ease readers into the story, which otherwise could be considered to start a bit abruptly. However, since the picture is of a man waving from a moving car to three people on a porch, it is still hard to be sure what is happening. The story can be considered complete without that first page, however, as the picture doesn't add any new element or twist to the story.

Several times in the story, Nathan wants to know about his daddy when he was Nathan's age. He wants to know what he liked to do, and how he liked to do it, and he wants to do it the same way. His grandmother compares him to his father several times as well. Some children notice this and launch inquiries into why this might be. Is Nathan missing his father? Did his father tell him so many stories of when he was little that it got Nathan all excited? Does Nathan consider his father a hero he wants to imitate? Is Nathan's father dead? Some of these questions can be addressed in part by the text and some cannot, but the search for evidence around these questions (or many other possible questions about other aspects of the book) can help students read carefully and thoughtfully and give them skills in hunting for evidence to support their ideas.

Some teachers use *Fireflies for Nathan* again in a writing workshop, to give students examples of how writers can slow down time by giving extra detail about what is going on, or by using repetition and other techniques. Oppenheim achieves this slowing down of time when she describes Nathan sitting in the grass with Nana and Poppy waiting for the fireflies to come out.

The realistic illustrations of Nathan and his grandparents finding something special in ordinary nature help impart one of the book's main messages. Anyone, it seems, can make a magic night-you don't need fancy equipment, a lot of preparation and hoopla. You need only to savor what's around you with a few special people. On the other hand, some students find the main message to be that people ought to slow down and appreciate the country more, because it'll give them a good feeling. Other students believe the message is that it's possible to have a good time with your grandparents, even if they don't have a lot of toys around for kids to play with. As long as the children have reasons and textual evidence for their ideas, they can have excellent discussions based on their thoughts.

Genre
Picture Book

Teaching Uses
Independent Reading; Teaching Writing; Read Aloud

Flight: The Journey of Charles Lindberg

Robert Burleigh

FIELD GUIDE

E F G

Illustrator
Mike Wimmer

Publisher
Putnam Publishing, 1991

ISBN
0399222723

TC Level
12

Book Summary

This Nonfiction book is the story of Charles Lindberg's first flight across the Atlantic. It tells the story from the moment just before he gets into the plane until he finally falls asleep after his arrival. The amazing thing about this beautiful picture book is the author's style and voice. The book is beautifully written. It begins, "It is 1927." The book incorporates Lindberg's actual words from the diary he kept as he crossed the Atlantic.

Basic Book Information

The book deserves to be categorized as a sophisticated biographical picture book. It has full-page paintings that capture the mood and make us feel as if we are standing in the world of the story.

The print is set rather like a poem without stanzas and it may be that the author intends for this to be read not only as a biography but also a romantic poem.

Noteworthy Features

This book is an extraordinary read-aloud text. The words, written with lyrical lilt and intimacy, create a mood and draw readers into a drama. The language is heart-shaping. The pictures are breathtaking. Meanwhile, every bit of the text is informational: "Lindberg is nearly as tall as the plane itself."

Burleigh gives us the precise time, down to the minute, throughout the text (e.g., 7:52, 12:08), so that we can sense how slowly time passes during this 33-hour flight. We are there with him looking at his watch.

Teaching Ideas

This book could be one of several texts that weave its way across the entire school year, serving as a mentor text to teach children countless lessons about the craft of good writing. For the text to work as a mentor text, however, children must first fall in love with it. This is sure to happen if a teacher rises to the occasion of reading it aloud. Practice reading it. Read it slowly. Read it with your mind fully attuned to what the book is saying, pausing with the line breaks, "Across the Atlantic / Alone."

The line break requires that we pause-pause and think about making a flight clear across that wide, wide sea. Then we add the word "alone," a word that says it all.

This is probably not a book that provides stopping points for mid-way conversations. Read it in one long luxurious read. And then be silent. On another day, re-read it and invite kids to re-read their favorite pages to feel this text in their mouths. Invite them to find the lines they love most and to write them in their writer's notebook.

Later, return to sections to study the craft. Your writers will notice the repetition, which at times is almost like an echo. "Later, they will call him" (1). There is other more subtle repetition such as the repetition of the time and date. The end then circles back to the beginning. Because this is a true Nonfiction biography, this is surprising.

Burleigh uses the craft that one might expect in a pretty fictional picture book, but there aren't many true Nonfiction books that are written with these craft elements. Burleigh chooses simple but powerful words, often selecting particularly precise verbs. He savors detail. Burleigh balances short and long sentences. He makes readers read quickly, then slowly, then pause. His punctuation is worth noting, and young readers could profit from discussion about why he chose a dash instead of a comma, or why he chose a fragment instead of a whole sentence.

This text could teach fluent readers a great deal about how to read with phrasing and intonation. "Find a page you love and practice reading it aloud so, so well." We could also ask children to do the same with a page of their own writing. This may make them want to revise their own text.

Book Connections

This book could initiate independent studies of the complex character of Charles Lindberg. Readers may want to read James Cross Giblin's marvelous book, *Charles A. Lindberg: A Human Hero*.

Burleigh is the author of other books, and all deserve to be studied and admired. He's written *Black Whiteness* about Admiral Perry in the Antarctic and *Home Run* about Babe Ruth, where again, he chooses individuals who are independent.

Genre
Nonfiction; Biography; Picture Book; Poetry

Teaching Uses
Read Aloud; Independent Reading; Teaching Writing; Language Conventions

For the Love of the Game: Michael Jordan and Me

FIELD GUIDE

E

Eloise Greenfield

Illustrator
Jan Spivey Gilchrist

Publisher
HarperCollins, 1997

ISBN
0064435555

TC Level
8

Book Summary

This is a two-part story. The first part describes the skill of Michael Jordan, and how the renowned basketball player can fly. The second part is an analogy. Just as Jordan can fly in basketball, just as he has a love of the game, so do the characters show this same love, this same enthusiasm for life. "For the love of the game of life I rise from my bed and greet the world," Greenfield writes. The children learn that they, like Jordan, can learn to fly if they overcome the obstacles that lie in their path. The text and illustrations together deliver a strong message to readers about the power that is within everyone.

Basic Book Information

Eloise Greenfield and Jan Spivey Gilchrist have collaborated on more than 16 award-winning books, including *William and the Good Old Days* and *Nathaniel Talking*. Although *For the Love of the Game* is a picture book, the story is best understood by students above the primary grades.

The text is a narrative poem, written in short, choppy phrases like, "he steps to the court and he greets his team." The majority of the text is written in free verse with some rhyme, as in, "stands right there / on a little piece of air." Gilchrist's illustrations perfectly depict the meaning the text conveys. In characteristic two-page spreads, the artist provides a colorful background for the printed words. On some pages there are as few as four lines of text, while on other pages there are as many as nine lines of text in varied places.

Noteworthy Features

The author uses little punctuation. The text is presented in thought units rather than formal sentences, for this is more a poem with a message than a story. This might make comprehension difficult for a less able reader. The pictures do help support understanding. With the exception perhaps of the word *naysayer*, the vocabulary is made up of words that are familiar to most English-speaking third and fourth graders. However, the way the words describe the world is far from basic. For example, "... he lands, smooth as a gliding plane, then turns and smiles at the memory of flying."

Teaching Ideas

Eloise Greenfield's writing-whether prose or poetry-always exhibits the craft of a seasoned writer. This book is no exception. If a teacher suggests that a child reread this book and use Post-its to note particular things the author has done, the child will probably notice that the first part of the book has pictures of Michael Jordan, while the second part emphasizes ordinary boys and girls. Through discussion students may discover that the focus changes in this two-part story. The first part records how Jordan "scores" in basketball; the second part shows how one must "score" in the same way in life and suggests the exhilaration that will follow.

Students may also notice that Greenfield writes in ways that aren't always clear. For example, they may wonder what exactly she means when she says, "the sun is at midmorning. The time to prepare is now." They might wonder, "What does 'he takes his stance' mean?" This may prompt great discussion and analysis.

Students may also note the use of rhyme, metaphor and alliteration, and discuss how these poetic devices contribute to the text.

Many readers prefer nonfiction reading to fiction reading, and it's important that all readers have a balanced reading life, one that includes information books. This book, then, could simply be one among many on the library shelf.

If a teacher sees that the class as a whole tends to select only fiction books during independent reading, the teacher may institute some rituals that steer children toward nonfiction. The least intrusive would simply be to do promotional book-talks in which one "sells" nonfiction books. It's also possible to go a step further and to talk to children about the importance of having a balanced reading life. They can suggest to children that if they have a personal book bin in this classroom with four to five books they're reading or planning to read, that at least one book might be a nonfiction text. Finally, it's possible to go a step further and suggest that for a designated length of time, all children need to read only nonfiction texts during independent reading.

Teachers will want to do mini-lessons about the strategies of skilled nonfiction reading. One mini-lesson may let children know that nonfiction readers sometimes read like magnets, looking for intriguing details that they pull from a text. One teacher told her students that highly literate people then fact-drop these little bits of information into conversations, sharing in passing whatever they've learned. A reader of this book would be full of such facts.

Another mini-lesson might show children that if a person read this book and loved it, the logical thing to do would be to collect other texts on the same topic. Over time, information from one text and another accumulates. Some of that information will overlap and some of it may be contradictory, leaving readers to determine the truth in what they read.

Book Connections

Eloise Greenfield and Jan Spivey Gilchrist have collaborated on more than 16 award-winning books, including *William and the Good Old Days* and *Nathaniel Talking*.

Genre

Poetry; Picture Book

Teaching Uses
Author Study; Independent Reading; Teaching Writing; Partnerships

Fourth Grade Rats

Jerry Spinelli

FIELD GUIDE

E

Book Summary

This is a coming of age story . . . age 9, that is. In Suds' school there is a chant, "First grade babies! Second grade cats! Third grade angels! Fourth grade rats!" As Suds enters fourth grade, he isn't quite sure he wants to give up being an "angel." His friend Joey convinces him that being a fourth grade rat means having a messy room, disobeying your mother, not being scared of spiders, and pushing first graders off their swings. This doesn't sound too good to Suds. He finally gives in, though, to win the heart of Judy Billings (who has a fondness for rats). After experiencing what it is to be a rat, Suds realizes that it's no fun and admits it to his mom. His mother tells him, "As soon as you stopped trying to be a man, you became one . . . admitting you were wrong, that's grownup stuff." For now, Suds decides that being a kid is enough.

Illustrator
Paul Casale

Publisher
Scholastic, 1991

ISBN
0590442449

TC Level
10

Basic Book Information

Jerry Spinelli won the Newbery Award for *Maniac Magee*. In addition to *Fourth Grade Rats*, Spinelli has written *Who Put That Hair in My Toothbrush?*, *Dump Days*, *Wringer*, *Space Station Seventh Grade* and *Jason and Marceline*.

Noteworthy Features

This is an early chapter book with chapters as short as four pages. All chapters are outlined in the Table of Contents at the beginning of the book.

Like other early chapter books, this one is illustrated. The illustrations are very detailed and realistic; however, there are only five of them in the book. These pictures do not always match the text on the opposite page, and so they provide limited support to the reader.

Jerry Spinelli uses a lot of dialogue throughout *Fourth Grade Rats*. This may be confusing for early readers of chapter books, since the speaker is not always noted.

Overall, the dialogue is true to how many fourth graders throughout America speak. The characters use phrases like "Yo" and "C'mon, man." The book is told in first-person narration, which again situates it in the culture of some American fourth graders. These devices give *Fourth Grade Rats* an authenticity that may help readers identify with the characters.

Throughout the story there are many changes in setting, which may be confusing for some readers. The story mainly takes place in three settings: school, Joey's house, and Suds' house. However, the story jumps back and forth between these settings quite often.

The passage of time throughout the story is chronological. There are no flashbacks or major jumps in time, and most of the shifts in time are indicated in the text.

Teaching Ideas

One of the most defining features of *Fourth Grade Rats* is its heavy use of dialogue. This can be a source of a lot of confusion for readers and a lot of learning for them as well. The speaker is not often identified directly. For example, Chapter 2 begins, "'Okay,' I said, 'now what?' He pointed. 'That.' 'My sandwich?' 'You gonna eat peanut butter and jelly all your life?'" If children are new to books with a lot of dialogue, this may be a great book to use in a read aloud. The teacher could model the way a reader provides different voices for each character to distinguish who is speaking. Alternatively, a teacher may want to use just a few pages of this book and do some small group strategy lessons to help children keep track of who is talking. In these small groups, it may help for a reader to read the text aloud to a partner who follows along, agreeing with or revising the intonation. As teachers ultimately want children to read dialogue like this silently and easily, role-playing in their mind's eye, so some externalized role-playing can help scaffold what must soon become an internalized process.

Another way that readers can keep track of the speakers is by building theories about how the main characters are different. Readers can compare and contrast the way that Joey and Suds are reacting to their new life as fourth graders. Once defining character traits have been established, how they talk and what they talk about become an extension of these traits.

Teachers may also want to make a list of the characters in the book during a read aloud. Like the Fudge series by Judy Blume, the Morton family uses weird nicknames to refer to each other like Sudsie, Zippernose and Bubba. These nicknames are genderless so it may confuse readers.

The setting changes many times throughout the book as Joey and Suds go back and forth from school to home. Teachers can guide students to notice that every time there is a setting change in the story the author is signaling to readers that a new significant event will take place. Readers, whether independent or in partnerships, can use post-its to mark setting changes throughout the book. When they have read the new scene they can do a retelling, either right on the post-it or to their partners, about the event that took place. This device will help readers stay focused on the scene changes and events of the story.

Spinelli does a wonderful job at capturing the essence of fourth grade life. If children's books are any indication, going into fourth grade seems like a major milestone in elementary school life. Other important books on the topic include *Tales of a Fourth Grade Nothing* and *Amber Brown Goes Fourth. Fourth Grade Rats* is written from the perspective of the main character, Suds. The narrator lets you know how Suds is feeling. How he feels is quite often very different from the way that he acts. Readers, whether in partnerships or individually, can note places where Suds is acting like a "rat" but still is torn by feelings of wanting to be an "angel." One of the reasons Suds does not act in accordance with his true feelings is because he is struggling to be popular. Other reasons include peer pressure and having a crush on a girl. Readers of this book may be very familiar with Suds' issues.

Another way that Spinelli indicates how a character is feeling is through the use of notes in parentheses. For example, when his friend Joey is stung by a bee and Judy Billings is impressed, Suds provides the following commentary: "'Joey can I see it?' (For the millionth time.) 'Ouu, it gives me the shivers.' (It is not even visible)." It should be pointed out to readers, especially those fairly new to chapter books, that the quotes in the parentheses represent Suds' inner thoughts.

In a writing workshop, students may want to study *Fourth Grade Rats* in order to understand how to use dialogue in their writing. Another focus in a craft study could be Spinelli's use of italics. He often puts words in italics for emphasis. Such as, "You're going to wear an earring?" Teachers can model the intonation with their voice so students understand how italics add emphasis to written words the same way volume adds emphasis to spoken words. Students may want to look for places in their own writing where they can use italics to emphasize a word or phrase.

Book Connections

Jerry Spinelli won the Newbery Award for *Maniac Magee*. In addition to *Fourth Grade Rats*, Spinelli has written *Who Put That Hair in My Toothbrush?*, *Dump Days*, *Wringer*, *Space Station Seventh Grade* and *Jason and Marceline*.

Genre
Chapter Book

Teaching Uses
Independent Reading; Character Study; Language Conventions

Fox in Love

Edward Marshall

FIELD GUIDE

E

Book Summary

In *Fox in Love*, Fox is once again asked to watch his little sister, Louise. He puts up a fuss each time, until he figures out that he can use Louise's presence to his benefit. He takes her to the park where Raisin, the cute little fox, thinks he is a kind person for taking her there. He takes Louise to a dance contest because his original partner gets sick and he needs a new one. In the end, Fox is genuinely nice to Louise because they win second place in the contest.

Series
The Fox Books

Illustrator
James Marshall

Publisher
Puffin Books, 1994

ISBN
0140368434

TC Level
7

Basic Book Information

Fox in Love is 48 pages long. The book is divided into 3 chapters, all approximately 16 pages in length. The chapter titles are supportive. There are helpful, humorous pictures on every page. This text has a simple sentence structure with all dialogue attributed to a speaker explicitly.

The *Fox* books do not need to be read in any particular order. However, it might be wise to have a child read *Fox Be Nimble* last, because in it Fox seems older and he is a bit more disrespectful toward his mother. Even his clothes are more hip than in the other books. Fox's mom is pregnant in three of the other books. In this apparently earlier book, *Fox in Love*, she is not pregnant, nor does she have twins. Fox's fear of heights is woven into several of the *Fox* books including *Fox and His Friends* and *Fox on Wheels*.

Noteworthy Features

Although there are many characters introduced in this short chapter book, they remain consistent and are heard from often in the series. The detailed pictures help the reader envision the characters and hold them in their mind as they read. Raisin, Rose and Lola are new characters that are only mentioned in this book. The second chapter is the most complex. Fox goes to the fair with a different girl each day. The girls find this out and Fox ends up going to the fair by himself on the last day. This book deals with many boy-girl issues.

Fox is a funny character. Readers will find themselves identifying with his sense of self. It's not that he is totally selfish, he just thinks of his own enjoyment before his responsibilities. Fox does at times accept responsibility, yet he does it in his own way. For example, he argues with his mom when she asks him to take Louise to the park. Once he meets Raisin, the cute little fox, he begs Louise to go to the park the next day so he can see Raisin, even though Louise is busy. It is evident that Fox has a crush on Raisin.Teachers may want to explain this and do some teaching around it.

The storyline is consistent with the other books in the series. Fox always has to take care of Louise, and he usually puts his own needs first. The reader can count on him to be a bit selfish in most of what he does. This can make for lively discussions of the merits (or flaws) of his character.

There are italics on a few pages for the purpose of emphasizing a specific word. The readers know that in some texts, italics mean that a character is thinking. In this book, they place emphasis on a certain word. Kids can be told this at the outset, or come to it on their own.

Teaching Ideas

There are many characters in this book, as well as throughout the series, to remember. Seven characters are mentioned in the first two pages alone. It would help readers if they kept track of the characters as they came up by viewing the pictures and saying the names aloud. The names, however, seem to be a bit tricky to pronounce. Therefore, it would probably benefit some readers if the names were introduced during a pre-reading picture walk of the text.

Inferential thinking is a must if the reader is to comprehend the underlying meaning of the chapters. The most interesting points for inferential thinking are places that require the reader to ask why Fox does what he does. A few examples:

Why does Fox want to go back to the park and Louise doesn't? He seems not to be acting like himself (pg. 15). Why does Fox lie about watching television (pg. 16)? Why does Fox say this is his lucky day when Raisin announces that she is rich (pg. 22)? Why does Fox end up going to the fair by himself instead of with his friends (pg. 34)?

There are many commonalities in the series. It is suggested that readers keep track of Fox's personality throughout each book and after reading a few, discuss when he acts most like himself and when he is acting out of character, and why? Students may use Post-its and/or discuss: times when Fox is acting selfish and when he is acting responsibly/selfless (it is always helful in a character study to look a places where the character seems to be acting oddly); parts that reveal the kind of character Fox is; parts that seem to be fair and unfair to Fox (fairness is also always a good topic for discussion in books); that something always seems to happen to Louise when Fox is watching her because he is not the most attentive caregiver. This can lead to cross-text conversations about Fox's sense of responsibility. (It is always useful to talk across texts-what tends to happen with this character or this writer?)

Students will undoubtedly come up with many other aspects of Fox that might be studied.

Book Connections

Fox Be Nimble is similar in difficulty to *Frog and Toad* by Arnold Lobel, the *Nate the Great* series by Marjorie Weinman Sharmat, and *The Little Bear* series by Else Holmelund Minarik. *Fox Be Nimble* is harder than books like *Sammy the Seal* by Syd Hoff, and *When Will I Read?* by Miriam Cohen. Once children have read the *Fox* series, they may profit from turning next to *The One in the Middle Is the Green Kangaroo* by Judy Blume, *Rollo and Tweedy and the Ghost at Dougal Castle* by Laura Jean Allen, or to the *Pinky and Rex* series by James Howe.

Genre
Short Chapter Book

Teaching Uses
Independent Reading

Freckle Juice

Judy Blume

FIELD GUIDE

E

Book Summary

Andrew Marcus wants freckles more than anything and Nicky Lane, who sits in front of him, has millions of them. Andrew thinks that if he had freckles like Nicky, then his mom would never know if his neck were dirty.

One day Andrew asks Nicky how he got his freckles. "You get born with them. That's how!" Sharon overhears their conversation and offers to sell Andrew her "secret freckle recipe" for fifty cents.

Andrew is intent on having freckles and believes that Sharon's secret recipe will help him. When he doesn't get the freckles after drinking the "freckle juice" he is embarrassed and angry.

Publisher
A Yearling Book, 1971

ISBN
0440428130

TC Level
8

Basic Book Information

Freckle Juice is a 47-page chapter book divided into 5 short untitled chapters all of which build on each other. The black-and-white illustrations throughout the text help support the single plot line. The sentence length varies. Most pages end with a period, but there are several wrap-around sentences that carry over to another page. The pictures provide wonderful visual aids for each scene.

Noteworthy Features

The biggest difficulty in this text is the print size. Print and spacing are disappointingly small for a book of this level. Additionally, the pictures aren't always placed beside the text they illustrate so at times the reader must turn to the next page for the appropriate picture.

Teaching Ideas

There are many characters with somewhat complex character traits in this book and there are many scene changes as well. There are many themes in the story that students can relate to: jealousy, envy, blind trust and getting even.

This book can be used in a variety of ways, especially to study the elements of story and character. *Freckle Juice* is a good example of a book in which aspects of a character's personality aren't directly stated, but must be inferred. In addition, because the book lends itself easily to debate, it would also be good for early book clubs.

When students are at first trying to make personal connections with the characters in the story, they may be stuck. Some will think that because they themselves have never wanted freckles, or have never been tricked into buying a recipe for them, they can't relate to Andrew. This is a common thought for readers at first: "I'm not exactly the same as the characters, so I can't relate." Teachers can show students that situations and feelings can be connected to each other even when they aren't identical. "How do you think you would feel in the same situation?" "Would your feelings be the same (or different) than the character's feelings?" or "What kind of situations have made you feel the way the character is feeling?" "What is the same about what made you both feel that way?" are good questions to start with.

In teaching readers to relate to characters different from them in books, teachers are also giving students ways to relate to people in the world who are different from them. Some teachers try to emphasize this application of their teaching by having students use the same strategies in their own lives, with real people they know.

Book Connections

This book is similar to *Molly's Pilgrim* by Barbara Cohen. It may be helpful if the reader first experiences success with *The One in the Middle Is the Green Kangaroo*, also by Judy Blume. A nice book to serve as a transition is *Lavender* by Karen Hesse.

Genre
Short Chapter Book

Teaching Uses
Independent Reading; Character Study; Book Clubs

Frog and Toad Are Friends

Arnold Lobel

FIELD GUIDE
C E

Book Summary

Frog and Toad Are Friends has two interesting characters, Frog and Toad. At first, Frog wakes up to a new Spring and does his best to get his good friend, Toad, to wake up and enjoy it with him. Some of the traits of Frog and Toad are scientific traits of frogs and toads in nature: their colors, some personality traits, and the fact that frogs are out first in the Spring before toads. Frog and Toad are great friends, yet very different in character. In the second chapter, "The Story," the reader will see how caring Toad can be when he wants to help Frog feel better. Frog asks him to tell a story but Toad cannot remember one to tell. He does everything he can to remember a story to tell Frog. Each chapter shows how caring, thoughtful, serious, and funny each character can be but also shows the differences between Frog and Toad. The author may want his readers to notice the differences between these two animals because many people confuse the two with one another. Frog and Toad act just like human beings. Sometimes they are happy, sometimes sad, angry or embarrassed. In the fourth chapter, "The Swim," Toad doesn't feel good wearing his bathing suit in front of people. The other animals wait for Toad to come out of the water to see how funny he looks, so Toad tries to stay in the water as long as he can. He gets so cold that he starts to shiver and sneeze. Toad does eventually get out, and finds that his friends-the snail, the snake, the turtles, and the lizards -are all having a good laugh at his expense.

Series
Frog and Toad books

Publisher
Harper Trophy, 1979

ISBN
0064440206

TC Level
6

Basic Book Information

Frog and Toad Are Friends is 64 pages long and divided into 5 chapters, each chapter approximately 12 pages in length. There are detailed supportive pictures on every other page. This book is a Caldecott Honor book. The chapter titles are not overly supportive due to their brevity, such as "Spring the Letter." The chapter titles are printed in green or brown, matching the color of the characters' (Frog and Toad's) bodies,and each chapter title's color matches the significant character in the spotlight. Of the four *Frog and Toad* books, this has the earliest copyright date and seems to be the first in the series.

Frog and Toad Are Friends by Arnold Lobel is a book in the four-book series *Frog and Toad*. Frog and Toad are the best of friends. They have distinctive personalities, which unfold as the reader journeys though the episodic chapters. Frog is always responsible, reasonable, looks for solutions when there is a problem, and doesn't get ruffled very easily. Toad is more nervous, demanding and impatient. He's easily discouraged and often gives up quickly. He doesn't seem to have a very strong work ethic. The friends have many adventures together and the reader will find that, no matter what, they remain forever friends.

Noteworthy Features

The main characters, Frog and Toad, are portrayed similarly in all of the titles in this series. A reader can count on the characters to act and react to situations accordingly. There are a few surprising moments in the book when Frog and Toad act out of character. For example, Toad is usually grumpy and a bit lazy. Yet, in Chapter2, "The Story," Toad wants to make Frog feel better and puts forth great effort to remember a story to tell Frog.

Dialogue is used for each character. It is easy for readers to practice voice inflections with these characters as they each have very distinctive voices. The dialogue is always referenced.

The color-coded chapter titles clue the reader as to which character is going to be in the spotlight with a problem. The other character will be the one who tries to help him solve the dilemma, or just feel better.

The big idea in this series is always the same: good friends help each other all of the time. Sometimes they get mad at each other, but in the end they always make up.

At times, the vocabulary seems specialized when dealing with other characters, scenes, and settings. For example, in Chapter3, "A Lost Button," Frog and Toad are walking in a meadow. They meet a sparrow and a raccoon that help look for Toad's lost button. Frog decides to sew many buttons onto a jacket for Toad. These days, sewing is not a part of most children's vocabulary or everyday life as much as a bathing suit or writing a letter, the subjects of two other chapters.

Teaching Ideas

Character development is a strong part of this text and series. It would be wise to follow each character and his actions and reactions to situations as a way of exploring different traits of each friend. It can be interesting to notice the similarities of each character to the scientific animal. Students may use Post-its to mark and discuss:

*Places where they feel most like a certain character

*Places where they disagree with the way a character responded

*Parts that show friendship between Frog and Toad

*Parts that support a theory the reader is developing about Frog or Toad. (For example, Frog is a responsible, neat, or obsessive character. Toad is a lazy, grumpy, or self-conscious character.)

Children who study and compare Frog and Toad will notice that Frog is the more proactive one in this book. When Frog gets sick, Toad is expected to rise to the occasion of being proactive. Frog asks for a story, and Toad feels the pressure mount and responds by doing a lot of silly things. He throws water on his face, bangs his head against the wall and so forth. In the end, Toad is in bed needing support and Frog, not surprisingly, meets this challenge and tells Toad a story.

Some teachers have found it powerful to use this book to teach children that it's important to make connections across the pages within a text or even within a chapter. Quite often children are taught instead to connect text to life or text to text. Sometimes the intra-text connections do the most for comprehension. One way to teach this is to pull readers together for a mini-lesson and to read the book aloud while showing pages on an overhead projector, or to distribute copies of the text for children to refer to.

On page 7, Frog pushes Toad out of bed, and out of the house. The children may conclude that Frog is being mean. Teachers could then ask, "Are there other places where you see this?" Soon students will find pages 12-14, where Frog is trying to trick his friend into not sleeping. Some children will say, "This isn't being mean. He's being a good friend and trying to wake Toad up to enjoy Spring." Students can celebrate this difference of opinion. As children look more closely to see if there is evidence that shows Frog's motivation, they'll cite page 12 where Frog admits that he wants Toad to wake up so that he (Frog) won't be lonely.

Book Connections

Frog and Toad Are Friends is similar in difficulty to *Tales of Amanda Pig* by Jean Van Leeuwen, *Bully Trouble* by Joanna Cole, *The Adventures of Benny and Watch*, created by Gertrude Chandler Warner and the Early Boxcar series. It is more difficult than *Sammy the Seal* by Syd Hoff, *Joe and Betsy the Dinosaur* by Lilian Hoban, and *No More Monsters for Me!* by Peggy Parish. Once children can successfully read *Frog and Toad Are Friends* and other books of comparable difficulty, they may find themselves well prepared to read *Pinky and Rex* by James Howe and *The One in the Middle Is the Green Kangaroo* by Judy Blume.

Genre
Chapter Book

Teaching Uses
Independent Reading; Character Study; Partnerships; Read Aloud

Fur, Feathers and Flippers: How Animals Live Where They Do

Patricia Lauber

FIELD GUIDE

E

Book Summary

This carefully written scientific text does not talk down to the reader as it describes animals that live in various regions of the world. The first section describes creatures that have adapted to the waters and frozen lands of the Antarctic. The text then moves to the grasslands of Africa, to the forests of New England, to the deserts of the Southwest and to the tundra of the Far North. In each area, the text details the ingenious traits of the animals that live and flourish in the difficult or unique conditions described. The book's conclusion is that the world is a better place because of the diversity of the creatures that inhabit it. Understanding how they survive and thrive may help keep humans from destroying habitats.

This book is particularly well suited to studies not of particular animals, but animals in general and how they have adapted or evolved to suit their environments. This is a book about animals in context; understanding the habitat is important to understanding the animal. Though it's not clear from the title, the book is nearly as helpful as a resource for learning about geography and ecology as it is for learning about animal features. Its list-like text allows readers to learn about a cross-section of life in an area, to begin to understand the biodiversity of an area instead of focusing on just one creature at a time.

Publisher
Scholastic, 1994

ISBN
0590450719

TC Level
12

Basic Book Information

There is a table of contents showing that the book is divided into sections based on geographical regions of the world. Each section begins with a panoramic photograph of the region as well as a map. There is also a beginning section that serves as an introduction to the topic and ending section that serves as a conclusion to the book.

Each of the 50 pages is about one-third text (about five to ten paragraphs) and two-thirds photographs. The captions are lengthy and continue the work of the text exclusively-they may not, for example, tell the reader where exactly the photos were taken.

Noteworthy Features

The clear and extensively labeled photographs help readers attach to the text and picture the lands described. They also break up visually and physically lengthy, serious chunks of text. At the book's end, the text expresses a refreshingly clear, understated hope that readers will continue to learn about the interdependence and intriguing variety of life on our planet. This conclusion can serve as a model for budding writers of nonfiction who want to make definite conclusions but want to avoid overstating.

Teaching Ideas

Fur, Feathers and Flippers: How Animals Live Where They Do, is an example of nonfiction writing at its best. This text has none of the usual gimmicks that nonfiction authors sometimes use to try to draw young readers into an interest in a topic. It's not jazzy or interactive or full of hip references or spiced with comics. It does the job it set out to do and does it well, and as such is worthy of study and appreciation.

This book addresses concepts that are absolutely essential to an understanding both of geography and of biology. It's important that readers encounter these ideas during their independent reading time. If a teacher wanted to ensure that her class read independently around a particular concept, such as animal adaptation or diverse ecosystems, the teacher could say to her class, "During independent reading over the next two weeks, be sure you have read at least two books from such-and-such shelf, and be prepared for a small group or whole class book talk on [whatever angle the teacher wants to highlight]."

Alternatively, a teacher could talk with readers about the importance of a balanced reading life, one that includes nonfiction as well as fiction. Many adults read nonfiction books around a particular life interest, such as gardening, or raising orchids or parenting boys. The teacher could ask kids to develop their own life topics and "advertise" a few by promoting several collections of texts. One of these might be the way our stewardship of the earth is putting species at risk. For this or any topic it would be important to remind readers that even when pursuing a life passion, it's best to choose texts that are within one's reach as a reader. The texts they look at around a particular topic can also include magazines as well as books.

This book could be used as a companion to a picture atlas of the world, to help readers understand more about the fauna that inhabit various regions of the planet.

Since the index and table of contents are clear and well designed, readers can easily use this book as a resource to find particular bits of information about animals or lands. Note-taking is also easier here than in some other similar books.

If a teacher sees that the class as a whole tends to select fiction books only during independent reading, the teacher may institute some rituals that steer children towards nonfiction. The least intrusive would be to do promotional "booktalks" in which one "sells" nonfiction books. It's also possible to go a step further and to talk to children about the importance of having a balanced reading life. They can ask students to make sure that if they have a personal book self with four to five books they're reading or planning to read, that at least one of them be nonfiction. Finally, it's possible to go a step further and to suggest that, for a specified time, all children read only nonfiction texts during independent reading.

Teachers may want to do mini-lessons on strategies for skilled nonfiction reading. Many nonfiction readers read like magnets, looking for intriguing details that they pull from a text. One teacher told her students that some people then fact-drop these little bits of information into conversations, sharing in passing whatever they've been learning. The reader of this book would be full of such facts.

Another mini-lesson might show children that if a person read this book and loves it, they might collect other texts on the same topic.

Book Connections

Other nonfiction texts about animals in this library include: *What is a Primate?* and *What is a Rodent?* by Bobbie Kalman, and *Whales* by Deborah Hodge. These books could be displayed in a general book basket for animal texts, or in a collection of nonfiction texts about animals. Children can read them alongside fiction books and compare the information contained in each.

Genre
Nonfiction; Picture Book

Teaching Uses
Content Area Study; Reading and Writing Nonfiction; Book Clubs

George's Marvelous Medicine

Roald Dahl

FIELD GUIDE

D E

Illustrator
Quentin Blake

Publisher
Penguin Group, 1981

ISBN
0140346414

TC Level
9

Book Summary

George Kranky does not have a sweet, kindly grandmother. George's grandma is a "selfish, grumpy old woman" with "pale brown teeth and a small puckered-up mouth like a dog's bottom." In retaliation for her constant bossing, George replaces his grandmother's medicine with a potion that he hopes will blow off the top of her head. After his grandmother takes a spoonful, her innards catch on fire. She inflates and then grows so tall that she sticks out of the chimney.

George's father, after recovering from the shock, realizes just how "marvelous" this medicine could be to a farmer. In an attempt to have the biggest cows and hens (maybe he could cure world hunger with their eggs) in the county, he gets George to mix him up a batch. The only problem is that George cannot remember all of the ingredients in his concoction. George's failed attempts create a farm of misshapen animals and eventually shrink his grandmother into nothingness.

Basic Book Information

The 89-page book contains 15 chapters that are outlined in the table of contents. There are humorous illustrations by Quentin Blake on every other page. Roald Dahlis the author of the acclaimed *Matilda, James and the Giant Peach* and *Charlie and the Chocolate Factory.*

Noteworthy Features

The structure of *George's Marvelous Medicine* generally supports readers since it is in chronological order and all jumps in time are explained in the text. It contains a single plot line and only four characters. The entire book is set on the Krankys' farm.

The story itself is told by a third-person narrator who gets inside George's head and tells readers just how the boy is feeling. The narrator also provides humorous commentary on the unfolding events.

For inexperienced readers, retaining the developing plot for the duration of the book may still be difficult, and so these readers may benefit from opportunities to meet with a partner, to page through what they've read so far and retell it. The chapter titles give a glimpse of what the upcoming chapter will be about.

Teaching Ideas

This book contains all of the trademark features of a Roald Dahl book, including silly rhyming songs, concoctions that disfigure nasty people, a protagonist who rises from poverty to do something extraordinary, and

Quentin Blake's marvelously funny illustrations. It would be a good idea to group all of Dahl's books together in a classroom library, much like you would a chapter book series. Since there is such a formula to his books a child can get hooked on reading all of them.

At first, teachers may think that the best way to introduce this text is with the big disclaimer, "Kids, don't try this at home." Feeding your grandma nail polish remover is never a solution to your problems, no matter how cantankerous she is. Dahl, however, does this work for us. He creates such ludicrous scenarios that children can easily infer that the story is in jest. As in *Charlie and the Chocolate Factory*, Dahl skillfully creates a world in which anything is possible. The cartoon-like illustrations further enhance the ridiculousness of the story.

Teachers may use *George's Marvelous Medicine* in a writing workshop to focus on how to write descriptively and humorously. Dahl uses many adjectives to create vivid and funny pictures in readers' heads. Students will be able to see that, when they write with many synonyms to describe the same thing, the adjectives intensify the description, the words "screechy," "shrill," "awful," "snapping" and "shouting" all work together to convey how horrible grandma's voice is.

A source of confusion for readers may be the dialogue throughout the book. Some children may develop an ear for Dahl's sarcasm, but others may not. Reading aloud can help, since a teacher can relay some of the sarcasm through vocal intonation. Children reading with partners may then pick up on the facetious outlook in Dahl's books, discussing what tone they would use if reading aloud.

There are also plays on words that the reader may not pick up on, such as when George is mixing the medicine and adds "half a pint of ENGINE OIL-to keep Grandma's engine running smoothly," and "Some ANTIFREEZE-to keep her radiator from freezing up in the winter." During independent reading conferences or whole-class read alouds, teachers may want to monitor whether students understand these double meanings.

Book Connections

George's Marvelous Medicine may excite children to read *Matilda*, *Charlie and the Chocolate Factory* and other Roald Dahl books.

Genre

Chapter Book

Teaching Uses

Independent Reading; Book Clubs

Grandpa's Face

Eloise Greenfield

FIELD GUIDE

E

Book Summary

Tamika loved her Grandpa and his very expressive face. She loved taking "talk-walks" with him. But one day when Grandpa, an actor, was practicing, Tamika, peeking in to watch, saw the reflection of his face, and it was mean: a tight face with cold, cold eyes-a face that, some day, would not love her. Tamika wouldn't tell anyone what she had seen, but fretted. When Grandpa realized something was wrong, he invited Tamika to take a "talk-walk" with him and coaxed her worries out. Grandpa promised that he was only pretending and that he could never look at Tamika like that. Encouraged, Tamika once more felt safe and once more watched Grandpa's expressive face.

Illustrator
Floyd Cooper

Publisher
Philomel Books, 1988

ISBN
0698113810

TC Level
8

Basic Book Information

This is a 29-page book. The text is set up on every other page with soft, grainy oversized illustrations depicting the story with precision. Sentence length varies. Some, like the first sentence in the book, are only 4 words long while others range from 10 to 20 words. The syntax presents ideas in a logical, forward direction, making them easy to process. The illustrations also assist the young reader in interpreting Greenfield's writing. There are between 6 and 14 lines of text on each page. The page division is determined by the plot line. Each page tells one episode in the story, the completeness of which makes comprehension easier. Text is superimposed on the illustrations, which bleed to the edge of both pages. This may make reading more difficult for children used to dark print on a white background. This book is by Eloise Greenfield, whose award-winning poetry and picture books always present wonderful characters.

Noteworthy Features

This picture book story is told in the third person. The sentence structure is varied but the ideas are easy to follow. Passage of time markers are present when needed. After giving a brief background of the relationship between Tamika and her grandfather, Greenfield begins to tell the story with the phrase, "One day. . . ." All the action that follows occurs in that day-the problem, the events and the resolution. The story is told in straightforward language without requiring inferences that might challenge younger readers. The dialogue is lively.

Teaching Ideas

When children write their own fictional stories, they tend to stuff each page full of one melodramatic event after another. The boy and his father hike in the hills and the lion attacks them; there is an avalanche and a forest fire and a rabid raccoon and the father falls from a cliff... What a powerful statement Greenfield makes when she creates this gorgeous and important picture book out of one of the countless tiny misunderstandings people live through each day. It's important for children to see that all the ingredients of a great story are here in this tiny incident: Tamika peeks in on her Grandpa while he's acting out a part; she is frightened by his mean expression and holds her fear in; Grandpa creates the solution of a "talk-walk," and the story ends with a resolution.

Children can study Greenfield's skill in creating literature out of tiny moments. They can try to see vignettes from their own lives as rich material for stories, too. "What does Greenfield do to make her moment matter?" children can ask, and they can try to emulate her craft, and write by her example.

Book Connections

Eloise Greenfield has written a number of critically acclaimed books. Students will enjoy reading her poetry in such titles as *Honey I Love*, *Night on Neighborhood Street* and *Under the Sunday Tree*. They will also enjoy the vignettes she tells in *Childtimes*. Teachers might introduce other intergenerational books in relation to this one, such as Howard's *Aunt Flossie's Hats*, Ackerman's *Song and Dance Man*, Patricia MacLachlan's *Through Grandpa's Eyes* or *Abuela* by Dorros.

Genre

Picture Book

Teaching Uses

Author Study; Read Aloud; Partnerships; Teaching Writing

Heidi

Johanna Spyri

FIELD GUIDE

E

Publisher
Puffin, 1999

ISBN
0789453908

TC Level
10

Book Summary

This is the classic story of Heidi, who as a five year old is sent to live with her paternal grandfather, after being an orphan under the care of her aunt. Heidi's grandfather, or Uncle Alp, lives in Switzerland's Alps, and is feared by all because he is cross. Heidi soon conquers him through her attentions and love, as she makes friends with Peter, the goatherd, and with Peter's grandmother.

Heidi is later taken from this mountain paradise because her aunt wants her to live as a companion to a rich but invalid girl, Clara Sesemann, in Frankfurt, Germany. Here, Miss Rottenmeier is appalled by Heidi's simplicity, and harshly strives to make her a lady who is suitable for her new position. Heidi is comforted by Clara's sincere friendship, Mr. Sesemann's kindness and Grandmother Sesemann's sympathetic advice.

Upon a doctor's advice, Mr. Sesemann allows Heidi to return to her home in the Alps to improve her now poor state of health due to homesickness. Later, the Sesemanns visit Heidi, where Clara miraculously fosters the energy to walk. Heidi stays with her grandfather, Clara, and her beloved mountains.

Basic Book Information

This book is a classic that has been treasured by generations of readers. It is long-almost 300 pages-and will therefore require students who are reading it independently or in a partnership to read with some speed and stamina. Some editions are abridged. The book was originally written in German. There are many different English translations.

Noteworthy Features

Some of the words here are archaic. Many of them, such as *darning*, introduce the reader to the vocabulary of the country and the time period. Since it was written in the 19th century, many very old-fashioned gender roles persist throughout the book. For example, Heidi does the cleaning in the house in the Alps, the goatherd is male, the governess is female, and the tutor is male. Partners may want to discuss this, and to question the gender roles in the world of this story.

A respect for the elderly is also woven into this book, and an emphasis on being considerate of others. At times, the book can be moralistic, declaring that everything happens for a reason and that God knows best.

Teaching Ideas

Setting is very important in this text, since it defines the society of characters and their values. Uncle Alp lives in the secluded Alps, where he may meditate apart from the world. Life here is presented as being very pure. The family lives off the land; Heidi is calm, happy and at peace. On the other hand, at the Sesemann's home in Frankfurt, Heidi is always agitated because of the different schedules and the many, seemingly tedious, things to remember and ways to act. The reader may want to compare the two settings and relate them to the book's larger ideas. What do the big differences between the two locations say about what kind of a person Heidi is and what she learns? How do the settings affect the actions in the book? Does this glorified description of the home in the Alps and more cynical view of the home in the village buy into stereotypes about town and country life?

The book introduces many memorable characters: Heidi, Grandfather, Peter, Peter's Grannie, Clara, Mr. Sesemann, Dr. Classen, Grandmother Sesemann, and Miss Rottenmeier are all vital to the story. A reader might jot down notes about each character: What are the character's goals? What's the character's relationship to Heidi? Where does this character live and how does this affect his or her goals and perspectives? Over the course of the story, Heidi comes to live in very different contexts, and she changes as the contexts change. A reader might want to jot down bits of thinking under the headings "Heidi in the Alps" or "Heidi in the Town." The reader can draw up two lists for the characters, one for the character when they are introduced, and another for when they exit. Have they grown? How? Have their goals worked out? How has this affected them? Do they seem to fit conventional character types?

Since the book follows some conventions, and sets up others, the reader may want to discuss these in a partnership. Does the plot structure remind the reader of any other story he or she has heard? Any fairy tale? What makes this plot structure different from what one finds in fairy tales? Has either partner read a recent book that has a similar plot structure? The readers will recognize that writers borrow plot structures and adapt them for their own works. Do any entries in the student's writers' notebooks reflect this plot structure? What plot structures can they find in their entries?

Readers can take this further and ask themselves why the author would want to use this plot structure. They should think about the big ideas of the text and see how they relate to the plot structure. For example, one of the big ideas relates to how Heidi must say good-bye to her grandfather for a while, and she is sad. She eventually becomes happier because she meets many people while away. Heidi's happiness grows when she later returns to her grandfather in the Alps because she introduces all her new friends to her old ones. This big idea seems to rise and fall, much like the plot structure.

The book uses a fair number of Christian references. For example, Heidi recites the New Testament story of the prodigal son to her grandfather. Obviously, this story can be seen as a metaphor for her grandfather's life. Readers can learn from this example how authors make literary allusions.

Genre
Chapter Book

Teaching Uses

Independent Reading; Book Clubs; Partnerships; Character Study

Here Comes McBroom

Sid Fleischman

FIELD GUIDE

E

Book Summary

Here Comes McBroom is a trilogy of short stories: "McBroom the Rainmaker," "McBroom's Ghost" and "McBroom's Zoo." On Josh McBroom's one-acre farm the soil is so rich that "anything would grow in it-lickety bang." One day, even a dollar pocket watch takes root and grows into a three-dollar alarm clock. In "McBroom the Rainmaker," Farmer McBroom reverses a drought by causing a swarm of mosquitoes to cry (using super-sized onions of course!). "McBroom's Ghost" tells about a winter so cold "that catfish had grown a coat of winter fur" and all the sounds on the farm freeze. And, in the last story, a tornado spins all sorts of strange creatures like a Teakettler, Desert Vamooser, and Great Seventeen-Toed Hairy Parried Hidebehind into McBroom's life. Regardless of the tale, laughs are always abloom with Farmer Josh McBroom.

Illustrator
Quentin Blake

Publisher
William Morrow, 1992

ISBN
0688163645

TC Level
9

Basic Book Information

Here Comes McBroom was first published as a trilogy in 1992, almost twenty years after the individual publication dates of the three stories. Sid Fleischman is also the author of the Newbery Medal-winning book, *The Whipping Boy*. Fleischman's other books include: *Jim Ugly*, *The Midnight Horse*, *The Ghost in the Noonday Sun*, *Mr. Mysterious & Company*, *Chancy and the Grand Rascal Humbug Mountain*, *The Scarebird* and *The Hey Hey Man*. Quentin Blake is the well known illustrator of books by Roald Dahl, Joan Aiken and Russell Hoban.

Noteworthy Features

Readers who are fans of Roald Dahl books will surely recognize Quentin Blake's illustrations. They create a cartoonish quality and help to accentuate the absurdity and humor of the book. For example, there are pictures of fireworks growing out of a garden, crying mosquitoes, and a catfish swimming backwards through the dust.

All of the stories have the same line-up of characters. Also, they take place on or around McBroom's one-acre farm. This repetition may help readers get a stronger sense of the characters and setting.

Josh McBroom is the narrator of all three stories. When he talks to his audience of readers no quotation marks are used, but when he is speaking to another character they are. As the title page states, McBroom is the teller of "tall tales" and is prone to major exaggeration. Even though McBroom says, "I'd as soon grab a skunk by the tail as tell a falsehood," readers can easily figure out that even as he vows he'd never lie, he's lying to them. Some readers who do not understand this may be confused.

McBroom speaks like a stereotypical farmer. He uses words like "skeeters," "young'uns," and "rapscallions." Also, "em" is added after many words in lieu of "them" -i.e., "pound em," "magnetize em." Readers will enjoy the rich dialect and playful use of words, and will probably want to get their own mouths around what McBroom says when he calls the children: "Willjillhesterchesterpeterpollytimtommarylarry andlittleclarinda."

Teaching Ideas

Here Comes McBroom is full of laughs. Kids will delight in the humor of the book, whether it's read independently or during a read aloud. As a teller of tall tales, McBroom is never content with a single adjective. Oftentimes, he'll use a string of descriptive words like that "lost-looking, scared-looking, long-tailed" creature. McBroom also likes to use words that are just plain funny sounding, like "bamboozled" and "hornswoggle." Fleischman creates exaggerated scenarios like a heat wave that causes cows to give powdered milk. To accentuate the humor of the book readers may want to give a voice to McBroom that mirrors his cartoonish character. They may want to take note of specific elements of craft in a funny book like this one and use them in their own writing.

The three stories in this book were not originally intended to be part of one volume, yet there are common elements in all of the stories. Besides character and setting, the plots are very similar. In each of the stories, McBroom turns a bad situation into a good one through outrageous ingenuity. In the first story, McBroom is faced with a drought and mosquito infestation. So he hunts down a rain cloud with the help of a rain crow and wets some topsoil to bring home. There, he grows barn-sized onions that cause the swarm of mosquitoes to wet his soil with their tears. The crying mosquitoes leave the farm in haste and McBroom gets to grow fireworks in time for the Fourth of July.McBroom comes up with similarly ridiculous schemes in all of the stories. Readers may want to compare the stories to see how McBroom deals with different situations in a similar way; from this, they can begin to develop a strong sense of his character traits.

If a child is reading *Here Comes McBroom* with classmates or by themselves they may want to find support for McBroom's tall tale telling. McBroom frequently reiterates that he is not lying. Over and over again he says, "that's the sworn truth" and that he wouldn't tell a "falsehood." Readers may find his insistence proof to the contrary. If he were confident that his readers believed him, why would he have to keep reminding the reader that he's not a liar? Readers might also want to find textual support that McBroom tells tall tales and make the argument that this is not the same as lying. For example, does McBroom's telling a tall tale hurt anyone? Does exaggeration just make for a better story?

Reading the stories involves a thorough workout of the imagination. Children will have to suspend disbelief when reading the stories. A bird has backwards feet (so hunters won't be able to follow his tracks) and the rich topsoil grows trowels into shovels and pocket watches into alarm clocks. A literal reading of the book will leave readers perplexed.

Book Connections

All of the McBroom stories are flat-out ridiculous and should keep readers in stitches. Fans of Roald Dahl will probably enjoy these stories, too. In addition to sharing an illustrator, they are humorous tales of absurd events. In Dahl's *Charlie and the Chocolate Factory* and *George's Marvelous Medicine*, strange potions cause people to grow to ludicrous sizes. On McBroom's farm, it's the topsoil that is rich enough to be put into a bank that causes vegetables to grow to the size of barns. Both Dahl and Fleischman are masters at creating humorous children's fiction.

Genre
Anthology of Short Stories

Teaching Uses
Independent Reading; Read Aloud; Small Group Strategy Instruction; Teaching Writing

Honey, I Love

Eloise Greenfield

FIELD GUIDE

C E

Illustrator
Jan Spivey Gilchrist

Publisher
HarperCollins, 1978

ISBN
0064430979

TC Level
8

Book Summary

This poem was originally published in a collection of Greenfield's poems, then republished in this book by itself. Each five-line verse tells something the narrator loves: the way her cousin talks, the laughing sound she and her best friend make, the things she sees while riding in the family car and her mother's arm. The only thing the narrator does not love is going to sleep early. The poem ends with the line, "And honey, I love ME, too," a change from the original version, "And honey, I love you, too."

Basic Book Information

This 16-page poem has been a favorite since its initial publication. Each stanza has a five-line format, with the first and second lines and third and fourth lines rhyming. The stanzas are linked to one another by the word "and." The vocabulary is simple and easily understood by young children. Although the lines tend to be long-about twelve words -the syntax is not complex. Each stanza of the poem is given its own page on a reddish-brown background. The soft illustrations, with minimal detail, merge with each stanza and enhance the meaning. The fact that this poem, part of a collection of poems in the original printing, now has its own book allows the publisher to place each stanza on its own page. Gilchrist's illustrations, specific to the text, help young readers more easily comprehend the actions described. The placement of the text varies-stanzas appear at top left, others at bottom right. Greenfield has received numerous awards for her writing for children, including recognition by the Council on Interracial Books for Children for her "outstanding and exemplary contributions in children's literature."

Noteworthy Features

Each stanza tells its own "story" in rhyme. The narrator tells of things she loves: listening to her cousin's way of speaking, racing under a hose on a hot summer day, and laughing with her friend. The repetition of the phrase, "Honey, let me tell you" in each verse accents the rhythm that flows through the words: "Honey, let me tell you that I love to take a ride, I love to take a family ride." The poem can be interpreted on two levels. For the younger reader, it might be a list of things that are fun to do. The more perceptive reader will detect the underlying message of love: each of the verses describes an activity that costs nothing, that includes family members and friends, that defines love of family, of neighbor and of self. The one verse that describes something that the narrator does not love-going to sleep early, an action that separates her from family-also fits that pattern.

Teaching Ideas

Readers might discuss the underlying ideas each stanza emphasizes. Perhaps they'll come to see that the poet is saying that love, not material things, is important. Teachers might ask students to compare the activities in each verse to see if there is an underlying theme that runs through the poem. "What is the one important thing that Greenfield mentions in each verse?"

Teachers might want to have students explore the craft Greenfield uses in this poem. Her use of rhythm, repetition, and rhyme are worth admiring, and the poem becomes yet another example of the list structure (see also Butterworth's *My Mom Is Excellent*, Rylant's *When I Was Young in the Mountains*, and Howard's *When I Was Five*).

Poetry is best appreciated when it is read aloud. Students might work together to prepare a choral reading of the poem, deciding when to read lines as a chorus, when to use solo readers, etc. One or two members of the group might pantomime the action as the rest of the group repeats the lines.

Book Connections

If students enjoy this poem, they might enjoy reading the original collection by Greenfield, *Honey, I Love and Other Love Poems*.

Genre
Poetry; Picture Book

Teaching Uses
Teaching Writing; Interpretation; Read Aloud

Horrible Harry and the Ant Invasion

Suzy Kline

FIELD GUIDE

E

Series
Horrible Harry

Illustrator
Frank Remkiewicz

Publisher
Scholastic, New York, 1989

ISBN
0141300825

TC Level
8

Book Summary

Horrible Harry and the Ant Invasion is the story of Harry and an incident that involves his classmates in Room 2B over the course of several days. When Miss Mackle, Harry's teacher, orders ants and an ant farm for the class to study, Harry is thrilled. Harry loves all sorts of horrible, slimy, crawly things-he wants to be a scientist when he grows up. Harry also loves his classmate, Song Lee. One day, when the class is practicing the "Virginia Reel" together in the gym, Sidney, the class troublemaker, bangs into Song Lee while fooling around. Harry gets revenge on Sidney after school and Sidney, in turn, gets his own revenge by making it look like Harry has purposely killed a fish in the class fish tank. When Harry is about to be unfairly punished, Song Lee saves him by telling the truth. Finally, on picture day, Harry gets to stand next to Song Lee, who is beautifully dressed in her native Korean dress. Harry is happier than ever.

Basic Book Information

Horrible Harry and the Ant Invasion is one of a series of books about Harry and his classmates in Room 2B. It is 56 pages long with 4 chapters. The chapters have titles and are listed in a table of contents. The titles of the chapters help readers anticipate the plot in each chapter. The chapters are about 10 pages long, except for the first chapter, which is twice that. There are several small black-and-white illustrations per chapter. These illustrations do not support readers with difficult words or with content. There is dialogue throughout the text and most of it is clearly referenced. There is a lot of text on each page and the font is smaller than the font in many early chapter books. Some pages have sentences that begin on one page and continue to the next.

Noteworthy Features

The characters of Harry, his teachers and his friends are believable. The voices of the second-grade characters are authentic and readers rarely have a problem relating to the children in Room 2B. The text is usually straightforward and direct and doesn't include a great many words that are challenging to readers at this general level.

The *Horrible Harry* books are narrated by Harry's best friend, Doug. In this particular book, however, it is not very clear that Doug is the one telling the story. The story begins: "When Harry and I walked into Room 2B, we couldn't believe our eyes. 'Look at that!' I said. 'Wow! What is it, Doug?' Harry asked me. 'It's an ant city.'" This lead can disorient some readers who may not be clear as to who is doing the talking.

In some chapters, the passage of time is marked by a break in the text or a space between paragraphs. Changes in scene (between the classroom, the principal's office, etc.) are delineated in a similarly clear fashion.

The character of Song Lee is written as though she is a somewhat recent immigrant from Korea. Her speech is written to sound like the speech of someone who does not use English as her first language. For example, on page 44, Song Lee says: "I see Sidney by the tank just before bell ring. He reach behind where knob is." For early chapter book readers, this change in syntax and grammar can be difficult to recognize and understand.

Teaching Ideas

Horrible Harry is called "horrible" because he likes slimy, creepy things, horrible noises and so forth. He is not horrible because he is bad, mean or otherwise horrible. Although this is well explained in the text, some readers form an expectation for the book based on the title and cling doggedly to it in the face of much contradictory evidence. If a child claims that Harry is horrible, a teacher may want to support the fact that the child is developing theories about the characters. But it may help the child to see that, although it's wise to read along with the idea that Harry is a horrible kid, when one confronts evidence to the contrary the skilled reader stops and says, "Wait a minute," and revises his or her initial idea. It may be new for readers to realize that revision is as important to readers as it is to writers. Of course, there are times in the story when Harry's feelings get the best of him and he does misbehave. But a close inspection will show readers that Harry's intentions are always good.

There are two small school-related sections in the story that might cause some challenges for less experienced readers. In one section, the class tries to generate a list of words that include the vowel cluster -ant. Some of the words are obvious, like Antarctica, but many of the words include -ant in a much more subtle way, like giant, antipasti and panther. In another section, the class is learning how to dance the "Virginia Reel." Some of the dancing terms such as *curtsy, bow, sashayed, curtsied* and *square dance* could be unfamiliar to many readers.

Although the story is pretty straightforward and not particularly complex, some teachers and children find it hard to connect the plot line through the four chapters. The chapters seem to stand on their own as four separate events in Harry's life. The series of events that lead from beginning to end is clear, but an overlying bigger plot is hard to define. For example, there is no real mention of the ants or the ant farm after the first chapter, and yet the title of the book is *Horrible Harry and the Ant Invasion*.

Readers at this level often tend to focus on just getting through the words and the pages. As a result, they may race through the book and forget to construct a coherent meaning or to laugh at the funny parts or to reflect on the themes. A teacher might talk to a reader about this, and invite him or her to approach a book having already selected a few places to stop. Then the teacher could suggest some of the things a good reader might do at these pause points. "Sometimes I just stop and think-so what's happened so far? I try to retell the story to myself and it's like I'm giving myself a retelling test because if I can't do this, I know I need to reread." At some pause points, readers might say, "So what am I realizing about each of the characters?" or "So, let me picture this . . .." Of course, these pauses to reflect can be appointments for partner conversations, or simply occasions to do the mind-work of reading. Teachers may say to readers, "Before you begin reading today, look through the book and put a Post-it or a bookmark on a good place to stop for a moment. If you are reading with a partner, look over the book and think together about a good place to stop and talk." At this stopping point, readers can use a thinking-as-you-read strategy.

Horrible Harry and the Ant Invasion can be used by readers who are getting better at inferring characters' motivations and feelings. At many times in the story, Harry does or says things that are not spelled out in the text. In order to understand the character and the story, readers must be able to infer. Strategies that support inference include studying the dialogue more closely, paying attention to one part of the story and asking, "How does this fit with the whole text?" and looking for evidence in the text to explain why a character is doing or saying a particular thing. Readers need to become good at asking themselves questions such as: "Why is the character acting like that? How is the character feeling? Is the character acting or saying something that seems different from the way they usually act or the things they usually say? Has the character gone through some kind of change? Does that make sense to me?"

Readers can use *Horrible Harry and the Ant Invasion* to do character studies. Students can think about the characters' relationships to one another as they read. They can study the various traits of a character. (For example, Sidney is the class troublemaker. Song Lee is gentle and shy.) Readers can compare the characters in the stories to themselves, to other people they know and to characters in other books they've read. These are great opportunities for readers to reread, write and have relevant discussions with reading partners or members of a reading group.

In *Horrible Harry and the Ant Invasion* (as in other books about the same character) Harry struggles with some kind of moral dilemma based on his misbehaving, acting impulsively or trying to make up for some wrongdoing. Through his own reflection, talking with friends or teachers or just plain feeling sorry, he always ends up resolving his dilemma and doing the right thing and the story has a satisfying resolution. This is a great topic of discussion for the whole class, reading partners or book clubs.

Teachers may also do a strategy lesson on how to use Post-its and notebooks to chart when, how and why the character has grown or changed. Teachers may want to discuss with readers how, why and when the character solves his or her problem. Teachers may say, "Harry knows that he is the one who is telling the truth about the fish tank, but no one believes him because he is usually doing something wrong. Do you think anyone in the class will believe Harry? How will he keep from being unfairly punished? What is he learning from being unfairly accused? As you are reading today, see if you get a hunch about what will happen next or what Harry will learn about himself from this. Talk with someone about what you read that made you think the way you did." The teacher can instruct or model how to find places in the text that support the reader's questions or predictions.

These are also great opportunities for the teacher to model how readers think as they read, their "internal dialogue" with the book. As the teacher is reading she can "think out loud" for the children to notice. For example, when Harry does something that seems out of character a teacher may say (as if talking to herself): "That is so strange. I wonder why Harry isn't sticking up for himself the way he usually does? Maybe he thinks no one will believe him." Or, more simply, a teacher may (with exaggeration) laugh out loud or show a shocked face at a part that is important to the story.

All of the features mentioned in the above "Teaching Ideas" are excellent opportunities for teachers to do strategy lessons with the class, with a small, guided reading group, with a partnership pair or with an individual conferring during independent reading. Teachers can make copies of parts of the text that may cause some difficulty for readers or copy a section of text on overhead projector paper to look at with a larger group.

Book Connections

Horrible Harry and the Ant Invasion is part of a series by Suzy Kline. Other titles include: *Horrible Harry in Room 2B, Horrible Harry and the Dungeon,* and *Horrible Harry and the Christmas Surprise.* Other chapter books that are similar to this one are the *Mary Marony* series by Suzy Kline and *The Kids of the Polk Street School* by Patricia Reilly Giff.

Genre

Short Chapter Book

Teaching Uses

Independent Reading; Small Group Strategy Instruction; Partnerships; Character Study

House on Mango Street

Sandra Cisneros

FIELD GUIDE

E G

Publisher

Random House, 1991

ISBN

0679734775

TC Level

11

Book Summary

This book consists of a series of vignettes of Esperanza Cordero, a young MexicanAmerican girl coming of age in the Hispanic quarter of Chicago. For her, Mango Street is a barren landscape consisting of concrete and dilapidated tenements. It is here that she discovers life's most trying realities: the chains of class, gender, and racial hatred.

The house in which the Corderos live is falling apart physically. Esperanza describes it as "the house I belong but do not belong to." She desires a house she takes pride in. At the end of the book, she vows not to let her sad memories prevent her from living in a way that will result in her personal satisfaction.

Basic Book Information

Sandra Cisneros was born in Chicago in 1954. Acclaimed internationally for her poems and non-fiction, as well as the recipient of many awards, she has also written *Woman Hollering Creek and Other Stories* and two collections of poetry, *My Wicked, Wicked Ways* and *Loose Woman*.

This is a novel written from the point of view of an adolescent, Esperanza Cordero but teachers and children often rely upon this as an example of memoir writing at its best. Each vignette is approximately one page long and can stand on its own as an example of how writers can make literature out of the fine detail of their lives. One of these vignettes, "Hairs" has been printed in English and Spanish as a self-standing picture book.

Noteworthy Features

One important aspect of this text is Cisneros' use of carefully chosen, spare prose. She succeeds in creating unforgettable characters. One example of such a character is Minerva who is "only a little bit older than (Esperanza) but already she has two kids and a husband who left... Minerva cries because her luck is unlucky. Every night and every day. And prays. But when the kids are asleep after she's fed them pancake dinner, she writes poems on little pieces of paper that she folds over and over and holds in her hands a long time, little pieces of paper that smell like a dime."

Along with creating characters who will remain indelible on the mind of the reader, her use of words also endears the reader to Esperanza's plight. Esperanza desperately wants "a house. A real house. One that I could point to. But this isn't it. The house on Mango Street isn't it. For the time being, Mama says. Temporary, says Papa. But I know how those things go." Ultimately, Esperanza succeeds in realizing for herself, if only in her mind, "a house all of [her] own...quiet as snow, a space for [herself] to go," despite the restrictive nature of her surroundings.

Cisneros also presents the craft of writing as liberating. It is the poetry that allows Minerva to escape her plight as a struggling single mother. Similarly, it is when Esperanza puts her story down on paper that Mango Street sets her free. She vows one day to leave with books and paper to "come back. For the ones [she] left behind. For the ones who cannot out."

Teaching Ideas

Though this book was not written for young children, it can be used selectively in all classrooms. Many of the short vignettes are both the length and the tone of the writing that students can do in elementary school. Pieces (such as "Hairs") are simple enough and short enough to be read aloud and again re-read independently by students in grades two or three and above. Teachers may not want to put this book on the shelves of their classroom library (unless they are in middle school) because for most classrooms of children this will be a teaching resource more than a good independent read.

This book contains many injustices that the discerning reader will recognize. These include issues such as racism, discrimination based on class and gender, and roles in families based on cultural beliefs. One example of this racism is Cathy, Queen of Cats, who moves a little father away north from Mango Street every time "people like [the Corderos] move in." If the piece is at the center of a book clubs discussion, children often notice and begin to discuss this issue.

This text would work well as a text for children to imitate in their own writing. Cisneros writes in a very controlled manner, sometimes with very sparse, almost staccato sentences and other times with fabulous description, in long word-filled sentences. Children can try this in their own writing, often with extraordinary results.

"Those Who Don't" is an extraordinary statement about the world and teachers have often used it as a short text when they want to begin a unit of study focusing on improving the quality of their book talks. It invites students to say something about home, and family and fear and prejudice.

Many teachers pull together "Laughter," "Hairs," "My Name," "The House on Mango Street," "Bums in the Attic," "Smart Cookie," "A House of My Own," and "Mango Says Good-bye Sometimes" so that together they provide an example of memoir in vignette form. The beginning of this text and the ending are so closely matched that they help us teach that the beginnings and endings of memoir often fold back on each other.

We also use this book in a study of the list as a structure for writing. Although some of the vignettes are stories, they combine in a list-like way. Teachers show students that these episodes are not arranged chronologically, though some of them individually may be stories.

Many teachers of writing have put selected pages from this book on overheads and projected them for the class to see, to study, and to emulate. "Papa wakes up tired in the dark," for example retells five minutes in time, and yet within these five minutes the narrator does a lot of internal thinking, enriching the story. Children benefit from seeing that they can retell a tiny vignette and weave memories into it. (i.e., "I stood at the edge of the sea, my toes dug into the sand. Nearby I saw a shell. I picked it up and remember a stormy August morning two years ago when. ..." "Papa who wakes up tired..." is worth studying.) Cisneros collects tiny detail to bring her characters to life, and she reveals one character through the point of view of another (e.g., Her papa "crumples like a coat and cries").

Book Connections

List books for the older, more sophisticated writer would include: this text, *Childtimes* by Eloise Greenfield, *Flora and Tiger* by Eric Carle, and *Walking the Log* by Bessie Nickens. The study of these more sophisticated books would come after studies of simpler list books such as *When I Was Young In the Mountains* by Cynthia Rylant and *Uptown* by Bryan Collier.

Genre
Short Chapter Book; Memoir

Teaching Uses
Teaching Writing; Partnerships; Read Aloud; Book Clubs

How Do Dogs Really Work?

Alan Snow

FIELD GUIDE

E

Book Summary

This is a humorous book of nonfiction. In it, the habits and peculiarities of dogs are described in unusual or ironic language. The subjects the book takes on range from communication, to legs and getting around, to the vet and general maintenance, to the brain and central nervous system and even the dog family tree.

Illustrator
Alan Snow

Publisher
Little, Brown and Company, 1993

ISBN
0316801348

TC Level
11

Basic Book Information

This picture book is about 30 pages long. It won the New York Times Book Review award for Best Illustrated Children's Book of 1993. The book begins with a table of contents listing the ten subjects related to dogs discussed in the text. The whimsical illustrations are detailed and sometimes contain extensive labels. The text is all hand-lettered, and of varying size and layout. Sometimes the text is in the form of a list of steps, sometimes in a series of examples with headings, sometimes as a paragraph laid out in the shape of a triangle to fit alongside the pictures. The last page of the book is a one-page index that offers the page numbers of peculiar, funny subjects related to dogs.

Noteworthy Features

The illustrations in this book really give it its charm and attraction. Many are depictions of machines that supposedly live inside the dogs, making them do the crazy, funny things they do.

This probably isn't a book one would want to turn to for hard information about dogs. Rather it's a humorous examination of the animals, meant for dog owners or dog lovers. In many ways the book is funny while still being true. It implies that the dogs are machines, for example, and describes in great detail a funny habit or characteristic dogs have, like sticky tongues. Sometimes just having a particular aspect of dog behavior that seems so familiar put into words makes readers smile.

Teaching Ideas

Kids who are reading the book literally will obviously be very confused. If they don't see the humor, the mechanical language and other tongue-in-cheek descriptions will be misleading and hard to understand. Sometimes reading parts of the book aloud to the reader and laughing when appropriate will be all the student needs to set him or her on the track toward understanding what kind of book this is. Sometimes, however, a little more explicit explanation of how the author is trying to create the humor helps the reader make sense of the words he is reading. Sometimes the book should simply be put aside until the reader is more experienced.

Often, the text changes abruptly from explaining a dog behavior to describing what it is like for the dog itself, in its mind. There is no overt signal that this is happening, so the transition is confusing for some readers. For example, "What happens when the eyes pick up the image of another dog? The brain checks it against memories. Is it a bone? No. Is it a cat? No. Is it a plate of dog food? No." and so forth. Many readers don't "get" to imagine that this is a dialogue that is inside a dog's head; they see it only as the author telling the reader what the dog is not. A teacher can confer with a reader about these instances of transition and teach him how to recognize them.

The readers who will enjoy this book the most, who will understand it best, are those for whom the habits and traits of dogs are already very familiar. Since they will know all the factual information in the book already, those readers are then free to revel in the idiosyncratic way the writer expresses those traits, and to have fun.

It can be interesting for children to discuss what they believe is the overall message of the book. What exactly is the author trying to make fun of, if anything? Is this book poking fun at people who tend to see everything as logical and mechanical? Is he mocking the genre of nonfiction books themselves? Is he just enjoying with the reader how silly dogs can be?

Book Connections

There are other nonfiction picture books about animals in this library that also have great illustrations: *Animal Defenses* by Etta Kaner is about different types of animals and how they protect themselves. *No One Told the Aardvark* by Deborah Eaton and Susan Halter combines a story with facts about animals. *Catbirds & Dogfish* by Bernard Most is a picture book filled with interesting information about rare animals.

Genre
Nonfiction; Picture Book

Teaching Uses
Independent Reading; Partnerships; Teaching Writing; Interpretation

I Wish I Were a Butterfly

James Howe

FIELD GUIDE

E

Illustrator
Ed Young

Publisher
Harcourt Brace, 1994

ISBN
015200470X

Book Summary

The littlest cricket in Swampswallow Pond is sad because a frog told him crickets are ugly. Now he feels ashamed and wishes to be a butterfly. The other insects around the pond try to console him, urging him not to wish for something he can never have. Finally, the old wise spider makes him feel okay about himself again by telling him she has also been called ugly, but that she believes him when he says she is beautiful. She tells him he, too, is beautiful and he believes her in return. A butterfly passing by hears the cricket chirping and longs to be a chirping cricket herself.

Basic Book Information

The well-known author of *Bunnicula* and many other books for children, James Howe has now written this straightforward picture book.

Noteworthy Features

The introductory author's note may answer questions that readers have about Howe's inspirations for creating the book; however, most children will appropriately skip over it, and perhaps return to it after reading the text.

The pastel illustrations by Caldecott award-winner Ed Young lend light and soft color to the pond creatures, while allowing enough ambiguity for children to envision some of their own images. Teachers may find that a book introduction will ease readers into the illustrations and the plot.

Teaching Ideas

I Wish I Were a Butterfly can be an excellent tool for helping kids learn interpretation and critique. Some teachers repeat three questions with each book they bring their students into: 1) What kind of people are the characters in the story? 2) What would their actions stand for in the real world? 3) What are the consequences of their actions in the book (and what would they be in the real world)? Kids may eventually internalize these questions and use them as an entryway into interpretation.

After readers are given the opportunity to support their answers to the above questions, they will develop a general sense of the book's message. Some may say it's about how important it is that other people think you are beautiful-since the cricket can only rest when the spider tells him he is beautiful. After looking more closely at the book, students may be able to enter into a broader discussion about the definition of beauty. Is it so necessary to be beautiful in the eyes of others? Can it not be that the cricket finds beauty in himself? Beyond this, could he have found happiness without being beautifulie., is outer beauty so important? As each child comes to a conclusion, it's important to develop the habit of critiquing it. Even if it's as simple as saying that the book's message is "when you don't feel happy with how you are, a good and wise friend can really help," children should know how to support their conclusion with examples from the text.

Some children need support in the middle of the story so that they understand that the long dashes are used to show interruption. When the cricket is talking to himself, saying "Why can't I be--?" the dragonfly completes his sentence with, "A dragonfly like me?" Still, it is unlikely that children will lose the thread of the story, as it is clear on the next page what is happening. In most of the other dialogue in the book, the character that is speaking is identified.

Book Connections

James Howe is also the author of *Bunnicula: A Rabbit-Tale of Mystery* and *Bunnicula strikes again*!

Genre

Picture Book

Teaching Uses

Critique; Interpretation

In the Dinosaur's Paw

Patricia Reilly Giff

FIELD GUIDE

E

Series
The Kids of the Polk Street School

Illustrator
Blanche Sims

Publisher
Bantam Doubleday, 1985

ISBN
0440441501

TC Level
8

Book Summary

In the Dinosaur's Paw is the fifth book in *The Kids of the Polk Street School* series. The characters in the series are the thirteen kids in Ms Rooney's class: Emily, Richard, Matthew, Jill, Alex, Timothy, Noah, Derrick, Wayne, Linda, Sherri, Jason and Dawn. Each numbered book in the series takes place in a different month of the year-this story occurs in January. Richard Best, also known as Beast, is having a hard month. He already feels bad about being left back, he forgot to bring a ruler for a special project in school, there hasn't been any snow all winter, he can't think of "five facts about dinosaurs" for his homework assignment, and Drake Evans, the bully from his old class, will not leave him alone. When Richard finds a cool dinosaur ruler in his desk, he thinks it might be magic, and starts wishing for his luck to turn around. It immediately snows all day and he comes up with great answers for his homework assignment. But when Drake Evans becomes too sick to join a class trip, Richard starts to feel afraid that he has gone too far. He "wishes" that he would lose his power for making wishes come true. As he takes back his wish, he realizes he has mistakenly judged Drake. When Drake shows up for the trip, Richard makes a first attempt to become his friend.

Basic Book Information

In the Dinosaur's Paw is 72 pages long, divided into 10 numbered, untitled chapters. There is one full-page illustration in each chapter that represents a small part of the action; the rest of the book is all text. This book involves several January days, and it is set in and around both Ms. Rooney's classroom at the Polk Street School and Richard's home. If a scene changes, it always happens at the start of a chapter.

Noteworthy Features

Patricia Reilly Giff does a good job of getting into the heads and hearts of the characters in the story. The voices of the children are quite authentic, as is the voice of the teacher, Ms. Rooney. The untitled chapters don't foreshadow the upcoming events or entice readers on, as books at this level so often do. On the other hand, chapter titles can also be puzzling or distracting for readers at this level, setting up expectations that aren't always met.

The vocabulary in the text tends to be simple but some of the text can be tricky for less experienced readers. Throughout the story, Richard's thoughts are written into the text, so readers must be able to keep straight whether they are reading dialogue, internal thought or actions. For example, on page 47 the text states: "Richard looked across the table. Matthew was still a little wet. Drake Evans had probably pushed him. If only Drake weren't going on the trip. If only Drake would move before Friday."

Although most of the dialogue is written simply and always referenced, some passages have dialogue that tends to jump around a bit. There are also times when characters interrupt each other or their sentences drift off as they think.

Teaching Ideas

In the Dinosaur's Paw is a great book for readers who have begun to read early chapter books independently, in a fluent and sustained way. A teacher may, in a conference, want to remind such a reader of his or her jobs as a chapter-book reader. Because readers of early chapter books are often focused on processing all that print, they sometimes can read along without doing the mind-work that reading involves. Sometimes when teachers ask these readers about the book, they say, "I read it, honest. I just can't remember it." Readers can be reminded that reading is comprehension. It's not an extra credit option for readers to read with accuracy and intonation!

If a teacher wants to prepare a child to be actively thinking as he or she reads, it sometimes helps to look over the book together in order to activate a child's expectations and involvement in the story. Because this book has no chapter titles, a teacher might suggest dipping in to read a few excerpts and using those passages to conjure up expectations for the text. Then, too, teachers will want to encourage readers to use all they know from other books in the series to generate expectations for this book.

Teachers may also want to talk with a child about the fact that, when reading a story, one generally expects to learn the characters, setting and basic plot by the end of the first chapter. If one comes to the end of the first chapter without knowing these things, it's often a good sign that some rereading is in order.

It could be, for example, that the teacher reads a book aloud and during the following book talk, shows children some of the ways good readers think about character. Afterwards, when children disperse for their independent reading, the teacher might remind them to do some of this work with characters as they read independently. Alternatively, the idea of reading with an eye towards understanding the characters could simply emerge out of a one-to-one conference between the teacher and a reader. The teacher could suggest that students read like magnets, collecting bits of information about each character so that early on in their reading, they could pause and create a tiny character sketch of each character.

The readers of *In the Dinosaur's Paw* could be coached to read entirely with an eye towards getting to know the characters. Readers will probably note that Richard is embarrassed about being held back, and sometimes acts mean to other kids when he feels this way. Dawn Bosco is a "know-it-all." Matthew is one of the nicest kids in class, but he wets the bed. Readers who've read other books in the series can compare the specific characters in this book to characters in other titles from the series. Readers can also compare the characters in this story to themselves, to other people they know, and to characters in other books they've read or heard read to them.

A teacher might suggest that good readers think about the characters in a story the way they think about the people in their lives. "Why don't you read on, but pause every few pages to think about Richard?" If a child did this, he or she would soon have a theory about the kind of person Richard seems to be. The great thing about taking the time to crystallize a theory is that often this allows readers to revise old theories. "Why don't you continue to read and see if Richard stays this way, or if he changes?" a teacher might say.

Throughout this series, the main character tends to undergo some kind of change. Although at the beginning of *In the Dinosaur's Paw* the main character, Richard Best, is convinced that his life would be a lot easier if Drake Evans would get sick or move, Richard changes. When he finds out that Drake has been helpful to his friend Matthew, he feels badly about wishing the worst on him. By the end of the story, when Drake reciprocates Richard's attempts at friendship, Richard's feelings about him have changed. Teachers may show readers how they can use Post-its to make notes of the places in the text where a character has changed.

A teacher may also want to help readers of this book predict what is going to happen to the character, or within the story. Teachers may set readers up with a brief introduction, such as: "In this story, Richard believes he has a magic ruler that allows him to make wishes that will come true. He decides to wish that Drake Evans, the bully, would get sick so that he won't come on the class trip. But when Richard finds out that Drake is sick, he doesn't feel happy at all. As you read today, try to find the place where Richard feels differently than he thought he would. When you find that place, see if you can guess how Richard will really feel and what you think he will do." Alternatively, the teacher could say, "I wonder why Richard has changed his mind and now he wishes that he didn't have magic powers?" Yet another option would be to say, "I think Richard is going to be brave next time he walks by the dog, because he is not taking the long way around." Teachers can also demonstrate for readers "out loud" some of the questions, predictions and feelings that they, as readers, have as they read.

Because *In the Dinosaur's Paw* is longer than the very early chapter books that children may have been reading recently, teachers may want to work with students on the ending or resolution of the story, and discuss where that actually occurs. The resolution of the story does not always happen in the last sentences or on the last page of the book. Teachers can work with readers on noticing parts in their reading where the character has fully changed, or the main events of the story have come together, or the "problem" has been resolved. It is important for the teacher to lead readers to discover where these things happen in the story, and how it is revealed in the text.

Book Connections

There are many titles in *The Kids of the Polk Street School* series including: The *Beast in Ms. Rooney's Room*, *December Secrets*, *Snaggle Doodles*, and *Lazy Lions, Lucky Lambs*. Other chapter book series similar to this one are: *The Pee Wee Scouts*, *The Bailey School Kids*, and *The New Kids of the Polk Street School*, which is about Emily Arrow's little sister and her friends. (This series though, is easier than *The Kids of the Polk Street School*.)

Genre
Short Chapter Book

Teaching Uses
Independent Reading; Character Study

Into the Sea

Brenda Z. Guiberson

FIELD GUIDE

E

Book Summary

This book follows a sea turtle through her first moments out of her egg and into the deep sea. She feeds, rests, encounters other plants and creatures and even manages to escape both a shark and a fishing net. In the end, she follows the patterns of her ancestors and returns to the same beach on which she herself hatched twenty years earlier. There, she lays her eggs and slowly makes her way back into the ocean.

Illustrator
Alix Berenzy

Publisher
Henry Holt and Company, 1996

ISBN
0805064818

TC Level
10; 11; 12

Basic Book Information

This nonfiction picture book is about 25 pages long. In it, the author tells the continuous narrative story of one sea turtle. Each double-page spread is composed of one or two large illustrations and one or two paragraphs of text. The book is formatted like a fictional picture book, with no table of contents or index. The book does end with a one-page note from the author that offers more details about the plight of endangered sea turtles. This note is longer than the text on any of the other pages, and it isn't accompanied by a full-page illustration. For this reason, some children may skip reading it, although the font size is the same as that in the story itself. The information in the note is pertinent to the story and understandable to readers of the book, generally.

Noteworthy Features

The smooth flow of this narrative may make it especially easy for readers more accustomed to fiction than nonfiction. The fact that the narrative follows one sea turtle in particular, instead of listing facts about many, also attracts certain kinds of readers who are used to allowing character attachments to pull them through stories.

This book not only offers lots of factual details about the sea turtle in the midst of the narrative, but it also offers information about the habitat of the sea turtle. It puts the sea turtle directly into her own environment and describes her part in it. This contextualization is not often found in many nonfiction books for this age group, and is appreciated especially by teachers who are helping students learn about interdependence in nature. The narrative form also allows the author to create a sense of place for the sea turtle, not only with facts but with carefully chosen language. There is an artistic element to this book that imparts more than an encyclopedia could.

Some children have discovered the dedication from the author to the "toothless turtle." This has led to many discussions about aggression and survival and the author's choice of the word "toothless," which seems to be favorable in the author's opinion.

Teaching Ideas

Although it is not an extreme example, some teachers use this book as an example of how people tend to put human emotions and thoughts into animals-a practice called anthropomorphizing-that has its advantages and disadvantages. On one hand, it can help humans come to understand the world of animals, to feel for them and care for their circumstances. On the other hand, since most animals don't feel human emotions or have human thoughts, to present them this way too strongly is not scientifically accurate or helpful to research.

This is one of those hard-to-find nonfiction picture books that can make an excellent read aloud book. The information about the sea turtle and her habitat come in the form of a smooth and interesting narrative that reads like fiction, and pays careful attention to language and imagery.

The author's note in the back gives specific examples of practices that are harmful to the future existence of sea turtles, and these examples sometimes make children irate and upset. For this reason, this book can easily lead students to further research about sea turtles, and can certainly spur them on to taking social action to try to protect these creatures and their habitats.

Genre

Nonfiction; Picture Book

Teaching Uses

Independent Reading; Read Aloud; Book Clubs; Teaching Writing; Critique

Ira Says Goodbye

Bernard Waber

FIELD GUIDE

E

Illustrator
Bernard Waber

Publisher
Houghton Mifflin, 1988

ISBN
0395584132

TC Level
8

Book Summary

Ira hears from his sister that his best friend Reggie is moving away in two weeks. He is heartbroken. At first his friend seems heartbroken, too, but then he begins to talk nonstop about how fun and perfect his new town is going to be. It makes Ira hurt and angry to hear his friend sound so happy to move; he begins to think of how happy he will be when Reggie moves. The two don't seem to get along any more. On the day of the move, Reggie starts to cry uncontrollably. Ira is surprised that Reggie cares. The two boys exchange some of their treasures. That night Reggie invites Ira to visit that weekend. In his excitement, Ira begins packing immediately, although the visit is days away.

Basic Book Information

Bernard Waber is the author and illustrator of more than thirty picture books for children, including such favorites as *Lyle*, *Lyle Crocodile* and *Ira Sleeps Over*.

Noteworthy Features

The essence of this book is the emotional story of two friends moving apart. The words themselves tell how the characters feel on the surface, or simply what they say and do. In order to read this book well, readers will need to penetrate the words, actions, and surface level emotions to try to figure out why the characters are speaking and behaving the way they are and what they are really thinking and feeling. Sometimes, this is easy to do just on the basis of what the reader thinks the character must be feeling, given what he has already said and done. Sometimes it is easier to do if the reader thinks about times he himself has had a similar experience. This kind of personal response can help readers understand how Ira and Reggie are feeling. At the same time, understanding what Ira and Reggie are feeling can help readers understand their own feelings.

Teaching Ideas

Much of this book is written in dialogue, and to follow it, children need to be able to know who is speaking, even when the dialogue isn't tagged with "he said." This may require a reminder about how paragraphs change when the speaker changes. Children who get confused time and time again might even use pencil to make light markings in the story with the initials of the character who is speaking, once they figure it out. This can work with any book that poses this sort of difficulty.

The part of the story that involves Ira and his turtles can be a great episode for kids to examine in depth because of its layered significance. When Ira claims that turtles can die from losing their friends, kids might at first think Ira is being ridiculous, and an examination of that can eventually bring them to understand how Ira is feeling about losing his own friend. Studying this event can be a bridge for helping children realize that characters sometimes do and say things with hidden meanings that take a little thinking to figure out.

The opening of the story, when Ira's sister tells him Reggie is going to move, can be difficult for some children because of the emotions and teasing that are going on beneath the surface between Ira and his sister. Some children don't understand why Ira keeps saying "Goodbye" to his sister. They need several reads or a discussion with their group to understand that Ira is trying to get his sister to tell him the news quickly. This part, too, takes thinking on the part of the reader to understand why Ira and his sister behave the way they do. Again, personal response may be helpful in comprehension here.

Along the same vein, some children don't understand why Ira's mother suggests the family bake a cake just after the sad move of Reggie and his family. Kids will have to wonder what Ira's mother must be thinking, and they must try to figure out her motive in suggesting they bake at this moment.

To help readers begin to get underneath the dialogue to the emotional truth it covers, children might start by reading and asking, "Could that be true?" When they come to the parts in which Reggie says that people in his new town smile all the time and are always friendly one hundred percent of the time, and do nothing but play games and watch fireworks, readers have to say to themselves, "That's not possible. No town is full of people who are always happy and always having fun." When readers come to that conclusion, it is not much of a leap for them to ask themselves, "Why would Reggie say that when it isn't true?" And then they are well on their way toward an emotional analysis of that character. The same thing will happen when readers come to parts in which Ira claims that turtles mope when they lose their friends. When readers say to themselves that can't be true, their next question can easily be, "Why would the character say that?" Even when Ira claims he will be happy when Reggie moves, readers can question the truth of the statement and wonder why Ira would say that. All of this questioning is not necessarily easy for students-doubting the truth of the words a narrator says is not an automatic impulse for many children. If it proves unduly difficult, it might be best for the teacher to read the book aloud to the children, thinking and explaining aloud for them their own thoughts.

Book Connections

Bernard Waber is the author and illustrator of more than thirty picture books for children, including such favorites as *Lyle, Lyle Crocodile* and *Ira Sleeps Over.*

Genre

Picture Book

Teaching Uses
Independent Reading; Read Aloud; Character Study; Partnerships

Island Boy

Barbara Cooney

FIELD GUIDE

E

Book Summary

This is the story of the life and death ofMatthias, the youngest of twelve children, on an island where his father had made a home for all of them. During both times of prosperity and times of hardship, his work is constant, and eventually there are the children, grandchildren and the beauty and ways of the island that he loves.

Illustrator
Barbara Cooney

Publisher
Penguin Books, 1988

ISBN
0140507566

Basic Book Information

Barbara Cooney has won two Caldecott awards for *Chanticleerand the Fox* and *Ox-Cart Man*. Cooney has illustrated more than 100 books, as well as written many of her own, including *Miss Rumphius*, for which she won the American Book Award.

Noteworthy Features

One of the most remarkable aspects of this book is the way the narrator tells of nature and of country life with a touch of the romantic, but without sentimentality. There are good times and bad in everyone's life. The fact that the cycle of life always goes on is the dominant theme of the book.

Some readers find it a little confusing to keep track of the characters in the story, since there are several generations and wives and uncles and children to account for. In some books with many characters, keeping track of them all is necessary to the story. In this one, however, that would probably detract from an understanding of the text. Instead, readers can be advised to keep track of the one central character, Matthias, as he grows, and only hold other characters in mind as they relate to him. The confusion of characters, too, may be a way of communicating the cycle of life and how one generation blends into another. Once again, when students call attention to the ways the text works, they are calling attention to clues that can point to or support the book's theme. In the first two pages, Matthias has not yet emerged as the central character, so this poses an additional challenge. If readers can contain their confusion and be patient until they think they have found a character they can hold on to, they will be all set.

Readers sometimes get very interested in who is telling this story, since they have to focus on characters in order to keep them straight. Many decide it is an outside, unrelated narrator telling all that has happened. A few readers, however, find the personal "Pa" on the first page, which reveals that the story is being told by one of the twelve children, a brother or sister to Matthias, not featured in the story, or perhaps referred to later in the third person; (there is no "I" anywhere in the work).

Children often speculate on whether or not this is a true story since it has the ring of truth, and because of the detailed, realistic maps on the inside front and back covers. But there really is little evidence to base a conclusion on from the text, one way or the other.

Teaching Ideas

Sometimes there are details within a story that seem to echo or emphasize the story's message or themes. Oftentimes, if a detail seems to be getting more space or words than other details, it's a sign that this is one of those emblematic details. When experienced readers read along and come to a part that is told in greater detail than other parts, they often ask themselves, "What makes this part so special?" This kind of flag goes up when the student reads about the little gull that Matthias tames and teaches to fly, who eventually takes to the skies. Some readers may ask themselves, "Why so much about the gull, will he come back later in the story and become important?" But when he does not, the experienced reader will probably say, "Why did the author give so much space to telling about the gull? And why is it on the cover of the book?" For many, the answer is that in the detail of the gull is the heart of the book, about growing up and changing and moving on to what you must do. The gull and Matthias himself both do these things.

Since the emblematic detail stands out so well in this book, it may be the kind teachers read aloud, stopping to explain why a particular detail might reveal the theme of the book. On the other hand, the ease with which this detail comes to light may make the book a good choice for students independently trying to find details that reveal theme. This will depend on how experienced children are at interpreting. Of course, children may find other details that emphasize what they believe the themes are as well. The learning comes in the decision making about which details count and which don't, not in the finding of the gull, exactly.

Some children are shocked by the deaths in the story that are told about in passing, or without much apparent effect on the other characters. Some are surprised that the storm that took Matthias' life isn't described in detail. Noticing these details points yet again to an interpretation of the book. One thing many experienced readers do is turn to where the text didn't go as expected and ask why it didn't. What made the author take that turn instead of the one that was expected? Discussions of why the author chose to write this way often lead to interpretations of the themes of the book -in this case, of accepting and relishing and not fearing the cycle of birth, life and death.

This book can also be used in a writing workshop to provide examples for children of the conscious decisions an author has to make about how much importance to give each event in his or her story. It's easy for children to imagine how this book could have been written differently, with Matthias' adventures on the high seas as the primary events, or with the deaths as central to the story. They may even understand why writing the book in these other ways wouldn't communicate the themes about the cycle of life that are so important.

Book Connections

Barbara Cooney has won two Caldecott awards for *Chanticleer and the Fox* and *Ox-Cart Man*. Cooney has illustrated more than 100 books, as well as written many of her own, including *Miss Rumphius*, for which she won the American Book Award.

Genre
Picture Book

Teaching Uses
Independent Reading; Interpretation; Teaching Writing

J.T.

Jane Wagner

FIELD GUIDE

E F

Illustrator
Gordon Parks Jr.

Publisher
Dell, 1969

ISBN
0440442753

TC Level
10

Book Summary

J.T. is a ten-year-old boy who feels lonely around the Christmas holidays until he finds a badly injured alley cat and is distracted from his own sadness. J.T. identifies with the cat's external injuries as he battles with his own internal conflicts around being poor and abandoned by his father. To make matters worse, J.T.'s teacher does not understand what he is going through, and there are two neighborhood bullies after him. J.T.'s relationship with his mother is tenuous, and although he feels more comfortable because his grandmother from the South is staying for the holidays, he is still unable to express his deep feelings of longing. However, through his desire and attempt to care for the badly injured cat, J.T. begins to learn that he can share his feelings with those around him.

Basic Book Information

This book is written by Jane Wagner and illustrated with photography by the well-known photographer Gordon Parks, Jr. This book originated as a ballad, and then as an award-winning CBS Children's Television Special. The book tells the story of a young ten-year-old boy living in the inner city with uncertainty and loss. The photographic illustrations make real the plight of this vulnerable ten year old. J.T. is a sensitive but conflicted boy who, on the one hand, is able to show love and concern towards a wounded animal, yet on the other hand, leans toward crime and dishonesty when he steals a radio and buys on credit at the grocery store without his mother's permission.

J.T. is 125 pages in length and it is not divided into chapters or sections. The story has a serious tone as well as a mixture of mystery and conflict. *J.T.* is not exactly a happy story, but represents what could be considered realism.

Noteworthy Features

The book is written in narrative form and includes dialogue between the characters. Some very challenging words are used, withmeanings not easily identified through context such as *antimacassar*, *valiant*, and *meticulously*. Colloquial speech is also used.

The book lends itself to great book talks because it deals with some difficult life themes, e.g., loneliness, poverty, abandonment and death.

It may be difficult for a child to keep up with the events because the book is not divided into chapters or sections. Children may benefit most by stopping to define, discuss and interpret major events as they happen in the book. This may make it easier for the child to group or organize ideas about the book for greater understanding of the plot.

Teaching Ideas

J.T's character is complex and many-sided; readers will want to think about him for a while. Is he a good boy? After all, he feels sympathy for the injured cat. Or is he a bad boy? After all, he steals, lies and stays out of school. To what extent has his environment made J.T. the person he seems to be?

Readers may ponder over how other characters fit into J.T.'s story. A reader might choose just one of these supporting characters and reread to notice and analyze his or her relationship with J.T and the minor character's role in the book. What would this book be like without this character? This, of course, is a move readers can learn to make with any book they read.

Genre
Chapter Book

Teaching Uses
Independent Reading; Character Study; Partnerships

*Junebug

Alice Mead

FIELD GUIDE

E F

Publisher
Bantam Doubleday Dell, 1995

ISBN
0440412455

TC Level
9

Book Summary

Junebug is the story of an almost-ten-year-old kid nicknamed Junebug who lives with his mom and his little sister in a pretty scary housing project. He has a lot to deal with in his life-gangs, bullies, worries about his family-and he wishes he could do something to make his family's life easier.

Basic Book Information

This realistic fiction book is 102 pages in length with 11 chapters. Each chapter is about 10 pages. A former art teacher, Alice Mead has written more than seven books for young adults. Some of her other titles include *Adem's Cross*, *Junebug and the Reverend*, *Walking the Edge*, *Crossing the Starlight Bridge*, and *Soldier Mom*.

Noteworthy Features

This story is told chronologically and is very easy to follow. It doesn't have many characters to keep track of and is told in the first person from Junebug's perspective.

The text poses few difficulties, although there are many serious issues for Junebug and the reader to think about and wrestle with throughout the story.

Junebug is a good book to make available early in the year. It has a sequel, which is good for students to know since it helps them with book choice. It could be a good read aloud in fourth or fifth grade-it offers a lot to think about. Junebug has to deal with living in a rough neighborhood; harassment and peer pressure from older kids about gangs and drugs; his mother being hospitalized, etc. It offers a nice mix of both plot and character-action definitely happens here, but there is also a very thoughtful narrator.

Teaching Ideas

Junebug is a great book for readers who have begun to read independently, in a fluent and sustained way. A teacher may, in a conference, want to remind readers of the challenges of chapter book reading. Because readers of early chapter books are often focused on processing all that print, they sometimes can read along without doing the mind-work that reading involves. Sometimes when teachers ask such readers about the book, they say, "I read it, honest. I just can't remember it." Readers can be reminded that reading is comprehension; it's not an extra credit option to read with accuracy and intonation.

It is essential that all students are working with books that they can read and process independently if they are reading them on their own. Students with serious comprehension problems should be encouraged to "shelve" the book until later in the year, and then try again.

If a teacher wants to prepare a child to be actively thinking while reading, it sometimes helps to look over the book together in order to activate a child's expectations and involvement in the story.

Then, too, teachers may want to talk with readers about the fact that when reading a story, one should generally expect to learn the characters, setting and basic plot by the end of chapter one. If one comes to the end of the first chapter without knowing these things, it's often a good sign that some rereading is in order.

It could be, for example, that the teacher reads a book aloud and during the following book talk, shows children some of the ways good readers think about character. Afterwards, when children disperse for their independent reading, the teacher might remind them to do some of this work with characters as they read independently. Alternatively, the idea of reading with an eye towards understanding the characters could simply emerge out of a one-to-one conference between teacher and reader. Teachers could suggest that readers read like magnets, collecting bits of information about each character so that early on in reading, students pause and create a tiny character sketch of each character.

Book Connections

Several books that could be read alongside this one are: *Junebug and the Reverend* by Alice Mead (the sequel to this book), *Chevrolet Saturdays* by Candy Dawson Boyd, *Miracle's Boys* by Jacqueline Woodson, and *Scorpions* by Walter Dean Myers (a harder read than this book).

Genre
Chapter Book

Teaching Uses
Independent Reading

Koala Lou

Mem Fox

FIELD GUIDE

A E

Illustrator
Pamela Lofts

Publisher
Harcourt, Brace & Company, 1988

ISBN
0152005021

TC Level
8

Book Summary

A young koala bear, longing to hear her mother speak lovingly to her as she did before all the other children came along, plans to win her distracted parent's attention. Little Koala Lou enters the Bush Olympics gum tree climbing event, but only comes in second. Her mother finds and comforts her with the words she had been waiting for, and reassurance that Koala Lou is as loved as ever.

Basic Book Information

This is an extremely popular book among both adults and children. The realistic and adorable illustrations, poignant story and the easy-to-identify-with feelings in the story, seem to appeal to everyone.

Mem Fox has written more than twenty-five picture books for children, including *Zoo-Looking*, *Feathers and Fools*, andHattie *and the Fox*. More information about Mem Fox can be found on her website at www.memfox.net.

Noteworthy Features

The story is straightforward, and the pictures in the text provide support to children trying to figure out the general storyline. However, in most cases the pictures won't help children with particular words, and the vocabulary is both lyrical and occasionally sophisticated. All of the animal characters are species native to Australia, and some may be unknown to the American reader. Occasionally in the story, there are some words written as they sound phonetically, in order to communicate the animals' Australian way of speaking English. Readers can usually figure these out on their own by reading them aloud a time or two like *platypus*, *emu*, and *kookaburra*.

The story revolves around the "Bush Olympics" with the "gum tree climbing event," but neither one is explained. Readers who hold on to the story can formulate guesses as to what the Bush Olympics will involve and what the gum tree climbing event will entail. As they read on the story will support these guesses.

The story is filled with literary language and is written for the ear. "At last the day of the Olympics arrived." Hearing books like this one read aloud many times will help readers develop a sense of literary story language.

Teaching Ideas

This is an all-time favorite read aloud book for many teachers. The book's lyrical language, drama and pace all combine to make it the sort of book that children long to hear over and over. No one should hesitate to give in to everyone's fondest hopes and do just that, for children benefit from hearing books such as this one read aloud so often that the structure and music of stories is internalized. It is from hearing stories like this read aloud that children come to sense that there's a time, in a story, for something to happen, that they learn to feel tension mounting, to catch their breath in suspense, to turn the page just a little bit faster because soon they'll know how it all turns out. When children grow up with a sense for how good stories flow, they'll instinctively write and tell their own stories that work for readers, and they'll read books expecting to find those elements that good authors always include.

A teacher won't want to read this aloud without reading it herself first several times, learning to hurry the pacing in some places and to slow it down in others. By reading a book such as this one well, teachers can help children fall in love with all books.

The first time a teacher reads *Koala Lou* to a group, she may want to read it straight through. Then the teacher may read it again to give children opportunities to talk to partners, or to listen for what Mem Fox has done as a writer so they can emulate her, etc.

Some teachers encourage listeners to talk early and often about the connections between a text and their own lives. One of the big life themes for many children is the arrival of siblings who compete for attention. It may be wise, however, to postpone this discussion and to first help children linger over and attend to the story at hand and perhaps the characters. What kind of characters are these? How do you know this? In this story, the main character is Koala Lou and she's a koala, but children can begin to think, "If she were a person, what kind of a person would she be?" A reader might say, "We don't know," because her characteristics are not spelled out in the text. But the reader can get to know a character by her actions, and surely Koala Lou's actions show determination, resolve, energy and a longing to be loved. The reader also gets to know a character by seeing what others think of them, and this book says that she was so soft and round that all who saw her loved her.

More sophisticated readers can notice not only the traits of characters, but the ways authors help readers know and care about the characters they create. Koala Lou is a richly developed character because she isn't just one thing. She isn't just lovely, brave and good. She's also brooding and able to sulk and be competitive. It's not important for children to produce these adjectives to describe her, but it is important for them to see they care about her all the more because she's complex and life-like; she's what some might call "human."

A teacher may want to point out that one of the most memorable lines in the story is the line Koala Lou's mother says (and then, as Koala Lou got older, doesn't say) "Koala Lou, I do love you!" Mem Fox could have written this differently. She could have had the mother say, "Koala Lou, I love you." But Mem knows how to write for the ear, to write so this and countless other passages of the text have an irresistible rhythm.

In their own writing, children may want to find an important section and to rewrite it so that it sounds good to the ear. Mem Fox rewrote her opening more than 50 times before she had it right! The passage is also memorable because these are the actual words a character says. Throughout the text, there aren't a lot of quotes, but the quoted passages are very important, each one helping to explain much about the character speaking. The way characters talk (as well as the content of the talk) reveals them. Again, children may want to reread their own writing and consider, "Do I have any characters talking from time to time? Does the way they talk reveal their characters?"

This book clearly conveys messages. With younger readers a teacher might simply ask, "What is the whole story trying to tell us?" With older, more experienced readers, the book can provide an opportunity for teachers to help them interpret texts.

Many readers feel that the book's message is that a child will get sad when another child is born and the parent has less time to spend, but that the parent really loves the first child as much as ever. Or, readers might decide the message is that even if someone has no time to tell you she loves you, she does love you, and you needn't try to win a big prize to gain her love.

If teachers want to push their student's thinking about the book, and give them reason to find textual support for their ideas, they may want to offer alternate conclusions about the message of the story. When they do this, students have to turn to the text to decide which interpretation fits best, and why. Perhaps the message of the story is that you need to at least try for the big prize to get the attention, or perhaps it is that only when you feel really low down will you finally get the affection you need. Perhaps the message, intended or not, is about what happens when you strive for attention for yourself, instead of simply asking for more or sharing in whatever is keeping the attention-giver so busy! In any case, students can discuss and find evidence to support their interpretations and decide what they think about the truth or justness of the messages they find.

Book Connections

Mem Fox has written more than twenty-five picture books for children, including

Zoo-Looking, *Feathers and Fools*, and *Hattie and the Fox*. More information about Mem Fox can be found on her website at www.memfox.net.

Genre

Picture Book

Teaching Uses

Author Study; Read Aloud; Interpretation; Critique

Let's Go, Philadelphia!

Patricia Reilly Giff

FIELD GUIDE

E

Book Summary

In *Let's Go, Philadelphia!*, Richard "Beast" Best and Ms. Rooney's class head off to Philadelphia. It is "Something New Week" at the Polk Street School. While painting his father's garage, Richard spills paint and ruins his sister Holly's bike. He wants to win the prize of "a new bike" that his substitute teacher has offered to the student who writes the best report about someone from Philadelphia. As his class visits the historic and famous sights of that city, Richard slowly realizes that his report is full of misinformation and his friend Dawn's report is bound to win the prize. When he finally tells Holly that he has ruined her bike, he is surprised that she doesn't really mind. Things continue to improve: Mrs. Miller isn't as mean a teacher as he thought; several kids in his class tell him that he is just like Benjamin Franklin because he is always inventing things; and the prize, which is really a book about Benjamin Franklin, is won by each kid in the class.

Series
The Kids of the Polk Street School (The Polk Street Kids on Tour)

Illustrator
Blanche Sims

Publisher
Bantam Doubleday Dell, 1998

ISBN
0440413680

TC Level
9

Basic Book Information

Let's Go, Philadelphia! is part of a series called *A Polk Street Special, The Polk Street Kids on Tour*. This series is an extension of the series known as *The Kids of the Polk Street School* and is a bit more challenging. The main characters in the series are the 13 kids in Ms. Rooney's class: Alex, Timothy, Noah, Matthew, Derrick, Jill, Wayne, Linda, Sherri, Richard, Jason, Dawn and Emily. Richard Best is the main character in this book. Each book in this series takes place in a different part of the United States. In this book, Ms. Rooney's class takes an overnight field trip to Philadelphia.

Let's Go, Philadelphia! is 80 pages long with 10 chapters. There is a "prologue" to the story, the text from a book being read to the class by Mrs. Miller. The prologue is entitled: "From Mrs. Miller's Book: Olden Days in Old Philadelphia." The chapters are numbered and each one averages six to seven pages in length. The books in this series are slightly more difficult than *The Kids of the Polk Street School* series. There is more dialogue in each chapter, sentence structure is slightly more complex and there are many scene changes.

In this book, as well as in all the other titles in the *Polk Street Kids on Tour* series, there is a guide to the city at the end of the book. The guide is 22 pages long and includes two simple street maps of neighborhoods in Philadelphia; a list of "The Polk Street Kids' Favorite Places to See and Things to Do in Philadelphia (listed in Alphabetical Order);" important addresses and phone numbers for information; and "quotes" from the Polk Street kids about their favorite attractions.

Noteworthy Features

Throughout the story, Richard's thoughts are written into the text, so the reader has to be able to decipher when this is happening. For example, on pages 55-56, Richard is imagining he is flying a plane at the Franklin Institute. The text states: "He could see the ground falling away. He felt as if he were in the clouds. ... Beast saw a building coming up. He pushed another button fast. He could hear a bell. 'Splat,' he said."

As mentioned above, the books in this series are slightly more challenging than *The Kids of the Polk Street School* series. The most challenging aspect of this book is that there are three equally important plot lines. First, Richard has accidentally ruined his sister Holly's bike by spilling paint all over it while trying to paint the garage as a surprise for his father. Readers also need to attend to the fact that Richard's substitute teacher for the day, Mrs. Miller, has "promised" the class that whoever writes the best report about someone from Philadelphia will win a prize. Richard mistakenly believes the prize is a new bike, because Mrs. Miller says that writing the report will be "as easy as riding a bike." Richard desperately wants to win the new bike to replace Holly's. At the same time, Richard thinks Ben Franklin (who is frequently referred to by Mrs. Miller and Richard's classmates) is the new kid in the class next door. Only when it is too late, does Richard realize that his report, which he initially thought was terrific, is filled with erroneous information. Meanwhile, the class takes a whole day field trip to Philadelphia and visits many historical sights.

Because the book is based around a class field trip to Philadelphia, there is a lot of historical and factual information woven into the story. References are made to important events in American history and the children visit various points of interest. A lot of ground is covered in one day. There is also quite a lot of information that is interesting, but unrelated to Richard's story. Unfortunately, the main plot, Richard's mistakes, and the factual information about Ben Franklin and Philadelphia's famous sights, are very hard to follow simultaneously. The author tries to weave them together, but the writing is sometimes awkward and may be quite confusing.

Teaching Ideas

Like many chapter books at this level, *Let's Go, Philadelphia!*, as well as all the titles in *The Kids of the Polk Street School* series, is a great book for readers who are comfortable reading independently in a fluid and sustained way. There are many "jobs" readers at this level need to practice and *Let's Go, Philadelphia!* affords the opportunity to do several of them. Teachers can use this book as a read aloud to model good independent reading strategies, as well as strategies for readers who are reading this book (or series) with a partner or groups.

Many readers at this level tend to race through their books and often miss information, meaning, humor and the more subtle themes. Some overestimate their reading ability and establish reading goals that are toolarge. This usually happens when the reader is not quite ready for a certain level book and needs to practice a while longer with shorter and/or easier books.

As readers at this level become good at setting reading goals for reflection, discussion with a partner or group member, note taking on Post-its, or developing a big idea about what the story is about, they may begin to practice and develop the above-mentioned skills. Readers may develop their ideas through "writing off" Post-its in their notebooks. For example, students may be putting Post-its on parts of the text they find exciting. They may use the Post-its as a starting off point to develop and defend why they found that part exciting. Readers may ask themselves, or reading partners, leading, open-ended questions that enable them to further develop their ideas. Some of these questions may include: "What is happening in this part that makes me feel excited? Is the author telling me that it is an exciting part or is it something else that makes me feel this way? Is this the place in the books in this series where it always gets exciting?" Children can write their answers, predictions and reflections based on the note they have jotted on the Post-it.

Readers at this level can use *Let's Go, Philadelphia!* to begin making deeper character studies. Readers can learn the names of characters, the traits (both good and bad) and the relationships between characters (e.g., Beast is easily confused and has a hard time in school; Dawn is a tattletale; Matthew is Beast's best friend). Because this is one book in a series, readers can compare specific characters to ones in other titles from the series. Readers can write a list of characteristics. They can also compare the characters in this story to themselves, other people they know, or characters in other books they've read and heard. These are great opportunities for the student to reread, write, and have relevant discussions with reading partners or members of a reading group.

Children at this level are ready to become more thoughtful about their responses. As children read about a character they are studying, they may want to use Post-its to mark places as "evidence" of a character's personality change, actions that are typical of that specific character or motivation for a character to do or say what he or she does or says. For example, in *Let's Go, Philadelphia!* Beast continually confuses Benjamin Franklin, the historical figure, with a new kid in school, whom Beast starts to believe is a great inventor. Readers can mark all those places in the text where Beast has gotten mixed up and, ultimately, the place in the text where he realizes his mistake. This will not only help readers keep information straight in their own minds, it will enable them to have relevant discussions about the development of Beast's character throughout the story.

Because there are several intertwined plot lines in the story, it would be a good idea for readers to learn how to attend to and organize information that "belongs to" each specific plot. As readers begin the story, they need to frequently discuss what is going on. As they begin to formulate ideas about what is happening in Richard's life, readers may want to use a graphic organizer to keep the varied information separate and clear. For example, readers may separate a notebook page into four different boxes. One box could be devoted to notes about all the mistakes Richard keeps making about believing that Mrs. Miller's prize for the best report is actually a bicycle. In a second box, readers can list all the historical places, figures and information the kids from Ms. Rooney's class are learning about on their trip to Philadelphia. In another box, they can list places in the text where Richard confuses Benjamin Franklin with the new kid in school, etc. As children read, they can use Post-its or copy notes from the text that belong in each box. In this way, they will be more apt to pay close attention to the various plot lines and will have the events organized in front of them, rather than having to retain and organize them all in their heads.

Book Connections

There are several titles in this series including: *Look Out, Washington, D.C.!*; *Next Stop, New York City!*; *Oh Boy, Boston!*; *Turkey Trouble* and *The Postcard Pest*. *The Kids of the Polk Street School* series are about the same characters and are slightly easier. Some of the titles in that series are: *The Beast in Ms. Rooney's Room*, *Pickle Puss*, *December Secrets* and *In the Dinosaur's Paw*.

Genre
Chapter Book

Teaching Uses
Independent Reading; Partnerships; Book Clubs

Lights, Action, Land-Ho!

Judy Delton

FIELD GUIDE

E

Book Summary

Lights, Action, Land-Ho! is the eighteenth book in the *Pee Wee Scouts* series. The story opens with the Pee Wees walking home from school, longing for the next school holiday, Columbus Day. A conversation ensues about Columbus discovering, or not discovering, America. The kids say goodbye and meet again on the day of their scout meeting. Mrs. Peters, their leader, tells them a movie will be filmed in their town and the kids decide to practice their skills and talents in order to be chosen for the movie. Rachel is a talented tap dancer, and Molly tries to learn how to dance in hopes of being better than Rachel. Molly realizes that Rachel is more talented than she, and will probably be chosen over her for the movie. When they find out that everyone is just going to be an extra, Molly devises a secret plan so that she can stand out. Through this drama, Molly learns that Rachel has another side to her and thinks that maybe she isn't as bad as she first thought.

Series
Pee Wee Scouts

Illustrator
Alan Tiegreen

Publisher
Dell Publishing, 1992

ISBN
044040732X

TC Level
8

Basic Book Information

Lights, Action, Land-Ho! is 99 pages long. The chapters are each about 15 pages in length. Print size is medium and the spacing between the words and lines is medium as well. The sentence structure is a combination of simple and complex sentences. The pictures are scattered throughout the book; usually there are two to three pictures in each chapter. As with other *Pee Wee Scout* illustrations, they support the plot, but often lag behind the text by a page or so.

This book is harder than the earlier books in the series-it's longer and there's no spacing between paragraphs as in previous books. Reading the books in order matters in this series, since a lot of background is given in earlier books.

Noteworthy Features

There is one plot line in this story and it unfolds chronologically. There are several scene changes, which occur in the middle of chapters. This is a different pattern than in earlier *Pee Wee Scout* books. There is some heavy dialogue in certain sections, with little accompanying narration. It is easy for a reader to lose track of the story in these areas.

Teaching Ideas

Since characters are a central part of these books, readers often decide to study them. Sometimes the studies take the form of collecting notes in a chart; sometimes it involves putting a mark or Post-it in the text where a character does something important that is representative of him or her. Sometimes, readers even choose to pretend to be that character for a scene or two as a way of understanding them better.

Book Connections

Similar series books are the *Junie B. Jones* series by Barbara Park and the *Marvin Redpost* series by Louis Sachar. Books that could be read before reading this one are the *M&M* series by Pat Ross and *Pinky and Rex* by James Howe. *Sweet & Sour Lily* by Sally Warner, the *Magic Tree House* series by Mary Pope Osborne, and *The Littles* by John Peterson are great books for follow-up.

Genre
Chapter Book

Teaching Uses
Character Study; Independent Reading; Partnerships

Look to the North: A Wolf Pup Diary

Jean Craighead George

FIELD GUIDE

E

Book Summary

The pages of this wolf diary tell the story of three wolf pups-Boulder, Scree and Talus-from the time they are born until the time they are nearly a year old. The author chooses particular days on which the pups are doing something especially noteworthy and describes those days in depth. She shows how the pups establish their order in the pack, how they roughhouse with each other, how they eat and how they relate to the others around them.

Illustrator
Lucia Washburn

Publisher
Harper Trophy, 1997

ISBN
0064435105

Basic Book Information

This nonfiction picture book is about 30 pages long. Although it has no table of contents or index, its organization is clear from the headings on each double-page spread. The book is organized according to the developmental stages of a young wolf's life, from birth to ten-and-a-half months old. The headings are large and printed in bold colors with the words "10 Days Old" or "7 Weeks Old" so readers always know just where they are in the chronology of the wolf's development. On every spread, there is a sentence to let the reader know what time of year it is, and then there are about two paragraphs describing, in poetic language, the kinds of things the wolves are doing or learning to do at that stage of their lives. The book opens with a short, easy-to-read note from the Newbery Award-winning author talking about her passion for wolves and wolf pups.

Noteworthy Features

The book is written with careful attention to language. The words convey not only factual information, but a sense of admiration for the animals as well. The story is compelling and helps the reader create a strong sensory impression of the wolf pups themselves.

Each diary entry begins with a notation about what happens during a particular season, and what stage of development the wolf pups are experiencing at that time. This allows readers to connect more easily their own changing world with the world of the growing pups.

In some of the entries in the text, parts of the descriptions of the pups' activities are distinguished by a small blue design element. Children may not be familiar with this convention of book design, which usually symbolizes time passing. They may be intrigued by it and try to figure it out with a partner, or they may simply ask for a teacher's help in understanding its meaning.

Because the text is divided into small chunks with clearly defined beginning points and rest points, readers don't have to "chunk" the text themselves. They can see an amount of text and know that in one sitting they must get through at least that much-a page's worth-before it makes sense to stop reading.

Teaching Ideas

Children sometimes find the information in this book surprising. They have often pictured wolves as dangerous and violent creatures. There is no evidence of that side of the animals in this book, and that may lead readers to ask questions. What is true and what is misleading? Are wolves really dangerous, or are they more like dogs, as they appear to be in this book? Some students, after reading this book, even begin a crusade to free the wolf from its big bad stereotypes and educate people about their gentler sides.

Because of the well-crafted writing and the narrative character of this nonfiction text, some teachers do use it very successfully as a read aloud book.

Because the text has clear sections, it makes it particularly easy for children to stop and talk in the midst of reading. These mid-book conversations can be focused simply on retelling the book or part so far, or they can have a more complicated purpose. Perhaps readers will be developing theories about the characters of the different wolf pups. Perhaps readers will be collecting factual information about wolves and their habitat. Readers might even stop and talk about particular observations they 've made regarding Jean Craighead George's writing style.

Genre
Nonfiction; Picture Book

Teaching Uses
Independent Reading; Teaching Writing; Read Aloud; Partnerships

M&M and the Santa Secrets

Pat Ross

FIELD GUIDE

E

Book Summary

Every year, Mandy and Mimi surprise each other with a special Christmas present. This year, Mimi wants a tarantula and Mandy wants a silver ring. Both girls make the mistake of assuming that, for some reason, the other has not bought a gift this Christmas. Then, to make matters worse, they argue. When the friends do exchange gifts-one day early-they quickly forget their hurt feelings and become best friends again.

Series
M&M

Illustrator
Marylin Hafner

Publisher
Puffin Books, 1998

ISBN
0141300949

TC Level
7

Basic Book Information

M&M and the Santa Secrets is part of a series of books about two best friends, Mandy and Mimi. This text has 43 pages with 5 untitled chapters, each almost six to ten pages long. There are black-and-white illustrations on every page that support some part of the book. There is simple dialogue throughout the text. The dialogue is referenced at either the beginnings or end of the sentences.

Teaching Ideas

As a read aloud, a teacher may do a short mini-lesson on how to use one's voice appropriately when reading text that is italicized (or text that is in word balloons). A teacher may show part of the text on an overhead projector or provide enough copies for children to look at individually. While reading the text aloud, the teacher can ask the readers to listen to how and when her voice is changing. Children can practice reading alongside the teacher or in partnerships with their copies of the text.

Another opportunity for the teacher to do some direct instruction using an overhead projector or multiple copies is with the dialogue in the story. Teachers can instruct children to notice quotation marks, read with expression in the characters' voice, and to notice where the references are in relation to the dialogue. It is important for them to become proficient at strategies that help them figure out who is talking.

M&M and the Santa Secrets is a great book for children who are ready to develop and practice strategies that enable them to read longer books in a fluent and sustained way. Some of the many "jobs" children can practice while reading this book include: paying attention to punctuation in longer sentences, and using it to promote understanding; reading more quickly and smoothly without the help of a "pointing finger" or bookmark under each line; not reading out loud; reading phrases or whole sentences in "one voice" (phrasing), rather than word-by-word; reading dialogue in a character's voice; and self-checking their miscues by asking themselves "Does that make sense to me?" Teachers can do a mini-lesson with the whole class or confer with independent readers one-on-one, about how to practice one of the strategies that he or she may be struggling with.

Teachers may use this book to teach children how to practice "knowing" themselves as readers. Teachers may say to readers, "Before you begin reading today, look through the part you are about to read and put a Post-it or bookmark on a good place to stop for a moment and talk with your partner."

Teachers may use this book to teach about feeling a personal connection to a story or a character. *M&M and the Santa Secrets* is based on a universal experience of childhood-having a friend you feel as close to as a sister or brother, fighting with that friend and the desolation that ensues. Readers at this level (and age) are going to recognize themselves and will enjoy empathizing with the friends in this story.

Book Connections

There are many other books about M&M, all by Pat Ross, including: *M&M and the Bad News Babies*, *M&M and the Mummy Mess*, *M&M and the Big Bag*, and *Meet M&M*.

Genre

Short Chapter Book

Teaching Uses

Independent Reading; Read Aloud

Malcolm X

Arnold Adoff

FIELD GUIDE

E

Book Summary

This biography of Malcolm X gives an overview of his childhood, his involvement and break with the Nation of Islam, how he became El-Hajj Malik El-Shabazz and his importance to the social struggle of the 1950s and 1960s. The book covers the events that led up to his assassination and his effect on American society.

Publisher
Harper Trophy, 2000

ISBN
006442118X

TC Level
9; 10

Basic Book Information

Arnold Adoff wrote the original text in 1970. Rudy Gutierrez' illustrations are newer. A single black-and-white charcoal drawing represents the main idea of each of the 9 chapters in this 52-page book.

Noteworthy Features

Adoff's simple, direct language can help readers grasp the basic history of Malcolm X's complicated life. The author defines most potentially unfamiliar vocabulary internally, within the sentences in which the challenging words appear. Adoff also tends to indicate cause-and-effect relationships (e.g., "It was difficult for Malcolm to understand many of the words he read, so he got a dictionary") which makes the text yet more accessible.

One of the possible complications of the text is that Adoff bases his book on Alex Haley's *The Autobiography of Malcolm X*. Adoff recounts many of the same stories as Haley, but Adoff condenses Malcolm X's life such that the major events of his adulthood shrink to the same scale as more minor details. For example, both Haley and Adoff begin their books with a story of Klansmen setting fire to Malcolm's parents' home. While Haley tells this story in three paragraphs, Adoff does so over five pages, thereby giving much more weight to an event before Malcolm's birth than to his pilgrimage to Mecca or break with the Elijah Mohammed-two of the most seminal moments in his life. Such uneven proportion may confuse readers about Malcolm's shifting ideology or the roots of his eventual assassination.

While the drawings all relate to major events in each chapter, some of the illustrations, such as the one of pall bearers holding a casket or Malcolm reading in jail, provide more obvious textual support than others, such as the streaky image of Malcolm hovering over the head of Elijah Mohammed, whom many readers might not recognize. Readers without foreknowledge of Malcolm X's life will not necessarily be able to skim quickly to predict or to support their comprehension.

Teaching Ideas

Part of a broader module on nonfiction, this book is an excellent example of biography. Students can use this text to explore some of the features of this genre. Other books in this module, such as *Richard Wright and the Library Card* or *A Boy Named Boomer*, describe incidents in only one part of their subjects' lives; *Malcolm X* follows a life in its entirety. As students study this genre, they might contrast it with others that they know, such as memoir. Do biographies have distinct tones? How does it affect the text if the biographer did not know the subject personally? How did the biographer determine what the subject thought and believed?

Some biographies for children relay anecdotes from the subject's childhood without connecting those events to the rest of their subject's life. When students try to write their own biographies, they often retell these anecdotes at length, giving equal attention to what happened on a future president's first day of kindergarten as to his foreign policy. While *Malcolm X* does not explicitly name how its subject's childhood affected his adulthood, it offers students a great opportunity to infer the connections. In teacher-student conferences or reading partnerships, students can speculate about such matters as how Malcolm X's beliefs were similar to and different from his father's; how the prejudice of the adults who ran his detention home and his teacher shaped Malcolm; why Malcolm became involved with crime; and why he began to read in prison.

Though knowing who Malcolm X was is not essential background knowledge for understanding this book, knowing something about the context of his life will help students considerably. Students should be familiar with American racism and segregation in the 1920s, 1930s, and 1940s, and with the civil rights movement that emerged in the decades thereafter. It would be helpful for readers to be able to contrast Malcolm X's religious and political ideology with the Christian-based, nonviolent resistance espoused by Dr. Martin Luther King, Jr. and others.

Book Connections

There are many biographies of social and political pioneers written for readers at this level. Lucille Davis' *Eleanor Roosevelt* and *Elizabeth Cady Stanton*, Eloise Greenfield's *Mary McLeod Bethune*, Margaret Davidson's *The Story of Jackie Robinson, Bravest Man in Baseball* and Rosa Parks' own *I Am Rosa Parks* chronicle the lives of such figures. David A. Adler's *A Picture Book of Simón Bolívar*, Barbara Mitchell's *A Pocketful of Goobers: A Story about George Washington Carver* and *Walking the Road to Freedom: A Story about Sojourner Truth* by Jeri Ferris are just slightly more challenging.

Genre

Biography

Teaching Uses
Content Area Study; Book Clubs; Independent Reading; Reading and Writing Nonfiction

Marvin Redpost: Alone in His Teacher's House

FIELD GUIDE

E

Louis Sachar

Book Summary

Marvin Redpost is the main character in *Alone in His Teacher's House*. When Marvin's third grade teacher, Mrs. North, has to go away for a week, she asks Marvin to dog-sit for her dog Waldo. Mrs. North pays Marvin three dollars a day, plus a four-dollar bonus if all goes well. Marvin accepts the job, but his two best friends, Nick and Stuart, are jealous that Marvin will be alone in their teacher's house. Marvin takes his job very seriously, but he runs into a number of problems. First, his friends become mad at him when he does not allow them inside the teacher's house. Then, Miss Hillway, the substitute teacher takes everything he says the wrong way. Worst of all, Waldo is not eating! When Marvin calls Dr. Charles the veterinarian about Waldo, he suggests feeding him liver. Waldo eats the liver that night, but the next morning, Marvin finds Waldo dead. The worst part for Marvin is waiting for Mrs. North to return while his friends taunt him, "She'll flunk you for sure." When Mrs. North returns, she, surprisingly, is the one apologizing.

Series
Marvin Redpost

Illustrator
Barbara Sullivan

Publisher
Scholastic, 1994

ISBN
0679819495

TC Level
8

Basic Book Information

Alone in His Teacher's House is an 83-page chapter book. The text is divided into 12 short chapters with supportive titles that clue the reader in to what the chapter will be about. There is at least one black-and-white picture in each chapter, which help to support the plot and define the characters. Most of the sentences are simple, but there are some complex sentences in the book. For example: "He was already downstairs, eating breakfast, when his mother knocked on his bedroom door and said, 'Marvin, time to get up'."

Currently, this series has seven books, all of which star Marvin and are told through a third-person narrator. The books do not need to be read in sequence. For the reader to get "hooked" on the *Marvin Redpost* series, however, Book #1(*Kidnapped at Birth*) probably should not be read first. *Kidnapped at Birth* is more difficult than the rest of the series because of its references to royalty and to medical lab testing. The other books contain storylines and themes that are easier for kids to relate to and understand (especially *Why Pick on Me?* and *Is He a Girl?*). Louis Sachar is also known for his *Holes*, which won the 1999 Newbery Medal. The *Marvin Redpost* series can introduce a reader to Sachar's style and humor by way of shorter chapters and less sophisticated plot structure.

Noteworthy Features

The reader is supported in this book because the story is a series of chronological events following a single plot line. Students can relate to Marvin's friends and family issues and look forward to his next "situation" in subsequent books. The main characters are recurring throughout the series, so students can keep track of any new characters who appear.

This series will be accessible to readers who cannot yet read some of Sachar's more complex books, yet they haven't been stripped of all colorful, fun language. The story includes some rich and challenging words such as *hooligan*, and *coincidence*. Readers will need to be resourceful in their reading, and not let themselves be totally stymied by a few words that may prove beyond their reach.

There are many characters mentioned in this story. This, of course, is more challenging for readers than books like *Frog and Toad*, which don't require readers to keep lots of characters straight. It's worthwhile for readers of this series to take some time to study the characters (who are mostly Marvin's classmates) since most of them appear again in other books in this series. There is a lot of dialogue in the text, some of it not referenced. The book is humorous, and not every reader will "get the joke" every time. For example, some students might not pick up on Mrs. North's sarcasm when she asks Marvin, "What did you expect? A blackboard in the living room?"

Teaching Ideas

Readers at this level often tend to focus on getting through the words and the pages. As a result, they can race through the book and forget to construct a coherent meaning, or to laugh at the funny parts or reflect on the themes. A teacher might talk to a reader about this, and ask him or her to approach a book having already selected a few places to stop. Then the teacher could suggest some of the things a good reader might do at these pause points. "Sometimes I just stop and think-so what's happened so far? I try to retell the story to myself, and it's like I'm giving myself a retelling test because if I can't do this, I know I need to reread." At some pause points, readers might say, "So what am I realizing about each of the characters?" or, "So, let me picture this...." Of course, these pauses to reflect can be opportunities for partner conversations, or they can simply be occasions to do the mind work of reading. Teachers may say to a reader, "Before you begin reading today, look through the book and put a Post-it or a bookmark on a good place to stop for a moment. If you are reading with a partner, look over the book and think together about a good place to stop and talk." At this stopping point, readers can use a thinking-as-you-read strategy.

Marvin Redpost: Alone in His Teacher's House is a great book for readers who have begun to read slightly longer chapter books independently, in a fluent and sustained way. A teacher may, in a conference, want to remind such a student of his or her jobs as a chapter-book reader. Because readers of early chapter books are often focused on processing all that print, they sometimes read along without doing the mind work that careful reading involves. Sometimes when teachers ask these readers about the book, they say, "I read it, honest. I just can't remember it." Readers need to be reminded that reading is comprehension. It's not an extra credit option to read with accuracy and intonation!

If a teacher wants to prepare a child to be actively thinking as he or she reads, it sometimes helps to look over the book together in order to activate a child's expectations and involvement in the story.

Teachers may want to talk with a child about the fact that, when reading a story, they generally expect to learn the characters, setting, and basic plot by the end of chapter one. If they come to the end of the first chapter without knowing these things, it's often a good sign that some rereading is in order.

A teacher might read a book aloud and during the book talk following, show children some of the ways good readers think about character. Afterwards, when children disperse for their independent reading, the teacher might remind them to do some of this work with characters as they read independently. Alternatively, the idea of reading with an eye towards understanding the characters could simply emerge out of a one-to-one conference between the teacher and reader. The teacher could suggest that students read like magnets, collecting bits of information about each character so that early on in their reading, they could pause and create a tiny character sketch of each character.

Readers may end up talking about some of the book's issues: the sharing, passing and taking of responsibility; the phenomenon of being or seeming a "teacher's pet;" and other subjects such as these.

Book Connections

This series is comparable in difficulty to the *Flower Girls* series and the *Ballet Slippers* series. If a child can successfully read the *Junie B. Jones* series and the *Adam Joshua* series, this series would make a good next step. After reading the *Marvin Redpost* series, this reader might turn next to the *Amber Brown* series or the *Aldo* series. Readers who have loved the *Marvin Redpost* series may soon feel ready to tackle Sachar's humorous *Wayside School* series.

Genre

Chapter Book

Teaching Uses

Independent Reading; Read Aloud

Marvin Redpost: Kidnapped at Birth?

Louis Sachar

FIELD GUIDE

E

Series
Marvin Redpost

Illustrator
Neal Hughes

Publisher
Scholastic, 1992

ISBN
0679819460

TC Level
8

Book Summary

After writing his current events report, Marvin is convinced that he is Prince Robert, the lost son of the King of Shampoon, and that he was kidnapped at birth. After all, he has red hair, unlike anyone else in his family. His friends start treating him like royalty and, surprisingly, his parents don't disagree with him either. His mom agrees to take him for a blood test; if Marvin has blood type O, he could be a match for the king. Suddenly he remembers something. "The King of Shampoon spoke with a weird accent! Marvin didn't talk like that. So that meant he couldn't be Prince Robert!" The possibility remains that he could be, but ultimately Marvin decides he doesn't even want to know if he is related to the king or not. He just wants to stay with his family. By the end of the story Marvin realizes, "He was different. Special. He was the one and only Marvin Redpost."

Basic Book Information

Kidnapped at Birth? is a 68-page chapter book. The text is divided into 10 short chapters, the titles of which clue the reader in as to what the chapter will be about. There is at least one black-and-white picture in each chapter, which helps to support the plot and define the characters. Most of the sentences are simple.

Currently, this series has seven books, all of which star Marvin and are told through a third-person narrator. The books do not need to be read in sequence. Some teachers suggest that for the reader to get "hooked" on the *Marvin Redpost* series, this book should not be read first. Some teachers found *Kidnapped at Birth?* to be more difficult than the rest of the series because of its references to royalty and to medical lab testing. The other books contain storylines and themes that are easier to relate to and understand (especially *Why Pick on Me?* and *Is He a Girl?*). Louis Sachar is also known for his *Holes*, which won the 1999 Newbery Medal. The *Marvin Redpost* series can introduce a reader to Sachar's style and humor by way of shorter chapters and less sophisticated plot structure.

Noteworthy Features

Kidnapped at Birth? follows a single plot line. Marvin is a strong main character with whom readers can identify. The familiar setting of home and school, as well as the familiar characters, family members and classmates will support the reader's entry into this series. The dialogue is usually simple and the speaker is generally identified.

This book requires a higher level of sophistication than the other books in the series. Readers of this book need to be familiar with the concepts of royalty, the lab-test experience, blood type, and references to Marco Polo. However, if students are even slightly familiar with these ideas, they should still get the gist of the story. The idea of Marvin's mom agreeing to allow Marvin to have his blood tested is also an unusual concept. Marvin's ideas about being kidnapped don't change until the very end of the book, and it might be unclear to readers why he changes his mind. Marvin realizes that he was already special-he doesn't need to be a prince to be loved by his family.

Unlike other books in this series, there are characters here who are not consistent with other titles of the series. For example Arnold and Jennifer only appear in this book. Another source of difficulty is the King's accent: "I don't know eef my son ees alive or dead" and "Vee need you. Your kingdom avaits you." If this is the first book a student reads in the series, it may be important to discuss that the books are told through a third-person narrator, and that they do contain humor and sarcasm.

Teaching Ideas

This series has been used successfully in a variety of ways. Some teachers recommend using *Marvin Redpost* in a reading center that focuses on character. Because the books lend themselves easily to conversation, they would also be good for reading partnerships and early book clubs. This book can also be used to talk about dealing with difficult concepts. Teachers might discuss with readers what they can do when they are faced with difficulty or confusion in texts. The students can retell chunks of the story to their partner or to the teacher in a conference in order to monitor for comprehension. Can the students pull out the main idea, and are they aware of the important information in the story? Readers might be encouraged to read all the titles in the series and "talk across" the different books.

As in the other *Marvin Redpost* books, this one explores a central theme: the pull of family and belonging. Readers in book clubs often focus on these sorts of central issues in the book.

Book Connections

This series is comparable in difficulty to the *Flower Girls* series and the *Ballet Slippers* series. It might be good for a reader who first experiences success with the *Junie B. Jones* series and the *Adam Joshua* series before then going on to this one. A nice transition from this series would be to the *Amber Brown* series or the *Aldo* series.

Genre

Chapter Book

Teaching Uses

Independent Reading; Partnerships; Book Clubs; Read Aloud

Monarchs

Kathryn Lasky

FIELD GUIDE

E G

Illustrator
Christopher G. Knight

Publisher
Harcourt Brace & Company, 1993

ISBN
0152552960

TC Level
11; 12; 13

Book Summary

The text starts with a butterfly egg. Each chapter takes the butterfly a step farther in its development, and each chapter also has at least one living human character who is admiring and studying the butterflies at this stage of their life. Sometimes these characters are the same as those in earlier chapters, sometimes they are not. The setting of each chapter depends on where the butterflies are in the world-from Maine to Mexico to California. The tone of the book, while it imparts enormous quantities of information about the monarch, is not strictly scientific, but rather reverential and protective of the butterfly and its habitat. Figurative language abounds in the text, creating a mood of admiration for these beautiful and fragile creatures. The author also includes personal details about the lives of the people working with and for the butterflies, adding to the immediacy of the book's tone.

Basic Book Information

This Nonfiction book is a well-illustrated chapter book. It has no table of contents or index, but chapters are clearly defined with headings and often a changed story location or story character. The chapter titles are literary and interest-catching rather than informative about the subject of the chapter.

There are one or two large, clear photographs on every two-page spread. There are five to ten paragraphs of text per two pages. The photographs don't have captions or labels and there are no diagrams. Instead, the photographs serve to illustrate the story of the butterflies' migration-understanding the pictures' content comes from reading the whole text.

Noteworthy Features

Although each chapter is clearly separated from the one before it, it takes some reading concentration to make the changes between characters and settings in the narrative. These elements of the story are not central to the text and are therefore imbedded within it, not stated outright necessarily, making the work of setting them straight a bit more challenging for the reader.

There is quite a lot of information to process, but it is not presented raw. There is usually some comparison and processing done for the reader. For example, "If a six-pound human baby grew as fast as a caterpillar, it would weigh eight tons in twelve days." At other times the information is made easier to retain by having the implications of it affect the course of action taken by the people in the story. This makes understanding and retaining the information easier that it otherwise would be. The photographs are vivid and make for interesting browsing, although there are no captions or short chunks of text to explain them.

Teaching Ideas

Because of its literary quality, and its migration-driven plot line, this book is as suitable for a read aloud (probably only a few sections would be read, or perhaps the entire book) as it is for independent reading or group discussion.

Because the text has two structures to aid in its use as a reference book, children who are looking for specific bits of information may want to be ready with pencil and notebook in hand during the first read through. Otherwise, the entire text may have to be re-read to glean the information.

Many readers prefer Nonfiction reading to fiction reading, and it can be important for all readers to balance their reading with information books. This book, then, could simply be one among many on the library shelf.

If a teacher sees that the class as a whole tends to select fiction books only during independent reading, the teacher may institute some rituals that steer children toward Nonfiction. The least intrusive might simply be to do promotional book-talks in which one "sells" Nonfiction books. It's possible to go a step further and to suggest that for a time, all children might read only Nonfiction texts during independent reading.

Teachers might want to do minilessons about the strategies of skilled Nonfiction reading. One minilesson may teach children that Nonfiction readers sometimes read like magnets, looking for intriguing details that they pull from a text. One teacher told her students that highly literate people then fact-drop these little bits of information into conversations, sharing in passing whatever they've been learning. The reader of this book could be full of such facts.

Another minilesson might show children that if, for example, a person read this book and loved it, the logical thing to do would be to collect other texts on the same topic. Information can vary from one book to another, sometimes it will develop and other times it will contradict.

Genre

Nonfiction; Chapter Book; Picture Book

Teaching Uses

Reading and Writing Nonfiction; Content Area Study; Book Clubs

Mr. Popper's Penguins

Richard Atwater; Florence Atwater

FIELD GUIDE

B C E F

Publisher
Little Brown, 1938

ISBN
0590477331

TC Level
12

Book Summary

Mr. Popper's Penguins is the comic story of a semi-employed house painter whose passion for Admiral Byrd's polar adventures leads him (and his surprised family) to become caretaker of, at first one, and thentwelve, mischievous penguins.

With the help of practical Mrs. Popper and their children, Janie and Bill, Mr. Popper ingeniously creates a proper polar home in the basement of their house. It isn't long before the financial strain of a large, fresh-fish-eating family leads the Poppers to a brief career on the stage, and to a solution that pleases everyone.

Basic Book Information

This Newbery Honor book has 132 pages and 20 numbered, titled chapters of between four and nine pages each.

Noteworthy Features

Mr. Popper's Penguins is a rare combination of humor, science, history and fantasy. Although the slapstick antics of the Poppers and their penguins are in the foreground of the story, a reader also gets a taste of the 1930s atmosphere, learns something about the explorer Admiral Byrd, and gets information on penguin diet and behavior.

Set in a small town during the 1930s when Admiral Richard Drake was exploring Antarctica, *Mr. Popper's Penguins* contains what might be unfamiliar vocabulary and settings (e.g., "Pullman" train and "vaudeville" stage shows), but its delightful wackiness should keep readers involved. Engagingly comic illustrations, chronological narration, and short chapters will be assets to less patient readers. In general, there are fewer reading challenges (in terms of vocabulary, structure and dialogue) than in other books in this grouping.

Teaching Ideas

Mr. Popper's Penguins makes a good read aloud, but is also appropriate for independent reading.

Mr. Popper's Penguins can accompany other nonfiction research on the 1930s, penguins and the Antarctic. This research may help with comprehension of the book. For example, if readers collect information on penguins, they can then discuss how Mr. Popper accommodated the penguins' needs.

Kids can work on interpreting the message of the story. Commonly, students decide one message is that with enough enthusiasm, one can accomplish nearly anything. Mr. Popper's eccentricity and passion, while bringing strange looks from the plumber, are assets to himself, his family and the penguins. Other readers decide on different messages, for instance, that odd people learn more. As long as kids are supporting their interpretations with textual evidence all of the messages they point to are fair game, and should generate lively discussion.

The characters of Mr. and Mrs. Popper are well drawn. Mr. Popper remains an irrepressible dreamer while Mrs. Popper is an utterly down-to-earth woman who ends up sharing Mr. Popper's love of the penguins. Students may want to study these characters and come to these conclusions about Mr. and Mrs. Popper's natures. Some students even do little character studies about the individual penguins!

Genre

Chapter Book; Fantasy; Historical Fiction

Teaching Uses

Read Aloud; Independent Reading; Character Study; Content Area Study

My Mama Had a Dancing Heart

Libba Moore Gray

FIELD GUIDE

E

Illustrator
Raúl Colón

Publisher
Orchard Books, 1995

ISBN
0531071421

TC Level
8

Book Summary

In this picture book memoir, the narrator tells how she, the daughter, and her mother shared a dancing heart. She recalls times when she and her mother danced outdoors during each season of the year. At the end of the story readers learn that now the narrator is grown up and a ballet dancer.

Basic Book Information

This 29-page book with its musical text and soft, textured illustrations will capture any "dancing heart." It is an excellent choice for a read aloud session with second or third graders.

My Mama Had a Dancing Heart is an ALA Notable book and a Booklist Editor's Choice. It is also listed in the *New York Times* Best Illustrated list and the New York Public Library 100 Titles for Sharing. Libba Gray, a dancer, actress and high school English and drama teacher has written other books as lyrical as this one. In *Small Green Snake*, for instance, there are such phrases as "sassy, sassy, flashy, flashy" and "snippity, snippety, clippety, clippity."

Noteworthy Features

One reviewer aptly calls this book a "lyrical dance through the seasons." The text springs to life with word combinations like "song-singing, finger-snapping," and "up-and-down squish-squashing feet." The structure of the text follows the four seasons, beginning with spring. In each section Gray describes an action mother and daughter do. For example, in spring "we'd kick off our shoes and out into the rain we'd go." Repeatedly, there are lines with adjectives cleverly constructed from a noun and a verb: "a frog-hopping, leaf-growing, flower-opening hello spring ballet." The drinks mother and daughter have when they come inside match the season: sassafras tea in spring, cocoa in winter. These descriptions, too, break conventional rules to create a rhythm not always present in prose: "lemonade cold," "hot tea spiced." Such text begs to be read aloud, to be danced to, to be acted out.

Teaching Ideas

This memoir is a prime example of a list book. It's a very sophisticated list book, but its structure is nevertheless a list. The book could be taken apart and thrown up in the air with pages landing everywhere, and the sequence would still seem okay to a reader.

The book has been used in writing workshops to show youngsters that authors often create words they "need." Many of the words in this book are not really words in our language, but Libba uses them because they express what she truly means and say specifically what she and her mother were doing. Examples include: frog-hopping, leaf-growing, plash-splashing, and slip-swish. Children notice that this book asks for readers to be active. It's a get-up-and-do-it book!

The *ing* at the end of the words makes this a delicious read aloud text. Older students may pause to notice punctuation in this book. The hyphen is used numerous times in this book. No punctuation that appears so often should be ignored. What work is this mark doing for the writer? What work does it always do in our written language?

This book has been used often to show youngsters the value of writing with significant detail. For each season, Libba has chosen one thing to share with readers.

Then, too, this book can teach writers about the power of patterns in a text. The book is structured according to two patterns. One is the use of the seasons. The second reoccurring pattern is evident when the author shows what she and others do in each season. Every season, Libba and her mom first run outside and do something appropriate to the season, then come in and slow themselves down, and finally have a seasonal drink. This pattern is easily imitated by upper-elementary level students, but is a little complicated for primary students.

This book might be read aloud, then reread and savored, and finally studied as an example of beautifully and bravely crafted writing. Once the children have listened to the book, when the class is still gasping over the language, the discussion would probably lead to noticing how Libba Gray used the seasons of the year to tell the story in a pattern. In each season section, the mother and daughter go outside and do a "hello ballet," then they go indoors to have a drink and do an indoor activity.

This book could certainly be a powerful influence in a writing workshop, when students are concentrating on finding just the right words and tone in their writing.

Book Connections

Children interested in stories with ballet as the theme might also read the picture book *Honk!* by Pamela Duncan Edwards, the story of Mimi, a swan who tries her hardest to dance *Swan Lake* in the Paris Opera House.

Genre

Memoir; Picture Book

Teaching Uses

Teaching Writing; Read Aloud; Independent Reading

My Name Is María Isabel

Alma Flor Ada

FIELD GUIDE

D E

Illustrator

K. Dyble Thompson

Publisher

Aladdin, 1995

ISBN

068980217X

Book Summary

The first chapter opens with María Isabel eating breakfast and drinking coffee before school. The reader is not told anything about where she is from or why she is nervous about going to school. Slowly it is revealed that she is going to a new school, although it is two months into the school year. Her mother, father and brother Antonio are introduced in the first chapter through dialogue. At the end of Chapter1, María falls and skins her knee; the day is off to a rocky start.

María's family has arrived in New York from Puerto Rico two years earlier. This year, the family has moved to a new neighborhood and she must start school in a new place. In Chapter3, María remembers her old bilingual school where she took classes in both languages. As we find out in Chapter2, she is quite nervous, not only because she is new, but because she must learn English as well.

Throughout the story, there are many sub-plots that readers will need to follow closely. María finds out that there are two Marías in the class and the teacher decides to call her "Mary." She is uncomfortable with this name and does not know how to share this with the teacher. We find out the importance of her name as she describes its history.

Another plot line is that María is dealing with making new friends, struggling to fit in and to participate in the winter festival. She is also learning how to stand up for herself. María reads *Charlotte's Web* and thinks about her life and that of Charlotte and Wilbur. María gets inspiration from the adventures these characters have together and from their caring relationship.

Basic Book Information

My Name is María Isabel has 10 chapters, each about 6 pages long. There is one full-page picture in each chapter to support the text. Alma Flor Ada has worked on more than one hundred books, many of them in Spanish.

Noteworthy Features

The text uses a medium print size and the words and lines appear close together on the page. The sentence structure throughout the book tends to be simple. However, there are many instances of more complex sentences sprinkled throughout the chapters.

The chapters in this book follow each other chronologically. Time is organized by holidays such as Thanksgiving and the December holidays. Each chapter title suggests its major idea. There are many references to the past. The title leads the reader to believe that María will be telling the story. This is not the case; the story is actually told through a third-person narrator.

Teaching Ideas

At the end of a read aloud, students can turn to each other and talk about María's character. The story focuses on María's journey as she learns how to retain both her language and culture, while also integrating herself into her new experiences and finally becoming comfortable in her new school. Students may also connect María's experiences in school to their own. Many of her fears and her triumphs are universal, and students can understand her better by thinking of their own experience-and perhaps understand their own experiences better by thinking of hers.

When looking more closely at this book, readers may want to pay attention to the cultural setting. The book is about setting, an overlooked element in many stories. Children often read stories and focus on what happens, and perhaps the characters, but rarely the setting of a book. For this reason, teachers might ask children to listen to this book while thinking about how the author makes *place* come alive. What happens in children's minds as they read or hear these words? These prompts could, of course, lead a teacher to demonstrate the way a student can visualize a setting while reading or listening to a book: "Today, please pay special attention to the setting of the story. I'm going to stop after a while and ask you to talk in partners about what you're envisioning."

Book Connections

Good books to read before this would be *The Magic Shell* by Nicholasa Mohr, *Lavender* by Karen Hesse, and the *Flower Girls* series by Kathleen Leverich. Books on the same level as this are the *Amber Brown* series, *Sable* by Karen Hesse and the *Stories that Julian Tells* by Ann Cameron.

Genre
Chapter Book

Teaching Uses
Independent Reading; Read Aloud

My Rotten Redheaded Older Brother

FIELD GUIDE

E

Patricia Polacco

Illustrator
Patricia Polacco

Publisher
Bantam Doubleday Dell, 1994

ISBN
044083449X

TC Level
9

Book Summary

The little girl narrator of this story has an older brother Richard who loves to torment her. He can do everything better than she can. When her grandmother teaches her how to wish upon a falling star, the girl wishes that she were able to do something better than Richard. Not long after, she rides the merry-go-round long after her brother has gotten off. Next thing she knows, she's lying in bed with stitches. She had fallen off into some bottles, and her brother had carried her all the way home. Their relationship changes from that time on, perhaps because her brother acknowledges she has done something "special" or perhaps because of his caring for her. The story ends as the two of them fall asleep that night under the stars with their beloved grandmother.

Basic Book Information

This is a short picture book with Patricia Polacco's special style of illustration gracing each page.

Noteworthy Features

Like many Trumpet Club paperback books, this edition has a note from the author on the inside front cover. Kids love the fact that the author has written especially and directly to them, so if they miss the note, it may be worth pointing out. If the readers save the note until the end of their reading of the story, they may be happy to confirm their idea that it is all based on a true story-or at least based on true characters. The note can also be fuel for some discussion topics about the relationship between the girl and her brother, since she reveals that they are now best friends. In the same way, readers enjoy discovering that the dedication from the author is to a real "Rich."

Kids who are thinking that the girl is Patricia Polacco herself may assume that is the little girl's name. They may be excited to find the evidence, the subtle evidence, at one point near the end of the story. When the girl is on the merry-go-round, her grandmother calls her "Treesha." Kids who read that as "Tricia" with the grandmother's accent may see that it could be short for "Patricia" and feel like real sleuths.

Teaching Ideas

Character studies are usually interesting for readers of this book, in part because there are many different kinds of behaviors to hypothesize about, and in part because there is a change in both characters. Students who have or know siblings also find personal experience and connections helpful in analyzing the story's characters. Readers can make educated guesses as to the motivations and feelings of the characters based on their own experiences. This experience might help them to feel how literature can help a person understand one's own life and how one's own life can help a person understand literature. However, readers may need help checking their hypotheses against the textual evidence presented. Just because they have felt a certain way doesn't mean that the characters here necessarily feel the same way.

At one point during the story, the little girl taunts her brother that she can eat more raw rhubarb than he can. She can't, of course, but time and time again the captivation for readers is not the sibling rivalry, but instead this mysterious "rhubarb." If students are city kids, they may not be familiar with rhubarb and its sour taste, and that tends to capture their interest unduly. Still, it's the kind of detail that is overemphasized if the teacher explains it ahead of time, so it usually works best to let kids work it out after reading the book, if they need to.

This kind of word-fixation also sometimes happens around "Bubbie," the name the children have given their babushka, or grandmother. Kids sometimes ask why the characters call her that. A little guesswork around the word "babushka" can probably get them to the answer, so again, a teacher's explanation isn't really necessary. They'll probably be able to figure it out if they work at it. The same is true for the few other unusual words or phrases such as "he upped and did it," and the grandmother asking the girl if she had eaten any "angry apples" since she wasn't having any pie.

Book Connections

Judy Blume's book *The Pain and the Great One* also deals with a sibling relationship that is less than smooth. The two relationships might make an interesting basis for a compare and contrast study.

Readers who know Patricia Polacco's book *Thunder Cake* may be excited to notice (or discover for themselves with the artful yet casual juxtaposition of the two books on the shelf by the teacher) that the farm and family in both books appear to be the same. On the first page of *My Rotten Redheaded Older Brother*, the girl even says her grandmother makes the best chocolate cake in Michigan. The secret cake ingredient revealed in *Thunder Cake* is even sitting on the table in the other book with the other ingredients-tomatoes!

Genre
Picture Book

Teaching Uses
Character Study; Author Study; Read Aloud

Nate the Great and Me: The Case of the Fleeing Fang

FIELD GUIDE

D E

Marjorie Weinman Sharmat

Series
Nate the Great books

Illustrator
Marc Simont

Publisher
Dell Yearling, 1988

ISBN
0440413818

TC Level
7

Book Summary

Nate the Great, a self-proclaimed "detective," tries to solve the case of his friend Annie's missing dog. With help from his dog and his friends, Nate successfully solves the case. Nate thinks about the information; notices people, places and things; looks for facts and clues; asks questions and takes things apart in order to solve the case. After following a misleading clue about a mysterious lady wearing fluffy bunny shoes, Nate discovers that the missing dog, Fang, has been following newly learned tricks in backwards order. Nate realizes that Fang must be waiting in the park for Annie. Fang is found and there is a celebration for Nate at the end of the story.

Basic Book Information

Nate the Great and Me: The Case of the Fleeing Fang has 50 pages with six chapters. The text begins on page seven. The majority of the book is colorfully illustrated. There are additional sections at the end of the book that include a detective certificate for the reader that is "signed" by Nate the Great; a page written in secret code, with directions on how to read it and the actual secret code on the facing page; three recipes for meals that Nate the Great loves to eat; and a page with the answer to a riddle asked on the dedication page of the book.

Nate the Great detective stories have been a highly popular series for 25 years. The characters in this book are the same characters as in all the books in the series. The nature of the "case" and the way in which it is "solved" by Nate are also consistent with the other books in the series.

Noteworthy Features

Throughout the text, notes written directly to readers appear. These notes are set off from the regular text by a bold, seemingly handwritten font and narrow margins. These notes are like readers' Post-Its embedded within the text itself. They offer advice on how to read this mystery and mysteries in general, posing metacognitive questions and suggestions for comprehension.

The six chapters in *Nate the Great and Me: The Case of the Fleeing Fang* have titles that explain something that comes up in the chapter and are meant to intrigue readers. The story contains several flashbacks. The flashbacks throughout the story serve as explanatory commentary, told by one of the main characters. These often set the scene for the case. Although these literary devices may be fun and interesting for the more sophisticated reader, they can be very confusing to the early chapter book reader of this series. In addition, much of the book is written in Nate's dryly humorous voice. Again, for the early chapter book reader, this kind of humor may be confusing, or may simply go unnoticed. Even more sophisticated readers often fail to realize that in this book, like all of the books in the *Nate the Great* series, Nate does not really do a very good job at all of solving mysteries. Still, readers love the humor on some level, even if they do not fully understand the subtleties.

There are two handwritten, cursive notes within illustrations. These may be difficult for second-grade readers who in many cases have not yet studied cursive writing.

Teaching Ideas

Although the characters, story format, setting, and mystery are the same as in the other books in the *Nate the Great* series, this one seems somewhat more challenging and sophisticated. In this book, there is more text per page, the story is longer, the mystery itself is more complicated, and the added elements mentioned above (change of voice, wry humor, etc.) are noticeably more difficult than the preceding books in the series. If used as part of a study of the *Nate the Great* series, this would be a good book with which to end. If used in isolation, it would be more appropriate for a reader who has some knowledge of the genre and solid fluency at this level.

Independent readers should actually pause to address the bold asides in the text's second font, which appears first on page 12. These notes encourage excellent reading behaviors, such as rereading ("Did you notice that Fang wasn't there?"), determining which information is relevant ("Are dog rhymes and feather-dusting clues? I don't know yet") and visualization ("...draw a picture of a huge, fangy dog running away from two tiny poodles"). The book also encourages scrutiny, also a good skill for readers. For example, it promises that the answer to the missing six-letter word on the dedication page is "somewhere in this book," and points out the role of illustrations in supporting text by stating, "We might have a clue in this picture." Readers who stop to consider each of Nate's asides will practice good reading skills, especially around the genre of mystery.

Books from the *Nate the Great* series are probably most apt to be studied as examples of mystery. When children embark on early chapter books, most of what they will read are mystery stories. It makes a lot of sense, then, to work with children around the features of this genre. Readers will thus want to pay special attention to chapters three and four, in which Nate the Great calls attention to the idea of a "red herring." This staple of mystery writing is designed to throw off readers with clues that lead nowhere. During teacher-student conferences, students may want to strategize ways to detect false leads, and recall some red herrings they remember from other books they have read.

Book Connections

There are many other books in this series. Most of them are slightly easier than this one. Some titles include *Nate the Great, Nate the Great and the Lost List, Nate the Great Goes Undercover,* and *Nate the Great and the Sticky Case.*

This series tends to be more challenging than the *Young Cam Jansen* series, but easier than the regular *Cam Jansen* series, both by David A. Adler. *The A to Z Mysteries* series by Ron Roy are also more challenging.

Genre
Short Chapter Book; Mystery

Teaching Uses
Independent Reading; Small Group Strategy Instruction; Partnerships

Our Strange New Land: Elizabeth's Diary Jamestown, Virginia, 1609

FIELD GUIDE

E

Patricia Hermes

Series
My America

Publisher
Scholastic, 2000

ISBN
0439112087

TC Level
12

Book Summary

This is a book of historical fiction about Elizabeth Barker, who sailed with her family on a ship from Plymouth, England to Jamestown, Virginia in 1609. Her diary documents the beauty, toil and hardships she and the other settlers faced in the New World. Through this portrayal readers learn about her friendships with Captain John Smith and Pocahontas, as well as see her help to build a house and care for the sick. Through ten-year-old Elizabeth's eyes, readers can realize some of the challenges facing these early settlers.

Basic Book Information

This is a 105-page book set in diary format. For most of the book, Elizabeth writes diary entries, and then for the final few pages she writes letters to her twin brother, Caleb, who has stayed behind in England. There are six pages of "Historical Notes" at the end of the book, which gives some background on the Jamestown settlements in an expository manner.

Noteworthy Features

Because this is the diary of a girl from 1609, Hermes has used a style of writing that will at first seem foreign to readers who are accustomed to reading American books with modern colloquialisms. Elizabeth's writing is a little flowery, yet it does not have the "thee" and "thou" that were part of the prevalent speech patterns of that time. Readers will find it easy to adapt to this style.

The diary entries act as small chapters and can give struggling readers additional support. Diary entries are short, usually one page in length. A reader can feel a great deal of success, as he or she will be able to read many of the entries at one sitting.

Elizabeth Barker is the central character. She writes the diary in the first person, and admits to being less than perfect quite early on as she stole the notebook from her brother, Caleb. Elizabeth's human foibles are the strong suit of her character. She expresses happiness upon her release from the confines of the ship, curiosity when confronted with Indians, anger at the laziness of some of the settlers, and fear in facing the deaths of her new friends. Understanding Elizabeth's character will give readers insight into her environment.

Teaching Ideas

These historical fiction books can help readers understand colonial times. To help a child read *Our Strange New Land*, a teacher might first talk about or read aloud the historical notes at the end of the book. A reader will most easily make sense of Elizabeth's letters by understanding their historical context. The reader learns in these notes that the Jamestown settlement floundered in the beginning, and had actually disappeared when more settlers arrived. Elizabeth could have died from illness, starvation or Indian attack. This will add an air of mystery and adventure to the book. Readers will want to read more about the Jamestown settlements to see what happened to these people. They can find out in Book Two of Elizabeth's diary, entitled *The Starving Time: Elizabeth's Diary, Book Two, Jamestown, Virginia 1609.*

The *My America* series contains some characters who later appear, older, in the *Dear America* series. Once readers have moved to more advanced levels, their knowledge of these characters will support them as they read the *Dear America* books.

Book Connections

Our Strange New Land is a book in the new *My America* series, which is a spin-off of the successful *Dear America* series published by Scholastic. Patricia Hermes, who has written more than 30 books for children, and Mary Pope Osborne (author of the *Magic Tree House* series), as well as other well known writers of historical fiction for children, have been commissioned to write this series, which will contain characters that are also in the *Dear America* series. *My America* is designed for earlier readers and to provide more historical context for the stories. Currently there are five other titles in this series, including *My Brother's Keeper: Virginia's Diary Gettysburg, Pennsylvania, 1863*, and *The Starving Time: Elizabeth's Diary, Book Two, Jamestown, Virginia 1609.*

Genre

Historical Fiction; Chapter Book

Teaching Uses

Independent Reading

Owl Moon

Jane Yolen

FIELD GUIDE

B E

Illustrator
John Schoenherr

Publisher
Scholastic Inc., 1987

ISBN
0590420445

TC Level
10

Book Summary

In this Caldecott Award-winning picture book, a young boy goes out on a winter night to go owling with his father. The two walk quietly through the dark forest, the father occasionally whoo-whooing to call the great horned owl. Finally one answers the call and flies to a nearby branch. The boy's father catches the owl in the beam of his flashlight, and they look at the magnificent creature in the eye for a moment before it flies away. They walk home together silently, full of the warmth of excitement and wonder.

Basic Book Information

This large picture book is a breathtakingly wonderful Caldecott Medal-winner.

Noteworthy Features

This is an enormously popular book among children and teachers alike. Because of its quiet excitement and slow pace, and because teachers tend to like it so much themselves, many teachers choose to read the book aloud, and to return to the book often.

Teaching Ideas

Reading the book aloud helps set the pace of the story for subsequent independent readings. Although the text is laid out in short bits at a time, like short lines of poetry, some children do not take this cue to read slowly, and instead read at their usual rapid clip. When this is done, the line breaks only succeed in making the sentences and meanings choppy. When it's read aloud first, at a slow pace, children can hear the elegance of the words and the story.

For some children, the scene and ideas may be difficult to take in. Many children have never gone for a night walk with their father. Many have never walked through the country in the snow. To some, this event may seem as strange and hard to imagine as an exotic ceremony in a faraway land, and readers may need just as much support in envisioning it. Still, the many metaphors will pull the reader in, and the pictures certainly help set the mood.

Many readers and teachers prefer not to work on interpreting a book like *Owl Moon* because it feels like too technical a thing to do to such a beautiful book. However, if children are thinking about the messages that the book sends, work on interpreting may help them come away feeling that the book is even more beautiful. They may find that the book sends messages about patience and hope and other things that are important in life.

As in any book, exotic setting or not, some readers will feel a personal response related to *Owl Moon* that may need an avenue for expression. Others will read the book and say, "What's the big deal, they saw an owl!" This very comment can reveal a great deal about the particular child and his or her reading and writing. It may also mean that *Owl Moon* is not a book that the child can easily connect with. Instead, another kind of book may be needed to help the child learn to appreciate literature. Later, the child may come back to books like *Owl Moon* and love them.

After the content has been discussed, the pace of the story might be a worthwhile conversation topic, whether the children have heard the book read to them or they've read it on their own. Why the line breaks? If the line breaks do indeed slow the pace, why the slower pace? Some children will point out that the beautiful language is more easily appreciated that way, and others may notice that the pace of the reading matches the pace of a walk in the deep snow, when you are on the lookout for the wonders around you.

Children writing their own stories or poems might well find help in referring back to this book to guide them when they make their own decisions about line breaks, use of metaphors, etc.

Genre
Picture Book; Memoir; Nonfiction

Teaching Uses
Read Aloud; Teaching Writing; Small Group Strategy Instruction

Pigs Might Fly

Dick King-Smith

FIELD GUIDE

E

Illustrator
Mary Rayner

Publisher
Penguin, 1990

ISBN
014034537X

TC Level
12

Book Summary

Daggie Dogfoot is the runt of Mrs. Barleylove's pig litter. When he escapes the death usually reserved for runts from the Pigman, Mrs. Barleylove begins to see her son as extraordinary. She even tells her neighbors that Daggie's deformed feet are for some special purpose. When one replies that's as likely as "pigs might fly," Daggie Dogfoot overhears them and becomes convinced it is true. In a failed attempt to fly, Daggie learns that his feet can help him swim. With the help of a friendly otter and duck he becomes a skilled swimmer. This special talent helps Daggie Dogfoot heroically save the entire pig farm when it floods. When a rescue mission thinks Daggie's dead, they decide to give him a hero's return back to the farm and string him from the helicopter. Daggie comes to as he is suspended in air over the farm and realizes that pigs not only "might fly"...they can.

Basic Book Information

Pigs Might Fly is written by Dick King-Smith. It was selected as an ALA Notable Book, and the ALA Booklist called it the "Best of the Decade." King-Smith also wrote *Babe,* another wonderful book about a spunky, little pig. The illustrations are by Mary Rayner, who has created the artwork for other children's books about pigs.

Noteworthy Features

The book contains 21 chapters with titles that will spark readers' interest about their contents. Some chapter titles include such teasers as "Gosh!" and "The Truth Comes Out." Since there are so many chapter divisions it may give children who are working on reading stamina to set small goals for themselves. It may also give less confident readers a sense of accomplishment since they will complete chapters at a more rapid pace.

The book contains many characters. The only human character is Pigman, but there are so many other pigs in the story that readers may find it hard to keep track of them all. Most of these characters are united in the common setting of the farm, where most of the events of the story take place. Ike (the otter) and Felicity (the duck) join Daggie in the water scenes, since none of the other pigs can swim.

The language in the book reflects the English background of Dick King-Smith. "No fish in there, old pig," says the otter. Often characters refer to each other as "old," as is common in England. There is also other terminology particular to British English such as *rows* for *fights.*

The story is told in the third person. Most of the jumps in time are noted in the beginning of the chapters, i.e., "In the early light of the following morning...."

Teaching Ideas

Although *Pigs Might Fly* is a very lighthearted book, it deals with a very serious issue. Daggie Dogfoot is "deformed" and the runt of the litter. Because he is different, he is deemed inadequate and sentenced to death. Daggie escapes from the Pigman who uses a hardwood club to "deal out merciful death to the weak and the wounded." Readers can explore how the other characters react to Daggie's deformity and what it says about their character. Also, readers can discuss Daggie Dogfoot's accomplishments in light of the fact that he is the runt. Do his limitations influence the way the rest of the characters view his accomplishments?

There is a lot of humor in *Pigs Might Fly* that is targeted at humans. The author writes that the pigs call the farmer " 'Dirty Pig Man!' For just as people say 'dirty as a pig' or 'fat as a pig,' so pigs repay the insult the other way around." The farmer is also viewed as "the servant" because he tends to all the pigs' needs. Readers individually or in partnerships may note places in the text where the author turns the tables on the human and animal worlds.

Daggie Dogfoot is a delightful character who turns his misfortune around. Readers will probably become quite attached to this unlikely hero. They may feel he is heroic because he is blind to his limitations, a hard worker, or just lucky. Readers may also extend their discussion to what constitutes a hero in general and see if Daggie Dogfoot fits the bill.

There is a lot of dialogue throughout *Pigs Might Fly*. Many of the characters speak in a British dialect that may cause some confusion for readers. Teachers should point out the "About the Author" section at the back of the book. In it the students will learn that the author lives in the English countryside. Knowing this, readers may be able to hear the British dialect come through as they read the words. In addition, the character of the otter has an "odd way of speaking" and says things like "And don't think it isn't, 'cause it is. My friends call me Ike, and don't say they don't, 'cause they do." The dialect and otter's "odd way of speaking" make the book very colorful. However, it may also be a source of confusion for some readers.

In a writing workshop *Pigs Might Fly* can be used as a text to studyanthropomorphism. Many children will only be using human characters in their own pieces. This writing device of embodying animals with human traits and voices can open up their interpretation of what a character can be. Since a lot of children at the primary levels are very interested in animals, giving them a voice in their stories may unleash their imaginations. Children can identify specific ways in which King-Smith gives his pigs human characteristics and study this craft.

Book Connections

Children who enjoy this book may find delight in other tales of courageous and kindhearted pigs. Both *Babe* and the classic story about another runt in *Charlotte's Web* would be wonderful related books to read. Children can compare and contrast the characters in the books.

Genre
Chapter Book

Teaching Uses
Independent Reading; Teaching Writing

Pinky and Rex and the Double-Dad Weekend

FIELD GUIDE
E

James Howe

Book Summary

Pinky and Rex and their dads are going on a weekend camping trip-just the four of them, without Rex's baby brother or Pinky's little sister. As the trip begins, so does the rain. They plan great indoor activities. They visit a cavern with stalactites (rock formations hanging down); they stay in a motel and set it up like a campsite (they call it "camping in"); and they put bats in Rex's dad's tent to scare him. They're having a great time until the last day of the trip, when Pinky and Rex each want to visit a different place. Pinky wants to go to a puppet-making shop, and Rex wants to go to a reptile museum. In the book, readers learn how these two best friends solve their problem and have the best camping trip ever.

Series
Pinky and Rex

Illustrator
Melissa Sweet

Publisher
Aladdin, 1996

ISBN
0689808356

TC Level
8

Basic Book Information

Pinky and Rex and the Double-Dad Weekend is 40 pages long and each chapter is about 5 to 6 pages in length. The print size is large, and the spacing between the words and lines makes things easy for readers of early chapter books. All the pictures depict events in the plot. They appear on every spread.

Reading the books in this series in order only matters because characters are introduced in certain books and then go through changes in future books. Each book can make sense on its own. Pinky and Rex are the main characters in all of them. Readers eventually keep it straight that Pinky is a boy and Rex is a girl, but the names do sometimes confuse readers.

Noteworthy Features

There is one main storyline in this book and the series of events happen in chronological sequence. There are just two main characters (Pinky and Rex) who are reintroduced in all the books. If there is a change of scene, it occurs at the beginning of the chapter. Each chapter title names the main idea of the chapter.

The dialogue in this book is not always referenced, and even when it is, it is often referenced with pronouns. This can be especially confusing for readers who get confused and think Pinky is a girl and Rex, a boy.

Teaching Ideas

Children who are reading this book will be fairly new to chapter books, and so it is conceivable that a teacher may want to support the reader by giving an introduction to the text. Just as high school students benefit from watching the movie of a Shakespeare play before tackling the text, so young readers sometimes benefit from hearing a bit about a story before they embark on it. The book summary (above) can also be used as an introduction.

In this book, as in other early chapter books, children will need to keep track of who is saying what, as the dialogue is often not referenced. A teacher may want to display one page of the text using an overhead projector, and to demonstrate how she reads it, mentally supplying the "said Pinky," or "said Amanda" when they're called for. Then the teacher could ask children to do this as they read silently and, when they meet with their reading partners, to go over a page of the text together delineating who is saying what.

In this book, as in many other early chapter books, the text contains a very large amount of dialogue. Readers, ideally, will follow the dialogue and actions and infer character traits, emotions and implied changes. Readers benefit from a teacher suggesting they pause as they are reading, and say to themselves, "So I guess this means that. . . ." or "I'm realizing that. . . ." In this book, readers are required to do a lot of inferring about Pinky's sister, who appears only at the beginning and end of the story. To an active reader , Pinky's sister's actions and speech could convey a lot about her relationship to Pinky .

On page 4, Amanda runs out to the yard where Pinky and Rex are waiting for their dads to pack the camping car. She says, "Look what I got! You don't have new sneakers!" On page 37, when they return from the trip, Amanda bursts out of the house saying, "It rained the whole trip! Ha! Ha! Ha!" A teacher might display these excerpts through use of an overhead projector and discuss what isn't explicitly stated, but could be inferred, about Amanda's feelings. This book can be used alongside other *Pinky and Rex* books to develop a theory about Pinky's sister. *Pinky and Rex Go to Camp* is another title in which readers learn about Amanda's personality and relationship to Pinky.

Book Connections

Similar books are the *M & M* series and the *Little Bill* series by Bill Cosby. *Henry and Mudge*, *Poppleton*, *Mr. Putter and Tabby*, and *Minnie and Moo* are all books that would be great to read before the *Pinky and Rex* series. As a follow-up, readers could try *Junie B. Jones*, the *Pee Wee Scouts* and *Triplet Trouble*.

Genre

Short Chapter Book

Teaching Uses
Independent Reading

Pinky and Rex and the School Play

James Howe

FIELD GUIDE

E

Book Summary

Pinky and Rex are best friends who live across the street from each other. Pinky is a boy and Rex is a girl. Pinky has his heart set on becoming the lead in the school play "Davi, Boy of the Rain Forest," but he's too nervous to audition. He convinces Rex to audition with him, for moral support. She does, and is so good that she gets the lead, while Pinky ends up with a supporting role as the monkey. Pinky's jealousy leads him to treat his best friend cruelly, but he doesn't stay angry for long. When the two friends perform on opening night, Pinky's quick thinking saves the play from disaster. Pinky realizes in the end that, although he ended up happy in the play after all, what he really wants to be is a director!

Series
Pinky and Rex

Illustrator
Melissa Sweet

Publisher
Simon & Schuster, 1998

ISBN
0689817045

TC Level
8

Basic Book Information

Pinky and Rex and the School Play is part of a series of books about the two main characters, Pinky and Rex. It is 40 pages long with 6 chapters. The chapters have titles and are listed in a table of contents. The titles of the chapters support the content and give the reader something to hold onto when reading ahead. Each chapter is 7 to 10 pages long (including pages with full-page illustrations). The story takes place over several days and is set at school or in Pinky's home. There is dialogue throughout the text. Most of it is referenced with proper names and pronouns.

Noteworthy Features

Pinky and Rex and the School Play is a good example of a chapter book that is at an "in-between" level-that is, more difficult than very early chapter books and not quite as difficult as late second-/early third-grade level books that are longer, more complex and mostly all text. Here there is a good deal of text on many pages (2-6 short paragraphs per page); every page is not illustrated; there is dialogue; and there are several characters to keep track of. And yet, the text is quite straightforward; the vocabulary and concepts are appropriate and direct; there are not many subtleties in the plot and/or the characters; there are many illustrations; and the font is large.

When introducing the series, the teacher may want to point out the twist in the names of the main characters. The girl has a typically boy's name-Rex, and the boy (because of stereotypical associations with the color pink, which this character loves) has a more typical girl's name-Pinky.

The author frequently uses italics for emphasis, which may be unfamiliar to early chapter book readers.

There are many theater terms throughout the story, which may be unfamiliar to young or less experienced readers.

Teaching Ideas

Pinky and Rex and the School Play can be used as a read aloud, a partner-reading book or an independent reading book. Teachers can use this book to model good reading behaviors for any of these uses.

As a read aloud, a teacher may do a short mini-lesson on how to use your voice appropriately when reading text that is italicized. A teacher may show part of the text on an overhead projector or have enough copies for children to look at individually. While reading the text aloud, the teacher can ask the readers to listen to how and when her voice is changing. Children can practice reading alongside the teacher or in partnerships with their copies of the text.

Another opportunity for teachers to do direct instruction using an overhead projector or multiple copies is with the dialogue in the story. Teachers can instruct children to notice quotation marks, read with expression in the characters' voice, and to notice where the references are in relation to the dialogue. Although much of the dialogue is referenced, there are places in the text where no references are used. This can be confusing for early readers.

Pinky and Rex and the School Play is a great book for children who are ready to develop and practice strategies that enable them to read longer books in a fluent and sustained way. Some of the many "jobs" children can practice while reading this book include: paying attention to punctuation in longer sentences and using it to promote understanding; reading more quickly and smoothly without the help of a "pointing finger" or bookmark under each line; not reading out loud; reading phrases or whole sentences in "one voice" (phrasing), rather than word-by-word; reading dialogue in a character's voice; and self-checking their miscues by asking themselves, "Does that make sense to me?" Teachers can do a mini-lesson with the whole class, or confer with independent readers one-on-one, about how to practice a strategy he or she may he struggling with.

Teachers may use this book to teach the children to practice "knowing" themselves as readers. One of the ways to do this is to learn how to assess where a good "stopping point" is before they begin reading independently. This stopping point can be used to reflect, retell, and reread interesting, funny or confusing parts, or to discuss their reading with a partner or group. This is a very sophisticated skill and readers at this level need a lot of practice to do it well. Teachers may say to readers: "Before you begin reading today, look through the part you are about to read and put a Post-it or bookmark on a good place to stop for a moment and practice the strategy we learned today. If you are reading with a partner, discuss with him or her where would be a good place to stop and talk."

Although the characters of Pinky and Rex are not deeply developed, they do have noticeable and recurring characteristics that readers may become aware of and use in a character study. (For example, Pinky loves pink things. Rex loves dinosaurs. Amanda, Pinky's little sister, is always trying to tag along.) Because this is one book in a series, readers can compare character traits, likes and dislikes, attitudes, etc., from one title to another. Readers can write a list of characteristics. They can also compare characters in this story to themselves, other people they know, or characters in other books they've read or heard. These are great opportunities for the reader to reread, write and have discussions with reading partners or members of a reading group.

In *Pinky and Rex and the School Play*, there are also opportunities for readers to feel some personal connection to the charactersas their experiences mirror the lives of children enough to generate some good discussions. (For example, Pinky is so jealous of Rex, he feels like he doesn't want to be her friend anymore.) Teachers may lead the discussion by responding aloud to the text as she is reading, about a time in her life when her jealousy of a friend caused her to not want to be friends with that person anymore.

Book Connections

Pinky and Rex and the School Play is part of a series of books about the two main characters. Other titles include: *Pinky and Rex*, *Pinky and Rex Get Married*, *Pinky and Rex and the Double-Dad Weekend* and *Pinky and Rex and the New Baby*. Other series books at a similar level include: the *New Kids of the Polk Street School*, *M&M* books, and the *Pee Wee Scouts* series.

Genre
Short Chapter Book

Teaching Uses
Independent Reading; Read Aloud; Partnerships; Character Study

Pinky and Rex and the Spelling Bee

James Howe

FIELD GUIDE

E

Series
Pinky and Rex

Illustrator
Melissa Sweet

Publisher
Aladdin, 1999

ISBN
0689828802

TC Level
8

Book Summary

Pinky is really excited about getting to school because there's going to be a spelling bee, and he's a really great speller. Rex, on the other hand, wants to pretend to be sick and go home so that she doesn't have to be embarrassed; she's an awful speller! Rex gets out on her first try, but Pinky gets all the words right. Pinky notices how good a speller Anthony is. At the lunchtime break, Pinky is so nervous he can't eat; he can only drink three cartons of milk and two glasses of juice. Rex tries to make him feel less nervous and says, "I can think of lots of worse things than losing a spelling bee." Pinky finds out that Rex is right, as he forgets to go to the bathroom after lunch and doesn't remember until the spelling bee has resumed. And then he can't go to the bathroom unless he wants to risk not winning. Finally Anthony misspells "excuse" and Pinky gets it right! He's the champion and he is thrilled until he feels "something warm and wet down his leg." Rex was right, there are worse things than losing a spelling bee-Pinky has wet his pants!

Basic Book Information

Pinky and Rex and the Spelling Bee is 40 pages long and each chapter is about 5 pages in length. The chapter titles are supportive, as are the pictures, which appear on every two-page spread. The print size is large, with medium-sized spacing between the words and lines. The sentence structure is a combination of simple and complex sentences.

Noteworthy Features

There is one storyline for the plot and it progresses in chronological sequence. There are two main characters who have clearly defined and well developed characteristics. The setting of the story will be familiar to most students, as it takes place at school. The illustrations support the scene changes, which always occur at the beginnings of chapters. All readers will be acquainted with a variety of embarrassing situations described here and will be able to connect with Pinky and Rex.

As with all the books in this series, *Pinky and Rex and the Spelling Bee* has dialogue that is referenced inconsistently. Some lines are referenced with pronouns and some are not referenced at all.

Teaching Ideas

Pinky takes on different roles in this story; he moves from feeling self-absorbed to being conscious of others' feelings. This makes for a dynamic, yet accessible character. Pinky is also not someone who fits the stereotype of a boy.

A reader might benefit from charting Pinky's feelings on one side of a T chart, and on the other side citing the page numbers where they find textual evidence of that feeling. Some readers could add a third column to the chart that is a place for their own ideas relating to that finding. Of course, this method of conducting a character study need not be confined to only charting Pinky's feelings. It can be used with other characters and other focuses.

Book Connections

Similar books to this one are the *M & M* series by Pat Ross and *Little Bill* series by Bill Cosby. *Henry and Mudge*, *Poppleton*, *Minnie and Moo* and *Mr. Putter and Tabby* are all precursors to the books in the *Pinky and Rex* series. Follow up this read with *Junie B. Jones*, *Pee Wee Scouts* and *Triplet Trouble*.

Genre
Short Chapter Book

Teaching Uses
Independent Reading

Pinky and Rex Go to Camp

James Howe

FIELD GUIDE

E

Series
Pinky and Rex

Illustrator
Melissa Sweet

Publisher
Simon & Schuster, 1992

ISBN
0689825889

TC Level
8

Book Summary

In this story, Rex is really excited about going to sleep away camp for the summer at Camp Wackatootchee. Pinky, on the other hand, is really nervous about going away. He writes a letter to "Dear Arnie," an advice column, asking for help. He tells Arnie that if he has to go to camp, he'll run away! Of course, he doesn't sign his real name. When he doesn't hear from Arnie, Pinky gets more and more nervous. His sister, Amanda, teases him, telling him he'll be eaten by camp counselors, or fall in the lake and be killed by piranhas. Nobody seems to be listening to Pinky's feelings. Rex wants him to practice his baseball for camp, his mom takes him to buy camp clothes, and Amanda reminds him he can't take his stuffed animals! The day finally comes when a response to Pinky's letter appears in Arnie's column. Even though Pinky used a fake name, his mom figures out that it is Pinky who wrote about his camp fears to Arnie. She finally asks Pinky if he wants to go to camp. When he admits he doesn't, his mom tells him the decision to go is his.

Basic Book Information

This is a 40-page chapter book. There are 7 chapters that vary in length from 4 to 8 pages. The print size is large, but the spacing between words and lines is small. The volume of text on the page varies. There is at least one picture on each two-page spread, which supports the plot. The chapter titles and the pictures support the main idea of each chapter.

Noteworthy Features

Going to camp is familiar to many readers-the subject is sure to generate personal connections and lively conversations. Many children who have younger siblings will be able to recognize the way Pinky's younger sister behaves toward him. Her character appears in several books in the series, so readers can develop hunches about her and follow her across several books. *Pinky and Rex and the Double Dad Weekend* is another book where Amanda's character and her relationship to Pinky are developed.

The chapter titles and pictures offer the reader a clue as to what each chapter is about. The story presents a series of events in sequence and has one plot line. Many chapters begin with a clear time marker, such as, "That night after dinner....," The next day....," and "It was the day before camp...."

Teaching Ideas

Readers often get confused about the gender of Pinky and Rex. (They automatically assume Pinky is the girl and Rex is the boy.) There is a lot of dialogue in the book and it is not always referenced. Sometimes the dialogue is referenced with a pronoun, sometimes the dialogue reference is embedded in the text, and sometimes the reader has to infer who is talking by what follows in the text.

The reader needs to infer a lot about the characters' feelings based on whatthey say and do. For example, it is not until page 9 that readers learn outright that Pinky is nervous about camp. But there are many clues that readers can use to infer his feelings prior to that. For example, when Rex asks Pinky, "'Isn't that the greatest song?' 'Uh-huh,' said Pinky flatly, 'the greatest. Um, Rex, I have to clean up my room now.' "

This book would make a great read aloud because it can spark conversations about a variety of topics. Children can talk about being afraid of something, not wanting to disappoint friends and family, about younger siblings, about taking a risk, etc. Many teachers also use books in this series for partnership reading and reading centers based on character. This book is also rich in ways the reader can learn about the characters: through what they say, what they do, how they feel, what others say about them, etc. Teachers might also introduce inference by rereading parts of the book that give clues as to Pinky's feelings. Students reading the book independently are able to hold the story in their heads because of the text supports: the chapter titles, pictures, recurring characters, familiar setting and storyline.

Book Connections

Pinky and Rex Go to Camp is comparable in difficulty to the *Little Bill* series by Bill Cosby, and the *M&M* series by Pat Ross. It is harder than *Henry and Mudge*, *Poppleton*, and *Mr. Putter and Tabby*, all by Cynthia Rylant. Good follow-up books to this text are: *Junie B. Jones* by Barbara Park, *Horrible Harry* by Suzy Kline, and *Triplet Trouble* by Debbie Dadey.

Genre

Short Chapter Book

Teaching Uses

Independent Reading; Character Study

Poppleton

Cynthia Rylant

FIELD GUIDE

C D E

Book Summary

Poppleton is the first book in a series about a pig and his friends. There are three separate, yet connected, stories in the book. In the first story, "Neighbors," Poppleton the pig moves from the city to the country. He thoroughly enjoys his new life, which includes napping in the sunroom, planting in the garden and sharing meals with his new neighbor, Cherry Sue (a goat). When Poppleton begins to tire of eating every meal with Cherry Sue, they discover that they both want to be alone sometimes, but have been afraid to hurt one another's feelings by saying so. After their talk, they become even better friends. In the second story, "Library Day," the reader learns about Poppleton's passion for spending Mondays at the library reading his favorite books. Poppleton follows the same routine, brings the same reading "tools" (such as a tissue, in case there is a sad part in the book he's reading), and buries his head in a good adventure for the day. In the third story, "The Pill," Poppleton cares for his sick friend Fillmore (another goat), who refuses to take his medicine until Poppleton hides it in a piece of Cherry Sue's heavenly cake. Fillmore proceeds to eat the whole cake to "find the pill." When Fillmore says he still needs a whole *other* cake to get his pill down, Poppleton decides to become sick too! The two friends spend the next few days in bed together and "polish off" 27 cakes.

Series
Poppleton books

Illustrator
Mark Teague

Publisher
Scholastic, 1997

ISBN
059084783X

TC Level
7

Basic Book Information

Poppleton is the first in a series of books about Poppleton and his friends. The book is 48 pages long and separated into three stories listed in a table of contents. The stories stand alone and can be read separately or as part of a larger story. Every page is illustrated.

This wonderful series does not have to be read in any particular order, but students should read several *Poppleton* books because the characters reveal themselves across the series. Readers will come to know Poppleton so well that they'll find themselves smiling when he returns to old antics we've seen in earlier books.

The *Poppleton* series has a great deal in common with *Frog and Toad* because both series tell of friendships that endure ups and downs, which result from the differences between the friends. The *Poppleton* series should be read after readers have experienced *Henry and Mudge* and *Mr. Putter and Tabby* (also written by Cynthia Rylant), as *Poppleton* is more complex. Over the course of the series we get to know not only Poppleton but also his friends Hudson, Cherry Sue, Marsha, Gus and Fillmore.

Noteworthy Features

The text of *Poppleton* is simply written but hilarious and heart-warming.

Most of the humor is readily accessible to the early reader, but some of the more subtle humor (e.g., when Poppleton reads, he holds "lip balm for a dry part") may go unnoticed.

Most of the story lines are simple and easily understood. There are some sections, however, in which the young reader will have to infer the motivation behind a character's actions, for motivations are not explicitly written into the text. Young readers may have trouble understanding that Poppleton soaks Cherry Sue with a hose because he is frustrated that she once again wants to eat with him, or that Fillmore refuses to hear in *which* piece of cake his pill is hidden in so that he will have an excuse to eat as much cake as possible.

This book, like the others in the series, is episodic, meaning each chapter stands on its own; young readers need not remember a continuous plot for the entire book. Each chapter has a supportive title. The illustrations support some part of the text on each page. Pages have anywhere from two to five sentences of text. There is dialogue throughout the book, all of which is referenced at the beginning or end of the sentence.

Teaching Ideas

Because this is the first book in a wonderful series, teachers will probably want to do some small group work to support children as they read it, setting the stage for them to read the remaining books more independently. In a book introduction, a teacher might say, "This is a book about Poppleton. Poppleton is a pig who loves naps, gardening, reading books at the library and chocolate cake. He has just moved from the city to the country and is becoming friends with his new neighbors, Cherry Sue and Fillmore. Just like when we make new friends, Poppleton doesn't always know what to say or how to act."

The straightforward humor is a great topic for discussion in read aloud and partnerships. For example, when Poppleton soaks *himself* with the hose to apologize for soaking Cherry Sue, the teacher and students can all have a good laugh and talk about why that's funny. The more subtly humorous parts can be discussed at greater length. For example, a teacher may say, "It's funny, but a little surprising, when Poppleton soaks Cherry Sue with the hose after she invites him over for lunch. Cherry Sue is being nice. Why is Poppleton acting like that? How do we know?" This discussion may inform children trying to write humor, and it may also give them new ways to think and talk about humor in their own, independent reading.

Poppleton presents several opportunities for readers to make some personal connection to the characters. Their experiences are not especially deep, but they do mirror the lives of children enough for some discussion. For example, in the story called "Library Day," Poppleton is totally committed to and invested in his love of books. A teacher may say to young readers, "I know exactly how Poppleton feels when he packs the same things each time he goes to the library. Every time I sit down to read my favorite book, I have my favorite bookmark in my hand and I always drink a cup of tea."

Book Connections

Other titles in the Poppleton series include *Poppleton and Friends* and *Poppleton Forever.* Cynthia Rylant's *Henry and Mudge* and *Mr. Putter and Tabby* series are comparably difficult. Arnold Lobel's *Frog and Toad* books touch on similar themes of friendship.

Genre

Short Chapter Book

Teaching Uses

Independent Reading; Character Study; Partnerships; Small Group Strategy Instruction; Critique

Poppleton and Friends

Cynthia Rylant

FIELD GUIDE

D E

Series
Poppleton

Illustrator
Mark Teague

Publisher
Scholastic, 1998

ISBN
0590847880

TC Level
7

Book Summary

In the first story in *Poppleton and Friends*, Poppleton the pig has been feeling landlocked, so he decides to go to the beach for a day with his friend Hudson. He wants to sit on the sand, watch the waves and collect shells. Poppleton and Hudson have a great time and tell Cherry Sue all about it.

Poppleton's next problem is that he can't get rid of his dry skin. Cherry Sue tells him to put oil on it, but that doesn't work. He is still as dry as a dandelion. Next Cherry Sue tells him to put honey on his skin. All that does is make him want some biscuits. Will Poppleton ever get rid of his dry skin?

In the third and final story, Poppleton discovers that eating grapefruit is supposed to make you live long. However, Poppleton hates grapefruit. It makes his eyes tear up, his lips turn outside in, and his face turn green. After learning a valuable lesson from Hudson's 100-year-old Uncle Bill, Poppleton throws out all the grapefruit he bought.

About the Series

This wonderful series doesn't have to be read in any particular order, but it is good for students to read many of the books in the series because Poppleton's character reveals itself across the series. Readers will come to know Poppleton so well that they'll find themselves smiling when he returns to old anticsthey've seen in earlier books. "There he goes again," some children say.

The *Poppleton* series has a great deal in common with Arnold Lobel's *Frog and Toad* - both series tell of a friendship that endures ups and downs, which occur because of the differences between the friends. As *Poppleton* is more complex, the *Poppleton* series should be read after readers have experienced *Henry and Mudge* and *Mr. Putter and Tabby,* also written by Cynthia Rylant.

Basic Book Information

Poppleton and Friends is 48 pages long. Most sentences are short and simple, but there are sentences that are long and descriptive.

There are lively pictures on every page, most of which match and enhance the text. This is an episodic chapter book. Because each chapter stands on its own, it is easier for young readers to hold onto the plot over the course of the book. Each chapter has a supportive title as well.

Poppleton is a lovable, warm character who isn't afraid of sharing his feelings and laughing at himself. Over the course of the series, readers also get to know his friends Hudson, Cherry Sue and Fillmore.

Noteworthy Features

There are three main characters that recur in the series: Poppleton, Hudson and Cherry Sue. Other characters are introduced, but names are not usually given (e.g., the saleslady and the tree doctor). This helps students remember them and hold onto the story better.

There is much more dialogue in this series than in *Henry and Mudge*. However, it is always referenced. The reference is also a little more difficult than in *Henry and Mudge* because pronouns, rather than proper names, are used.

Children will have no problem relating to the feelings exhibited by Poppleton, and how he and his friends help and hurt each other. Some of the situations are rather bizarre-like dry skin and grapefruit-but kids find them funny and point out that Poppleton is not always the smartest pig on the block.

There is some vocabulary that might stump young readers, such as *lint*. Understanding what lint is will help your readers understand that Poppleton is mistaken-he really doesn't have dry skin. Rather it is the lint from the sweater he has been wearing for the past three days.

The humor here can be difficult in spots and many readers find Chapter2, "Dry Skin," particularly hard. For example, Poppleton says, "putting on oil only made me hungry for French fries." Asking why Poppleton is hungry for French fries yields rather interesting responses. It is important to explain why that is funny, and then ask them why Poppleton is hungry for biscuits after he puts on the honey. See if they can make the connection.

Teaching Ideas

Since the dialogue is a bit complex, teachers can make overhead transparencies of these pages and teach kids how the names or pronouns reference the dialogue (e.g., page 42 and 45 versus the embedded references on page 16). It is really important to know who is talking when a pronoun is used.

During the reading, students can look for and make note of: the times when Poppleton is acting smart or silly; the parts that reveal Poppleton's character; the times when Poppleton acts like a pig; the parts that show friendship between Poppleton and Hudson and/or Cherry Sue; and the funny parts.

For discussion, students may wish to talk about: what Poppleton likes to do; the lessons that Poppleton learns; who is a better friend (Hudson or Cherry Sue); whether Cherry Sue is helpful or mean in "Dry Skin"; and if they would be friends with Poppleton.

Teachers may want to encourage students who have read other books by Cynthia Rylant to do an author study and notice aspects of her craft, the characters she creates and the themes that reappear in her work.

Book Connections

Poppleton and Friends is an early chapter book comparable in difficulty to *And I Mean It, Stanley* by Crosby Bonsall, *Owl at Home* by Arnold Lobel and *Minnie and Moo* by Denys Cazet. *Albert the Albatross* by Syd Hoff, *Hattie and the Fox* by Mem Fox and *Noisy Nora* by Rosemary Wells are good precursors to this series. *Arthur's Honey Bear* and the rest of the books in this series by Lillian Hoban would be good follow-ups.

Poppleton should be read after readers have experienced other Cynthia Rylant series books such as *Henry and Mudge* and *Mr. Putter and Tabby*, because it is more complex.

Genre
Short Chapter Book

Teaching Uses
Independent Reading

Poppleton in Spring

Cynthia Rylant

FIELD GUIDE

C E

Book Summary

Poppleton in Spring is a collection of stories about Poppleton the pig and his animal friends doing springtime activities. Poppleton decides to have a spring-cleaning. He can't bring himself to throw out things like unmatched socks, old buttons and rocks, so he brings them to his neighbor and friend, Cherry Sue, who also happens to be cleaning. In the end, Cherry Sue ends up with a clean attic and Poppleton ends up with a house overflowing with things. Then Poppleton goes to buy a new red bike from his friend, Marsha. He gets overwhelmed by too many choices and can't make a decision. In the final story, Poppleton buys a new tent in order to sleep outside. All his friends, except Cherry Sue, think he is silly, and Gus thinks that Poppleton will catch pneumonia. But Poppleton doesn't care what they think because he read some good books by flashlight and he paid attention. . . and saw a new flower open up that night.

Series
Poppleton

Illustrator
Mark Teague

Publisher
Scholastic, 1999

ISBN
0590848224

TC Level
7

Basic Book Information

Poppleton in Spring is the fifth book in the *Poppleton* series. It is 48 pages long. There are lively pictures on every page, most matching the text. Occasionally the text and illustrations do not match. On page 46, the text says, "Then Poppleton went back inside, and closed his blinds and slept in his bed all day," but nowhere in the picture are blinds shown. Also, on page 27, the text reads, " 'Red,' croaked Poppleton." The picture shows Poppleton looking very sad. Children may not be able to figure out what croaked means and it is repeated three times.

This wonderful series doesn't have to be read in any particular order, but it is good for students to read many of the books in the series because Poppleton's character reveals itself across the series. Readers will come to know Poppleton so well that they'll find themselves smiling when he returns to old antics they've seen in earlier books. "There he goes again," they might say.

The *Poppleton* series has a great deal in common with Lobel's *Frog and Toad*-both series tell of a friendship that endures ups and downs that occur because of the differences between the friends. As Poppleton is more complex, the *Poppleton* series should be read after readers have experienced *Henry and Mudge* and *Mr. Putter and Tabby* (also written by Cynthia Rylant). Over the course of the series readers get to know not only Poppleton but also his friends Hudson, Cherry Sue, Marsha, Gus and Fillmore.

The books in this series are episodic chapter books that make it easier for young readers to hold on to the plot because each chapter stands on its own. Readers don't have to hold onto one plot line that unfolds slowly over the course of the book. Each chapter has a supportive title.

Noteworthy Features

This book is in many ways characteristic of Rylant's writing. She uses lots of lists and her books often have echoes, with early events reoccurring in later parts. The first list in this book comes when Poppleton looks at all his things. "Things and things" Rylant writes. Then she says, "There was a box of unmatched socks. There were jars of old buttons. One whole shelf was full of rocks." One of the first patterns in the book begins on page 13, when Poppleton, after spring-cleaning his junk, eyes Cherry Sue's yarn. "May I have it?" Poppleton asks, and Cherry Sue-who is also spring-cleaning-says, "Of course." Next Poppleton sees her thumbtacks, then her shoelaces, and each time he asks, "May I have it?" and each time Cherry Sue says, "Of course."

In this book, new friends of Poppleton are introduced: Marsha, who works at the bicycle store, and Gus, the mail carrier. The reader can't help but notice that everywhere Poppleton goes, he deals with friends-his friend the librarian, his friend the bike store sales clerk, his friend the mail carrier.

Each episode is set in Poppleton's familiar neighborhood and the cover of the book shows a map of this small town. Neither the bike store nor Poppleton's house are shown on the map, although the library is there, as are both Poppleton and Cherry Sue.

A third-person, omniscient narrator describes each character's actions and feelings. For example, on page 10, the narrator says that Cherry Sue "couldn't hurt Poppleton's feelings," and on page 15, Cherry Sue "was so nice."

Teaching Ideas

In *Poppleton in Spring*, Poppleton the pig has three different experiences: he and Cherry Sue decide to do some spring cleaning, he goes to buy a new red bike; and he sleeps out in his back yard in a tent to "pay attention" to spring.

There is much more dialogue in this series than in *Henry and Mudge* and *Mr. Putter and Tabby*. Occasionally the dialogue reference is embedded in the text and not at the ends of lines. This will probably be new for readers at this level. The dialogue is also more difficult because pronouns, rather than proper names, are used to identify who is speaking. There is some vocabulary that might challenge readers. *Attic* might be difficult for urban students, while many readers will have difficulty with *croaked*, *blinds*, and *pneumonia*.

The humor is also a source of some challenge for readers. Many students may not "get" the section that starts on page 13, when Poppleton covets Cherry Sue's yarn, her thumbtacks and her shoelaces, all of which she never uses. It helps to clue readers into the humor as they read by telling them that Poppleton is funny, and suggesting they be on the lookout for humor as they read. Still other readers will need more scaffolding. Some teachers have found it helps to simply have them put a Post-it note on pages 13 to 16 labeled "funny." When conferring with individual readers, teachers will often ask students what was so funny about these pages. Students can then find and put Post-its on other parts that are funny in this book or books in the series.

Poppleton is a rich character who doesn't change greatly in any one book, but is revealed in the way he handles everyday situations. Some students jot down what they learn about Poppleton and notice when Poppleton acts in characteristic ways across several stories. In *Poppleton*, he gets more and more frustrated over Cherry Sue's invitations to eat every meal together, and finally explodes, dousing her with water. In *Poppleton in Spring*, his frustrations grow when he is in the bike shop, and he finally explodes, running out of the shop in a fit. In *Poppleton*, Poppleton's love of books is evident, and this again is the theme in one of the chapters in *Poppleton in Spring*.

Poppleton in Spring is a great book for working with students on phrasing and fluency, as well as reading dialogue. A teacher might gather students together for a small strategy lesson. One teacher pointed out that the narrator sounds like he or she is talking to the reader. "We're going to read pages 5, 6 and 7 aloud to ourselves. Listen to yourself and make it sound like a story is being told," she said. "First, let's look on pages 6 and 7. There are words that repeat themselves here. Our eyes can pick up on that quickly." Each student then read aloud side-by-side (but not in unison; their starting times were staggered a bit to keep them out of sync with each other). The teacher listened in for students who needed coaching. One teacher said to a reader, "Put your words closer together, read faster, faster." Another asked a child to remove her finger, as it was slowing her down.

After a bit, the teacher told readers that reading fluently and smoothly is easier if you think about what the character is probably feeling. To read page 11 accurately, for instance, it is important to know that Cherry Sue doesn't want to hurt Poppleton's feelings. "Of course," said Cherry Sue. "We'll put them in my attic."The same work can be done with pages 12-15. Children can then disperse to read the next chapters on their own, trying to maintain fluency and phrasing. The group would probably need to reconvene several times for more of the same work.

Book Connections

Poppleton in Spring is similar in difficulty to *Henry and Mudge* and *Mr. Putter and Tabby*, also by Cynthia Rylant. The first story in this book is very similar to Pat Hutchins' book *Tidy Titch*. Readers might have a great time noticing ways the two stories are similar and different. After children have read the *Poppleton* series, teachers might recommend that they move to any book in the *Nate the Great* series by Marjorie Weinman Sharmat.

Genre

Short Chapter Book

Teaching Uses
Independent Reading; Character Study; Language Conventions

Possum Magic

Mem Fox

FIELD GUIDE

E

Illustrator
Julie Vivas

Publisher
Trumpet Club, 1983

ISBN
0440843820

TC Level
8

Book Summary

Hush, the little possum, has a magical grandmother who keeps her safe by making her invisible. She has lots of adventures, but one day wants to see herself again. Grandma Poss looks everywhere but can't find the spell that will turn Hush back the way she was. Hush is sad but tells her grandma that it's okay. Finally, Grandma Poss remembers the spell is something about eating food, so the two travel to Australia eating and eating until the little possum finally can be seen again. Every year, they eat a little of the particular Australian food that turned Hush visible, just to be sure she stays that way.

Basic Book Information

The book's quaint illustrations and animals particular to Australia, as well as its endearing story, have made it well loved in the world of children's books.

Mem Fox has written more than twenty-five picture books for children including *Zoo-Looking*, *Feathers and Fools*, and *Koala Lou*. More information about Mem Fox can be found on her website at www.memfox.net.

Noteworthy Features

Although the setting of the book, Australia, is foreign to most American readers, the book aids readers in feeling at home while reading. First of all, the book starts out clearly introducing the setting and characters in the first sentence. Second, the pictures help the reader know what is going on. When the text reads, "Grandma Poss made bush magic. She made wombats blue and kookaburras pink" the pictures show those animals in their respective colors, leaving no doubt for the reader what a "kookaburra" or a "wombat" is. As a final aid to the reader, the back page has a map of Australia with the cities the two possums travel to labeled, along with the food the two ate there. Also on the back page is a glossary describing six of the foods the possums ate.

Teaching Ideas

Readers who feel uncomfortable with the strange setting-despite the first two props from the text-might benefit from the teacher pointing at the map and glossary at the back, so they can refer to them as they read. Teachers could add that since they are the kinds of readers who like to know a lot about a book before they start, they may want to get into the habit of checking the backs of books before they begin reading to see if there are additional bits of information that might help them feel comfortable as they read.

Readers sometimes relish Hush's invisibility and her invisible adventures. A few children don't quite understand how the illustrations, in which you can see the outline of Hush, can represent Hush in her invisible state, but usually in groups there is a reader who understands that the other characters cannot see the outline the reader can see, that it is only there to help the reader picture her. Conversations sometimes come up about what the readers themselves would do if they, too, were invisible. These conversations can help children read more deeply if the talk turns to what might be hard about being invisible, or why Hush started to want to be seen. This kind of personal connection can even get children started toward forming an interpretation of the book.

If children aren't headed in that direction, and they need to be interpreting the story, they could again turn to the starter questions for interpretation in books with animal or toy characters: What would the characters be like if they were real people? What would the change or decision represent if they were real people? What would the real-world equivalent be of the consequence or solution?

If readers try to figure out these questions in relation to *Possum Magic*, they may come to the conclusion that Hush is the kind of being who was taught by her grandmother to be very shy, to be the kind of person that nobody notices in order to protect herself from meanness (like the snakes) in the world. Readers might also posit that this "invisibility" worked for a time, but that Hush feels, as she grows up, that she doesn't like always being in the background, that she wants to let her personality show more in order to see for herself who she really is. When she brings this news to her grandmother, her grandmother doesn't know what to do-she can't find the spell. Maybe it was always that way; the grandmother didn't know how to help Hush stop being shy and retiring. Eventually, the two characters figure out that traveling around and seeing the world and taking in new things (like eating new food) can bring out Hush's sense of self, and her sense of adventure. Ever since then, the two have made sure to always have a little adventure, to take in a little of the new and wonderful to make sure Hush can always feel her sense of self. Of course, readers can easily come to other conclusions about interpretations of the story, as long as they have textual evidence to support their ideas.

The occasional rhyming sections of the text often give readers a lot of pleasure, but sometimes they are only found when readers take the time to read aloud, or reread several times. Of course, it isn't necessary to the comprehension of the book to notice the rhyming parts. But the more "treasures" children uncover in books, the more they can be on alert for them in their next reads, so it may be worthwhile to point them out by reading these parts aloud, with relish.

Book Connections

Mem Fox has written more than twenty-five picture books for children including

Zoo-Looking, *Feathers and Fools*, and *Koala Lou*. More information about Mem Fox can be found on her website at www.memfox.net.

Genre
Picture Book

Teaching Uses
Author Study; Independent Reading; Interpretation; Critique

Ragweed

Avi

FIELD GUIDE

E F

Book Summary

Ragweed is the third book in Avi's *Tales from Dimwood Forest* series, which tells the story of a family of mice. In the first book, *Poppy*, Ragweed is killed by Mr. Ocax, the owl, for dancing in the moonlight with his fiancée, Poppy. Poppy takes on some of Ragweed's reckless bravery by fighting Mr. Ocax and getting her family to fight back. *Ragweed* is a flashback, to a time when Ragweed first went from his family nest to the big city. It is about how Ragweed acquired his own bravery and outspokenness. At the beginning of the book, the reader is introduced to Ragweed and his family. This flashback will seem logical to series readers because Ragweed's big city adventure was alluded to in *Poppy* and readers have been waiting for this story.

Series
Tales from Dimwood Forest

Illustrator
Brian Floca

Publisher
Harper Trophy, 1999

ISBN
0380801671

TC Level
13

Basic Book Information

There are 178 pages and 27 chapters in this book. Chapters are short and can usually be read in one sitting. Chapter titles are supportive and preview the main idea or event in the chapter. There is a map in the front of the book. The illustrations are by Brian Floca and are consistent with the pictures and style of the other *Dimwood Forest* books. At least one picture appears in each chapter, and supports the text well. A chapter usually contains only one scene, and when the scenes change within a chapter, the new scene is set off with extra spacing.

Ragweed is the third book in the *Tales from Dimwood Forest* series, but it can be read as if it followed *Poppy*, the first book. The other books include *Poppy and Rye* and *Ereth's Birthday*.

Noteworthy Features

There are a lot of colloquialisms and slang terms used in this book. Readers can grasp the cadence once they get accustomed to the patterns of speaking. It may be helpful to read certain sections aloud to students.

There are also a lot of characters in this story. Members of Ragweed's family are present in this book and not in other books in the series. The point of view varies; different chapters are written from the point of view of different characters. Usually this shift occurs with a new chapter, but sometimes it happens within a chapter, most notably on page 127 in chapter 19. That chapter starts out being told through a third-person narrator who observes the cat. After double spacing and a new paragraph, the point of view changes from a narrator who observes the cat to the cat itself, voicing its thoughts.

The pictures are helpful in envisioning the story. They appear frequently and correspond to the text on that page. There's a lot of action in this story, which will keep the reader attentive and motivated to read on.

Teaching Ideas

This book works very well in studies of either point of view or setting. They can do this independently, in read alouds or in book clubs or partnerships. Students can use sketches, Post-its, highlighters or various other reading workshop tools to help them focus on these elements. If, for example, students are investigating how the setting affects the mood of the story, the teacher might say, "As you read this book, each time you come to a place where you can really picture in your mind where the story is happening, mark it with a Post-it. Take a moment to jot down the moods and feelings it brings up. How are the characters feeling? How are you feeling? By looking at these markers, students realize that the mood of the book changes when the setting moves from the city to the country.

Book Connections

More advanced readers can be pointed to *Mrs. Frisby and the Rats of NIMH* as a follow-up to this series.

Genre
Chapter Book; Fantasy

Teaching Uses
Independent Reading; Book Clubs

Ramona and Her Father

Beverly Cleary

FIELD GUIDE

E

Series
Ramona

Illustrator
Alan Tiegreen

Publisher
Morrow, 1977

ISBN
0688221149

TC Level
9

Book Summary

Just as Ramona Quimby eagerly begins second grade, the family learns that Mr. Quimby has lost his job. Ramona tries to think of ways to make money, comes up with a campaign to get her father to stop smoking, and tries her best to be a good sport. As comically irrepressible as ever, Ramona confronts the obstacles in her way and ends up with a joyful sense of accomplishment.

Basic Book Information

This Newbery Honor book has 186 pages, with 7 titled and numbered chapters of between 21 and 30 pages. Illustrations are by Alan Tiegreen.

Cleary has written over 30 books and received many honors. She won the Newbery Medal for *Dear Mr. Henshaw*. Besides the *Ramona* series, she has also written a series about Henry Huggins, the eponymous protagonist of her first published title. Cleary's own memoir can be found in *A Girl from Yamhill*.

Ramona and Her Father is the third of seven books predominantly about Ramona. (*Beezus and Ramona* introduces Ramona, but focuses on Beezus, the older sister. It is an easier book than most in the series.) If these books are read in order, they give a year-by-year accounting of Ramona's life from kindergarten through fourth grade. However, each book can also stand alone.

Noteworthy Features

The text is clear, lively and well written, and the characters are multi-dimensional. As in earlier *Ramona* books, the incidents described in the story will be familiar to many readers and exemplify how vivid writing and a sense of humor can make even mundane events-such as having an inadequate costume for the play-truly engaging for many readers. The plot is straightforward and chronological.

Cleary manages to use simple vocabulary in a way that does not diminish the complexity of her subjects. Compared to books on the same level, such as those in the *Horrible Harry* series, *Ramona* books use long sentences with more complicated syntax. This kind of difficulty should provide a great learning opportunity for many readers.

As is usually the case with Beverly Cleary's writing, paragraphs tend to be longer than is now the norm for this reading level, but they are still quite accessible. Chapters, too, are fairly long and meandering: the lack of obvious focus may put off some readers, but could help other readers develop patience.

The setting is Klickitat Street, a neighborhood of single-family houses within a small city. Ample information is provided about the physical setting and the background details of the Quimbys' lives: their economic status, what they eat and wear and drive, where they work. This realistic detail, concerning everything from Mr. Quimby's having to wait in line to collect unemployment, to the faded pink rabbits on Ramona's pajamas-turned-lamb-costume, gives the book a concreteness that contributes to its meaningfulness.

While the overall theme concerns the challenges and satisfactions of growing up, each chapter has its own smaller theme. While some of the *Ramona* books deal more exclusively with her problems at school and with her family members, *Ramona and Her Father* brings up "adult" issues, such as employment, smoking and financial problems. The story makes clear that the family's financial trouble means that everyone has to give up certain things, but that it is being together that truly makes them happy.

Teaching Ideas

This book is a fine example of how writing about ordinary life can be made interesting by attention to detail, language, dialogue and characterization. A teacher may help a child to take note of the level of detail in *Ramona and Her Father*, and to see that all of it contributes to the reader's understanding of Ramona's world.

One of the special features of this series is that Ramona and her family are dynamic (not static) characters, meaning that they change across the books. This happens most noticeably because Ramona is growing older, but as years go by in any of our families, other things change as well. Students who've read earlier *Ramona* books will find it worthwhile to talk and think about how Ramona is changing, and perhaps to compare the younger and older Ramonas.

In this book, an important theme is the idea that it isn't necessary to have money in order to be happy. Readers can look at what Ramona goes without, and when she is most content.

Book Connections

Cleary has written over thirty books and received many honors. She won the Newbery Medal for *Dear Mr. Henshaw*. Besides the *Ramona* series, she has also written a series about Henry Huggins, the eponymous protagonist of her first published title. Cleary's own memoir can be found in *A Girl from Yamhill*.

Genre

Chapter Book

Teaching Uses
Independent Reading; Partnerships; Interpretation; Teaching Writing

Ramona Forever

Beverly Cleary

FIELD GUIDE

E

Book Summary

The unconquerable Ramona is in the third grade. She's excited about meeting Hobart Kemp, the rich uncle of her best friend, Howie. She cannot figure out what is so special about him, though, until her mother and her Aunt Bea start to whisper. She discovers they have two life-changing secrets for her: she will have another sibling, and her Aunt Bea is going to marry Hobart and move to Alaska with him. Also, her father will not get a job as an art teacher, for which he studied, to the disappointment of the whole family. Ramona's world is turned upside-down, until she learns to happily go with the flow. Thus, she discovers that she and her family can positively deal with such mishaps together, and that she is "wonderful" because she is so resilient.

Series
Ramona

Illustrator
Alan Tiegreen

Publisher
Avon Camelot, 1984

ISBN
03800709600

TC Level
10

Basic Book Information

This classic book continues the *Ramona* saga. The book will be somewhat long for many third graders, but it develops further the circumstances surrounding Ramona's understanding of her world and her family.

There is a contents page that lists the 10 chapters with their titles. This helps readers keep track of the plot's many events, which may get confusing, since each chapter has its own smaller plot.

Noteworthy Features

In this book, the uplifting themes of self-esteem and family support blend well. As a third grader, Ramona is ever dependent on her family for her adventures and for stability as she grows up.

Teaching Ideas

This text deals with more serious issues and themes than previous *Ramona* books. Ramona has to deal with death and birth, "hellos" and "good-byes."

When Picky-Picky, the family cat, dies, Ramona and her sister Beezus go through a stage of mourning. They had just had an argument, but their similar feelings bring them closer together. Hard times, they realize, have some redeeming features. This happens again when Ramona's father does not get the job he desired. He responds realistically, saying, "We can't always do what we want in life . . . so we do the best we can." In partnerships, readers could discuss what Cleary seems to want to teach her readers.

The author also deals with other issues that some children avoid addressing, issues such as disliking adults and being uncomfortable about adult disagreements. Ramona does not like Mrs. Kemp, Howie's grandmother, who looks after Ramona and Beezus after school. Ramona, shamefully and with tears in her eyes, reveals these feelings to her family and is surprised that the family accepts her feelings. In a one-on-one conference, a teacher could ask a reader, "What is the author saying about what makes relationships between people successful?"

In all the *Ramona* books, it's worthwhile for readers to follow Ramona's changes as she grows up. In this book, she develops a more mature perception of herself and a keener awareness of others.

Book Connections

Cleary has written over thirty books and received many honors. She won the Newbery Medal for *Dear Mr. Henshaw*. Besides the *Ramona* series, she has also written a series about Henry Huggins, the eponymous protagonist of her first published title. Cleary's own memoir can be found in *A Girl from Yamhill*.

Genre
Chapter Book

Teaching Uses
Independent Reading; Character Study

Ramona Quimby, Age 8

Beverly Cleary

FIELD GUIDE

E

Book Summary

Eight-year-old Ramona Quimby is starting third grade at a new school and getting used to some changes in the family. Mrs. Quimby works full time, and Mr. Quimby is studying to be a teacher, so Ramona must endure a cranky babysitter on top of the usual embarrassments at school, parents who sometimes quarrel, minor economic hardship and rainy days. Ramona's humorous, quirky point of view, however, makes her ordinary life a delight to read about.

Series
Ramona

Illustrator
Alan Tiegreen

Publisher
Dell, 1981

ISBN
0440473500

TC Level
10

Basic Book Information

This Newbery Honor book has 190 pages, with 9 titled and numbered chapters of between 17 and 26 pages.

Ramona Quimby, Age 8 is the fifth of seven books predominantly about Ramona. (*Beezus and Ramona* introduces Ramona but focuses on Beezus, the older sister.) Read in order, the books give a year-by-year accounting of Ramona's life from kindergarten to fourth grade. However, each book can also stand alone.

Noteworthy Features

The text is clear, lively and well written, and the characters are multi-dimensional. As in earlier *Ramona* books, the incidents described in the story will be familiar to many readers and exemplify how vivid writing and a sense of humor can make even mundane events-such as getting sick at school, dealing with a tough babysitter-truly engaging for many readers. The plot is straightforward and chronological.

Cleary manages to use simple vocabulary in a way that does not diminish the complexity of her subjects. Compared to books on the same level, such as those in the *Horrible Harry* series, *Ramona* books use longer sentences with more complicated syntax. For example, Cleary writes, "When lunchtime came, Ramona collected her lunch box and went off to the cafeteria where, after waiting in line for her milk, she sat at a table with Sara, Janet, Marsha, and other third grade girls." This kind of sentence complexity should provide opportunities for many readers to grow.

As is usually the case with Beverly Cleary's writing, paragraphs tend to be longer than is now the norm for this reading level, but they are quite accessible. Chapters, too, are fairly long and meandering: the lack of obvious focus may put off some readers, but could help others develop patience.

The setting is Klickitat Street, a neighborhood of single-family houses within a small city. Ample information is provided about the physical setting and the background details of the Quimby's lives: their economic status, what they eat and wear and drive, where they work.

While the overall theme concerns the challenges and satisfactions of growing up, each chapter has its own smaller theme. For example, "The Hard-Boiled Egg Fad" involves the wish to fit in at school and the pain of being met with disapproval. Ramona finds that friendship and a sense of independence help one make it through.

Teaching Ideas

This book is a fine example of how writing about ordinary life can be made interesting by attention to detail, language, dialogue and characterization. Students can use Post-its to mark their favorite incidents from the book, and then use those sections as models for their own writing. Students should take note of the level of detail in *Ramona Quimby, Age 8*, and how it contributes to their understanding of Ramona's world.

In partnership conversations, children may find it worthwhile to talk about the ways Ramona's character develops. Readers might compare Ramona with another character who changes, such as *Amber Brown* of the series by Paula Danziger. In a comparison with a less complex character, such as *Cam Jansen*, readers might discuss the differences in how problems are resolved. Cam's problems are neatly tied up, while Ramona's are usually only partially solved.

Book Connections

Cleary has written over thirty books and received many honors. She won the Newbery Medal for *Dear Mr. Henshaw*. Besides the *Ramona* series, she has also written a series about Henry Huggins, the eponymous protagonist of her first published title. Cleary's own memoir can be found in *A Girl from Yamhill*.

Genre
Chapter Book

Teaching Uses
Teaching Writing; Independent Reading; Character Study; Partnerships

Richard Wright and the Library Card

William Miller

FIELD GUIDE

E

Illustrator
Gregory Christie

Publisher
Lee & Low Books, Inc., 1997

ISBN
1880000881

TC Level
10

Book Summary

This biographical picture book is focused on the final chapters of Richard Wright's famous autobiography *Black Boy*. It begins with Richard Wright's mother telling him stories of her childhood on a farm, and his grandfather telling him of how he ran away from his master and fought the rebel army. Young Richard is developing a love of words and reading, but his family is poor and frequently moves to follow work. He has little chance to go to school, but when they can, his parents teach him to read from the funny papers. The libraries are closed to Richard because he is African American. "So Richard read whatever he could find-old newspapers, books without covers pulled from trash cans...."

At the age of seventeen Richard catches a bus to Memphis, Tennessee, so he can find work. He dreams of saving enough money to move north to Chicago. While working at an optician's office, Richard learns that "as long as he kept his head down, as long as he began every sentence with 'sir,' he was safe." Richard finally manages to persuade a co-worker, Mr. Falk, to cooperate with him so that he can check out books at the library. The author describes this important moment saying, "On the way to the library, Richard felt as if he were on a train to Chicago, as if he were traveling north already." The prose changes when Richard is finally in the library, glorying in all it holds for him.

Basic Book Information

Richard Wright and the Library Card is an award-winning picture book. It has received the Notable Children's Book Award from the Smithsonian and the Honor Book Award from the Society of School Libraries. *Kirkus Reviews* describes the book as "skillfully fictionalized, resulting in a suspenseful and gratifying story about the power of reading." Each page of text is accompanied by an illustration that appropriately captures its main concept. The illustrations seem to capture the emotion of Richard and those he encounters in a way that contributes significant meaning to the story.

Noteworthy Features

The story is straightforward, and is best read in one sitting. Although it follows a definite chronology, it makes some very large leaps in the age of the character. Richard begins as a young boy and in the text quickly matures into young adulthood, moving away from home. Many of the sentences are somewhat challenging, containing complex clauses that may be tricky at first-they will likely cause the reader to reread for appropriate meaning. The expressive illustrations support the emotions of the characters and make the task of inferring emotion easier for the reader.

Because the setting of the story is so important to the understanding of the text, it may be appropriate to begin the reading of the story with the "Author's Note" to provide students with information about the time and place in which the story occurs.

Teaching Ideas

The story, as it is written, begins without providing any historically relevant context. However, reading it this way may offer a valuable opportunity to teach. Although the book does not explicitly state the year and place it begins, references to slavery, the rebel army, and the library being off limits to African Americans all offer valuable information from which students may make inferences. A close look at the illustrations will provide readers with more information about when and where this story is taking place.

Students might reflect upon each of the characters and how they either acted or reacted within the racist society. Important discussion may emerge from a number of instances in the story. Some questions for talks might include: Why was it important for Richard to go north to Chicago? Why weren't Black people allowed to use the library? What happened to the relationship between Mr. Falk and Richard? What a jolt it is to find that Richard learns to survive by looking down at the floor. Why is it that the only man who befriends Richard is someone who seems to be a social outcast? What is meant by the last line, "Every page was a ticket to freedom, to the place where he would always be free"?

Mortimer Adler said, "Some people think a good book is one you can't put down, but me, I think a good book is one you must put down." The book begs to be discussed, and can be read without having any prior knowledge of the injustices that have been committed against Black people throughout America's history.

This book could be used to help students write their own memoir. Instead of attempting to summarize Richard Wright's whole life, it focuses on a single episode, yet manages to reveal much about the person and the times.

Genre
Biography; Picture Book

Teaching Uses
Independent Reading; Read Aloud; Content Area Study; Teaching Writing

Rip-Roaring Russell

Johanna Hurwitz

FIELD GUIDE

E

Book Summary

In *Rip-Roaring Russell*, four-year-old Russell Michaels is starting nursery school. These stories show Russell's antics at school with lost teeth, his friends, and how he copes with his new baby sister Elisa as he comes to accept his new role as big brother.

Basic Book Information

Rip-Roaring Russell has 80 pages with 6 episodic chapters that stand alone as stories. The stories move forward in time and are linked by the theme of Russell's growing up. There is a table of contents and chapter titles announce the focus of each chapter (e.g., "Lost and Found" and "Columbus Day"). Pictures appear at the beginning of each chapter, but they do not always match the facing text. *Rip-Roaring Russell* is also available as a 1999 Beech Tree Chapter book (an imprint of William Morrow).

The books can be read out of order, but because Russell ages in the series, the reading of these books should follow him through his growing pains (*Rip-Roaring Russell* (age 4); *Russell Rides Again* (age 5); *Russell Sprouts,* (age 6); and *Russell and Elisa*). All of the books in this series have the same structure, episodic chapters, and are similar to short stories linked by the passage of time.

Noteworthy Features

This was an ALA Notable Book of the Year when it was published. The sentence structure is very supportive to young readers. Stand-alone chapters make it possible to get the story in a short take without having to carry the plot for a long time. For readers who are following the growing-up theme in these books, the passage of time is marked by seasonal events (e.g., the beginning of the school year, Columbus Day, a cold day and spring). Though it is written in the third person, the narration helps the reader know what Russell is thinking as he changes: "Russell didn't know why she was crying. She didn't even understand about the parade. It was all her fault that they weren't going to see it."

The titles in this series may need some explaining. Readers might not know that *rip-roaring* means *whopping*, nor that the titles *Russell Rides Again* and *Russell Sprouts* use word play.

There is a discrepancy between the book's generally easy reading level and its occasionally difficult vocabulary, which includes *insisted* and *reassuringly*. In several instances, parents use "A-B-C talk," spelling out words so that

Series
Russell

Illustrator
Debbie Tiley

Publisher
Puffin, 1983

ISBN
0140329390

TC Level
8

Russell will not understand. Readers may need help in understanding this. Both the vocabulary and layout features may present problems for "easy book" readers. Regardless, Russell's four-year-old antics should keep most readers engaged.

Teaching Ideas

Many teachers find it helpful to introduce a book when it is the first of a series. One teacher introduced this one by talking first about Russell: "Russell Michaels is four, going on five. He has to cope with going to nursery school for the first time and with having a new baby sister. He isn't sure he wants to follow the rules all the time, or that he likes someone else in the house getting attention and staying home all day with Mom."

This teacher then explained that each chapter is like a little story and that chapters don't build from one to the next: "The chapters are all about Russell and his growing-up problems, but they are not one story from the beginning to the end of the book. For example, the second chapter, 'Columbus Day' is all about Russell's disappointment about missing a parade because of his sister. At the end, his dad promises to take him to another parade. But the beginning of the next chapter isn't about the parade. Instead, it is about a different problem Russell has-a Chinese dinner." (Later the book mentions that Russell has already gone to the parade.)

Another teacher introduced the book by highlighting and comparing the opposing development of Russell, who changes, with Junie B. Jones (a character in another series by Barbara Park) who stays the same. Students might notice and record places where Russell acts like a baby and places where he seems more grown up. They might list the "lessons" Russell learns throughout the book, and might note how the sympathetic adults in his life help him grow up.

Young chapter-book readers can read *Rip-Roaring Russell* independently or in partnerships. Readers will have an extra layer of understanding and enjoyment if they can step back from Russell's egocentricity and remember that he is only four. He's simply acting his age when he says his little sister's at fault for him missing the parade. Four year olds can't be expected to know that a baby doesn't do things on purpose. If readers don't realize this, they may think Russell is a bit of a brat.

Book Connections

Students who enjoy this book might want to read the *Amber Brown* series by Paula Danziger or the *Julian* series by Ann Cameron. Other books by Johanna Hurwitz include *Class Clown*, *Spring Break*, *Baseball Fever* and the *Aldo* series, but these are more advanced and not immediate follow-ups to this book.

Genre

Chapter Book

Teaching Uses

Independent Reading; Partnerships; Character Study

Rose

Kathleen Leverich

FIELD GUIDE

E

Book Summary

Rose and her friends Violet, Daisy, and Heather have formed a club called the flower girls because they all have flower names and each girl dreams of being in a wedding. Every weekend, the girls meet at Pleasant Park where all the bridal parties in town come to take pictures. Rose is the last of all her friends to be a flower girl. Rose has dreamed of this day, but is not as happy as she thought she'd be because it is her mother who is getting married, to Mike Mello, the owner of Mike's Garage and Classic Cars.

We find that all her life Rose has envied kids who had a mother and a father. Rose's father left them a long time ago and she doesn't remember him at all. But now that she is going to have a father, Rose doesn't want one. She doesn't like the way Mike is starting to take care of her mother, because that has always been Rose's job. Rose is grown up for her age and is the one that runs the home.

On page 53, Rose, who has been holding in how upset she is about her mother getting married, finally explodes. She yells, "I'm sick of hearing about Mike. I wish we had never met him." Rose is sick about the wedding, about being a flower girl and about finding a decent dress. On top of everything, her friends feel they have outgrown the flower girl club.

Series
Flower Girls

Illustrator
Lynne Woodcock

Publisher
Harper Trophy, 1997

ISBN
0064420205

TC Level
9

Basic Book Information

Rose is 90 pages long. The sentences are short and simple. There are a few pictures scattered throughout the book that provide some picture support for comprehension.

Noteworthy Features

Each book in the *Flower Girls* series starts the same way so that any reader entering the series learns about how the club came to be, and who has already been a flower girl. There is also a little summary of each girl's experience. However, reading the series in order lets the reader live through the excitement and anticipation of each of the girls. Since Rose is the last to be a flower girl, readers will be better able to understand her dilemma if they have already seen how much Rose has yearned for this day and has supported Violet, Daisy and Heather through their flower girl experiences.

Each character has a particular personality and the reader gets to know them through the series. The characters are all well developed, lovable, strong female characters. Each reader will no doubt have a favorite flower girl. In each book one of the characters rises up and is the focal point of the book. Young readers are not faced with holding four complex characters in their minds as they read. In reading *Rose*, one doesn't confuse Rose with other characters because they are secondary, yet their presence is central to the plot.

A good tip to give students who are starting off on this series is that there is a third-person narrator who tells the story from each of the flower girls' point of view. For instance, it's very important for teachers to tell students leaving Violet's story that now it is Daisy's story, and the reader will now be in on Daisy's inner thoughts and feelings.

Teaching Ideas

Internal thinking drives this text, so it is easy for the reader to understand what Rose is going through; readers are aware of her every thought. The internal thinking is not presented in a dense fashion, but is broken up nicely by dialogue that is easy to read and sounds authentic. The author is also careful to note who is speaking.

Rose deals with sophisticated issues like remarriage, parenting, growing up and the fear of change. It's easy to see why older struggling readers would love this series. *Rose* is a high interest, low vocabulary book, as is the whole series. The flower girl theme, on the other hand, may appeal to younger readers.

Teachers can use this book to help readers' transition from simple single plots to multiple plots. There are great, lovable characters here-teachers can help students connect to them and empathize with them. The series would be great for a character study on Rose, Violet, Daisy or Heather because in each of these books, the reader learns new information about each of the girls. Across the series the characters grow and change. This series prompts lively conversation because each of the girls faces a dilemma, which makes for a great partnership or book club book.

Some readers might shy away from the series because it sounds so *girl-ish.* But some teachers have found that if they read the book aloud, the series starts to fly off the shelf, chosen by boys and girls alike.

Book Connections

Rose is comparable in difficulty to the *Ballet Slippers* series by Patricia Reilly Giff. It is also similar to *The Littles* by John Peterson. The *Horrible Harry* series and the *Song Lee* series, both by Suzy Kline, are good precursors to this series. Paula Danziger's *Amber Brown* series would be a good series to follow *Rose.*

Genre
Chapter Book

Teaching Uses
Independent Reading; Read Aloud

Rosie's Big City Ballet

Patricia Reilly Giff

FIELD GUIDE

E

Series
Ballet Slippers

Illustrator
Julie Durrell

Publisher
Penguin, 1999

ISBN
0141301678

TC Level
9

Book Summary

Rosie O'Meara and her friend go to see the ballet *Romeo and Juliet*. Rosie is mesmerized. By the end of the show she wants to be Juliet someday and takes to heart what the Juliet dancer told her: "Believing in yourself is the most important part of it all."

Rosie wants to be picked for the ballet, even though she knows the other girls are more talented. She vows to spend the next three weeks practicing during every waking moment. Tommy Murphy, her best friend, wants her to help him build a tree house, but she dedicates herself to ballet practice and Murphy works on the tree house alone.

Rosie is torn because she realizes, "He will never get that tree house finished without me." As Tommy is finishing the tree house, he falls and sprains his ankle. Rosie feels so terrible that she overcomes her fear of heights and decides to help him finish it. But this means there is no time to practice.

Rosie is a lovable, complex character. She is not merely a stereotype of a girl but has a diversity of interests. Rosie enjoys climbing trees. She has scraped knees as well as tutus. In *Rosie's Big City Ballet* readers see Rosie struggling between her commitment to dancing and to her best friend.

Basic Book Information

Rosie's Big City Ballet by Patricia Reilly Giff is 73 pages long. It is part of the *Ballet Slippers* series. Its sentences are short and simple with only an occasional complex one. There are just a few pictures scattered throughout the book. They are there to catch the reader's eye, but do not support comprehension.

Rosie's Big City Ballet uses authentic dialogue that is, in most cases, easy to read, though it can be confusing. The references to the speaker occur before, after and in between their words. Dialogue is also embedded in some paragraphs.

This series has five other books: *Dance with Rosie*, *A Glass Slipper for Rosie*, *Not-So-Perfect Rosie*, *Rosie's Nutcracker Dreams*, and *Starring Rosie*. Each book follows the escapades of Rosie and her dream of becoming a ballerina. The main

storylines are all stated early in the text. The grandfather's love and support for Rosie and her brother Andrew are prevalent throughout the texts. Nearly all the characters are present throughout the entire series.

Noteworthy Features

Rosie's character is the most developed in the story. She perseveres and is learning to believe in herself. Readers will not have to carry as many characters in their heads as they do in the *Pee Wee Scouts* series or the *Polk Street* series. The secondary characters-Miss Deirdre, Miss Elise, Andrew, Grandpa, Amy and Rosie's parents-are very minor.

As in the rest of the series, the book's premise is laid out early: Will Rosie get the part? The minor plot lines involve building the tree house and going to see *Romeo and Juliet*. All of these threads come together in the last two chapters.

Teaching Ideas

This text makes for a good read aloud. As students come across ballet terms (e.g., boureed, pirouetted, plies, and grand battement), teachers can remind them to check the book's glossary, which is called "From Rosie's Notebook." This section gives both the pronunciations and definitions of ballet terms.

Rosie narrates this whole series. Teachers should make sure that readers know who the "I" is in the story. Many readers think Patricia Reilly Giff is the narrator. In an early conference, the teacher might ask who is speaking: "It wasn't a dream after all. I was in the big city to see the ballet, the story of *Romeo and Juliet*."

Readers might have trouble grasping how much time has past. Many readers think it is taking place in the summer, which is why it is important to point out the passage of time.

Because Rosie changes in each book, a character study would be worthwhile. What makes Rosie more confident? What does she begin to appreciate?

Book Connections

A study of Rose in the *Flower Girls* series might make for an interesting comparison with Rosie in this *Ballet Slippers* series.

Genre
Short Chapter Book

Teaching Uses
Independent Reading; Read Aloud

Russell Sprouts

Johanna Hurwitz

FIELD GUIDE

E

Series
Russell

Publisher
Puffin Penguin, 1987

ISBN
0140329420

TC Level
8

Book Summary

Russell Michaels is now six and in first grade. He keeps working on growing up, but sometimes he doesn't get it right. He does and says funny things that kids his age might do. This book is like the others: instead of one long story, the six chapters can stand alone like short stories.

Basic Book Information

Russell Sprouts has 68 pages and 6 chapters of 8 to13 pages each. All the dialogue is referenced. Each chapter has one small picture at the beginning that refers to an event further into the chapter, as well as a full-page picture with matching text opposite. Pictures show the action clearly. There are some big words, like *especially*, and *impatient.* Some can be figured out from the context, like "a large container of popcorn."

Russell Sprouts is the third book in this series. Although it is not crucial to readers' understanding of any individual book, it makes sense to follow the series in order as Russell and his sister Elisa get older.

Noteworthy Features

Readers can empathize with, but feel superior to Russell as he goes through the familiar stages of growing up. The book has a home-school setting. Although it is set in a large apartment building in New York City, readers unfamiliar with this lifestyle will have no problems, since setting here is incidental. The text is manageable by most readers of early chapter books because the sentences are simple, and because a lot of Russell's internal thinking is included to help them understand his motivations. Readers will not have much inferring to do.

The word play in the title may need explaining: it's a pun on "Brussels sprouts," a reference to the last chapter in which Russell's plant sprouts, as well as the growing up theme. The teacher may need to help students with some vocabulary.

Teaching Ideas

Russell Sprouts lends itself to character study very well for several reasons. He and his struggles are familiar to kids; the text makes his thinking very clear; and he changes and grows up through some of the plots in the stories. Character work can be done on several levels: identifying character traits, digging for motivations; following a line of thinking about Russell's changes and the reasons for them; and stepping back to develop a sympathetic understanding of how a little boy thinks and the conflicts and confusion heendures. A series of mini-lessons about character could include:

Make a list of favorite characters in books; show an overhead projection of pages that scaffold narrative, internal thinking and dialogue; ask students to tell you what they have learned about Russell from the page; list ways we learn about character: what they say, think, feel, do, what others say to them and about them.

Stories in the other *Russell* books, such as "The Birthday Monster" in *Russell Rides Again* show Russell's bad side and the complexity of his character. Students can continue their character work during reading in partnerships or book clubs of four.

Students could have a copy of a chapter that shows Russell changing, e.g., "The Costume Party." They can start with identifying Russell's traits: he is sensitive to his friend's teasing about his costume; he is thoughtful; he tries to problem-solve; he likes being a man for Halloween. Students could then search the text for ways Russell changes and what causes it (he keeps trying to find a solution, he likes identifying with his grown-up dad).

Vocabulary work would be appropriate, since there are some big words in an otherwise accessible book. The teacher could model how to decide if a word is important to know by reading the paragraph with and without the word. "You certainly did" makes sense without "certainly," but when his dad says, "And I can't help it if I get impatient with you sometimes." Impatientneeds more attention because it is central to understanding the sentence. Some words need to be inferred. For example when Russell sees *Needs Improvement* on his report card, his mother explains that his calling out in school is not good behavior. Teachers can help readers link the words with the meaning. Readers can infer the meaning of *excellent* because in that paragraph Russell understands he is one of the best readers.

Book Connections

This book is comparable in difficulty to other books in the *Russell* series, the *Marvin Redpost* series by Louis Sachar, *The Polk Street School* series by Patricia Reilly Giff, and the *Magic Tree House* series by Mary Pope Osborne. Precursor books could be the *Cam Jansen* series by David Adler, or the *Little Bill* series by Bill Cosby. For follow-up, students could read the *Amber Brown* series by Paula Danziger or the *Julian* series by Ann Cameron. Other books by this author-*Class Clown*, *Spring Break*, *Baseball Fever*, the *Aldo* series-are more advanced and do not make good, immediate follow-ups.

Genre

Short Chapter Book

Teaching Uses

Character Study; Independent Reading

Shiloh

Phyllis Reynolds Naylor

FIELD GUIDE

E F

Book Summary

When eleven-year-old Marty Preston befriends a young beagle near his home in rural West Virginia, he suspects that the dog has been badly mistreated. Marty hides the dog in the woods and cares for him while he wrestles with a wrenching question: Should he be honest with his parents and return the dog, or will returning the dog to its owner, Judd Travers, mean the dog's death? Marty finds his way through his ethical dilemma, works out a bargain with the owner, and saves the dog's life.

Series
Shiloh

Publisher
Bantam Doubleday Dell, 1991

ISBN
0440407524

TC Level
11

Basic Book Information

Shiloh, winner of a Newbery Medal, is a 144-page book divided into 15 untitled chapters. There are no illustrations.

Naylor's work includes several series-the *Alice* books (*The Agony of Alice*, *Alice In Between* and *Reluctantly Alice*), the *Magruder* series (*Bernie Magruder and the Haunted Hotel*, *Bernie Magruder and the Disappearing Bodies*, and *Bernie Magruder and the Case of the Big Stink* among others) as well as the *Shiloh* trilogy, which includes *Shiloh Season* and *Saving Shiloh*, along with *Shiloh*. Some of her other titles include *Jade Green:A Ghost Story*, *Carlotta's Kittens* and *Walker's Crossing*.

Noteworthy Features

This suspenseful, well-written and thought-provoking story will hold the attention of many children, particularly animal lovers. Written in the first person, it has an intimacy that keeps readers close to the concerns of the narrator, Marty. The setting-rural West Virginia-is clearly evoked, and the unobtrusively colloquial speech contributes to the mood and setting.

Suspense drives the story forward. Will Marty get caught? Will his parents see through his lies? Will his lies about having the dog hidden backfire? The resolution of the story is uncertain until the last few pages, and should keep readers glued to the page. Because the suspense involves not just action, but Marty's internal dilemmas, there is always a sense of complexity that is convincingly "real-life."

The characterization of Marty is subtle, yet from it readers can sense the complexity of his feelings: his love for the dog; his guilt about lying to his parents; his interactions with family, friends and the dog's owner; and his relationship to the outdoors. Marty's growing maturity is unforced and his realizations are convincing. Judd Travers, the dog's owner, appears at first to be purely evil, but through Marty's eyes, readers come to see his frailty, and his capacity for change.

The language is simple and evocative, with a few difficult words and phrases (such as *groveling*) but most of the language is clear enough from the context. Colloquial language, such as "You never eat more'n a couple of bites," may be difficult for many readers, and some teachers find that presenting a few examples of Marty's dialect to the group before they start reading can head off a lot of confusion.

Teaching Ideas

Shiloh is appropriate both as a read aloud and for individual reading. Children can consider and discuss the themes and ethical issues. Are there instances in which they are torn between conflicting feelings? Have they suffered negative consequences from lying? Have they ever felt lying was necessary?

The mistreatment of the dog and the attitude of Judd Travers may disturb readers, just as Marty is disturbed. However, this is a necessary part of understanding *Shiloh*. One theme involves how Marty learns to confront and understand evil, as personified by Travers, and not simply fear it. Marty must give up his fantasies of avoiding Travers, escaping with Shiloh or keeping Shiloh hidden.

A related theme involves honesty, as it relates to Travers, Marty and his parents. During the course of the book, Marty's lies cause trouble for Marty, his parents, Shiloh and Judd Travers, while honesty proves to be the key to rescuing Shiloh from danger. As a study of cause and effect, readers can collect instances of Marty's dishonesty and discuss the effects.

A third related theme worthy of discussion involves the conflict between personal conviction and the rules of family or society. Marty feels a sense of obligation toward the helpless dog, but his obligation runs counter to the wishes of his parents and the laws of society.

The changes in Marty's character might be another area of discussion. Some categories to look into include Marty's attitude toward Travers, his view of his father and his mother, his relationship with Shiloh, his attitude toward work and his attitude toward honesty.

Book Connections

Naylor's work includes several series-the *Alice* books (*The Agony of Alice*, *Alice In Between* and *Reluctantly Alice*), the *Magruder* series (*Bernie Magruder and the Haunted Hotel*, *Bernie Magruder and the Disappearing Bodies*, and *Bernie Magruder and the Case of the Big Stink* among others) as well as the *Shiloh* trilogy, which includes *Shiloh Season* and *Saving Shiloh*, along with *Shiloh*. Some of Naylor's other titles include *Jade Green: A Ghost Story*, *Carlotta's Kittens* and *Walker's Crossing*.

Genre

Chapter Book

Teaching Uses

Independent Reading; Read Aloud; Interpretation; Critique

Shoeshine Girl

Clyde Robert Bulla

FIELD GUIDE

D E

Illustrator
Jim Burke

Publisher
Harper Trophy, 1973

ISBN
0064402282

TC Level
9

Book Summary

Ten-year-old Sarah Ida arrives in Palmville to stay with her Aunt Claudia for the summer. Her mother is sick, but her parents also wanted to get her away from a friend who has been shoplifting. Sarah Ida does not want to be in Palmville, and she makes this clear with anger and rudeness. When she pressures a neighbor girl into giving her money, Aunt Claudia confronts Sarah Ida. Angry that she is not given any money to spend during the summer, Sarah Ida rushes out to get a job just to spite Aunt Claudia. This new job and her relationship with her boss change her forever.

Basic Book Information

Shoeshine Girl is 84 pages long. There is a picture in every chapter and some of them give information that is not explicit in the text. Clyde Robert Bulla has written dozens of books in several different genres, including *The Chalk Box Kid* and *The Paint Brush Kid,* which are as emotionally authentic as *Shoeshine Girl.*

Noteworthy Features

The realistic depiction of the changes in Sarah Ida helps readers to recognize familiar human behavior in the story. There is only a single storyline, although some events cause surprising turns. There are few characters: Sarah Ida, her Aunt Claudia, her neighbor Rossi, and Al, the shoeshine stand owner. The whole story takes place in the same location. Time is structured clearly: breaks on the page and asterisks indicate chronological leaps forward.

Teaching Ideas

An introduction to a character is one way a teacher can help readers become involved with this book. *Shoeshine Girl's* most significant challenge is that it requires readers to infer carefully. For instance, readers must understand *why* Sarah Ida is scared to cry when she settles into her new bed at Aunt Claudia's.

Because Sarah Ida 's sullen anger gives way to sensitivity, Shoeshine *Girl* has the emotional complexity to lend itself to character study. Whole-class mini-lessons can model how to look for moments when characters change and why, which students can label with Post-its. During the independent reading that follows such mini-lessons, students reading *Shoeshine Girl* can notice and record the places where Sarah Ida changes, and why. A Post-it might read: "As soon as she called Al's medal a piece of tin, she was sorry. Now Sarah Ida is learning how to care."

This book can also serve during a reading workshop mini-lesson to practice discerning which characters speak which lines of dialogue. Page 19, for example, is mostly dialogue, but there are only two references to speakers. By studying the page together with an overhead projector, students can notice that it alternates between Aunt Claudia and Sarah Ida. They can follow it if they are careful to note the pattern and ask themselves, "Whose voice is this? Who would say that?"

Clyde Robert Bulla's books span different reading levels. Once a book like *Shoeshine Girl* has been featured in a read aloud or in a class study, an author collection of his books is very popular in the class library.

Book Connections

Shoeshine Girl is comparable in difficulty to the *Amber Brown* series by Paula Danziger and the *Julian* series by Ann Cameron. The *Ramona* series by Beverly Cleary and the *Elisa* series by Johanna Hurwitz would be good follow-ups.

Genre

Short Chapter Book

Teaching Uses

Independent Reading; Read Aloud; Partnerships; Character Study

Soccer Sam

Jean Marzollo

FIELD GUIDE

E

Book Summary

A boy named Sam is meeting his cousin from Mexico for the first time. Sam's cousin, Marco, is coming to stay with Sam and his family, and doesn't speak much English. Sam loves the sports he has been brought up to know, especially basketball, and is confused that his cousin has different images of what one does with a ball. Marco uses a basketball as one might use a soccer ball, bouncing it with his head and knees. Some of his friends fail to see this as a legitimate thing to do with a ball; they laugh at Marco, making Sam ashamed of his cousin.

Meanwhile, Marco seems to be homesick. To cheer him up, Sam's mother suggests a trip to the mall to buy Marco a Giants football shirt. At the mall, Marco sees a soccer ball in the window. When Sam sees Marco playing with the soccer ball, the tables turn and now Marco becomes the instructor to Sam and his friends. Pretty soon Sam and all his friends are involved in soccer, and again they are competitive and quick to laugh at others who are just learning. With Marco's help, the third grade wins the soccer game. The book ends with the second graders challenging the third graders to another game, and this time the second graders win.

Illustrator
Blanche Sims

Publisher
Random House, Inc., 1987

ISBN
039488406X

TC Level
8

Basic Book Information

Soccer Sam uses a large font on its 48 pages, and a large illustration matching the text on every page. Marco speaks a few Spanish words (i.e., "¡hola!" and "si"). Spanish punctuation may intrigue the reader. For instance, the upside down exclamation point before "¡hola!" and the exclamation point afterward. The book is not divided into chapters, but the storyline can be thought of as a sequence of problems and solutions.

Teaching Ideas

The book is one continuing story; that is, it isn't divided into chapters, but there are clearly sections that readers may want to earmark. "If I was going to divide it into chapters," one child said, "one chapter would be 'Marco Learning to Feel at Home in America,' or 'Marco Teaching Soccer to the Third Graders,' or 'The Third Graders Encounter the Second Graders' or 'The Big Game.'

Meanwhile, as a way to follow the plot, it might be helpful for students to graph Marco's happiness. What failed attempts are there to make him happy? What successful ones? Time passes in the book, and how the author communicates this could be worth noting. Sometimes the text is a summary of events and sometimes a series of vignettes; budding writers could study this technique to emulate in their own writing.

Above all, the text deserves to be read critically. Readers will benefit from asking, "What are the values of the characters and do I choose those same values in my life?" Sam's mother decides to cheer Marco up and make him less homesick by taking him to the mall and buying him a shirt that's used for a sport he doesn't like. Marco is accepted only when he reveals himself as a star soccer player. The third graders laugh at the second graders, just as they'd earlier laughed at Marco. The grand finale is a victory on the sports field. The last line of the book, too, is a revealing one-Sam speaks Marco's language for the first time.

Genre

Picture Book

Teaching Uses

Independent Reading; Critique

Spring Break

Johanna Hurwitz

FIELD GUIDE

E

Book Summary

Cricket Kaufmann is the protagonist in this tale about limitations and friendships. It begins with Cricket pretending to be blind, like Helen Keller, walking with her eyes closed in order to impress Lucas Cott. However, she falls off the sidewalk and breaks her ankle, leaving her suffering both from pain and a broken heart-she will no longer be able to go to Washington with her best friend, Zoe, over spring break. Instead, she must stay home and miss out on spring, which she considers the best time for being outdoors. To make matters worse, Zoe invites Sara Jane, a quiet girl whom Cricket had been indifferent about, to go in place of Cricket.

Though Cricket cannot skate outside as she would like, she does occupy her time well: she enters a stamp-designing contest; she makes a new friend, Sara Jane; and she tricks other friends, Lucas and Julio. In *Spring Break*, Cricket gains an understanding of what it means to be disabled and how she can still experience life dynamically.

Publisher
Beech Tree, 1997

ISBN
0688166725

TC Level
9

Basic Book Information

Spring Break has 129 pages, divided into 11 chapters. The chapters must be read sequentially to understand the bigger picture because they each build major themes. Each chapter, however, has its own lessons that connect to the book's overall themes. The chapter titles clearly indicate main events while not overstating the content.

Noteworthy Features

Hurwitz magnificently allows the reader to enter the mind of a fifth-grade girl-moods, emotions and all. Though one does not always agree with Cricket's behavior, the reader does see her perspective and reasoning. Cricket's egocentricity and moodiness are presented as natural characteristics for her age. Nonetheless, the reader is left waiting for some kind of reaction, which never happens. There is an opportunity for discussion here about how people should react to rudeness or selfishness.

One of *Spring Breaks'* great features is its simple yet powerful introduction to how people with disabilities experience and see the world. Because Cricket has trouble sleeping and cannot shower quickly, she will later go back to prior activities with more appreciation, recognizing all the freedom of movement she enjoyed. This may lead to a discussion about how people with long-term disabilities see the world, since they may not have all the choices others have.

Teaching Ideas

Hurwitz weaves together learning about friendship and learning about disabilities. She begins the novel with Cricket pretending to be blind and ends with Cricket having to curtail her activities. But she now has a new friend, Sara Jane, and a better understanding of Julio, as well as of all people with disabilities.

Also, Cricket gains a new friend but does not always treat her nicely. Why? What does friendship mean to Cricket? Like many girls her age, she seems to think that by being friends with Sara Jane, she will not be as good a friend to Zoe, even though Zoe likes Sara Jane a lot. She may also be jealous that Zoe pays attention to Sara Jane.

Cricket's moodiness may also be a topic for discussion. Cricket tells Sara Jane that they are in her kitchen so they must do as she says. She also tells her mother not to open her mail. How can Cricket be autonomous and assertive while still controlling her emotions?

All these are questions that are bound to come up during a discussion.

Book Connections

This is one of Johanna Hurwitz's books involving characters from Edison-Armstrong School. Others are *Class Clown*, which focuses on Lucas Cott as a younger student. *Class President* focuses on Julio, and comes before *Spring Break*. These books introduce the reader to the character's personalities and environment.

Genre
Chapter Book

Teaching Uses
Independent Reading

Superfudge

Judy Blume

FIELD GUIDE

E

Book Summary

Twelve-year-old Peter Hatcher is hardly over the shock of the news that his mother is going to have a baby when he learns that his family is moving out of New York City to Princeton, New Jersey, for a year. The changes are enough to make Peter consider running away. He fears that the new baby will turn out to be just like his four-year-old brother, Fudge, who is always causing commotion, and that he will not have any friends in the new school. Over the course of a year marked by Fudge's antics and the baby's birth, Peter struggles with and finally learns to accept the changes in his life.

Series
Fudge

Publisher
Yearling/Bantam
Doubleday Dell, 1980

ISBN
044048474X

TC Level
10

Basic Book Information

Superfudge contains 166 pages with 12 chapters, each ranging from 9 to 16 pages in length. The photo on the cover of the book alerts readers to some of the antics Peter will face with Fudge.

Superfudge is the second of a humorous and popular series of books by Blume featuring the Hatcher family. *Tales of a Fourth Grade Nothing* is the first book in the series and the third is *Fudge-a-mania*. The books can be read as a series or each book as a stand alone. Peter, the oldest brother, narrates the series, though Fudge is a central character.

Noteworthy Features

Several of the chapters simply describe various antics and messes that Fudge gets himself into, but the chapters do not work entirely independently of each other. Students will need to remember who certain peripheral characters are, as they will appear again. They will need to remember promises Peter makes to his friend, as later, those promises will be broken, and apologies offered. The new baby, Tootsie, will also be growing and learning, and students can mark the progress of the year by keeping in mind the various benchmarks of her development. The structure of the chapters in *Superfudge* encourages readers to hold bits of information in their heads as they progress through the story.

Teaching Ideas

Many issues pertinent to young readers are raised in this book and present discussion opportunities. Peter and his friend Jimmy fight, but then apologize to each other. Jimmy's parents are divorced, and Jimmy is seeing the school counselor for guidance in dealing with his anger over the divorce. But above all, the book spotlights Peter's relationship with his brother Fudge. Readers learn of Peter's envy and resentment for all the attention the younger sibling receives. Peter endures Fudge's constant questioning. The role of older brother as teacher can be discussed around those occasions.

Peter's private thoughts appear in italics. Italics are also used for emphasis in dialogue between other characters. These multiple uses of italics may be worth discussing.

Fudge is supposed to be a very funny character, but occasionally a reader finds his behavior more rude than funny. This might well be the spark that launches a group or partnership onto a character study of Fudge. He shouts at his parents, calls his teachers names, and is frequently disobedient and defiant. For some of his acts of disobedience he gets punished, but most of the other occasions go by without consequence. Students might want to talk about his behavior in a variety of ways. They may discuss what makes a child a 'brat' and determine whether Fudge is one or not. Some readers may think his behavior is acceptable because he is so young and doesn't know any better. Other readers may disagree and think that Fudge could be better behaved.

The emotions expressed in this book seem realistic. Students might recognize Peter's frustration with all the changes in his life. When Peter threatens to run away, surely many readers will recall their own moments when running away seemed the only solution. Peter also expresses embarrassment when his mother not only tells Fudge the facts of life in response to the question of how the baby got to be inside her, but also volunteers to make a presentation to Fudge's kindergarten class. This embarrassment will be familiar to readers, as will the occasions of Peter's disobedience. This is a great book to work on learning how to build personal connections with characters.

If students are reading these books as a series, they will see in *Superfudge* that the Hatcher family has grown, with the introduction of the baby, Tootsie. They can also note that Peter and Fudge have gotten older. They may want to compare the older Peter to the younger Peter, and the older Fudge to the younger Fudge. Also, Peter's great fear in *Superfudge* is that Tootsie the baby will turn out just like Fudge. For students who have met Fudge in *Tales of a Fourth Grade Nothing*, they can talk about what Fudge is like and why Peter would be upset if Tootsie did turn out to be just like Fudge.

In the opening pages of Chapter1, Peter begins packing. Soon after, readers learn that he is planning to run away. The fact that he was packing is meant to be a 'hint' and in a conference, a teacher might show readers that they are expected to add onto what the author explicitly says, to draw conclusions that she doesn't explicitly draw. This, of course, is what inference is all about. Teachers may also want to coach readers to carry unanswered questions with them, almost as if in an invisible reader's backpack, until those questions either turn out to be irrelevant to the story and can be dropped, or until they are answered. For example, late in Chapter 1when Fudge is told that his mother will be having a baby, Peter thinks to himself, "Here it comes . . . the big question." But Fudge doesn't ask 'the question' until Chapter2. This example shows not only that readers sometimes need to wait for questions to be answered, but it is also another example of readers needing to supply their own ideas as they read. The author doesn't explicitly state what 'the big question' is. Readers therefore are left to speculate and talk about the clues the author provides to help them make the inference. For example, not only does Peter start packing, but he has also been yelling, expressing his anger. And in regard to the 'big question,' Peter remembers that when he asked it, he was given the book *How Babies Are Made*.

Characters in *Superfudge* talk to the baby, Tootsie, in baby talk. Readers may end up talking a bit about why people use this kind of talk with babies, but the more relevant conversation will be about the way in which Tootsie, like most little babies, disrupts life-as-usual with the Hatchers.

Book Connections

Superfudge is the second of a humorous and popular series of books by Blume featuring the Hatcher family. *Tales of a Fourth Grade Nothing* is the first book in the series and the third is *Fudge-a-mania*. The books can be read as a series or each book as a stand alone.

Genre

Chapter Book

Teaching Uses

Character Study; Book Clubs; Independent Reading

Sweet and Sour Lily

Sally Warner

FIELD GUIDE

E

Series
Lily

Illustrator
Jacqueline Rogers

Publisher
Scholastic Inc., 1998

ISBN
0375800557

TC Level
9

Book Summary

Lily is a six-year-old girl who has had to make many changes in her life. Her father was sent to jail and her mother needs to find a job. So Lily, her brother Casey and her mother move from a house in the suburbs of New Jersey to an apartment in the city of Philadelphia. Lily has to attend a new school, make new friends and adjust to a working mom and a small apartment. In *Sweet and Sour Lily*, readers learn that Lily is willing to risk breaking a school rule in order to make friends with two girls, Daisy and LaVon.

Basic Book Information

Sweet and Sour Lily has 85 pages with 8 titled chapters. There is a table of contents. Some of the chapter titles are supportive, but others aren't clear until the end of the chapter. (Chapter 4 is called "Two Little Flowers" because the girls' teacher refers to them as "my two little flowers." Readers don't find this out until the last page of the chapter.) The early chapters are around 6 pages long, the later chapters range from 12 to 16 pages long. The story is cumulative and the reader needs to hold onto the events throughout the entire book. There are occasional pictures throughout the text that support the character's actions. The illustrations also clue the reader into the feelings and mood of the characters. The facial expressions are very clear.

This story-and all the titles in this series-is told in first-person narrative, from Lily's point of view. Readers learn a lot about Lily by what she says about herself and other characters, as well as through her internal thoughts.

There are four titles in this series. They are, in order: *Sweet and Sour Lily*, *Private Lily*, *Accidental Lily*, and *Leftover Lily*. It is recommended that *Sweet and Sour Lily* be read first so the reader understands Lily's background, how and why she came to Philadelphia and the relationship between Lily and her two new friends, LaVon and Daisy. The last title of the series, *Leftover Lily*, has 122 pages. It is much longer than the other titles, and there is more for the reader to hold onto. It is recommended that this title be read last. The characters in the series reappear; with each new title, readers learn more about their personalities and relationships. All the books in the series are cumulative chapter books, so that the reader of this series should have experience reading shorter cumulative texts.

Noteworthy Features

The type size is large, as is the spacing between lines. This feature supports a reader who is just going into this book. The copy on the back of this book offers no support to the reader. A book introduction giving some background information can support a reader in this book. (However, the other titles in the series all have excellent jacket copy.) There are clear time markers throughout the text so the reader will know the time span covered.

There is a lot of dialogue throughout the text; most of it is referenced with the character's name. Occasionally, the dialogue is referenced with a pronoun, but usually within a paragraph where the character is mentioned. This offers more support for the reader.

The school setting is a familiar one to readers. The main plot line, making new friends, is also one that all readers can relate to. The voice of Lily, the way she speaks and thinks, is very much like a typical elementary school student. This will allow readers to relate to her situation and understand what Lily is going through. The other plot line-her adjustment to her new home, the fact that her father is in jail, and her mother no longer has enough time for her-is more complicated to "get." Readers who will easily understand the story of making new friends might miss the story of Lily's adjustment to her new life. A lot of this story is told through Lily's internal thoughts. (On page 8 it says: "I hate Philadelphia. It smells bad. But I love my daddy. He smells good, I remember. Like shoe polish, which is number one of my three favorite smells.") Readers need to learn to linger on these parts to understand Lily's character and motivation.

Teaching Ideas

This series would be wonderful to have in a character center basket. Readers learn about the characters through what they say, what they do, the way they think and what other characters say about them. The characters also act out of character-students could study when this occurs as well. There are also many characters to study. Although Lily is the main character, you also learn a lot about her friends and her mom in the series.

The series lends itself to discussion on character motivation. Why does Lily act the way she does? How do characters change throughout the book or series? Children can chart ways that each character changes.

Junie B. Jones is another series written in first-person narrative. Children can juxtapose titles from this series and *Sweet and Sour Lily* and compare characters and character motivation.

There is a lot of dialogue throughout the series. Sally Warner uses italics frequently to help the reader use a certain tone when reading. It would be helpful to study the dialogue and learn how reading it properly helps the reader understand the character's mood or feelings. For example on page 6: "'Shut up,' I say a little louder... 'You shut up,' Case tells me, and he stretches and yawns."

In order for the readers to understand Lily's motivation and feelings, they will need to infer. Teachers can show certain parts of the text on the overhead projector and talk about how readers need to infer certain things about Lily from what the text says. For example this passage from page 49: "This is going to be the longest afternoon in my whole life so far. Everyone else is work-work working. They are minding their own beeswax, even Stevie and Marcus. I am only pretending to work, but I feel like bothering every single one of my neighbors with a big old stick." Readers need to learn to infer that Lily is upset about her teacher taking away her doll, so her feelings about school and working have changed. There are passages throughout the book that help students learn to infer.

Book Connections

The *M & M* series by Pat Ross, and the *Junie B. Jones* series by Barbara Park are good precursors to this series. The *Amber Brown* series, by Paula Danziger, would make a good follow-up to this one.

Genre
Chapter Book

Teaching Uses
Character Study; Independent Reading

The Absent Author

Ron Roy

FIELD GUIDE

D E

Book Summary

Dink, a.k.a., Donald David Duncan, loves mysteries and mystery stories. He writes to his favorite mystery author, Wallis Wallace, and invites him to visit Dink's home in Green Lawn. Remarkably, Wallace agrees-as long as no one kidnaps him along the way. When the big day comes, Wallis Wallace is nowhere to be found. The police think he just missed his plane, but Dink knows better. It's up to Dink and his two best friends, Josh and Ruth Rose, to find Wallace. As the three friends follow leads using their deductive detective skills, they uncover the truth: Wallis Wallace is a woman, *and* she's been planting clues and creating a mystery for them to solve all day long. In the end, Ruth Rose solves the mystery, and Wallis Wallace promises to dedicate her next book to the three pals.

Series
A to Z Mysteries

Illustrator
John Steven Gurney

Publisher
Random House, New York, 1997

ISBN
0679881689

TC Level
9

Basic Book Information

The Absent Author is the first book in the *A to Z Mysteries* series, which features one title for each letter in the alphabet. The series itself is part of *Stepping Stone Books*, published by Random House. The recurring main characters in the series are Dink, Ruth Rose and Josh. This book is 87 pages long, with 10 untitled chapters. The chapters average 8 to 12 pages in length and include small black-and-white illustrations that support one small portion of the text.

Noteworthy Features

The author, Ron Roy, does a good job of creating a mystery within a mystery by making the main characters mystery book lovers. As the story unfolds, the author introduces essential mystery book elements such as cliffhangers, mistaken identities and important clues embedded in seemingly trivial details.

There are many minor but important characters that are integrated throughout the story. This may be confusing to readers at this level. The text includes a lot of referenced and non-referenced dialogue, complex sentence structure, frequent and varied use of italics and capital letters as well as some challenging vocabulary.

Teaching Ideas

Most students reading at this level are already familiar with the mystery genre, so *The Absent Author* will help them practice some of the special strategies readers of mysteries use to "crack the case." To do so, students must be mindful of all of the details that do not seem to make sense, as these usually provide clues to the mystery.

This is also a good book for partner and independent reading for the reader who is beginning to read longer, more detailed and more complexly structured books. Partners can discuss their observations, make predictions, reread to find places where they may have missed a clue, and jot down the numbers of pages on which they find clues.

Teachers may also want to use this book to introduce children to, or have them practice using a kind of formal or informal graphic organizer in their notebooks or on chart paper. This can be used to keep the clues straight, to follow the plot, or to keep track of characters who may or may not be important. Readers can section their notes into boxes that contain the various characters' names and some detail that distinguishes that character's role. Or, readers can chart on a graph the way in which different elements of mystery are introduced into the text.

As readers become more familiar with the mystery genre, they may want to do a comparison across several series and explore ways in which the *A to Z Mysteries* resemble other books in this genre. Or, after reading other books in the same genre, they may come back to the series to reread and compare. They can look for, discuss and write about things that seem universal in all mystery stories. How do the detectives seem alike in their methods? What literary devices do the authors use consistently?

Book Connections

The Absent Author is part of the *A to Z Mysteries* series, which is organized by alphabet. Some of the other titles include *The Bald Bandit* and *The Jaguar's Jewel.* Other mystery series that are similar to this one include the *Magic Tree House* and *The Boxcar Children*.

Genre

Short Chapter Book; Mystery

Teaching Uses

Independent Reading

The Adventures of Captain Underpants

Dav Pilkey

FIELD GUIDE

E

Series
Captain Underpants

Publisher
Scholastic, 1997

ISBN
0590846280

TC Level
8

Book Summary

George and Harold are two adventurous boys who enjoy making trouble and tormenting their principal, Mr. Krupp, at the Jerome Horwitz Elementary School. One day George and Harold decide to hypnotize Mr. Krupp so that they won't be punished anymore. For fun, they tell him to be Captain Underpants, a fictional character in a comic strip that the two boys created. Incredibly, Mr. Krupp turns into Captain Underpants and goes off to save the world. Captain Underpants needs assistance, however, and so George and Harold, feeling responsible, follow him. And so the *Adventures of Captain Underpants* begin.

Since this series follows the time-honored serial format of building on the last episode, it is important that the books be read in order.

Basic Book Information

Dav Pilkey is well known for his zany humor from the books *Dogzilla*, *The Hallo-Wiener* and *The Dumb Bunnies*. *The Adventures of Captain Underpants* strikes the same chord, playing with words and situations. This humor is what some adults call adolescent or "bathroom" humor, but it's all in good fun and in surprisingly good taste with no gratuitous violence. There is a section in the book that follows a comic book format, with many boxes across the page, with action and bubble dialogue. The comic book section was written by George and Harold, the two boys, and is full of ridiculous spelling errors. There is a section called "Flip-o-rama" where the reader is encouraged to flip the pages of the book back and forth to create a moving picture, sort of like a flipbook.

Noteworthy Features

Kids love this book and the entire series, partly because it is irreverent and partly because it is interactive. *The Adventures of Captain Underpants* gives readers, most often boys, the sense of a comic book: It is easy to read, full of action, and it contains moments of pure fantasy. Dav Pilkey has given this book the appeal of a comic book with his wisecracking wit and sassy play on words.

George and Harold are very like the pesky boys we've all known growing up and seem a bit like our wilder selves, too. George has a flat top; Harold has a really bad haircut.

There is a lot of dialogue in this book that is easy to understand. All dialogue is either referenced or encased in bubbles. Readers moving from the systematically referenced dialogue of *Nate the Great* can transition well into *Captain Underpants.*

Teaching Ideas

Comic books are not held in much esteem these days, if they ever were. But they have always had a following among children, and even some adults, because they are action-oriented and easy to follow. Capitalizing on this interest can serve many classrooms and struggling readers well, and provide some great laughs. Like comic books, the *Captain Underpants* series moves quickly between students-children are always eagerly waiting for a classmate to finish reading. Dav Pilkey does a great job mimicking this genre, while also using it to the reader's advantage, by integrating the comic book format with that of a regular chapter book.

Captain Underpants can serve several purposes for developing readers. First, it appeals to reluctant and struggling readers because of its subversive content, and gets them to read. It can also be used to move readers stuck in easier, early chapter books like *Nate the Great,* on to more meaty reads like *Marvin Redpost* by Louis Sachar. *The Adventures of Captain Underpants* can also become part of an ongoing humor study that a partnership, class or book club undertakes. Dav Pilkey uses his illustrations to show more than his words reveal, as well as using words that could be taken in more than one way (double entendre).

Students may encounter difficulty with this text because of the varied format. An introduction to the book that addresses how to read the sections that are not narrated would be helpful to readers.

Teachers might refer back to this book during writing workshop to show how words can be placed in pictures, and also how students can vary format in their own writing.

Book Connections

Other Dav Pilkey books that readers will enjoy are *The Hallo-Wiener* and *The Dumb Bunnies.*

Genre
Chapter Book

Teaching Uses
Independent Reading; Partnerships

The Amazing Impossible Erie Canal

Cheryl Harness

FIELD GUIDE

E

Illustrator
Cheryl Harness

Publisher
Aladdin, Simon & Schuster, 1995

ISBN
0689825846

TC Level
10; 11; 12

Book Summary

This book tells the story of the Erie Canal, from the time it was merely an idea to the time it was paved over. Along the way, it tells of its construction, of what it was like to ride down it, and the celebrations that occurred when it was complete. The book explains how and why it was used, and why it has seen less and less usage in our present day.

Basic Book Information

This nonfiction picture book has about 30 pages. Each double-page spread has about two paragraphs of text, inset over full-page watercolor illustrations. These illustrations sometimes include maps with keys, diagrams with labels, and bits of written information blended together with the illustration. There is no table of contents or index. The last page of the book contains words and music to an old folk song about the canal.

Noteworthy Features

The organization of this text doesn't let the reader feel the overall structure of the book until it is over. As they find out about the construction of the Erie Canal, readers assume that the book is only about that mammoth endeavor. But the construction is soon over and readers embark on a trip down the canal, with a day-by-day accounting of the progress of the boat. They don't know how long the trip is going to last, and at every turn of the page, they expect that that, too, could be over. Even when the trip is complete, the book goes on, explaining what happened to the canal. This structure makes it hard to get into the proper flow of the book, and hard to know when to let the excitement build and when it is at its peak.

Even within the structure of the text, the story can be a bit hard to follow. Characters change, and events come and go. The opening sentence of the text, "After the second war against Great Britain, the War of 1812, the people of the United States were feeling confident about the future of their expanding nation" leaves readers uncertain about where the text is going and even where it has come from. Readers must be very persistent to plow through these kinds of questions and continue reading.

In addition to the structural oddities of the book, the illustrations are a bit hard to decipher. Maps blend into diagrams, which blend into illustrations, leaving none with particular impact, although the effect is generally pleasing to the eye. Diagrams have no titles, and don't explain their overall point. Readers learn how a lock on the canal works, but why are they needed at all? Maps are closely cropped and busy, so it takes hard work to gather an impression of where exactly the canal is in relation to the rest of the country. Readers who can learn what they need to know from these pages are certainly learning how to navigate information and how to skim text for a purpose.

Patient readers who are willing and able to go back and forth over both the illustrations and the text will find nearly everything they could ever want to know about the Erie Canal. What at first seems not to make sense becomes clear with rereading, and pictures that are hard to decipher reveal themselves to be amazing renditions of the canal's passageway and its series of locks. The author includes details about the weather and dialogue from the participants in the project, all of which make history come alive for the readers. Readers will learn that what at first seems a dense clutter of information can, with work, yield lots of fascinating information.

Teaching Ideas

This text would not be right as a read aloud, and is not recommended for readers who frustrate easily. For patient or diligent readers, or those striving to be so, or for readers who already have some background knowledge about the Erie Canal, this book could be perfect. Reading the book in a partnership or in a group would make working out the confusing parts easier.Without typical reference structures such as a table of contents and index, the book is difficult to use as a reference book about the topic. Readers would have to be prepared to read the entire book for information about the canal, but it could provide a good text for lessons on getting information out of difficult nonfiction. A teacher could say, "Sometimes when I'm reading nonfiction, the author gives me much more information than I need. One way I approach books like this is deciding early on what fascinates me and paying extra attention to those parts. I end up reading through the other parts more quickly." The teacher might then connect this to the strategies of skimming or using Post-its to mark specific information.

Book Connections

The Hudson River written by Melissa Whitcraft and Cobblestone's *New York City Reader* are two nonfiction picture books that introduce readers to New York.

Genre
Nonfiction; Picture Book

Teaching Uses
Content Area Study; Reading and Writing Nonfiction; Partnerships

The Best Christmas

Lee Kingman

FIELD GUIDE

E

Illustrator
Barbara Cooney

Publisher
Beech Tree, 1949

ISBN
0688118380

TC Level
9

Book Summary

The Best Christmas tells the story of a large Finnish family living in New England in the 1950s. It is the beginning of the Christmas season when the reader is introduced to the Seppala family. Eight of the nine children live at home with their parents, while the oldest child, Matti, is a sailor off at sea.

The story centers on one of the younger children, Erkki. Erkki is a bright, energetic ten-year-old boy who is particularly excited about Christmas. Erkki's parents cannot afford to buy all nine children Christmas gifts. Instead, Erkki's mother knits each of her children a pair of mittens, while his father puts a few coins and a peppermint stick in each of the mittens. It is Matti, however, who brings home gifts every Christmas for his siblings. In Erkki's eyes, Matti is Christmas.

The Seppala holiday spirit turns sour when they get word that Matti's boat is reportedly missing at sea. The entire family is sick with worry, and the children are also secretly crestfallen because without Matti, they won't have a Christmas full of gifts. Young Erkki decides he will take Matti's place this year as the gift-giver and he makes homemade, personalized gifts for his entire family. While the Seppalas are very glum as the days close in on Christmas, Erkki is exceptionally happy and excited because he can't wait for his family to see all of the gifts he has been secretly making for them during the past few weeks.

When Christmas Eve arrives, Erkki surprises his family with his gifts. His parents and siblings are delighted and touched that Erkki spent so much time and effort on them. The Seppala family is still upset, however, because they don't have Matti to share the holiday with them. As proud as Erkki is of having gifts for his family for Christmas, he realizes that having his entire family together is the best gift of all. Finally Matti returns home from his journey, and the family has the best Christmas ever!

Basic Book Information

The Best Christmas is broken down into nine chapters. Each chapter has a title that gives the reader a hint as to what will happen next. For instance, in the chapter "Erkki's Grand Idea" Erkki has the idea that he should make Christmas gifts for his whole family. Erkki is the main character in the book, followed by his mother and father. Readers have a better sense of his not-yet-seen brother, Matti, as opposed to his other siblings simply because they are not mentioned very frequently.

Noteworthy Features

Since the Seppala family is Finnish, their names may not be familiar to most American readers (Erkki, Matti, Saima, etc.). Children might have a difficult time when reading the characters' names. The teacher should remind the children to try their best when pronouncing them. The teacher could also mention that readers could think-up their own comparable names (e.g., Erik, Matt, Sam) to make their reading less difficult.

The story moves in a traditional linear direction and is told in the third person. There are black-and-white illustrations throughout. As the story revolves around Erkki, children may have a difficult time discerning between other characters, but this is not critical for understanding the text.

Teaching Ideas

This book is suitable for interpretation studies for young readers because the messages are not too far beneath the surface. Asking readers questions that encourage them to interpret the text, such as "What is the really important message here?" or "What do you think the author is trying to tell us?" or "What is this story really about?" is usually all they need to be launched into a discussion of the deeper meanings in the story.

Some teachers also choose to read this book during the December holidays so that students can focus on human values more easily than they might with books about Santa Claus or particular holidays.

Genre
Picture Book; Chapter Book

Teaching Uses
Interpretation; Independent Reading

The Chalk Box Kid

Clyde Robert Bulla

FIELD GUIDE

E F

Illustrator
Thomas B. Allen

Publisher
Scholastic, 1987

ISBN
0590485237

TC Level
9

Book Summary

Gregory moves to a new neighborhood on his ninth birthday. The new house is in an older section of town and does not have a yard. He has to share his new room with his uncle and has problems being accepted at his new school. Gregory consoles himself by drawing on a wall blackened by fire in his neighborhood. In school the class is given seeds to plant a garden. Gregory cannot plant seeds in his yard so he draws a garden on the wall. At first people doubt his claim that he has a garden, but when they see the wall, everyone is impressed by his "garden" and he is accepted by his new classmates.

Basic Book Information

The text spans 58 pages and is divided into 9 chapters with supportive titles that clue the reader into what the chapter will be about, such as "The New School" or "The Burned Building." Black-and-white pictures appear every few pages and support the written text on the page. The sentences are simple and not too long. The dialogue is clearly referenced and on separate lines. Time flows chronologically.

Noteworthy Features

Readers may have difficulty understanding the beginning of the story because it is written in the past perfect tense: "He had wanted to go with Mother and Daddy. They were moving to another house, and he hadn't even seen it yet." The tense then changes to the simple past and remains in this tense throughout the rest of the book: "The house was small and it needed paint.... There was no yard at all." Although the story is told in a straightforward way and does not require much inference, the ending is inconclusive. Children sometimes say, "Is that the end?" as it occurs in the middle of an unresolved conversation with Gregory's new friend. Although the text is written simply, there is a serious theme: how the character copes with disappointment and rejection by creating art.

Teaching Ideas

Readers of this book tend to spend a lot of time making personal connections to Gregory's situation. Being new, being placed in a disappointing situation, and finding acceptance are themes that many children readily relate to. Many teachers encourage their readers to develop these connections beyond the "me too" statements many readers make at this level. Having students develop the reasoning behind the similarities and differences they see with Gregory can deepen and build their personal response.

Because *The Chalk Box Kid* combines readability with a meaningful story, teachers may use this book for character study, theme work or read aloud with students of any age. The text is accessible enough for partner and or independent reading with newly fluent readers. This book is well written and offers the opportunity for young readers to experience the qualities of good writing and a universal theme.

Book Connections

Paint Brush Kid is the sequel to this book. Bulla also wrote the popular *Shoeshine Girl*, which also deals with the theme of a child finding a place in a new situation.

Genre
Short Chapter Book

Teaching Uses
Character Study; Read Aloud; Independent Reading

The Cloud Book

Tomie dePaola

FIELD GUIDE

E

Illustrator
Tomie dePaola

Publisher
Scholastic, 1975

ISBN
059008531X

TC Level
9; 10; 11

Book Summary

This book is made up largely of descriptions and definitions of the ten main types of clouds in the sky. The author first describes the three primary kinds, then describes combination clouds that result from a mixing of those three types. He also names and portrays less common kinds of clouds that observers have noted. Following this catalogue, the text offers myths peoples have created about clouds and images they have seen in them. The reader can then learn some popular sayings about clouds that have aided people in forecasting the weather. The text refers to several English language idioms that involve clouds and then ends with a silly story about a cloud.

Basic Book Information

This nonfiction picture book has about 30 pages. Each individual page has from one to eight sentences, written in short, declarative form with very few clauses. In order to more fully illustrate the text, the pictures are sometimes separated into separate boxes on the page, one for each big idea in the text. The text is a continuous narrative with no headings or chapters. There is a short, ten-entry index at the back of the book that helps readers find the pages on which each of the ten types of clouds in the book are described. There is no one character traveling throughout the book with the reader, and instead different characters appear in the pictures that illustrate different aspects of the text. Very few of the pictures are labeled.

Noteworthy Features

As mentioned before, there aren't textual markers, like headings, between the different kinds of information offered about clouds. This makes referring back to the text for information a little more difficult if the desired information is not referenced in the index.

Since the majority of the book is a description of the types of clouds, some readers may have difficulty holding all that information in their heads. One way to read the book is to not try to hold the information; just read to know that these categories exist and can be referred to when necessary. Another way is to stop and take notes and make diagrams to help the information stay in the reader's head. Yet a third way is to use it as a reference at various times of the day or week when there are clouds in the sky to be identified. Some readers find that talking over the text as they read is enough to help keep the terms and categories stuck in their minds for a while.

The three-sentence short story at the end of the book is very odd to some readers. Some understand that the very brevity and oddity in itself is what's silly about it, and some children are just flat out puzzled, thinking they missed some significance in it.

The familiar and entertaining pictures of Tomie dePaola usually make the book attractive and accessible to readers. The silly story at the book's end and the humorous comments at the bottom of some of the pages also make the book a fun choice for readers who don't even have a particular interest in clouds. The careful and thorough introduction of terms for clouds and sayings about clouds invites readers to add the words, sayings and idioms to their own conversations. It even invites children to predict the weather themselves using some of the sayings. Kids usually enjoy this newfound knowledge.

Teaching Ideas

Some teachers use this book as part of a larger study of clouds and the weather. In these cases, introduction of the book is usually unnecessary as readers are already familiar with the basics of weather and clouds, and the book itself will offer further details. Teachers who do feel an introduction to the book is necessary may want to flip through the book with the reader referring to the type of reading that will be necessary in each section. First, there is the listing of the types of clouds and what they look like; then there are the myths and images in the clouds; then the sayings that predict weather based on clouds; then the silly story. Readers who know that these categories of information are presented in this certain order may read with more ease.

After teachers and readers have used the book to learn about weather in general and clouds in particular, this book has some hidden but powerful uses in a writing workshop. The names people have given to clouds over time are powerful metaphors. Calling a particular kind of cloud a "sheep" when everyone knows it is not a sheep is a clear example of the use of metaphor. The descriptions of the clouds often contain examples of analogies and similes.

Genre

Picture Book; Nonfiction

Teaching Uses

Reading and Writing Nonfiction; Partnerships; Content Area Study

The Cuckoo Child

Dick King-Smith

FIELD GUIDE

E

Illustrator
Leslie W. Bowman

Publisher
Penguin, 1993

ISBN
0786813512

TC Level
10

Book Summary

When Oliver the ostrich is hatched, the geese, in whose nest his egg was placed, plainly see that their son is no ordinary goose-they think he's marvelous. Jack the human, who took the ostrich egg from a park ranger while on a class trip and put it in the nest, is also filled with pride in Ollie. He and the geese have wonderful escapades trying to understand this odd bird. Jack dreads the day he will have to give back the bird that is not rightfully his. When Ollie the ostrich becomes an adult, it is evident that he finally needs to be with his own kind and is brought back to a wildlife refuge. Jack has also become an adult in the process. Luckily, they never have to say goodbye. Jack is offered a job as a park ranger and gets to ride Ollie every day.

Basic Book Information

Dick King-Smith is the author of *Babe: The Gallant Pig* and *Pigs Might Fly*. He has received England's 1984 Guardian Award for excellence in children's literature. *The Cuckoo Child* is a children's chapter book.

Noteworthy Features

The Cuckoo Child is told in a third-person omniscient narration. The narrator provides commentary on the events of the story and also lets readers know what the characters are thinking.

There are only two main settings in the book-the farm and the Wildlife Refuge. Readers will not need to keep track of many locations throughout the book, this may be helpful for young readers.

There are quite a few characters throughout the book. One set of characters are the humans-Jack Daw, his family and the staff at the Wildlife Refuge. The other set of characters are the farm animals, including Lydia, Wilfred and Oliver. Both the animals and the humans speak in English, but humans and animals cannot understand each other.

Most of the major shifts in time are clearly noted in the text. However, sometimes time progression must be inferred, i.e., "Day followed day, week succeeded week." Usually the passage of years is marked by Jack Daw's birthdays, when his father measures Jack and Oliver against one another. Time goes forth in forward progression and moves quite rapidly at the end of the book. There is one chapter called "Time Flies" in which Jack essentially moves from childhood to adulthood in the course of just a few pages.

Dick King-Smith loves to play with language. He makes Lydia, the goose, into a sophisticated character by saying things such as, she "bestrode her colossus" instead of she sat on her egg. Sometimes the author's energetic word choice and delight in using precise bird terms, such as *struthio camelus*, may be challenging to younger readers.

Teaching Ideas

Dick King-Smith's books are beloved by children because of their humor, warmth, adventure, and wonderful animal characters. In most of his books, the "little guy" wins through perseverance and wit. In this story, the little guy is Jack Daw, a boy who falls head over heels in love with birds. He is a wonderful model for students the world over because he has a passion, and that passion leads him into a life of research-and risk. Jack knows he is breaking all the rules to bring an ostrich egg home from the bird park. But he takes the risk and soon joins Lydia, the goose, as the adoptive parents of a growing ostrich.

Children may want to use Post-its to mark instances in the book where the animals and humans can understand one another. They may see Jack's understanding of animal language as an extension of his animal expertise and compassion for pets. There are times when Jack swears that Lydia and Wilfred are saying "Oliver," and Jack and Oliver communicate somewhat with each other. Readers may notice that Oliver is a part of Jack's family and a part of Lydia and Wilfred's family. Despite the fact that he is loved by both, he is always the odd-bird out. Readers may want to explore what it takes to be "a family" and look for places in the book where Oliver has found family love, in its many forms.

Some readers may see humor in the way the geese talk and reason. The geese are not that clever, so their talk is very circular. Also, there are humorous references to Wilfred being a "goose-pecked husband." Readers who understand these puns will be sure to have a few laughs.

In a writing workshop, it may be interesting to notice Dick King-Smith's use of a full-circle ending. In the beginning of the book, Jack Daw is at the Wildlife Refuge with his school trip when he steals the ostrich egg from a park ranger. At the end of the book, Jack himself is a ranger working with the ostrich that was hatched from that very egg. Writers may want to take note of specific elements of this full-circle ending and practice a similar type of ending in their own pieces.

Book Connections

Readers who like to read books where the world of animals comes alive may delight in other Dick King-Smith books such as *Babe* and *Pigs Might Fly*. *The Mouse and the Motorcycle* and *Runaway Ralph* by Beverly Cleary and *Charlotte's Web* by E.B. White may also be books of interest for readers who would love to hear about a mouse's or a pig's perspective on the world of humans.

The Cuckoo Child also has many parallels to Oliver Butterworth's book, *The Enormous Egg.*

Genre

Chapter Book

Teaching Uses
Independent Reading; Teaching Writing; Partnerships

The Great Gilly Hopkins

Katherine Paterson

FIELD GUIDE

E F

Publisher
Harper Trophy, 1978

ISBN
0064402010

TC Level
12

Book Summary

Gilly has been shuttled from one foster home to the next since she was born, and has developed an armor of sarcasm and intimidation to protect her from being hurt repeatedly. This book is about the relationship between Gilly and her most recent foster family and about the loving relationships that eventually alter the way Gilly perceives and reacts to the world. Gilly comes to learn that, even though this foster parent is not the mother of her dreams, she is her family. By the time she realizes this, however, it is too late. She has already written a letter of complaint to her "real" mother (her birth mother), and is forced to leave the family she has grown to love.

But Gilly's birth mother does not live up to Gilly's fantasies either. She abandons the girl again, as she did when Gilly was born, and at the end of the book Gilly is living with her grandmother and writing letters to her foster family.

Although the primary plot line revolves around Gilly's struggles to find a family (as evidenced by her relationships to Trotter, her foster mother, and Courtney, her birth mother), the book is also about Gilly's relationships with several other people. Gilly learns important life lessons through her relationships with these other characters, such as her foster brother, William Ernest. She comes to realize that William is not a "wimp," but is scared because he has been hurt in the past by the people closest to him, just as Gilly has been. This book is about the relationships that allow Gilly to learn, change and grow.

Basic Book Information

This book is 148 pages long, with 15 chapters. The chapters are titled and vary in length from 6 to 18 pages. The chapters are episodic, and their titles foreshadow the events taking place within them. For example, in the chapter entitled "Welcome to Thomson Park," Gilly moves to Thomson Park. Italics set poems and letters apart from the rest of the text. There are no illustrations. The story is told in a first-person narrative, from Gilly's point of view.

Noteworthy Features

The Great Gilly Hopkins lends itself to a study of character, motivation and change. Gilly's actions and words clearly reflect the lessons she is learning on the inside, and thus provide strong textual support for readers' ideas about these changes. Her sarcastic, intimidating manner is easily traced to past experiences, providing a solid springboard for conversations around the reasons behind characters' choices and behaviors. This is an excellent opportunity to discuss the fact that readers can understand and feel compassion for characters, even when disagreeing with their choices. Because chapter titles foreshadow coming events, they lend themselves nicely to predictions and guesswork.

Gilly uses mildly offensive swear words, such as "dammit" and "hell," and refers to religious practices in less than flattering ways. The erroneous thinking caused by her past experience, or lack of experience, is responsible for the prejudiced attitudes and behaviors she demonstrates toward African American characters. When she first meets Mr. Randolph, Gilly thinks, "I never touched one of these people in all my life." Paterson writes, "It was bad enough having to come to this broken down old school but to be behind . . . to have to appear a fool in front of . . . almost half the class was black." Readers will protest Gilly's behavior and attitudes, rightly calling her racist, but as the story unfolds, Gilly becomes a more sympathetic character, leading readers to reach for explanations for her behavior. In time, Gilly shows signs of changing. "She's softening up," readers will probably say. "She's learning and letting her true feelings out." Readers will want to understand the various factors that contribute to Gilly's transformation, and to see how all elements of the story fit with this central plot line.

Some readers will want to puzzle over the rather complex (and significant) words of a poem recited by Mr. Randolph. Although the poem is clearly connected to Gilly's journey, it is not imperative for students to understand its every nuance. They need not be expected to, and it would take away from the real story to devote an inordinate amount of time to its interpretation. Gilly doesn't fully understand it herself.

Finally, readers will want to understand why Gilly holds so tightly to her fantasy of Courtney, her birth mother. It will be worthwhile for readers to spend some time on Courtney's letter to Gilly. She writes, "My Dearest Galadriel, the agency wrote to me that you had moved. I wish it were to here. All my love, Courtney." Students may come to understand that, although these are the words Gilly wants to hear, they are not supported by her mother's actions. Sometimes it's hard for readers (as it is for Gilly) to understand that when words are just words, unsupported by actions, they may not justify our putting too much trust in them.

Teaching Ideas

This book is so rich that it deserves to be the centerpiece of a daily, whole-class read aloud and book talk. Because the book is rich with literary themes, the book merits intense, teacher-supported conversations.

If the class develops the theory that Gilly is tough, students may be encouraged to stop and write at moments when Gilly's actions or words reflect inner change. For example, someone may claim that Gilly leaves people before they can leave her. Readers can find evidence for this. Paterson writes that the Nevinses "got rid of her. No. She'd got rid of them-the whole stinking place." And later she thinks, "But I can't stay. I might go soft and stupid, too. Like I did at Dixons'. I let her fool me with all that rocking and love talk. I called her Mama and crawled up on her lap when I had to cry . . . but when they moved to Florida, I was put out like the rest of the trash they left behind. I can't go soft-not as long as I'm nobody's real kid. . . ." Readers might also find and write about instances when it seems Gilly is starting to soften.

Book Connections

Gilly taps into more than one major literary theme and can be compared to several books along different lines. Texts addressing a search for home and family include *The Music of Dolphins* by Karen Hesse and Jerry Spinelli's *Maniac Magee*. The protagonists in Patricia MacLachlan's *Journey* and *Baby* are also forced to cope with loss and, in the process, ultimately learn to face and accept the truth.

Genre
Chapter Book

Teaching Uses
Independent Reading; Read Aloud; Book Clubs; Character Study

The Hundred Dresses

Eleanor Estes

FIELD GUIDE

C E

Book Summary

The Hundred Dresses won the Newbery Honor when it was first published in 1944, and has continued to offer insight and humility to children and adults alike. Wanda Petronski is different from all the other kids at school: she wears an old faded dress and muddy shoes; she has a funny name and lives in the poor part of town. Peggy and Maddie tease her daily, but miss her when she doesn't come to school because they must suspend their teasing game. The game is called the Hundred Dresses game, and in it Peggy repeatedly gets Wanda to tell everyone that she has a hundred dresses at home "all lined up in my closet." When Wanda wins the class competition for her drawings (of her hundred dresses), Maddie convinces Peggy that they must apologize. However, they are too late: the Petronskis have moved. As Wanda's absence extends into many days, the class receives a letter from Wanda's father telling them that Wanda will not return to school. They are moving to a big city where their name won't be made fun of and they won't be called "Polack." By the end of the book Maddie has become reflective, vowing never again to stand by and allow someone to be teased or bullied. Peggy, however, remains the same.

Illustrator
Louis Slobodkin

Publisher
Voyager Books, 1944

ISBN
0156423502

TC Level
9

Basic Book Information

This 80-page book has 7 chapters, with illustrations on nearly every page. The story is told in the third person from Maddie's point of view. There is frequent dialogue to show Wanda's and Maddie's interactions with others. Eleanor Estes is also known for her beloved *Ginger Pye*, which received the NewberyMedal, and for *The Moffats*.

Noteworthy Features

This book is available in several formats, ranging from a large picture book to a slim chapter book. Older children may feel that the large picture book looks babyish, and so perhaps using the 6" x 8" version, illustrated in full color, can solve this perceived problem.

Since this book was written in 1944, there is some language that will seem foreign to readers. At one point in the book, the narrator points out that Wanda's forehead shined, like she used "Sapolio" on it. Not many young people will know that sapolio was a form of margarine used in the 30s and 40s. The practice of oral reading in school may also need some explaining. Some readers may not know what "Polack" refers to and that it is a derogatory term for people of Polish descent.

The story begins almost immediately with a shift in time as Maddie remembers how the Hundred Dresses game began one day outside of school. This invites readers to do some good work right away, and encourages lively conversation. Readers may realize, at this point, that it'd be helpful to keep some record of the time line of the story.

Many readers do not catch on to the fact that Peggy is cruel, particularly those who do not yet realize that words in a book may not be true. Because the narrator states that Peggy would never think of herself as cruel, for she often defended those who were being bullied, readers tend to accept this as gospel. They don't read between the lines enough to see the real truth of the statement. Readers need to understand that even though Peggy may protect "small children from bullies" and cry for hours when she sees an animal mistreated, she doesn't hesitate to tease Wanda about her lie because Wanda isn't an "ordinary person." Peggy thinks it's okay to tease Wanda because she deserves it and because she's different. This goes to the root of cultural, racial and ethnic bias and should be pointed out to students if they don't see this.

Teaching Ideas

The Hundred Dresses is a book commonly used to address classroom community issues such as bullying. Rather than preach that bullying is wrong, this book tells the story of Wanda Petronski and humanizes the issue, letting readers draw their own conclusions. It is a great book for a read aloud, especially in the beginning of the school year or when the issue of bullying arises. It is short and can be read over a couple of days, and it can support a great deal of conversation that will probably center around the characters of Wanda, Maddie and Peggy. In almost any fictional story, readers could benefit from collecting information and growing theories about the main characters. Such a character study would be rich for readers of this book. The readers will benefit from being reminded that one gets to know a character by attending to what he or she says, does and does not say or do. One class, studying *The Hundred Dresses*, decided to use a T-chart, setting up the names of the characters on one side of the T and their personality traits on the other, referencing the pages they used for evidence.

Using a T-chart to list character traits can be very helpful in making the story more organized and concrete for unsophisticated readers. Many readers think that Wanda is lying and that Peggy is doing the right thing by showing her up to everyone. The story does move quickly, so using a T-chart will slow down the story and help clear up many readers' misconceptions. T-charts could be made for Wanda, Maddie and Peggy, listing on the right side their attributes and on the left, textual evidence to support it. When students think that Wanda is lying, they will need to prove it. This will keep the readers on track with what is really going on and cut down on confusion.

Readers could talk about Peggy as a character, or they could read aloud excerpts of the text in ways that show her character. One partnership of readers used photocopied pages of dialogue between Wanda and Peggy, talking about her voice inflection and meaning. One teacher who was trying to show her class that Peggy was not as nice as she appeared, asked, "Why does Peggy call Wanda 'the child'?" She went on to say, "When Peggy says, 'Your hundred dresses sound beautiful,' she says it like this, 'bee-you-tiful.' Look at that on the page. How does that sound when you say it like it is written?" The readers practiced saying "bee-you-tiful," and discovered that it sounded like Wanda was being mocked. From there the readers better understood the character of Peggy.

Book Connections

Other books by Eleanor Estes include *The Moffats* and *The Middle Moffat.* Though these Newbery Honor Books are somewhat longer and more challenging than *The Hundred Dresses*, the series is warm and humorous and a favorite of many third graders. Eleanor Estes also wrote *The Curious Adventures of Jimmy McGee*, *The Witch Family* and the Newbery Medal winner, *Ginger Pye.*

Genre
Short Chapter Book

Teaching Uses
Read Aloud; Character Study; Independent Reading

The Leaf Men: And the Brave Good Bugs

William Joyce

FIELD GUIDE

E

Book Summary

An old woman and her garden are dying. The bugs are sad and gather to see what can be done. The long-lost toy speaks for the first time, telling the bugs that they need to climb to the top of the tree in the full moon and call for the Leaf Men. The brave doodlebugs do just that, despite the terrible storm and the evil spider queen and her goblins. The tiny Leaf Men come and sew the leaves back on the bushes and turn the stems from brown to green, but they cannot help the old woman. All they can do is carry the lost toy to her bedside as she sleeps. When she wakes, the memories the toy awakens in her bring her back to life, and she goes outside with her grandchildren, reminding them that miraculous things can happen in the garden on a moonlit night.

Illustrator
William Joyce

Publisher
Scholastic, 1996

ISBN
0060272376

TC Level
8

Basic Book Information

This colorful picture book has the look of a graphic novel or picture book.

Noteworthy Features

The illustrations' bold and powerful realism appeals to many young readers, and promises action and adventure. Though the font is large and readable, some students might feel hesitant about reading so much print. But the story is action-packed like a comic book. The heroes slay the evil spider queen with a thistle. The brave doodlebugs venture to the top of the tree despite the pouring rain and thunder. And the lost toy is the only one who can save the day.

Any child who likes comic books or television cartoons could be drawn into the spell of this book (not to mention the similarities between this and movies like *Antz* or *Toy Story*). However, there isn't as much violence. On the contrary, the doodlebugs tickle a goblin to make their way past, and the main characters are all gentle bugs.

Teaching Ideas

Though the plot has some elements in common with most comic books and cartoon genres, the writing style is very crafted and poetic. At the beginning of the book, the author describes the old woman: "Though her skin was wrinkled with age, it was as soft as the petals of her favorite roses." Children who like the story can take such sentences aside and look closely at what makes them work, letting them be models for the metaphors and similes in their own writing.

Teachers often appreciate having a book like this to refer to when trying to explain word choice to young writers. William Joyce also has a talent for choosing precise verbs. The Spider Queen "sneers," her goblins "croak" with laughter, a storm "brews," and raindrops "smash down." Children can be guided to notice these strong, exact words and then try to focus on choosing stronger, perhaps more onomatopoetic words in their own writing.

The plot does have its complicated spots. Some readers don't understand right away that the Spider Queen is evil, and therefore don't know why it is ominous when she appears in front of the brave doodlebugs. This oversight is quickly corrected if readers go back looking for earlier parts in which the Spider Queen appears. Even if they don't turn back, they will come to the conclusion that she is evil when the Leaf Men spear her through the heart. But it helps the story along to be cheering with the Leaf Men when they do it.

It also can be confusing to some readers that the appearance of the lost toy makes the old woman feel better. Was it magic alone, or memories of her parents and her youth? What was the significance of the lost toy? Was it more than the toy that she lost? Why was she ready to forget the garden's magic at the beginning and yet tells the children about it at the end? Kids will have to explore the text and pictures for clues to these questions.

As children explore the illustrations, they'll be excited to find that in a picture hanging on a wall in one of the rooms, there is the old woman and her parents-and there is the little metal man who became the lost toy! They may also be excited to find faces in the clouds and the moon and other subtle, interesting details.

This book may well contain some words the young reader doesn't know, such as *perilous* or *guild*, but in all cases, these words can be passed over without interrupting the story, or its meaning will be clear from the context.

Genre

Picture Book

Teaching Uses

Independent Reading

The Lion, the Witch and the Wardrobe

C.S. Lewis

FIELD GUIDE

E F G

Series
The Chronicles of Narnia

Illustrator
Pauline Baynes

Publisher
Harper Trophy Edition, 2000

ISBN
0064409422

TC Level
12

Book Summary

This is Book Two of *The Chronicles of Narnia*, but it is generally regarded as the foundational book in the series because it is here that the reader is introduced to the four children: Lucy, Susan, Edmund, and Peter. Lucy discovers another world on the other side of a magic wardrobe in a friendly professor's house and she and her siblings begin their adventures in Narnia. Lucy's brother Edmund is enchanted by the White Witch, evil ruler of Narnia who has kept the land forever in a winter without Christmas. Together with Aslan, the magic lion, Lucy and her brothers and sister work to free the land and its inhabitants of their enslavement.

Basic Book Information

This book was originally published in 1950 and this edition is its 50th year anniversary. This is a full-color collector's edition, which, interestingly, is the first time that it has appeared with the complete interior illustrations and jacket that Pauline Baynes created for the book in 1950. Some of the illustrations (especially those of Mr. Tumnus) will look familiar to older readers because they have appeared in black and white in previous editions.

About This Series

Unlike many series, it is not necessary to read this series in order. For many years, it was thought that *The Lion, the Witch and the Wardrobe* was the first in the series, not the second. Although the children are introduced in *The Lion, the Witch and Wardrobe*, reading out of order will not have a detrimental effect. Rather, it makes for a more interesting, and sometimes more challenging read. *The Chronicles of Narnia* are considered classics. The United Kingdom thinks so, too, having bestowed the prestigious Carnegie Award in 1956 to the final book in the series, *The Last Battle.*

Noteworthy Features

There is a map of "Narnia and the Surrounding Counties" before the title page and it is worth examining and referring back to as the book is read. An island called "Terebinthia" appears within the Bight of Calormen and some readers may think of *The Bridge to Terebithia* by Katherine Paterson. Indeed, Paterson mentions Narnia as a reference point for both Leslie and Jess when they create their own magical land and it is no coincidence that the names are so similar.

There are seventeen chapters in this 189-page fantasy book, which is sometimes steeped not only in Briticisms, but sayings common to the 1950s.

The children speak proper English, "Do stop grumbling, Ed," and "Indeed, indeed, you really mustn't," and may seem impenetrable to young readers. Even those who have read *Harry Potter* haven't been exposed to true British colloquialisms because J.K. Rowling created an American version for readers west of the Atlantic. A few students may need help deciphering "wireless," a radio, and "row," a fight, both which appear within the first pages of the book. Probably, though, they can speed over these words without needing to know exactly what they mean.

There is sophisticated vocabulary that readers need to be encouraged to "have a go" with by relying on context clues. Sometimes children will puzzle over words because they've grown up in a modern culture, and are unfamiliar with "marmalade" and "pavilions."

Readers come to meet mythical creatures who often populate fairy tales and fantasy books: centaurs, dryads, dwarves, elves, talking animals, and bewitching witches. Lewis also incorporates some references to the Old Testament as he names the children the Sons of Adam and the Daughters of Eve. C.S. Lewis is a Christian theologian and these books can be read as allegories, with Aslan representing Christ. Unless an adult tells children that deeper meaning, it's doubtful a child will find it on his or her own. The story does not require this interpretation and most readers find abundant meaning and significance in the fantasy story itself.

Teaching Ideas

The Lion, the Witch and the Wardrobe marks another step up into higher-level fantasy for readers. Readers who have read some fairy tales and legends and perhaps fantasy books such as *The Search for Delicious* by Natalie Babbitt will find this background helps them when they turn to *The Chronicles of Narnia*. A genre study of fantasy and how it weaves in elements of other genres could be fascinating to fantasy enthusiasts. Lewis incorporates important features such as the battle between good and evil, enchantment, talking animals, magical powers, delicious foods, and believable characters. His rich portrayal of Lucy, Susan, Peter, and Edmund also affords a character study that could cross over into the other books of the series. Readers could follow Lucy, or any of the other characters, and see how they develop in the future.

There are several rather obvious lines of thinking that a reader might follow when reading this book. Early in the book, Edmund is lured onto the Evil Queen's sleigh by the taste of Turkish Delight, and after that much of the plotline involves the other three children's efforts to rescue their brother from the Queen's power. Many readers read to find out if Edmund is freed, even though he has done some things that could make readers wonder whether he is worth all the risk and effort the other children go through to rescue him. The core plot of this story is not unlike the plot of *The Wizard of Oz*. In both books a cluster of characters journey through an enchanted land en route to their goal. All such journeys have their ups and downs, their internal journeys paralleling the external ones, artifacts that do and don't accompany the travelers, and so on.

One sixth grade book club took on *The Chronicles of Narnia* as a project, and each of the club members studied a particular character (Lucy, Edmund, Peter, or Susan). During one of their meetings, the club was discussing the changes in Edmund. One member of the club said, "In *The Lion, the Witch and the Wardrobe*, Edmund is a weak and greedy boy. He just wants the candy, the 'Turkish Delight,' and to be a prince. He doesn't care about his sisters or brother. That's why Aslan dies, because of Edmund and his dumbness. But, at the end of the book Edmund seems a little different than in the first book." Another club member chimed in, saying, "Yeah, I think so. I think he's sorry. See how he acts, look at this page. . . ." Following this exchange, the club decided to make a chart for Edmund and one for each of the other characters, to follow how, or if, they change through the series.

Indeed, the club discovered that in later books, Edmund develops into a hard-working and wise young man. He has learned through his experience with Aslan's death. Susan, however, is shown to be a virtuous and open-minded character in *The Lion, the Witch and the Wardrobe*, but in later books, her character deteriorates. She becomes selfish and unwilling to use her imagination so as to be a part of the adventures in Narnia.

With the inclusion of the map of Narnia, *The Lion, the Witch and the Wardrobe* becomes part of a growing collection of books that have maps in their frontispieces. All of the *Tales of Dimwood Forest* (by Avi) contain maps, as do Lloyd Alexander books, *The Search for Delicious* (by Natalie Babbitt), the *Oz* books, and the *Redwall* books. A study of these books, which are mostly all fantasy books, could be a rich one. In each of these books, a new world is created. What do these worlds have in common? How does the skilled reader come to envision and care about these worlds and the characters who live in them? A book club or an individual may take on these maps that are present in all the books as a project, patching them together to create the whole world of Narnia. (Students can also undertake this study with the *Redwall* series by Brian Jacques.) While these books are fiction, they utilize many geographical principles that readers and students need to be acquainted with (like physical features such as rivers, mountains, oceans).

Book Connections

See above for many book connections. Edward Eager's *Tales of Magic*, including *Half Magic*, *Knight's Castle*, *The Time Garden*, and *Magic by the Lake*, is about siblings who embark on a variety of magical adventures and could be another good companion series to this one.

Genre

Fantasy; Chapter Book

Teaching Uses

Read Aloud; Book Clubs; Independent Reading

The Lucky Stone

Lucille Clifton

FIELD GUIDE

E

Publisher
Yearling Books, 1986

ISBN
0440451108

TC Level
8

Book Summary

Little Tee is sitting out on the porch with her great-grandmother, Ms. Elzie F. Pickens, who tells her stories about a lucky stone. The lucky stone benefited its owners for over a century. The stone's first owner, Miss Mandy, found freedom from slavery. The stone's next owner was Miss Mandy's daughter, Vashti, who survived a near-death experience during a prayer meeting at the time of emancipation. Vashti passed the stone on to Tee's great-grandmother, who survived a dog attack and met her husband. At fourteen, adolescent Tee becomes the new owner of the stone and has hopes for what the lucky stone will bring her.

Basic Book Information

The Lucky Stone is 62 pages long. There are pictures on almost every page and they are supportive. However, the plot structure and historical content make it a very challenging book. The book is written in dialogue format and follows the African American oral tradition of passing on stories. The story emphasizes both the historical life experiences of African Americans, as well as the richness of the intergenerational relationship between a girl and her great-grandmother.

Noteworthy Features

There is a preface that sets the reader up for the structure of the book. Some teachers suggest that this be read first by students, or read aloud by the teacher. The movement in time, with five different changes in setting and character, makes the book particularly difficult. The time span covered is great and an understanding of life in each era is helpful in truly appreciating the passing on of the stone from generation to generation. Fortunately, each chapter signifies a change in setting and there are many pictures to depict the variety of time periods.

The book is just as much an historical fiction piece as it is a warm family saga evoking the emotions and connections felt between Tee and her great-grandmother. The first two flashbacks (slavery and emancipation) are explicitly stated. While the subsequent flashbacks are not explicit, the pictures aid the reader in determining that they occur in chronological order up to the present day.

Teaching Ideas

Due to the complexity and richness of this book, teachers recommend it primarily as a read aloud or perhaps a book club selection for strong, upper elementary readers. To use it for read aloud, some teachers might read one chapter a day in order to organize the listeners' experience of the text so they understand that each new chapter represents a new time period. If children know about life during the time of slavery and emancipation, this will enrich their appreciation for the text. If they do not have this contextual knowledge, a teacher might want to say, "When you read historic fiction, it can help to know information about the time and place in which a story occurs." Then the teacher could either proceed to give children a tiny crash course, or could provide children with a parallel nonfiction text that could do some of the same job. "Let's listen to the story now and when I pause and ask you to turn and talk to your partner, please be sure to talk in part about how the information you know about slavery and emancipation connects with the passage from the story you've just heard."

Book Connections

The Lucky Stone is similar to *Mississippi Bridge* and *The Friendship*, both by Mildred D. Taylor, because of the vernacular and the historical time periods. But *The Lucky Stone* is more difficult because of the flashback and flash-forward plot structure.

Genre
Historical Fiction; Picture Book

Teaching Uses
Read Aloud; Book Clubs

The Magic School Bus series

Joanna Cole (adaptation by Patricia Relf)

FIELD GUIDE

E

Book Summary

Each *Magic School Bus* book is devoted to one particular science topic, such as animal habitats, decomposition, food chains or deserts. The books are set inMs. Frizzle's class, among students learning about the topic. The class always goes on an adventurous field trip on the magic school bus to learn more about the subject. The bus transforms, shrinks, flies and provides strange equipment so that the students on board can get first-hand experience with the subjects they are studying.

Basic Book Information

Each of the books in this series is about 30 pages long. They are each based on a nonfiction topic, but the storylines are fictional. Each has from one to ten sentences per page, and every page has a large illustration. On many of the pages, there are also speech balloons coming from the characters in the story that offer humorous asides or added information about the topic at hand. There are never tables of contents, indexes, or other text dividers such as chapters or headings. At the end of each book there are always two pages of non-story text. Sometimes this text takes the form of an activity that is somehow related to the concepts in the book, sometimes it is a bit of added information told in a new way, such as the transcribed telephone conversation of a *Magic School Bus* fan. Sometimes the page contains jokes or fictional letters from readers pointing out silly aspects of the story.

Noteworthy Features

In every book, the changes that the students undergo on the magic bus put them in some sort of danger. Now that they are as small as bullfrogs, will they be eaten by the approaching blue heron? Or, now that they are inside the rotting log, will they and their animal companions be victims of a chain saw? There are always several suspenseful escapes and near tragedies in each adventure.

There is also humor in every story. The kid characters make silly puns about the topic they're exploring, usually in the speech bubbles. The characters joke with each other and get into slapstick situations. Certain characters display the same characteristics in every book: Arnold complains about the field trips; Phoebe says she didn't have to do such outrageous things in her old school; Ms. Frizzle wears dresses with outrageous topical prints; and so on. Some readers find these inside jokes funny, and enjoy knowing the characters and their quirks.

The books all use a lot of dialogue in the text. The lines are usually followed by who said them, but not always. There are a lot of characters to keep straight, and the characters often refer to each other with

Series
The Magic School Bus

Illustrator
Bruce Degen (adaptation by Stevenson, Jocelyn)

Publisher
Scholastic, 1996

ISBN
0

TC Level
10

nicknames-"Friz" for Ms. Frizzle, "Pheebes" for Phoebe, etc. This, added together with the frequent jokes, sarcasm and speech bubbles, add frequent interruptions and can make for a very challenging read.

The pictures, like the text, offer a lot of factors to consider-all colorful, all eye-catching. Like the story itself, the pictures have many different elements vying to attract the reader's attention. They too require concentration and focus on the part of readers, as they can be a bit cluttered.

The activities suggested at the end of some of the books are not directly related to the topic and many teachers and readers ignore them.

Teaching Ideas

Usually, there is a small amount of factual information within the lengthy, elaborate plots of these books. A student solely interested in gathering information about her topic would probably be better off reading a more traditional, straightforward nonfiction book, as she will get more information for the same amount of reading. In these books, readers have to navigate subtle humor, dialogue, fast moving, fantastical plots and other devices in order to get the information they are looking for. It can sometimes be hard for readers to know which parts of the book to believe and which parts are made up.

The way these books are structured, the adventures and the silly interactions-not the factual information-are at the center of the text. They are what move the story along; they are the plot. Because of this, students who haven't found the topic interesting previously may learn about it in a painless fashion as they read of the adventures of this class. On the other hand, children who are drawn to the topic may find the books too lightweight.

These books can be read in conjunction with other books on the topics, as children will no doubt be excited to read about information they have already begun to study. This kind of reading can serve to reinforce what they already know, and can give them confidence in picking out facts in the midst of fiction.

Some aspects of these books are not tightly or carefully constructed. Children can develop careful reading skills by attending to some of the slips or soft spots in the text and illustrations. Why can the bus shrink and grow as the teacher commands in some instances, but not at other crucial moments? Why are the children saying there are no animals for the desert habitat they have created when there is a lizard right there in the picture? Why does the magic school bus have three sets of windows on the title page of some books and four sets on the pages of others?

Children can also develop their critiquing skills with these books. Teachers sometimes ask students if they agree or disagree with the conclusions and messages in the books. Should all decomposing matter be treasured and left alone as the book on the topic suggests? Can't decomposing matter also be a health hazard? Can't it also be damaging to the morale of a community? In the book about deserts, the girl who stands up and cries out for community action ends up being considered silly for her actions. What kind of a message does this send to readers about forming committees and making changes? Is it a fair message in this case? These nonfiction topics are never as simple as the books in the series tend to present them, and children who are willing to be thoughtful can often take the subjects much further by questioning the messages of the books.

Since these books are based on a television series, videos are available that are nearly identical to the books. The original *Magic School Bus* series-the one not based on the television series-is more challenging to read, in general.

Genre
Picture Book

Teaching Uses
Content Area Study; Independent Reading; Critique

The Music of Dolphins

Karen Hesse

FIELD GUIDE

E G

Book Summary

Mila is discovered in the waters between Florida and Cuba, where she has been raised by dolphins for as long as she can remember. She is taken to a Boston University research center, where she is observed by professors of cognitive and neural systems to determine "the role language and socialization play in the making of a human being." Mila is introduced to qualities of existence that are uniquely human: language, music, dance, the arts technology, and territory. Initially desiring only to please, Mila is a willing subject. She never suspects that she may be unable to return to the sea. This is the story of her growing awareness of being "trapped in the net of humans," and her growing awareness of self. By page 118, Mila has "decided to work hard at being human so they will let me go free." Although Mila delights in certain aspects of her human existence, she ultimately decides to escape to the sea and return to her dolphin family. Here she is occasionally "startled by the fierce and sudden hunger for things left behind," but she is home. This book is about Mila's internal movement and tension between the human and dolphin aspects of her self. Although this is never fully resolved, she has made her decision.

Publisher
Scholastic, 1996

ISBN
0590897985

TC Level
12

Basic Book Information

This book is 181 pages long and divided into sixty-two short chapters. Each chapter is a new entry in Mila's journal, and the story is told in the first-person narrative from her point of view. The beginning pages of Mila's journal are printed in large, bold letters, which gradually decrease in size as she acquires greater fluency and proficiency with the English language. Her syntax changes dramatically throughout the book. Initial journal entries consist of short, choppy, incomplete sentences. Mila's writing is most fluid about three quarters into the book. When she begins to feel she can no longer live in the human world, the print gradually becomes larger and sentences grow increasingly choppy until she finally returns to the sea. The font, syntax, and fluency of entries at the end of the book mirror those of the beginning.

The story begins with an italicized passage, written from Mila's point of view before she is taken from her dolphin family. Italicized passages throughout the text detail Mila's immediate experience of the sea, and are not part of her journal. The reader is listening to Mila's inner voice. The plot is revealed on pages four and five through a newspaper article chronicling the events behind Mila's rescue. The font of both the italicized passages and newspaper article are relatively small, as is the spacing between words and lines.

Noteworthy Features

This book offers an excellent opportunity to heighten students' awareness of voice. As Mila becomes more human, the syntax and fluency of her writing grow increasingly sophisticated. When she begins to yearn more deeply for her ocean life, her voice echoes that of her beginning journal entries. Mila's voice also shifts in italicized passages, when she is directly experiencing or remembering her life in the sea. The inner language of her thought and feelings is markedly different from her written language. There also exists strong evidence for the existence of both dolphin and human characteristics within Mila, allowing students to cite these and easily chronicle the evolution and resolution of the primary tension within the text.

There are three italicized passages in this text, at the beginning, the middle, and the end. These are set apart from the rest of the book because they are not part of Mila's journal. Instead, they are her inner, more immediate experiences of life with the dolphins. This may confuse readers, as both the journal and the italicized passages are written in the first person narrative, from Mila's point of view. To ponder this question for a considerable length of time would detract from the story and students' attention to the big question: Will Mila go back to the sea? Instead, it might be advisable to explain to students the function of the italicized passages, so they may be fully empowered to do the interpretive work intended by the author.

A teacher may not want to spend undue time focusing on the letter Mila receives from her father on page fifty-eight. Students tend to develop theories that Mila will return to her real family. This is not part of the story and, although it is a reasonable prediction, the author's intent is not to put this question into her readers' minds. Another potential stumbling block is the newspaper article at the beginning of the book. This is written in adult language that may be difficult for some students to comprehend. They might benefit from a simplified summary before approaching the body of the text.

Teaching Ideas

During daily read aloud conversations, the teacher can gently guide students to understand and articulate that, although Mila yearns to go back to the sea, she embraces those parts of her that are human as well. The teacher might explain that when two parts of a person or community are at odds with another, it is called *tension*. Tension within and between characters is a theme continually addressed by literature, and may be illustrated and chronicled with a T-chart. The teacher can instruct students to divide their papers into two sections, dolphin and human, then cite passages and page numbers which provide evidence for each of these aspects of Mila's character. For example, the following passages highlight the ways in which Mila is becoming human:

"Dr. Beck says, If you are waiting seven days for Sandy to come back and five days are finished, how many more days do you have left to wait? Dr. Beck shows with her fingers. I say two. I like to play these games." (p.41)

"Making progress is when I talk words. Making progress is when I wear clothes. Making progress is when I sleep in a bed and eat the fish." (p.50)

"I listen to the music. It is little sounds and little sounds all put together to make something so big. It is a bird singing and a whale singing and people singing. It is so many sounds I cannot name...I love the music." (p.53)

"I am happy. I love the lessons. I love my work with the computer. With the cards. With the paper and crayons and pencils and paint. We dance. We sing. We go different places. We swim. We play games." (p.75)

"I turn the radio off and on. If I move the knob so slow, I can find music, so much music hiding in the radio...And it is all human." (p.81)

"I know seven notes on the recorder now. They say I learn fast. They say I can catch up with others my age before too long. Good. I want to catch up. I want to be with others." (p.82)

"I love to use my hands. To play games, to make the music on the recorder...I like every little thing I am learning with my fingers and toes." (p.83)

On the other hand, there exists equally strong evidence to remind the reader that Mila possesses a dolphin's sensibility and love for the ocean. She has every intention to return to the sea:

"I am splashing water on Sandy. I am so happy. I say, Doctor Beck, I can stay here and sleep here in the water room with Sandy all the time?...I do not want to go." (p.27)

"I have another family too. Dolphin family. The ones who love and care for me. The ones I love and care for. Can they see me again? I say, Sandy, can the dolphins see me again?" (p.35)

"I am not listening. I see water. Water! It is not big like the ocean, but it is not little like the pool...I go over the road and into the water, swimming and swimming in my clothes, going with the good tide. I dive in the water. The water is not good to see in. It is all clouds. But it is much water. I call my dolphin name. I call again and wait." (p.45)

"The water sings in my ears. I feel the pull of the sea. I swim a long time. I swim very far. The cold water empties the strength from my bones. Again and again I make my dolphin name in my nose, but there is no answer. I cannot find the warm sea where the dolphins wait. It is too far, and I am too alone." (p.68)

"I feel the music inside me. It says something more than just the notes, more than just the sounds. It is hearing with more than the ears. Like the way it is when I am with the dolphins." (p.76)

"I beat my hands against the locked door...I look at the hands that held the fin of my dolphin mother. My hands bleed. I am trapped in the net of the room. In the net of humans. I think I may be drowning in the net of humans." (p.110)

"When I know the language, when I know the rules, when they unlock the door, I can run back to the warm sea. I can leave my human clothes on the beach. I can leave my human thought on the beach. I will go home." (p.117)

"I want to go back to the sea, where I do not feel the crushing of my heart by the ideas in my head." (p.131)

"My music is fading. Inside me everything is fading. When I make music on the recorder it is such sad music. It has nothing to do with dolphin life." (p.151)

"I have been coming back to the sea from the moment I left it." (p.175)

Book Connections

The fiction writer, John Gardiner, has said that all stories are about one of two themes: "the human search for home," or "a stranger comes to town." This book fits the former category, as do countless books including Voigt's *Homecoming* series, both *The Great Gilly Hopkins* and *Flip-Flop Girl* by Katherine Paterson, and Spinelli's *Maniac Magee*. In *The Invisible Thread*, Yoshiko Uchida experiences a similar tension between her Japanese heritage and American upbringing. This same tension is the theme of Fritz's *Homesick*. Like Mila, Jean Fritz feels torn between two worlds.

The Great Gilly Hopkins, by Katherine Paterson, and Jerry Spinelli's *Maniac Magee* are also stories of a search for home, family, and acceptance. In *The Invisible Thread* Yoshiko Uchida experiences a similar internal tension between her Japanese heritage and American upbringing. Like Mila, she feels torn between two worlds.

Genre

Short Chapter Book

Teaching Uses

Independent Reading; Language Conventions; Book Clubs; Read Aloud

The One in the Middle Is the Green Kangaroo

Judy Blume

FIELD GUIDE

D E

Book Summary

Freddy Dissel is in the second grade and he is the middle child in his family. Freddy feels like "the peanut butter part of a sandwich, squeezed between Mike and Ellen." Freddy worries that he will always be "a great big middle nothing," so he decides to do something that Mike and Ellen never have - he will try to be in the school play. Even though the play is only for fifth and sixth graders, Ms. Matson decides that Freddy should play a special part: the Green Kangaroo. During the performance, Freddy's nerves settle down as he realizes that his family is in the middle of the audience, but he is up on stage alone. When the play is over, the audience claps enthusiastically. Freddy feels "great being Freddy Dissel."

Illustrator
Irene Trivas

Publisher
Dell Publishing, 1981

ISBN
0440467314

TC Level
8

Basic Book Information

The One in the Middle Is the Green Kangaroo is a 40-page chapter book. The story is continuous, without chapter breaks. Color illustrations appear on every page.

Noteworthy Features

There are some expressions in the story that children may enjoy: "he felt like the peanut butter part of the sandwich" and "his stomach bounced up and down." The text is written simply and there is a special message-finding out that you truly are special.

Teaching Ideas

The theme of wanting to be special or wanting to stand out is one that many readers relate to easily. Often teachers use this book with partnerships and book clubs to encourage "conversation stamina." One way teachers do this is to have students mark places with Post-its where they have strong reactions or insights into Freddy's character. Students then take turns "talking off" each Post-it with the goal of discussing each point as deeply as possible.

Book Connections

This book is similar to the *Cam Jansen* series by David A. Adler. We recommend that the reader first experience success with the *Pinky and Rex* series by James Howe. A good follow-up would be *Freckle Juice*, also by Judy Blume.

Genre
Short Chapter Book

Teaching Uses
Independent Reading; Partnerships; Book Clubs

The Puppy Sister

S.E. Hinton

FIELD GUIDE

E

Book Summary

Aleasha was born an Australian Sheepdog, but she loves her new family so much that she wants to be human. Incredibly, over time, Aleasha transforms herself from a puppy to a little girl. Her metamorphosis is slow; first her ears change and her hands, then she can talk. Her family is overjoyed to have a real girl, and Aleasha, while sometimes confused by her human feelings, is thrilled to become a girl.

Basic Book Information

S.E. Hinton is best known for her young adult books *The Outsiders* and *That Was Then, This Is Now*. *The Puppy Sister* is a departure from her usual. It is a fantasy early chapter book that reads like *Charlotte's Web* by E.B. White or *Babe, the Gallant Pig* by Dick King-Smith. There are 11 chapters in this 122-page book, with black-and-white illustrations that appear only sporadically.

Noteworthy Features

The Puppy Sister is a more difficult early chapter book than most because of its fantasy elements, and because it relies so little on pictures to support the reader.

The Puppy Sister is written in the first person, with Aleasha the dog as the narrator. This can be very confusing when a child begins the book; a reader may need to reread the first paragraphs to get it right. Hinton does a great job of visualizing what it would be like to be a dog, and it's especially notable in the way in which the smells are brought out to match a dog's sensibilities. However, when Aleasha becomes more and more like a little girl, some readers feel that the narrator really doesn't feel as much like a little girl. The personality of Aleasha stays the same. She is interested in sensual delights and in creating happiness with her family.

Teaching Ideas

This is a great book for independent reading in grades three and four. It mixes in humor, which is fairly light, that most readers, especially those who love dogs, will appreciate.

The dog's name, Aleasha, is a pun on the word "leash," and there are several instances where Aleasha and the boy Nick poke fun at each other by using puns and double entendres. A fourth grade partnership worked with this idea; they reread the book, looking for all the places where Hinton used puns. The idea of puns especially appealed to these young readers because, "I never knew you could say two things at once, with the same words. Now

Illustrator
Jacqueline Rogers

Publisher
Bantam Doubleday Dell, 1995

ISBN
0440413842

TC Level
10

I'm studying other books I've already read to find places where the author made puns," one fourth grader said.

One partnership of third graders decided to study how the character Aleasha changes. "We think that as she changes from a dog into a girl, she will change how she talks," one of the readers said. As they read *The Puppy Sister*, they put Post-its on all the passages in which Aleasha spoke. When they finished the book, they went back and reviewed the passages. They determined that their theory about Aleasha was only partly right. She changed a little bit in how she spoke, but not entirely. This got them thinking about the character of Aleasha. Did she really change completely? Wasn't she still Aleasha no matter what kind of body she had?

Another pair of readers decided to parallel this book with *The Music of Dolphins*, in which Mila changes from being a dolphin, to being human, to being a dolphin again. How is Mila dolphin-like? How is Aleasha dog-like? For each of these characters, what does it mean to become more human?

Book Connections

S.E. Hinton is best known for her young adult books *The Outsiders* and *That Was Then, This Is Now*. *The Puppy Sister* is a departure from her usual. It is a fantasy early chapter book that reads like *Charlotte's Web* by E.B. White or *Babe, the Gallant Pig* by Dick King-Smith.

Genre

Chapter Book

Teaching Uses

Character Study; Independent Reading

The Seven Treasure Hunts

Betsy Byars

FIELD GUIDE

E

Book Summary

Jackie and his friend Goat are having a friendly contest. They are each planning treasure hunts with clues for the other boy to solve. When Jackie guesses from Goat's clues that there is a chocolate Popsicle waiting for him at Goat's house, he can't think of anything else until he gets it. But things start to go wrong when, by mistake, he eats the Popsicle that belonged to "the ogre," Goat's big sister Rachel. Her plans for revenge make the boys go on a treasure hunt they never planned to have.

Publisher

Harper Trophy, 1991

ISBN

0060208856

TC Level

8

Basic Book Information

Betsy Byars is a prolific author of books for middle-grade readers and has written a few books for younger children as well, including *My Brother, Ant* and *Daniel's Duck*, both easy readers, and *Beans on the Roof*, an early chapter book slightly easier than this book. These books have more of the qualities of real literature than some books for young readers: charming style, genuine characters who have feelings and relationships, and, in *The Seven Treasure* Hunts' case, humor.

The Seven Treasure Hunts has 74 pages. Each chapter is titled as a treasure hunt, for example, "The Hunt for the Stolen Treasure," or "The Hunt for the Garbage Treasure." The titles set up the expectation in the reader that there will be seven actual treasure hunts, but the expectation is not realized. There are two or three pictures in each chapter, mostly illustrating the action on the same or facing page. Dialogue is often not referenced.

Noteworthy Features

This story about kids is very engaging and funny. It draws the reader into the action and drama of the characters. The first-person narration helps readers follow the story, and Jackie's internal thinking helps explain what is happening and how he feels about it.

There are subtleties in this book not apparent from its easy chapter book format. The text structure is more complex than the chapter titles would lead readers to believe. After the first two treasures have been found in the first chapter, the plot turns to the problems that occur after Jackie eats Rachel's Popsicle. The rest of the story is about how the boys try to make restitution and how "the ogre" gets her revenge. The titles are tongue-in-cheek, and, after Chapter2, they refer not to treasure hunts the boys have planned, but to the other events in the story.

Sentence length is inconsistent. Many are simple, but dialogue sentences are sometimes fragmented, and there are some more complex sentences. The dialogue can be a problem. The teacher will need to go over the alternating dialogue, and students will need to read slowly and carefully to be sure they know who is talking.

There are a number of inferences readers must make and past events to hold in their heads. For example, on page 9, Jackie is puzzling over Goat's clues. When he mentions trees, "Goat stuck his hands in his pockets. It was a quick movement, and it gave him away just as the flower had given me away." Readers need to understand that Goat's gesture indicates that Jackie has guessed right about trees. They also need to remember from page 5 that a piece of pansy stuck in Jackie's watch told Goat where the treasure was. There are many inferences to make from the dialogue. After Goat deflates Jackie by denigrating the treasures Jackie gave him, Jackie's internal thinking tells the reader, "Now he had ruined it... I opened the front door... 'I'm bored with this,' Jackie says." Goat responds with, "So, Jackie, it's too tough for you, huh? Go ahead and quit." The reader needs to understand that Jackie isn't really bored-he is covering up his hurt feelings, and that Goat sees through this cover-up.

Teaching Ideas

This book is more complicated than it at first appears, but it's worth the work. Many teachers find an introduction to this book helpful. One teacher began by saying, "On page 30, we learn that Rachel is Goat's sister, and it was her Popsicle Jackie ate. But then on page 35, Goat says, 'It was the ogre's!' Who is this ogre? Then, on the next page, Goat says, 'I'll have to watch Rachel eat it.' Sometimes brothers and sisters have names they call each other. This is Goat's name for Rachel. When we read more, we find a clue to who the ogre is. When readers do this, putting two clues together to make sense, it's called inferring."

Because of the difficulties in this book, it's ideal for older struggling readers who can understand the subtleties and the tricky dialogue. When younger students read this book, the teacher should not assume they can handle it on their own.

Teacher dialogue could help also. Using an overhead projection of the bottom of pages 6 and7, a teacher could show how to follow unreferenced dialogue and how to recognize when the same speaker continues for two paragraphs (the close-quote is missing). While reading, students could work though the dialogue with a partner to be sure they agree on who is talking.

To keep the plot straight, especially after the story veers off the simple treasure hunt, readers could retell each chapter to a partner, or older readers could write a simple summary of the chapters to be sure they understood it, or explain what the chapter titles mean.

Book Connections

Books that are comparable in difficulty are the *Pee Wee Scouts* series by Judy Delton and the *Junie B. Jones* series by Barbara Park. The *Magic Tree House* series by Mary Pope Osborne and *The Littles* series by John Peterson would make for good follow-up books.

Genre

Mystery; Chapter Book

Teaching Uses
Independent Reading

The Snake Scientist

Sy Montgomery

FIELD GUIDE

E

Book Summary

This is the story of Bob Mason, a herpetologist (snake scientist). The book slowly unveils why he finds snakes so fascinating. This nonfiction narrative presents its facts artfully. There is little, if any, expository text. It is a story about snakes, but also about how scientists behave. Sy Montgomery is as entranced as Bob Mason about snakes, and their fascination is contagious for the reader. Bob Mason's story illustrates a truism of science: "finding that answer was the beginning of a whole new story" (page 30). This book is great for readers already interested in snakes; they'll learn an incredible amount. But it is also for people who know little about snakes-or don't like them at all! For these readers, the study of the snake can serve as a vehicle into a scientist's methods, thinking, and passion for a particular subject.

Illustrator
Nic Bishop

Publisher
Houghton Mifflin, 1999

ISBN
0395871697

TC Level
12; 13; 14

Basic Book Information

There is no table of contents here, but there are 6 chapters. Chapters range in length from 5 to 10 pages. Every page has at least one photo. The photos are clear and bright, and many are close-ups of snakes. There is an index in the book, and a "For Further Reading" page with four books' bibliographies given. The photos are captioned and support the text on the page. The print is medium sized with medium spacing between words and a lot of spacing between lines.

Noteworthy Features

In pages 3 to 38, the author details how Bob Mason is involved with snakes and how some of his experiments deal with snake pheromones-chemicals they release in certain situations. His methods are clearly stated and can be followed easily, creating a great model for scientific method illustrations. The narration makes for an engrossing story, and moves the reader painlessly through the scientific methodology. Sy Montgomery incorporates interesting details about Bob Mason's life at the relevant junctures. For instance, on page 29, Bob describes how he was once told he didn't have what it takes to be a scientist. "Even tests are sometimes wrong," he says later. This is an interesting insertion of a valuable life lesson, pertinent but not melodramatic.

There is a frequent use of quotations and dialogue, which makes the text come to life even further. "Snakes are first cowards, next bluffers, and last of all warriors," wrote snake scientist C.H. Pope, who studied some of the most dangerous African snakes.

Vocabulary is woven gently into the story. Seldom does the reader feel abandoned by the writer of the text regarding the meaning of words.

Teaching Ideas

This is a great book for content area reading on snakes, reptiles, endangered species and scientific method. The book could be used for partnership reading on persuasive voice and point of view recognition in reading.

Independent reading issues that could be explored include how well the reader is engaging with the text and the questions the narrative conjures up. For example, is the reader able to follow the dialogue and quotations? Can the reader relate both to the character of Bob Mason and the snakes' nature? Bob is the main character; he is visible, audible and present throughout the text. If a reader finds it difficult to hold onto the story, holding on to Bob would be helpful because Bob points the way of the story.

Genre

Chapter Book; Nonfiction

Teaching Uses

Content Area Study; Reading and Writing Nonfiction; Independent Reading

The Story of Rosy Dock

Jeannie Baker

FIELD GUIDE

E

Illustrator
Jeannie Baker

Publisher
Green Willow, 1995

ISBN
068811938

TC Level
7

Book Summary

The book starts with an elderly European woman planting some rosy dock seeds she has brought with her from her original country. The book then describes the cycles of rain and dryness and seed dispersal in the Australian desert. After a flood, and a new season of dryness many generations later, the desert is covered with the rosy dock flower. After the story ends, there is a paragraph about the plant called rosy dock, and a paragraph about the effects of introducing plants and animals to new environments.

Basic Book Information

This nonfiction picture book is about 30 pages long. Each page has a sentence or two of text, telling a continuous story about the cycle of nature in the desert of Australia. The book takes on a lyrical tone. At the end of the book, in a different, smaller font than the main text, there are two paragraphs offering further context for the happenings in the book.

Noteworthy Features

The collages that illustrate this text are astounding-intricate and mood setting. One can easily imagine the desert is very similar to the one the artist depicts. Readers are bound to be fascinated with this book for the pictures alone.

The pictures do compound some of the reading difficulties presented by the text, however. Since the text opens with one character creating a flowerbed, and the pictures continue to depict that character for the initial pages of the story, the reader is led to assume that that character is important to the story. However, it is only the seeds she planted that remain important. The reader needs to let go of that woman, not be concerned with what happens to her or her house in the flood, in order to understand the main idea of the story. This is a bit confusing for some readers.

In fact, the story actually moves on many years after the woman first planted those seeds, although the clues in the text that time has passed are very subtle. Readers who miss these clues are worried about the woman and her house when the desert flooding occurs. They need to reread to realize that the woman has died long before that point.

Another confusing aspect of the apparently simple text is that the spread of the flowers is made to look (and sound) beautiful at the end of the book. Readers may well conclude that the importation of foreign seeds to this land was a wonderful and beautifying event. Students who read the very last paragraph of the book, however, may realize that the spread of these flowers may very well have harmful effects on the environment.

Teaching Ideas

Is this book about desert seasons? Seed dispersal? The unintended effects of introducing new seeds to an environment? Is it about the hardships of living in the desert? Readers will have much to figure out at the story's end, and will need the teacher's guidance to explore all of these questions.

Although the book is short enough and lyrical enough to appeal to many teachers as a read aloud, that is probably not its best use. Truly, the collages are the highlight of this book, and a one-to-one scrutiny of the pictures is necessary to appreciate their finest qualities. Perhaps a partnership would be the best forum for reading this book. The two readers can enjoy the pictures, and also have someone with whom to discuss the inevitable questions that will arise after the book's reading.

Independent readers may well assume their initial confusion or reading of the book is the only way to understand it, and therefore may not move themselves to a deeper level of understanding of its possible messages.

Genre

Picture Book; Nonfiction

Teaching Uses

Content Area Study; Critique; Independent Reading

The Table Where Rich People Sit

Byrd Baylor

FIELD GUIDE

E

Illustrator
Peter Parnall

Publisher
Charles Scribner & Sons, 1994

ISBN
0689820089

Book Summary

As this book starts out, readers meet an unnamed girl who seems very concerned about her family's economic status. The girl begins to describe her family's kitchen table, and how her parents built it. She is certain that her family isn't rich, despite her father trying to convince her that they are. The girl cannot understand how her father can't see their "worn out shoes" and patched pants. The little girl pleads with her father, "Would rich people eat at a table like this?" Her parents have tried to explain that if everyone could eat and talk at a table like theirs, there wouldn't be any more fighting in the world.

The young girl decides to call a family meeting: There is going to be an argument at her family's wooden hand-made table. She is firm in her beliefs that her parents need ambition, drive and goals. She believes that with a little structure and regimen, her family could do better. She tells her parents that they could get better jobs instead of panning for gold together in the wilderness with coyotes. They should stop planting fields of sweet corn and alfalfa and hope it brings in enough money for food.

Her parents seem confused. They can't understand how they would experience the great outdoors if they were kept inside. Her father finally says, "How many people are as lucky as we are?" Her parents list their "rules for living" and the conditions that they are bound by, none of which include working in an office. The parents explain to the mountain girl how they figure out the value of things. Before you know it, the girl is putting price tags on things she never viewed as valuable. Mountain girl is tallying sunrises and sunsets, each color change in the mountains throughout the day. Her parents put prices on animal callings and flower blooms. Before the girl is close to finishing her calculations, she has over fifty thousand dollars. The entire family is worth over four million and sixty thousand dollars (and that's without adding cash). As her family goes outside to watch the sunset, she is left writing a book about the table where rich people sit.

Basic Book Information

This is Byrd Baylor's seventh book. All seven have been collaborations with Peter Parnall (the illustrator). There are Native American undertones throughout this and other of her children's books. There are 17 pages of text. The pictures support the text; however they would not be of much help in decoding some of the adult vocabulary.

Noteworthy Features

The book is eloquently written and makes readers think about their own values. The girl learns an important lesson about the true riches in life.

Teaching Ideas

This book could be used in myriad ways. One of the first things one notices is how the author begins the story. Who is the narrator? A discussion of point of view could be very helpful here. The next thing that jumps at the reader is the organization of the text: the words appear in columns, almost like a newspaper article. Does this serve a purpose? Why would an author choose to do this? Does it confuse the reader? Support their thinking?

As readers adjust to the narrative voice, they begin to notice the colors, illustrations. While the table is intricately drawn, the characters are done in outline form, using a minimalist style. Is this done to emphasize the table's significance? Word choice also seems important. The author chose the word *rich.* Why? Is there a play on words being used? Would the story change if another word had been substituted? Why are some of the words italicized? Is there a pattern to the italicized words? For instance the money seems to be italicized. Is this done for a reason? There is also the lesson that is to be learned from the mountain girl, and her eventual placing of material value on nonmaterial wealth. Perhaps this is something everyone could learn from.

Book Connections

This is Byrd Baylor's seventh book. All seven have been collaborations with Peter Parnall (the illustrator). There are Native American undertones throughout this and other of her children's books.

Genre
Picture Book

Teaching Uses
Interpretation; Teaching Writing; Book Clubs

The Trojan Horse

Emily Little

FIELD GUIDE

E

Illustrator
Michael Eagle

Publisher
Random House, 1988

ISBN
0394896742

TC Level
9; 10

Book Summary

This book tells the story of the ancient city of Troy. The war between the Greeks and the Trojans started with the taxing of the Greek ships and the kidnapping of the beautiful Helen. Most of all, the book describes the Trojan horse itself, and how the Greeks used it to trick the Trojans into bringing them into their well-protected city. At the end of the story, after the Greeks have won the war and reclaimed Helen, the author describes Homer and his telling of the entire tale. It also describes the work of historians trying to discover if the tale is true or fictional.

Basic Book Information

This nonfiction book is an early chapter book with illustrations. There is no table of contents or index. The last page of the book has a short pronunciation guide for some of the words in the text. There are between two to six paragraphs on every two-page spread, and there is always an illustration on at least one of the two pages. Each of the books in the series opens with a note to parents.

Noteworthy Features

This story offers a bit of history told with suspense and characters and action. Readers can enjoy the story as fiction, or can think about it as a retelling of a real event from long ago. The chapters break the story up into usable chunks, and the illustrations make the expanses of text easier on the eye. Most of the sentences are short and simple, making the story easy to follow.

Because the story is a simplified version of a much more complicated one, there are many of characters who are given names and referred to who don't end up being that important here. But if readers take a bit of care in keeping the characters straight, perhaps by keeping a short list beside them, that challenge shouldn't be too difficult to overcome.

The text also makes several statements that are supposed to be read as true to the time, but are actually matters of opinion. For example, the text says that if Athena liked the gift of the Greeks better than she liked the gift of the Trojans, she would favor them in war. Although the people of the day believed that, it isn't necessarily true. To read the story well, a reader has to understand what this apparent statement of fact means. The text also claims that Helen was the most beautiful woman in the land. Was this actually true? Was it just what the people of the time believed? Or was it only what the rulers believed? Readers will have to sort this out for themselves.

Teaching Ideas

There is much to discuss in this short history. Readers can be encouraged to think of history not as the only course actions and events could have taken, but as one of many. Readers tend to come up with questions such as: Why did the Greeks and Trojans fight for more than ten years? Was there no better solution to their problem? What do they think Helen herself thought about all this? Would they have been tricked by the wooden horse? What could the Trojans have done to avoid being tricked? What lessons can we learn for ourselves from this history? What evidence do scientists have that this city was real?

Book Connections

This book might pair well with D'Aulaires' *Book of Greek Myths* or with *How Would You Survive as an Ancient Greek?* from the *How Would You Survive* series.

Genre
Nonfiction; Chapter Book

Teaching Uses
Content Area Study; Independent Reading

The Van Gogh Café

Cynthia Rylant

FIELD GUIDE

E

Publisher
Scholastic, 1995

ISBN
0590907174

TC Level
11

Book Summary

Cynthia Rylant's magical creation, *The Van Gogh Café*, involves a 1920s theater-turned-café in Kansas, the crossroads between the West and the East. Here, "magic happens" to and for many: Clara, Clara's father and the café's guests. Each chapter unfolds a new, miraculous experience that involves seemingly normal as well as fantastical persons and objects (e.g., the elegant, older film star and the tiny but powerful muffins). The adventures also include a possum, a seagull, a writer and lightning. Readers ultimately are left questioning to what degree magic affects their own existence.

Basic Book Information

Though only 53 pages divided into 6 chapters or stories, this tale presents many sophisticated and intriguing ideas, which earned the book the 1996 Pen USA West Children's Award, and an ALA Notable Children's Book recognition. Though there is no table of contents, the chapter titles guide the reader to notice the story's important characters or objects.

Noteworthy Features

The first chapter begins some time before March and ends in the spring of the following year. The times of the year correspond to the events of the story: lightning strikes in March, and Marc is thus struck into writing poetry; Christmas time brings together old friends, such as the star and his dead friend; and in February, probably because of Valentine's Day, a gull and cat fall in love. Rylant probably wanted to reinforce how magic can occur all year, with everyday objects and events. Readers will want to further explore the other possible connections between the times of year and the events. They may also want to develop and test hypotheses about format, and why Rylant chose to begin before spring and end the following spring. Rylant does not begin including time references until the third chapter. Why does she begin to include them then? Do the seasons/months relate to small and big ideas in the text? It may be difficult for readers to recognize the seasonal symbols, unless they take each chapter and consider its time, plot, changes and big ideas. They will then be able to put each chapter's big ideas together, and make connections to discover any overall themes, such as the impact of change and the arts in magic creation.

The first chapter establishes the setting and helps readers determine the book's mood, with its description of the porcelain hen atop a cake carousel, phonograph, and sign above the register that reads, "Bless all Dogs." It foreshadows some of the bizarre events to come. Readers may question what these specific objects signify, and should not be discouraged if they find that they primarily serve to set up the unusual mood.

Older readers may notice the relationship between the movie star and his old, now-dead friend. Rylant presents such a relationship as loving and gentle.

Teaching Ideas

It's easy for readers to get confused in this book, since every chapter, and sometimes even paragraphs, offer their own detailed mini-story, and because the text is constantly playing between realistic fiction and fantasy. For example, the fact that there is a possum in flowers motivates people who are angry with one another to communicate. This is not so unlikely as the events in the next chapter, in which food begins to cook itself. Readers may not be sure whether to believe this, because the transition into fantasy is not clear. Students get to understand how genres mix, and may wonder if the subject of the text encourages this interweaving. Because of the complexity of the story, rereading is a good idea. Readers should first read the chapter or section of a chapter for the action, then re-read for the special details that make the stories so poetic and consider the larger themes.

Though the stories in every chapter are different, they are connected through their magic and the willingness of the characters to accept it, and even further it. These chapters will help readers who need to practice finding big ideas within a chapter. Readers may recognize that each chapter is like a short story. Because the chapters ask readers to refer back to previous chapters, students will strengthen their reference and inference skills. Readers can then begin to see connections between chapters and forge ideas.

The emphasis here on writing, which readers may find "cool," will prove beneficial now and throughout their academic and reading lives. For example, Marc writes poetry (adding to the many genres employed in the text) in the chapter, "Lightning Strikes." Also, the writer in the last chapter leads both a life as a writer and a reader. He takes the details in and, as the reader finds out, makes them into this story. Thus, the text can help the reader recognize a circular pattern, and the complicated relationships between the writer, text and reader. Students can realize that they, too, are authors and can make magic in their own lives.

Some readers may see *Van Gogh Café* as more of a fairy tale than a manual for creating magic. Rylant is always combining art, writing, reading, music and theatre with magic. The background music of the phonograph is a kind of magic. The source of all the magic, the Van Gogh Café was once an old theatre. Readers may want to think about why Rylant named it so, and do additional research on Van Gogh and his "magic" paintings.

Readers may find it worthwhile to question the role of school in Clara's life. They will notice that there is hardly any mention of Clara's school activities. Does this have to do with the genre? What are the goals of the author? What does she tell us, and why?

Book Connections

Rylant has written a variety of young adult novels, including *Missing May*, which won her a Newbery Medal in 1993. She also wrote the *Henry and*

Mudge series, for younger readers.

Genre
Short Chapter Book; Fantasy; Fairy and Folk Tale

Teaching Uses
Independent Reading; Teaching Writing; Book Clubs

The War with Grandpa

Robert Kimmel Smith

FIELD GUIDE

E F

Illustrator
Richard Lauter

Publisher
Yearling/Bantam
Doubleday Dell, 1984

ISBN
0440492769

TC Level
10

Book Summary

Fifth grader Peter Stokes loves his grandfather and is happy that he is coming to live with Peter's family. What he's not happy about is the fact that his grandfather will be moving into Peter's room, and Peter will be moving upstairs to a dingy room in the attic. When his grandfather arrives, Peter declares war on him and keeps up a series of playful "attacks" in an attempt to get his grandfather to surrender the room. Along the way, Peter learns that his grandfather is a good sport, that war is not a game, and that talking rather than fighting is a better way to handle problems.

Basic Book Information

The War with Grandpa has 140 pages divided into 37 very short chapters. There is a table of contents. The chapter titles are catchy and give an inkling of what a reader can expect. The cover drawing is more interesting than any of the interior illustrations. *The War with Grandpa* is the winner of ten state reading awards.

Noteworthy Features

Peter "writes" this story as he narrates it. "This is the true and real story of what happened when Grandpa came to live with us.... I am typing it out on paper without lines...." As he is writing his story, Peter talks about some writing techniques, such as the advantage of using short sentences. Several of the chapters open with Peter telling what the chapter is going to be about. This alerts the reader to the main idea of the chapter. That Peter is writing the story is a clever and effective device, but it's possible that a few students may be confused as to the role of the author, if it is Peter who is writing this book. It might be worth asking students: Who is Robert Kimmel Smith and what did he have to do with the book if Peter is the one writing it? A discussion about the distinction between narrators and authors could ensue; students could talk about the author's prerogative to pretend to be someone else while he or she writes. This, in turn could lead to a discussion of voice.

Important issues regarding the elderly-depression, illness, pain and loss-are raised in this book. These provide opportunities for students to discuss the discomforts many older people must struggle with, and to consider ways in which they may be made more comfortable.

Since Peter declared "war" on his grandfather, several references to real wars are brought up in the book. Peter's friends help him to strategize by recalling what they know about the Revolutionary War and WWII. The boys give clear explanations for all the terms they use: tyranny, Minuteman, Redcoats, Pearl Harbor. Teachers may want to make sure students understand the meanings or expand on the meanings. Also, one boy makes reference to Machiavelli. Though his explanation of who Machiavelli is will be sufficient for some readers, the teacher should be prepared for questions. What is noteworthy about these sections is that this knowledge of history is taken for granted. It is not just the smartest boy who knows about the American Revolution, etc.; all the boys clearly have an interest in history.

Teaching Ideas

The story should be read in just a few sittings. Momentum builds from chapter to chapter, and if the student reads only a two-page chapter a night on her or his own, that momentum will be lost. Weaker readers could also be paired with stronger readers to help them keep pace.

In Chapter 22, Grandpa tries to discourage Peter from his war. But Peter is adamant, claiming that war is just like the game of Risk and when a person's territory is taken, that person must retaliate. Grandpa gets very upset and slaps Peter. Students could be asked why they think Grandpa got so upset. They could also be encouraged to infer that Grandpa has actually been in a war and so knows that it's not a game. Students could discuss what they know of war and what any of their relatives have experienced of it.

Students can be asked if they feel Peter went too far when he stole Grandpa's false teeth. How do they think Grandpa felt? Why was Peter ashamed? How do they feel they treat their own grandparents? How do their grandparents treat them? Has the book helped them to understand their grandparents any better? This building of personal connections with a text can inform and change not only a reader's understanding of a book but of the real world.

Genre
Chapter Book

Teaching Uses
Independent Reading; Read Aloud; Critique; Character Study

The Whipping Boy

Sid Fleischman

FIELD GUIDE

E

Illustrator
Peter Sis

Publisher
Green Willow Books, 1986

ISBN
816710384

TC Level
12

Book Summary

Jemmy serves as the "Whipping Boy" to Prince Brat, and suffers the punishments for the prince's misbehavior due to an ancient law that forbids princes from being touched. Jemmy's dreams of running away are realized one day when Prince Brat decides to sneak away from the castle in an attempt to get his father, the king, to notice him. Their plan goes awry when they are captured by two villains, Hold-Your-Nose Billy and Cutwater, who in turn try to get a ransom out of the king. Through escaping, meeting new friends outside the castle and trying to return, each character learns lessons about himself that make lasting changes in his character.

Basic Book Information

The Whipping Boy has 90 pages. While some chapter headings signal important developments in a straightforward manner, such as "The Ransom Note" and "The Chase," many contain strange usages or puns. For example, the first chapter heading, "In which we observe a hair-raising event" concerns a prank in which members of the king's court lose their wigs. The title in this case does not really give an easily identifiable clue as to what is about to transpire. Others, such as the title of Chapter 11, "Containing a great deal of shouting," which is about an argument between the two main characters, while more direct, can still be difficult for some readers.

There are 10 illustrations that accurately depict what transpires in the plot, but they are not always matched up with corresponding text on the opposite page.

There is an author's note at the end of the book informing the reader that the practice of maintaining a whipping boy is true. "Some royal households of past centuries did keep whipping boys to suffer the punishments due a misbehaving prince." This is a remarkable fact to many readers.

Noteworthy Features

Many of the characters speak in an approximation of Old English, for example: "Catchpenny rogues! I will not be exchanged for such a trifle. My mere weight? A paltry treasure you could carry on you shoulder? How dare you insult me!" If students are not equipped with strategies for dealing with this particular dialect, they may get bogged down.

Much of the plot turns on cases of mistaken identity and the switches happen quickly. If, for example, one misses that the robbers mistakenly think that Jemmy is the prince, they might think that all of the robbers' comments directed to "His Lordship" are, in fact, aimed at the real prince, instead of Jemmy.

There are several distinct settings where the action takes place. The story moves from the castle, to the woods, to the open road and so on. Each change in setting marks a new development and plot point. If the change in locale is missed it could lead to confusion.

Teaching Ideas

This book provides many experiences in dealing with dialect. Some teachers choose to have children read the parts out loud until they get the flow of the sounds of the speech. This is especially true of the heavily accented speech of the villains Cutwater and Hold-Your-Nose Billy. The ungrammatical way these characters speak-"Now let me reckon out a safe spot"-can throw many readers. If the book is used as a read aloud or in a small group, conversation can focus around why an author might choose to use dialect, even though it can be difficult to read.

The text is also full of many medieval words, such as *scragged*, *plague* and *footmen*. Most of these words appear in such a way that they can be figured out through context. For example, "I'll be lucky if they don't whip me to the bone. More likely I'll be hung from the gallows. Scragged for sure!" In this case, the difficult word's meaning can be approximated, if not figured outright, by the way it is used.

Both main characters, and Prince Brat in particular, go through dramatic changes from the beginning of the story to the end. Many teachers spend time having readers create vivid examinations of character at the beginning of the book, then observe how the rest of the narrative holds up to these initial impressions. The prince transforms from being a selfish, spoiled and thoughtless individual to one who is caring, respectful of others and who has learned the value of being honorable. Jemmy learns to see past his initial dislike of the prince and to value and appreciate him as a friend.

All students are struck by the grave injustice of one person suffering the punishment for another's actions. Besides relating this to their own experiences, many students are shocked by the fact that this actually happened in the past. This can lead to conversation on the purpose and worth of punishment and the connection between responsibility and consequence.

Genre
Chapter Book

Teaching Uses
Independent Reading

The Winter Solstice

Ellen B. Jackson

FIELD GUIDE

E

Illustrator
Jan Davey Ellis

Publisher
Millbook Press, 1997

ISBN
0761302972

TC Level
9; 10; 11

Book Summary

This nonfiction book details various interpretations of the winter solstice, from the culture of the Druids through the Romans, Scandinavians, Europeans and various Native American societies. The book devotes at least one page to each of these cultures, revealing their beliefs and some general knowledge of the world they inhabited.

Basic Book Information

This 28-page book usually pairs a page of text with a full-color, realistic drawing. The pages are not numbered, or titled, and there is no table of contents or index.

Noteworthy Features

The book starts with a narrative about a Scottish family and then jumps to descriptions of numerous cultures. This may initially be confusing to a reader who continues looking for the Scottish family in the text. For interested readers this is a wonderful text to consult while doing an imaginary study, as it will cause the reader to question and dig further for answers. Since it is also well written, it may pull readers into the text, even if they are not interested in the content: "Today, when the earth is bare and brown and the cold vanilla taste of winter is in the air, no one worries about the darkness or the whistling wind. People simply turn on the lights, pour themselves a cup of hot chocolate, and go about their business."

There is an assumption by the author that the reader has at least a passing familiarity with many ancient cultures, as well as geography and the term *winter solstice* (nowhere in the text is the word solstice explained). This basic definition would go a long way toward supporting a reader with less background knowledge.

Also, difficult illustrations are not always explained. In the illustration of the Scandinavians, for instance, a man in the background is slumped over a chair with a cup falling out of his hand. Will readers know this is meant to show a man who has been drinking beer? Again, a certain level of background knowledge is assumed, perhaps too much for some younger readers.

There are two pages in the latter part of the book that explain the principles of rotation and revolution of the earth. When reading these pages, it's helpful to have the materials mentioned (orange, toothpicks, flashlight), or to have a globe, to help explain such things as the Northern Hemisphere.

Teaching Ideas

This book is good for studying the seasons or winter, as well as different cultures in relation to the seasons. Myth and superstition are also likely possibilities for subjects to study. On the page about the Scandinavians, one line reads: "During this feast, men (not the women) sat in a long hall...." This might be a good starting point for a discussion on cultural gender roles. Also, because of the Cherokee creation tale presented at the end, an inquiry into Native American legends and folk tales could be begun, centering on their response to nature.

Genre

Nonfiction; Picture Book

Teaching Uses

Content Area Study; Independent Reading

The Wise Woman and Her Secret

Eve Merriam

FIELD GUIDE

E G

Book Summary

This beautifully illustrated book tells the story of a very wise woman who lives alone in the country. People from surrounding towns know of her great wisdom and travel to her home to find her secret. Once there, they abruptly demand that she reveal herself. "We are here for your secret. We have come a long distance, and we wish to get home before dark, so give it to us without delay." Amused, the wise woman will not give them an answer, but allows them to search her house and property.

Frantically, the group goes from place to place looking for the secret, never stopping for more than a minute or two at each location. Meanwhile, a small girl named Jenny trails behind the rest of the group. She curiously observes all that is around her. The group is impatient with the girl. "Don't lag, don't loiter, don't dawdle," they scold. The little girl finally approaches the wise woman and excitedly asks her several questions about a penny the rest of the group discarded in disgust. The delighted woman reveals that Jenny already possesses the secret. Her curiosity and tendency to "wander and wonder" were all she needs to receive the gift of wisdom.

Illustrator
Linda Graves

Publisher
Aladdin Paperbacks, 1991

ISBN
067172603

Basic Book Information

The Wise Woman and Her Secret is a picture book that features lush language and illustrations and tells the message that "stopping to smell the roses" will bring wisdom and peace. Eve Merriam is the author of several children's picture books such as *Halloween ABC* as well as poetry collections such as *You Be Good & I'll Be Night: Jump-On The Bed Poems*. Her work as a poet is evident in the gorgeous language she uses throughout the text. Teachers can focus on Merriam in the beginning of the year to demonstrate how writers work in a variety of genres, showing students that Merriam writes poetry, list books, picture books, and ABC books. Eve Merriam's first book was published in the 1960s.

The illustrator, Linda Graves, has illustrated more than 25 books including *Frogs' Legs for Dinner?* Her illustrations have also appeared in major magazines.

Noteworthy Features

This 27-page picture book features idealistic, pastel illustrations that strongly support the text. True to the message of the story, if the reader looks slowly and carefully at each illustration, the wonders of nature can be discovered. A beautifully shaped leaf, curious cat or a bird preparing to take flight are just some of the surprises readers can encounter.

The illustrations could be analyzed to get deeper into the story because they are so detailed and expressive. For example, the illustrations could also be used to discuss the idea of following a crowd versus thinking as an individual. Throughout the book, the group looks like a frenzied and somewhat hostile mob than a group looking for answers. When a group member shouts out a wild theory about the woman, the others are shown joining in without hesitation. When the man shouts, "She may not be of our kind at all. Perhaps she isn't a human being like us, perhaps she is from another planet." The crowd looks both excited and enraged. "Yes, yes they began to whisper in excitement, that must be the answer that is why we can't find the secret." Students who are reading the book in partnerships or book clubs may stop to ask, "Is this book fair?" a question many readers ask as they critique their reading.

By contrast, illustrations of Jenny and the wise woman show them looking serene and content. Throughout the book they are both observing nature with a thoughtful gaze and knowing grin. Comparing the images within the same page would most likely produce a lively discussion among students, and encourage them to talk about why the illustrator chose to draw the characters so differently.

Teaching Ideas

There are many teaching points that can be explored with this book. Therefore, it would make a good choice to be a touchtone text, one that is revisited several times throughout the year. While first introduced as a read aloud in order to fully absorb the richness of the language used it could be read independently, in partnerships, or in small groups.

When first read aloud, the teacher could focus on the beautiful language highlighted by the use of metaphor. While that term wouldn't have to be used, a teacher could instead discuss how Eve Merriam helps put a picture in the reader's mind with descriptions such as "She had long, dark hair that was streaked with white, like patches of snow on the muddy spring ground," or "Her voice was soft as the fur of her cat, yet you could hear her every word from far away." During the first reading, the teacher could read these sentences a few times before showing them the illustrations and have students close their eyes and try to picture the woman. They could then discuss what they visualized with a partner. The teacher might later invite the students to try to use descriptive sentences such as these in their own writing.

There are several ways this text could lead children to write about their reading. It is important to note that in order for children to be able to write about their reading, they must first be able to talk about their reading. If studying character traits, for example, children could work with a partner to discuss their ideas about Jenny or another character. If a reader decides that Jenny is "curious," he might then go back with a partner and place post-it notes throughout the book whenever they notice Jenny being curious. They could, for instance, mark pictures of Jenny looking intently at a stick with cobwebs or when she asks the woman many questions about the found penny. The same could be done for the wise woman or for "the crowd."

This book is reminiscent of a folk tale in which a lesson has been learned, and could also be used as a reading center. A small group of children could compare *The Wise Woman and Her Secret* with folk/fairy tales and try to determine if the book would fit in with this category. Students could read through a selection of texts and decide how they would report what they discovered to the whole group. A comparison chart, summary of opinions, or oral presentation are just some of the ways children could share what they noticed in their reading.

Book Connections

Fairy tales by the Brothers Grimm such as *Hansel and Gretel, Little Red Riding Hood,* and *Rumplestiltskin* are tales where a lesson is learned. Books by Jan Brett, such as *The Mitten* and *The Gingerbread Baby* would also make good companions to this book because of the folk tale style and similar illustrations. A connection could also be made to *Wizard of Oz* because a character is seeking what she already possesses much like the characters journeying to the wizard.

Genre
Picture Book; Fairy and Folk Tale

Teaching Uses
Read Aloud; Independent Reading; Teaching Writing

Through My Eyes

Ruby Bridges

FIELD GUIDE

E F

Book Summary

As a six-year-old girl, Ruby Bridges was the first Black child to enter an all-White school in New Orleans. She was escorted to school by U.S. Marshals, who protected her from the violent, taunting crowd that opposed her attendance. This book tells of her life before that pivotal year, witnessed by the rest of the country; the experience of walking past those jeering crowds every day, and her time inside the school, learning alone with her first-grade teacher. The text also offers the story of what happened to her as she grew into an adult.

Publisher
Scholastic Press, 1999

ISBN
0590189239

TC Level
10; 11; 12

Noteworthy Features

This autobiographical picture book/chapter book is about 60 pages long. It is about two-thirds text and one-third photographs. There is no table of contents or index. The text is structured as a chronological narrative, with a focus on the details of Ruby's life that tell also of the times, and then of her year in first grade. It is divided into sections of about two pages each, with headings that clearly indicate what each section is about. The last page of the book presents the lyrics to a song about Ruby. Sidebars to the text offer quotations from civic leaders, writers and newspapers of the day describing the same events Ruby describes, but from an outsider's point of view.

Teaching Ideas

This book can be read aloud in grades two, three, and up. Many readers prefer fiction reading to nonfiction reading. It's important that all readers have a balanced reading life however, one that includes information books. This book, then, could simply be one among many on the library shelf.

If a teacher sees that the class as a whole tends to select fiction books only during independent reading, the teacher may institute some rituals that steer children towards nonfiction. The least intrusive would simply be to do promotional book-talks in which one "sells" nonfiction books. The teacher could go a step further and talk to children about the importance of having a balanced reading life. She could ask the students to make sure that if they have a personal book bin full of four to five books they're reading or planning to read, that at least one of these is nonfiction. Finally, it's possible to go a step further and to suggest that, for a time, all children need to read only nonfiction texts during independent reading.

Teachers may want to do mini-lessons on the strategies for skilled nonfiction reading. They could tell children that nonfiction readers sometimes read like magnets, looking for intriguing details that they pull from a text. One teacher told her students that highly literate people then fact-drop these little bits of information into conversations, sharing in passing whatever they've been learning. The reader of this book would be full of such facts.

Another mini-lesson might show children that if a person read this book and loved it, the logical thing to do would be to collect other texts on the same topic. Information from one text and then another cumulates; some of the information overlaps and some of it may be contradictory. Depending on the students and the grade level, the teacher would determine the length of time and frequency of discussion necessary to support comprehension. The ability to sustain a conversation on a topic will support comprehension as well.

This is a great book to engage students in conversation about civil rights, life in southern states in the 1950s-1960s, and how one person, a child, was affected. This text could support a number of units of study in the social studies curriculum. It could also be used in an interpretation unit of study in grades four and above. The setting (place and time) plays a major role in the way the events in the story unfold and is crucial to deep comprehension. Students can do further research about the time period and use it to support an interpretation. This could lead to developing an awareness of social action.

It is recommended that this text be included in the independent reading library in grades three and up. It could be chosen for a variety of reasons and purposes that would be determined by the reader. The teacher can support the book choice process by giving an orientation to the text as part of a mini-lesson. The teacher could show the students how to negotiate the text as well.

Through My Eyes is an example of narrative nonfiction. Therefore some reinforcement of the story elements would help students make meaning of the text. This book also contains many nonfiction text features (captions, subtitles, sidebars, graphs, diagrams, etc.) that make this genre seem dense.

Many teachers who have used this book have helped make it more accessible by doing mini-lessons on "how to navigate one's way through nonfiction." Students can use Post-its or other indicators to mark the many sections where news articles or quotes appear, and then in pairs help each other insert this information into the main text.

As a touchstone text in a writing workshop, sections can be pulled out as examples of personal narrative. The voice is clear and the language is simple enough for all students to try.

Ruby Bridges is an important historical figure. In the class's collection of books about important people, *Through My Eyes* will help introduce one of the many little-known heroes worth learning about.

Book Connections

This book goes well with *Walking For Freedom: The Montgomery Bus Boycott* edited by Richard Kelso.

Genre

Chapter Book; Biography; Memoir; Picture Book

Teaching Uses
Book Clubs; Read Aloud; Partnerships

Walking For Freedom: The Montgomery Bus Boycott

FIELD GUIDE

E

Richard Kelso

Book Summary

This book tells the story of the Montgomery, Alabama bus boycott in 1955. It is a nonfiction book written in narrative form. It focuses on Mrs. Jo An Robinson as the main character in the story. The illustrations and the dialogue make it feel real. The point of view in this book changes a lot from Mrs. Robinson to Dr. Martin Luther King. Getting inside their heads helps the reader to know all the issues they faced when they took this bold step.

Series
Stories of America

Publisher
Raintree Steck-Vaughn, 1993

ISBN
0811480585

TC Level
10; 11; 12

Basic Book Information

Alex Haley, the author of *Roots* among other titles, is the general editor of this book. He writes the introduction, which appears before the table of contents. There are 52 pages, with 4 chapters ranging from 9 to 12 pages in length. Titles are given but are not very supportive. There are black-and-white drawings by Michael Newton that appear every four or five pages. There is an epilogue and notes for each page of the text, which act as footnotes.

Noteworthy Features

Alex Haley's introduction acts as a preface and gives the reader some clues to the author's intent in writing the book. The narrative in this book makes it come alive for the reader. There is a lot of dialogue, which serves the same purpose. This book does not feel dry; instead it is populated with living, breathing people. This book can be read on two levels. The first is at the surface-little background knowledge is needed, except to know the major regions of the U.S. If a student reads the accompanying "Notes," however, then more information is given, and the book becomes a highly sophisticated read as well as a research source.

Teaching Ideas

Some common research topics that are addressed in this book are civil rights, The United States in the 1950s, nonviolent civil disobedience, Martin Luther King Jr., and Rosa Parks. This is also a good book to introduce embedded narrative to nonfiction readers.

Book Connections

The book goes well with *Through My Eyes* by Ruby Bridges.

Genre
Short Chapter Book; Nonfiction

Teaching Uses
Content Area Study; Partnerships

We Had a Picnic This Sunday Past

Jacqueline Woodson

FIELD GUIDE

D E

Illustrator
Diane Greenseid

Publisher
Hyperion, 1998

ISBN
0786802421

Book Summary

It is the day of the big family picnic and Teeka and her grandmother are buzzing with excitement. As members of the family arrive in the park, Teeka, the narrator, comments about each person and the food each has brought for the potluck. Teeka obviously enjoys herself, telling readers on the last page, "You should have been there."

Basic Book Information

This 27-page picture book contains bold illustrations on every page. There are roughly two paragraphs of text on one side of every two-page spread. A Coretta Scott King Honor recipient, Jacqueline Woodson has written many novels for older readers, including *I Hadn't Meant to Tell You This* and *If You Come Softly*. Woodson's *The Other Side* is another subtly crafted picture book, though the subject, illustrations and overall tone are far less exuberant than those of *We Had a Picnic This Sunday Past*.

Noteworthy Features

Set on a single afternoon, this story is structured simply and chronologically. Vocabulary should present most students with few challenges. Though many characters enter the park, readers can understand the story while remembering just three: Teeka, Grandma and Cousin Martha, whose arrival and notoriously dry apple pie are anticipated throughout the story.

In spite of these easier elements, *We Had a Picnic This Sunday Past* is fairly complex. Dialogue is set off from the rest of the text not by quotation marks, but by bold print. The speaker of the dialogue is rarely referenced, and sometimes the subject of the dialogue is also hard to discern. For example, some readers may not immediately understand that the "boy" whose baking skills Grandma praises is an adult, Uncle Luther. Reading aloud with inflection is important and helpful for students who are trying to reproduce the cadence of the text.

The figurative language of Teeka's narration also adds a layer of complexity to the story. Phrases such as "a pail of peaches fresh as summer" make her voice poetic. Students at first may not see the humorous word play in asides such as "the most delicious store-bought cake Cousin Martha **never** made" and "Reverend Luke can eat like the devil-strange, since he's such a holy man."

Teaching Ideas

Though technically a work of fiction, *We Had a Picnic This Sunday Past* has many of the elements of memoir. It is a first-person narrative that, through images and anecdotes, provides a window into the life of the narrator. Teeka's perspective and observations are central to this story. Used in the writing workshop, this book can serve as a model to which students refer while they write their own memoir. Mini-lessons can look at how Woodson creates Teeka's strong voice, how to show detail instead of telling it, and how to comment subtly on the action instead of just listing what happened next. Enlarging text on an overhead transparency or chart paper can help children see examples during these whole-class mini-lessons.

After students are familiar with the story, they might reread to examine the relationship between Teeka and her grandmother. Children may notice how Teeka's behavior mirrors Grandma's. The two whisper conspiratorially, and Teeka appears to share her grandmother's passion for gossip and judgment. Both of them enjoy bragging. In the illustration on the second page, their arms jut upward at complementary angles, and later they fold their arms and throw back their heads in identically indignant poses.

Negotiating the challenging dialogue is crucial for children's understanding. Some students will be able to imagine the book's natural inflection and to hear in their heads all of the characters' distinct voices. Others may need to hear someone else read it. Teachers who plan to read *We Had a Picnic This Sunday Past* aloud should prepare carefully first. They must plan how they will differentiate Teeka's narrative commentary from dialogue that the characters utter to each other; students may miss one of the key features of the book otherwise. Also, teachers must distinguish the voices of different characters. Slight adjustments in tone, pitch and pace can suggest everything from Auntie Kim's sweetness to Cousin Martha's frenetic energy. As both Teeka and Grandma whisper frequently, teachers should decide in advance when they plan to raise or lower their volume. Finally, teachers should plan to read sensitively. Reading any dialect well requires naturalism, not theatrical exaggeration. Hearing this story read in overblown accents will not enrich it for students, but distract them.

Book Connections

Shortcut, by Donald Crews; *Nana Upstairs & Nana Downstairs*, by Tomie dePaola; and *Home: A Collaboration of Thirty Distinguished Authors and Illustrators of Children's Books to Aid the Homeless*, edited by Michael J. Rosen and Franz Brandenberg, offer strong examples of memoir.

Genre
Memoir; Picture Book

Teaching Uses
Read Aloud; Independent Reading; Partnerships; Teaching Writing

Whales

FIELD GUIDE

E

Joan Short; Bettina Bird

Book Summary

This book presents facts and explanations about whales-their physical features, behavior, a history of the hunt for them, and measures to protect them.

Deborah Savin's illustrations in this book are clear, with captions that are easy to follow. There are also numerous photographs.

Basic Book Information

This archetypal nonfiction book about whales is about 30 pages long. A table of contents appears at the beginning of the book, and it is laid out like an outline--major sections in large bold font, sub-topics beneath in smaller font, and sub-sub-topics below them in even smaller, italicized font. The sections themselves are named succinctly to help students find information, for example, "Communication" or "Echo-Location." At the end of the book, there is a short glossary, an even shorter guide to pronunciation of terms, and a one-page index with photographs. In short, the book contains many of the elements common to nonfiction books.

Each section of the text is self-contained and set off by large bold headings. Within each one- to two-paragraph section, there are captioned photographs, diagrams and pictures to help explain the information given. These captions are in a smaller font than the rest of the text, and are generally short. The text of the sections is composed of listings and explanations of facts. There is no story or narrative device to make the text continuous, just a presentation of information, somewhat like an encyclopedia for children.

Noteworthy Features

The book will clearly be fascinating to children who are already interested in whales. Because there are no narrative devices to carry the text along, readers who aren't interested in whales will have little to grab hold of; the book is entirely composed of bits of information about whales.

This text presents a large amount of information in a relatively small number of words. Children can learn a lot without reading a lot and with very little searching, if they know how to use the table of contents and/or the index. This can be rare in nonfiction texts.

This text also provides a lot of visual representations of the topic, which help children feel connected to the subject they are studying, and help them understand the descriptions they are reading.

Series
Mondo Animals

Illustrator
Deborah Savin

Publisher
Mondo, 1996

ISBN
1572551909

TC Level
9; 10; 11

Teaching Ideas

Certainly, teachers often use this book in the classroom when children are studying the topic. The book also offers an excellent model of the parts of nonfiction books, and can be used as such once children are familiar with those various elements. Because of its thoroughly distinct and labeled parts, this is also an excellent book for children to use for note-taking and gathering information about a topic.

In many nonfiction children's books, the last sentences usually contain opinion or unproved conclusions. Here, the author writes that there are no reasons left to continue killing whales. This certainly is one point of view, but there are other points of view as well. Are there groups of purely evil, scheming whale-haters out on the seas? Probably not. One has to believe that there are still reasons to hunt whales. The reasons might not be good ones, but to say those reasons don't exist is to ignore reality. Children might swallow the conclusion whole, and the teacher will have to decide whether to let this go, or to direct the children to think about the book's conclusion further.

Book Connections

Interestingly, other books in this series are different. The *Mondo Animals* series has a number of authors. *Crocodilians*, also written by Short and Bird, is set up very similarly and readers could study the authors' technique and point of view in both books. *Platypus* is an easier read. *Insects* has a table of contents that is very easy to read and follows an outline.

Genre
Nonfiction; Picture Book

Teaching Uses
Independent Reading; Reading and Writing Nonfiction; Content Area Study; Critique

What You Know First

Patricia MacLachlan

FIELD GUIDE

C E G

Book Summary

What You Know First tells the story of a little girl and her family who are preparing to move away from the only home the girl has ever known. The farm she lives on is located on the prairie and holds some of her most cherished memories. The young girl reflects on all of the things she loves about this place and how she will say goodbye to them. The sky, the grass, and her tree, are all a part of her and hard to part with. The little girl wants to find a way to hold on to these things so she can share them with her baby brother when he grows up. She is determined to find a way to take these memories with her.

Illustrator
Barry Moser

Publisher
Harper Collins, 1995

ISBN
0064434923

TC Level
8

Basic Book Information

Patricia MacLachlan is the author of many well-loved novels and picture books, including *Sarah, Plain and Tall,* winner of the Newbery Medal; it's sequel, *Skylark,* and *All The Places To Love,* illustrated by Mike Wimmer.

Noteworthy Features

The dark, serious, dramatically cropped engravings on these pages lend the book an adult air, which attracts some children and repels others. The small amount of text per page may, for some children, counterbalance the sophisticated air lent by the illustrations. On the other hand, some children see the format of the copy on the page and think the book is poetry, and therefore (sadly) intimidating to read. In most classrooms, especially at the beginning of the year, this book could use an introduction or a promotion or at least a link to another book (perhaps one of MacLachlan's many others) to get it off the shelves and into children's hands.

What You Know First is really more a meditation than a story. It is the thoughts of a girl-a reader can only tell it is a girl from the pictures, not the text, so conceivably it could be a boy-as she adjusts to the fact that she is moving away from the place she loves.

This book is laden with farm-specific vocabulary and images, so, like any book, readers unfamiliar with the places described will undoubtedly have a harder time picturing it, and possibly understanding it, than other readers. Passages that describe the pipits feeding or the geese sky-talking may give some readers pause.

Some of the more interesting facts about this story are based in its creation. Patricia MacLachlan was born on the prairie, and to this day carries a small bag of prairie dirt with her wherever she goes to remind her of what she knew first. One day, shortly after a move to a new home MacLachlan felt unstable. She was having a hard time adjusting to her new surroundings and missed her old home. She was having trouble writing as well. At that very time she was to speak to a fourth grade class at the Jackson Street School and worried about what she would say to them in this state of mind. She wound up discussing heavily the topic of "place and landscape" and showed the students her bag of prairie dirt from where she was born. The children were very involved in the discussion because they could relate. Five were foster children, disconnected from their homes. One boy had recently lost everything he had to a fire in his home. Another told her that he was moving in a few days to a place he'd never been. MacLachlan suggested to these students that maybe she should take her prairie dirt and toss it in her new backyard so that the two places could mix together. The children's reactions to this were so strongly against this idea, fearful that the dirt might blow away. One small girl suggested placing the dirt in a bowl and keeping it on the window so that it would be a constant reminder of "what you knew first." When MacLachlan left the school she went home to write this book.

Teaching Ideas

This book starts right in the middle of her thoughts, with no explanation of the characters, situation or setting. If children are confused by this opening, or by books in general that open this way, it may help them to learn that all readers feel that sense of missing knowledge when a book starts in the middle like that. We can tell children that authors know the reader will be wondering about the details of the situation, and the authors use that to get the reader to read more in order to get their questions answered. In order for the words to make sense as the reader does read more, he or she has to read carefully and hold in mind the questions raised by the text. In this case the questions are probably the following: Who is the "I"? Where is it she won't go? Why?

In this book, some of the reader's questions are answered almost right away. It becomes clear that the place the girl doesn't want to go to is a new house, a new place, a land she's never seen. That quick answer to the reader's early question provides some support for the reader unused to reading with questions. For that reason, this book might make a good transitional read for kids who aren't yet able to read fantasy and other-world-type books that require the reader to hold in mind a lot of unanswered questions.

The book leaves some questions for readers to puzzle over, to discuss in groups or reread and think about. The narrator asks to herself why they must leave at all, and the reader may well try to figure that out from the story. It seems the family must leave for monetary reasons, but students can debate over the possibilities that are hinted at in the book.

Like many of MacLachlan's books, this one has a tone of nostalgia for the "good life," one where people live side by side with natural beauty and in perfect harmony with the land. The tone itself can provide fodder for discussion, especially if the tone in this book is compared to the tone in another book that presents another perspective on farm life-one that shows some of the hardships or negative aspects of country living.

This book could appear in a basket with multiple copies. Whether a teacher wishes to introduce Memoir, Poetry or an Author Study of Patricia MacLachlan's literary work, or if a teacher would rather discuss the beautiful language and vivid vocabulary or even the structure of this text, it would make a great mentor text. Not only is it a wonderfully structured book, but it can even be used to ease the anxiety of that new child that appears at each of our classroom doorways in the late winter or early spring. Surely a child such as this could immediately feel comforted after reading the first page ("I won't go, I'll say, To a new house, To a new place, To a land I've never seen").

This book also provides an outstanding opportunity for introducing the concept of studying artifacts in Memoir. The young girl will "take a twig of the cottonwood tree...take a little bag of prairie dirt." One can almost picture the girl sitting with these artifacts later in life and all of her original memories come flooding to her mind:

Or maybe
I'll live in a tree.
The tall cottonwood that was small when Papa was small,
But grew faster than he did.
Now it has branches
And crooks where I can sit
To look over the rooftop,
Over the windmill
Over the prairie...

Book Connections

Patricia MacLachlan is the author of many well-loved novels and picture books, including *Sarah, Plain and Tall,* winner of the Newbery Medal; it's sequel, *Skylark,* and *All The Places To Love,* illustrated by Mike Wimmer.

Genre

Picture Book

Teaching Uses

Read Aloud; Independent Reading; Partnerships; Critique; Teaching Writing

William Shakespeare & the Globe

Aliki

FIELD GUIDE

E

Illustrator
Aliki

Publisher
HarperCollins, 1999

ISBN
0064437221

TC Level
10; 11; 12

Book Summary

Well-known author and illustrator Aliki brings her knowledge and magic to Shakespeare with *William Shakespeare& the Globe*. This book is similar in format to *A Medieval Feast* (also by Aliki) and is a good resource to learn about Shakespeare's life, Elizabethan times and Elizabethan drama. Aliki sets up the book with acts and scenes, very much like the structure of a Shakespearean play. The book begins by explaining its structure and introducing the principal characters: Shakespeare, his contemporaries and Sam Wanamaker, the man who rebuilt the Globe Theater.

Basic Book Information

This book is 48 pages long and has a table of contents. Acts tend to be 5 to 6 pages long and scenes usually run 1 to 3 pages. The text follows the structure of a Shakespeare play(Act 1: Scene 1; Scene 2; Act 2; Scene 1; etc.) On every page, there is a line from a play that pertains directly to the content of that page, and is usually a well-known quote, such as "All the world's a stage." The pages are packed with facts, but they are not wordy.Pages run between 46 and 140 words each. There are full-color, and sometimes multiple, illustrations on every page, some of which are captioned. Aliki is an award-winning illustrator.

Noteworthy Features

Very often pages contain two to three illustrations arranged in large rectangular boxes, with captions beneath. The text on all pages is large with generous spacing between lines. The book is 11 x 8 1/2, which creates a large tableau and makes the text, which is filled with facts, welcoming to the reader.

This book is excellent for learning about captions. There are many captions on each page serving a variety of purposes. Sometimes the caption is a label. Other times, it conveys new information that the illustrations are highlighting.

Teaching Ideas

This book is a great one for students to use when they are studying subjects related to the book: Elizabethan times, Shakespeare, archeology, drama or a variety of other topics.

This book also serves as an example of a work that presents a variety of ways of communicating information. Teaches can help students learn ways of enjoying, and navigating, this kind of nonfiction.

Genre
Nonfiction; Picture Book

Teaching Uses
Reading and Writing Nonfiction; Content Area Study; Partnerships

Index